CENTENARY WOLVES

BY THE SAME AUTHOR:

A History of British Football.
    Stanley Paul & Co. Ltd., 1968.
    Arrow Books Ltd., 1973.

With Derek Dougan:
The Sash he never wore
    Allison & Busby Ltd., 1972.
    Mayflower Books Ltd., 1974.

On the Spot: Football as a Profession.
    Stanley Paul Ltd., 1974.

CENTENARY WOLVES

☆

BY
PERCY M. YOUNG

Published by Wolverhampton Wanderers F.C. (1923) Ltd.

Copyright © 1976 Wolverhampton Wanderers (1923) Ltd.
All rights reserved.

*Printed in Great Britain
by Sunderland Print Ltd., West Midlands
ISBN 0 9505245 0 6*

Contents

Foreword by:
Harry J. Marshall, Chairman, Wolverhampton Wanderers.

Illustrations

1	Pioneers	1
2	Wanderers	9
3	Last days at Dudley Road	22
4	Molineux	30
5	Breakers ahead	43
6	Decline and fall	54
7	Second Division	61
8	Hard times	69
9	Return journey	80
10	The Buckley era	92
11	War and peace	117
12	Rise and fall	125
13	Interregnum	138
14	Varied fortunes	142
15	Full circle	149
	Appendix	154
	Index of Proper Names	205

Illustrations in text

Goldthorn Football Club, Notice of General Meeting 1876	4
Annual Report of Wolverhampton Wanderers 1881-2	13
Letter concerning lease of Molineux Grounds 1889	31
Aston Villa v Wolves, October 1892	35
Blackburn Rovers v Wolves, March 1893	37
The Throstles v the Wolves, October 1893	44
Wolves v Newton Heath, November 1893	46
Cup Final Programme 1921	75
"Jackery" Jones, 1921	77
The cult of Emile Coué, 1922	79
August optimism 1923	81
Opening a new stand, August 29 1925	85
Programme design 1926	87
That unwelcome apparition, 1927	90
Red Riding Hood and the Wolf, 1929	96
"This season's 'it'", 1930	97
The Laws of the Game, 1930	99
Dinner menu, with autographs, 1932	102, 104

Illustrations in half-tone

between

Lake in grounds of Molineux House c. 1860
Molineux Pleasure Grounds c. 1860
Molineux Pleasure Grounds 1869 } 20-21
Birmingham F.A. Testimonial for E. Ray, G. H. Sellman, and J. Whitehead

The Wanderers c. 1890
Fred Leek's Share Certificate 1891
Cup Final at Fallowfield 1893 } 36-37
Wolverhampton Wanderers Football Club, Winners of English Cup 1892-3

The Wanderers 1907
Portrait studies 1908
From the Fixture Card 1908-9 } 52-53
Cup Final Officials 1921

Team of 1922
G. H. Marshall, S. Brooks, A. Riley
E. J. Peers, N. George, A. Potts } 68-69
J. E. Hodnett, T. Lea, G. Brewster

R. W. Richards, E. Morse, G. W. Edmonds
W. Hann, H. Scott, A. Canavon, M. Woodward
F.A. Cup-tie, Wolves v Wrexham, at Molineux 1931 } 84-85
T. Smalley, A. Tootill, C. Phillips

M. S. Crook, W. G. Lowton, D. Richards
Aerial view of Molineux c. 1925
Relaxing at Nice 1933
F. C. Buckley } 100-101
Pre-match courtesies, Nice 1933
Cup Final memories 1908, 1939

Cullis in defence, v Arsenal 1936
Dorsett in attack, v Stoke 1938 } 116-117

ILLUSTRATIONS

between

Team, Lady Day 1893
Cup Final procession 1939
S. Cullis with C. Chataway
Welcome home 1949

116-117

B. F. Williams and T. Phillipson
S. Smyth in action, Cup Final 1949
The Wolves, 1949 and 1951
The Wolves 1954
v Spartak, Moscow 1955
In Europe 1959-71

132-133

R. Flowers in action
Peak year 1958: G. Showell, E. Clamp, G. Harris, J. Gardiner, M. Finlayson, J. Murray, W. J. Slater, R. Flowers, E. A. Stuart, R. Mason, N. Deeley, W. A. Wright, S. Cullis, P. Broadbent, C. Booth, J. Mullen, J. Henderson.
Birmingham League, Football League, Worcestershire, F.A. Youth, Central League, Worcs. Combination Trophies.
F.A. Cup winners 1960
Molineux Grounds 1972

148-149

Wolves "offered classic teamwork"
UEFA journeys to Jena and Leipzig 1971-3
J. McAlle scores, v Coimbra
Ado scores penalty for Den Haag (1971, UEFA Cup)
A. D. Dougan in prayerful mood 1973
J. Richards scores v Ferencvaros, Budapest (UEFA Cup 1972)

164-165

Snow scene at Jena 1971
Defeat of Juventus 1972
Winning the League Cup 1974
Supporter power, Wembley 1974
Contrasts:1884 and 1974

180-181

Wolves v Porto 1974
Wolves Youth team, Switzerland 1976
"Test Match" 1976
Vale et ave: W. McGarry, S. Chung

196-197

Foreword

Those young men connected with St. Luke's School, Blakenhall, who met 100 years ago to form a football club could have had no idea of the consequences that would result from their action. The name by which their club was soon to be known (exactly how is uncertain) underlines the point. For over the years Wolverhampton Wanderers acquired not only national but international significance. In some senses the name came to denote Town as well as Club.

At the beginning of the second century of our history, we are very conscious of the responsibilities placed on us at Molineux, both by the past record and tradition of the Club, and by the expectations of Wulfrunians. We know that changes in the future are inevitable, both for the Club and for football itself. Sometimes the process of change is uncomfortable but we are not afraid of change.

A centenary celebration reminds us of tradition, and at Molineux we have a continuing tradition. There are some who have loyally worked with us for almost half a century. On the other hand, we have abundant promise and faith in the youth who will take us into the future. It would be rash to prophesy; but we believe that our Club as an institution of the town will go forward worthily to represent the town into the distant future.

When the second centenary year comes round we shall be absent. We hope, however, that those then concerned with the Wolves will look back on us with something of the amusement, affection, and perhaps even gratitude with which we regard the Brodies and Bayntons of long ago.

I have great pleasure in introducing this history of the Club written by one whose long affection for the Wolves is well known, and it is not only a tale of what has been, but also a spur to further effort in the future.

HARRY J. MARSHALL,

Chairman, Wolverhampton Wanderers.

Acknowledgements

The author wishes to thank the following for assistance in respect of the furnishing of information or illustrative material and for permission to use the same: Aerofilms Limited, Airviews Limited, G. J. Cooksey, S. Cullis, Fotosports International, V. Grebnev, Councillor Mrs. M. W. Hodson, M. Horne, the late J. Howley, J. H. Marshall, Councillor S. Martin, Photographic News Agency, Planet News, P.A.-Reuter, A. Wilkes and Son, Mrs. E. Woodward, the Estate of the late A. G. Taylor, The *Express and Star*, the Wolverhampton Art Gallery, past and present players, many supporters, and the officials of Wolverhampton Wanderers F.C. Ltd.

1

Pioneers

'John Baynton . . . commenced apprenticeship
John Brodie commenced as monitor'
Log Book of St. Luke's School, Blakenhall, January 15 1875.

ST. Luke's Church, Blakenhall, is the centre around which the story of Wolves began. It is a story full of twists and turns, and unexpected happenings; in short it is a romantic story.

The land on which St. Luke's Church stands was given by Jeremiah Mason, landlord of the King's Arms on the Dudley Road, by Sedgley Street. Opened in 1861, the church—like the pub—was built 'chiefly to meet the requirements of an artisan population which, through the operations of freehold building societies, have been enabled to migrate from the more densely occupied town and erect their own dwellings in this elevated and salubrious district'. This shift of population also necessitated additional educational provision and Mason sold a further patch of land—for 1/3d. a yard—for the 'commodious schools', to take 500 pupils, opened on 11 November 1861.

At that time football was beginning to establish itself as a national sport, a fact that was marked in 1863 by the institution of a Football Association in London. During the next ten years or so the need for healthy recreation was a cause pursued with some zeal by those principally responsible for the welfare of the young. These were clergymen and schoolmasters, who were specially active in industrialised areas like Wolverhampton and the Black Country.

In 1873 the staff of St. Luke's School was led by W. H. Barcroft (1852-1917), Alice Mary Harding, mistress of the infants' department, and Hester Tipper, mistress—presumably with special responsibility for the girls. The nominal direction of this collective was in the hands of Rev. John Parry, Vicar of the parish since 1861. An absent-minded gentleman who never managed to bring himself to fill out the forms requested by the compilers of the Clerical Directory, he lived on Goldthorn Hill on a stipend of £150 a year with the care of 4000 souls. From 1872 to 1874 he was assisted by Thomas Orrell, and from 1874 for some years by David Williams, who had served his probationary period as a curate in Pensnett.

The appointment of Harry Barcroft was an act of faith if not of genius. He was only 21 years of age, but what he achieved in the earlier part of his 44-year-long career was of monumental significance. He was himself an active footballer, and as soon as he took over responsibility for the further education of John Baynton and John Brodie—as apprentice and monitor respectively—he began a new chapter in the history of Wolverhampton.

Baynton, born at Rushock in Worcestershire, was brought to live at Lodge Farm, Goldthorn Hill, when he was an infant in arms. Brodie was born at Wightwick. On the day after they were entered as above in the St. Luke's Log Book, a lecture in aid of a Working Men's Club was given in Christ Church Schools by Thomas Hughes, Q.C., famous as the author of *Tom Brown's Schooldays*. His subject (as important now as then) was 'The Right Use of Leisure', and he emphasised the importance of cricket and football. These sports in his view had a moral influence, and it was this that influenced the clergy and schoolmasters of the day. While praising football and cricket, Hughes deplored the so-called field sports because they were associated with cruelty and death. His lecture was published more or less in full in the *Midland Counties Express* of January 16, 1875. On November 20 of the same year the same newspaper reprinted an article from the *Daily News*, entitled 'Football Vindicated', which brought the main advantage of the game once again to general notice in Wolverhampton:

> Out of door games there must be if the standard of health and strength is to be kept up . . . It is more properly encouraged at Public Schools, where almost the most dangerous tendency boys can have is to loaf about, banquet in confectioners' shops, and read yellow-backed novels. Football is a healthy corrective of these practices and tastes . . .

The newsworthy sports in Wolverhampton in 1875 were cricket and bicycling. There was a wide range of cricket clubs, the senior one bearing the name of the town. At full strength this club included in the team The 'Perpetual Curate' of Tettenhall—Rev. A. J. Van Straubenzee—and two curates from St. Peter's Church—Rev. G. Woodhouse and Rev. W. J. Price. At the Railway Works, on Stafford Road, cricket was encouraged at shop floor level, matches being arranged for workers who were not members of regular clubs—as between teams of fitters on the one hand and turners on the other. There was a Goldthorn Cricket Club, and among those who played against Mowbray House Past and Present on September 23 was J. Mason—no doubt the sporting landlord of the King's Arms. Bicycle races were big business and the chief promotor was Oliver Edge McGregor, who owned Molineux House and the Pleasure Grounds at the back, an ideal and most convenient venue for large-scale sporting activity. Molineux House was otherwise the headquarters of the Molineux Bowling Club.

To give a fuller dimension to the sporting opportunities for Wulfrunians a hundred years ago, the Wolverhampton Races, begun in 1825 and staged at Dunstall, and the Skating Rink in Darlington Street should also be mentioned.

Football—entirely amateur—was a going concern too, although receiving only casual treatment in the press, which relied for the most part on club secretaries to supply factual information. But in the West Midlands (as in other parts of the country) there was often difficulty in establishing what football was. There is a nice record of confusion in an account in the *Midland Counties Express*, even at the relatively late date of February 23 1876 of a match between Wednesbury Town and Edgbaston Proprietary School:

> The Wednesbury Club having sustained defeat at the first meeting by one goal to nothing, owing to their ignorance of the Rugby Union rules, now returned the compliment with interest, for when the game ended the umpire called two goals to love. But the Proprietary School was certainly not defeated for their lack of pluck, or for the inferiority of their play, but chiefly on account of being strange to the Association rules.

There was a Wolverhampton Football Club already in existence which played according to Rugby Union rules, as did the Cleveland Club which played at Dunstall, and Tettenhall College and the Grammar School.

But the Association game was making headway. The most active club was that at Stafford Road, which founded—it was said—in 1872 and which three years later was running two teams regularly. The ground of the Stafford Road club was on Fox's Lane. The amenities were minimal and for changing-rooms a Pumping Shed in the vicinity was used. Other prominent clubs included Aston Park Unity, Aston Villa, Birmingham Royal, Cannock, Lichfield, Rushall Rovers, Shropshire Wanderers (semi-finalists in the F.A. Cup in 1875), Walsall Victoria Swifts, Wednesbury Town, and West Bromwich Albion.

On Friday, November 10 1876, a meeting billed as the First General Meeting of the Goldthorn Football Club was held in St. Luke's School, Blakenhall, which 'any gentleman interested in the game' was invited to attend. Of what precisely transpired there is no record, but of the fact that the club came into effective being—and within it the inspiration of the Wolves-to-be—there is no doubt.

FOOTBALL.

THE FIRST GENERAL MEETING

OF THE

GOLDTHORN FOOTBALL CLUB

Will (by the kind permission of the Vicar) be held at

ST. LUKE'S SCHOOL, BLAKENHALL,

ON

Friday next, November 10, 1876,

AT 7·30 P.M.

Any Gentleman interested in the game is invited to attend.

The day after this First General Meeting those who were keen to see how football should be played took themselves to Fox's Lane to see the Works team defeat West Bromwich Albion 1-0 in a Birmingham and District F.A. Cup tie. The works team comprised:

> R. Gowland (goal); L. Gowland, G. Sel(l)man (backs); T. Whitehead, W. Grant, T. Wardle (half-backs); C. Crump, J. Whitehead, E. Davies, E. Jones, J. S. Ludlam, Rev. J. Lightfoot (forwards).

John Lightfoot, who had studied at Lichfield Theological College, was ordained deacon only in 1875 and he was appointed to his first curacy in Heath Town, where his participation in football was welcome. As was the case in those days, the Stafford Road—West Bromwich match required two umpires. G. McCann acted for the former, one Bache for the latter. Supervising them (umpires somewhat later on became linesmen) was the referee, in this case Rev. Francis Marshall (1845-1906). Marshall was an interesting scholar-sportsman typical of the age in which he lived. Born in West Bromwich (which no doubt tested his impartiality in the above-mentioned match), educated at Brewood Grammar School and Cambridge University, he distinguished himself as a mathematical scholar. In 1870 he became Headmaster of the Wednesbury Collegiate School, where he remained for eight years. A busy writer, he published text-books on the bible, literature, and mathematics. But of greater significance was his editing of *Football: the Rugby Union Game*, which first appeared in 1892, and was reissued in 1893, 1894, and 1925.

There were, it is clear, many and diverse talents on view on November 11 1876, but the most historic were those of Crump, the captain of the twelve-man Works team. He was to become a key figure not only in the record of Wolverhampton but also of English football.

On December 30 Stafford Road played against Cannock, the team being as before, except R. Gowland was replaced by E. Gowland, E. Davies by A. Nicholls. As the Cannock team arrived one man short their umpire took his place, while S. G. Crump, of the home team, stood in for the visiting umpire. Stafford Road won easily by 3-0.

On January 13 1877, at 3.30 p.m. a much more epoch-making match—although it did not then appear as such—began. The Stafford Road second team 'met the Goldthorn Hill team on their own ground, near the Orphanage . . . From the commencement it was evident that the superior strength and tactics of the Stafford Road team must result in an easy victory for them'. And an easy victory it was, the final score being 8-0. But the encouragement given to Goldthorn Hill from Stafford Road led to the eventual transfiguration of the former and the dissolution of the latter. The first recorded Goldthorn Hill team was:

> Barcroft, Hampton, Hodges, Adams, A. O. Robotham, T. Worrall, W. Kendrick, J. Boynton, E. Newman, Myatt, Jacks, and Foster, with J. Ward as umpire.

Adams, it may be surmised, was the same as in the Goldthorn Hill Cricket team, while T. Worrall putatively was a brother of George Worrall, a well-known pupil of St. Luke's School. The vagaries of printers being what they were one suspects that Hodges was the Hedges of the cricket team and J. Boynton identical with Baynton, now beginning his third year of teaching apprenticeship at St. Luke's. What is undeniable is, that the initiative for the foundation of the Goldthorn Hill F.C. was Harry Barcroft's, whose practical instruction in football was remembered by his former pupils and even now is within living memory. There is another note in the Log Book of St. Luke's School which is a milestone in the history of the Wolves; 'March 15 1877; Let the boys out earlier on Friday afternoon and they had a Football Match'. Next day Stafford Road—described simply as Wolverhampton—beat Shrewsbury 3-0. A week later they were beaten in the Final of the Birmingham Cup by Wednesbury Old Athletic, a team which several times put an end to the hopes of Wolverhampton teams in those early days.

Meanwhile the Goldthorn Hill Club had shown itself in no sense narrow-minded, having played against Cleveland on February 3 and losing by eight goals and three tries to nil! In the general upsurge of football interest Bushbury F.C. played Rugby rules for first choice, while Wolverhampton Lancers showed a marked indifference as to code. Stafford Road produced daughter clubs in Bushbury, Loco and Railway. On the eastern side of the town The Heath and Heath Town football clubs came into existence, the latter under the tutelage of Rev. J. Lightfoot, otherwise connected with Stafford Road. In an expanding district where a growing work force was being housed, Whitmore Reans F.C. began to attract promising players. Where there were schools or where there were factories footballers emerged and as soon as there were twelve (more often than not the statutory number on those days) there was a team. So at that time there were Graiseley F.C., Redcross Street F.C., Alexandria F.C., United Rovers F.C., Wednesbury Crown, and Fallings Park Britannia.

As to what happened in some matches one may guess from newspaper notices—or, rather, non-notices:

Graiseley-Hill v Redcross Street. A match between these clubs was played on Saturday last, but as the accounts sent by the representatives of the clubs are contradictory as to the result we must decline to insert either of them. *(Midland Counties Express,* December 10 1877).

The Graiseley team of that time included T. Cliff, who like Worrall of Goldthorn Hill was an alumnus of St. Luke's School, which also gave its name to a separate football team. In the late 70's, then, it is clear that those pupils of St. Luke's School who had football aspirations were well placed to realise them.

It is worth mentioning that a fresh stimulus to school football came in 1877 with the raising of the school-leaving age to 14—an edict that was objected to by many. (At the same time employment of children under the age of nine was outlawed). Among Barcroft's early pupils, in addition to those already named, were Thomas Arthur Blackham—who was born in Haggar Street in 1859, James George Hill, Arthur Lowder—in later life Chairman of Brewood Council, Dick Baugh, George Worrall, and John Addenbrooke—to become first Secretary of the Wolves, and Jeremiah Mason's son Charles. The last-named, born in 1863, was a valuable adjunct to any team in its infancy, in that his father's generosity was inevitably invested in his activities.

On May 10 1879 Barcroft sadly found it necessary to write in the Log Book: 'The teachers have not attended to their duties well this week. I have had to correct Baynton and Brodie several times within a few hours of neglect of duty—found Brodie on the floor and the boys laughing at him'.

But St. Luke's F.C., its ground on Goldthorn Hill, near the home of Alfred Hickman, owner of Spring Vale Iron Works, was a going concern which in the autumn of that year maintained two teams. On October 11 the first team played Heath Town first team, and although without three first team players, only lost 1-0. The depleted second team, away at Heath Town, won. On January 17, 1880 the St. Luke's second team played against Shifnal Wanderers first team. Shifnal won 2-1, 'but a pleasant evening was spent at the Wheatsheaf Inn, where a handsome cap was presented to the captain of the losing team'.

As educator, the head teacher of St. Luke's School could not have done other than welcome Baynton's departure and Brodie's entry to Saltley College in 1880. But he must have looked back with satisfaction at the sense of team spirit inculcated by the departing apprentice and monitor.

There are a few details of these early days which have been sieved through uncertain memories. Brodie and Jimmy Hill once threatened to desert the St. Luke's set-up in favour of that at Whitmore Reans (see p. 6). In time the 'old Windmill Field', on Goldthorn Hill was given up in favour of John Harper's field in Lower Villiers Street. Business affairs were transacted in a room in the King's Arms.

Amid the insecure parts of history some things stand firm; in this case the important fact is that St. Luke's School was, in truth, a 'nursery' for footballers. But between the endeavours of its young hopefuls and the achievements of the senior clubs there was a gap to be bridged.

2

Wanderers

Two of the goals, however, which counted for the Alma went off two of the Wanderers.
Midland Counties Express,
September 28 1880.

IN 1879 Stafford Road F.C., losing finalists in 1877, once again contested the Final of the Birmingham Cup. Once again the result was disappointing, victory being conceded to the old enemy, Wednesbury Old Athletic. In the next season ambition led to entry into the F.A. Cup competition, but here again there was disappointment. Stafford Road were not good enough for Aston Villa, who won 3-1. Nevertheless, there was quality in the team, as evidenced by the selection of three players—E. Ray, J. Whitehead, and G. H. Sellman—for the representative Birmingham F.A. team that played against London (twice), Sheffield, and Scottish Counties. To mark the contribution of these players the Birmingham Association presented to Stafford Road a handsomely inscribed and illuminated document of thanks on April 30 1880.

The next was the finest season to date in the history of football in Wolverhampton. Victories against Grantham (after a draw at the first attempt) and Aston Villa—between which there was a helpful bye—brought them up against the most famous team of the day: Old Etonians. On March 19 1881, a vast crowd (for those days) of 3,000 assembled at Fox's Lane. But alas for expectations! the home team played well, but not well enough. In the end, it was claimed, skill told and after a hard-fought match the visitors returned south with the 2-1 win that put them into the Final—a bye again assisting progress.

This was Charlie Crump's best season as a player and—apparently—his last as captain of Stafford Road. A remarkable man, and a typical Victorian, he deserves some separate mention, for without him neither English nor Wolverhampton football would have prospered as they did.

Crump was born near Leominster in 1840 and came to Wolverhampton when he was 17 as a clerk in the Railway Works. After eleven years he had worked his way up to being chief clerk, a post he held until his retirement in 1905. A well-built, active young man when he entered the works, and with an inclination to be among the leaders rather than the led, he encouraged his companions to go for long country walks. Next he developed an enthusiasm among them for bandy, a primitive kind of hockey. In 1872, inspired by the success of the railway men of Stoke-on-Trent in this respect, no doubt, he promoted organised football. The Stafford Road F.C. was his creation, as were other clubs in the neighbourhood set up on the 'permanent way'.

Under Crump's influence there was a combination of responsibility and opportunity in the fact that J. Jarrad, Hon., Sec., of the Bushbury F.C., conducted that club's business from Bushbury Railway Station. In 1875, on its foundation, Crump was elected President of the Birmingham F.A., and he retained this honour until his death in 1923. When he finished his career as a footballer he undertook refereeing duties and officiated at the celebrated F.A. Cup Final of 1883. The Old Etonians, against whom Crump had once played in the same competition were the winners, their opponents being Blackburn Olympic. In due course he was elected to the Council of the F.A. On his eightieth birthday the F.A. honoured Crump with a banquet, when a cheque for £4,000 presented to him was a substantial token of the nation-wide respect in which he was held. Like many pioneers of football, Crump had a strong religious sense, and for many years he was Superintendent of the Darlington Street Methodist Church Sunday School.

In 1879 (so far as can be deduced) a fresh alignment of existing talents brought a new name into the local football circuit. The best players of the Blakenhall group of clubs—St. Luke's, Goldthorn Hill, Graiseley—went into a separate organisation, which for no very good reason called itself Wolverhampton Wanderers. One theory was there was in existence a club named the Wanderers in Wolverhampton which (according to the obituary of J. H. Addenbrooke, printed in the *Express and Star* on September 7 1922) 'threw in its lot with St. Luke's— and the title then became that of Wolverhampton Wanderers'. This theory seemingly became dogma when it was given general currency in the magazine *Out of Doors* (April 1 1893) in an account of Wolves printed in honour of their appearance in the Cup Final. At the time there were many football teams in Wolverhampton; but none was called the Wanderers. However, undeterred by this fact, some raised a parallel thesis; that the football club attached to St. Luke's shared a field with a cricket club named Wanderers (of this team there is no evidence although there certainly was a Goldthorn Hill Cricket Club, as detailed on p. 3). This theory is nicely confused by a note in a compilation by the former sports journalist A. F. Taylor *(Wolverhampton Wanderers F. C. 1883-1913*, which is principally a list of cup-tie results and teams): 'The Wolves played cricket on Baynton's field, Goldthorn Hill, for 2 years before starting football'. That is interesting for the link with the Baynton family. Nor is it inherently improbable that *some* of those who became Wanderers had played cricket. The final proposition, and the likeliest, comes from the former Alderman Levi Johnson, himself in at the beginning of the Wolves. In the *Express and Star*, April 25 1932 he declared that the title Wanderers was adopted out of respect for the famous London team of that name which had won the F.A. Cup five times between 1872 and 1878.

Reports of the earliest matches of the Wanderers are thin on the ground. But as the 1879-80 season wore on their achievements began to receive notice. On April 9, 1880 Wednesfield Rovers found it prudent to strengthen their team, by bringing in a stalwart and experienced defender in the person of G. H. Sellman, before playing the Wanderers at Wednesfield. The Wanderers were compelled to travel from their new headquarters near the Fighting Cocks with three second team players. Nonetheless they won 2-1. The team that day was:

> Goal; W. Caddick; back: J. Baynton; half-backs; C. Mason, T. A. Blackham, B. Gill; forwards: J. Hill, G. Cadman, T. Stanford, T. Cliff, T. Handley, Belcher.

In the Wednesfield side, as well as Sellman, were three players who later cast in their lot with the Wanderers: E. Hadley, J. Griffiths and B. Griffiths.

Although most players seem to have been loyal to the clubs of their choice, there was a tendency to strengthen teams for important fixtures of local importance. So when Whitmore Reans played Stafford Road in March 1880 T. Cliff was to be found in the ranks of the first-named.

Other results that season included a double over All Saints Darlaston. When the autumn came around again the opening match of the 1880-81 season was played at Dudley Road against Walsall Alma. This ended in a 3-3 draw—but two of the Walsall goals were caused by the helpful if unwilling intervention of un-named Wanderers' players—something not unknown in later times. There is a good deal of interest about the description of the team: goal: J. Barlow; backs: Baynton (capt.), J. Brodie; half-backs: Cliff, Stanford, Blackham; forwards: R. Crichton (sub.), Hill, Gill, Handley, Cadman. Whether this is the first published mention of a substitute is unsure, but at least it appears a likely claimant for consideration.

While Wolverhampton Wanderers came into being as such in the 1879-80 season there was no reason for it to be more successful than more senior clubs. Wolverhampton Rangers had a growing reputation in case Stafford Road slipped from grace. And the composite Wolverhampton Association F.C., which became generally known simply as Wolverhampton F.C. was a formidable opponent. Between October 1881 and the early part of January 1882 Wolverhampton F.C. played eleven matches, of which eight were won, two drawn, and only one lost. Of these matches that were played at Saltley against the College on October 1 1881 one was of special interest, for Jack Brodie, Barcroft's protégé from St. Luke's School, and a founder member of the Wanderers, was playing at full back for the College. The Wolverhampton team, which won, was as follows:

Goal, H. Dean; backs, S. Dean, Aston; half-backs, F. McBean, H. Addenbrooke; left forwards, Bennett, F. Reynolds; centre forwards, R. Addenbrooke, J. Ludlam; right forwards, A. D. Bantock, T. J. Addenbrooke.

Another of Barcroft's boys went to Saltley College and became a member of the football team. This was J. H. Addenbrooke, who came back to Wolverhampton in order to pursue a teaching career. Two years of probationary teaching at Bushbury School—during which time he kept his interest in football alive by playing for the Wanderers' second team—convinced him that his vocation was not sufficiently strong to support him through a lifetime of pedagogy. In the Wolves programme of April 18 1922 it was said that in 1875 Addenbrooke was elected Secretary of St. Luke's F.C. "in the playground" of the school. At the time he was ten years of age! It is, however, certain that in 1885 he became the first paid secretary of the Wanderers, a post he held for 37 years. For the time being, however, the club was managed by its playing members—Baynton being captain and treasurer; Cliff, secretary; J. Hill (senior and junior). Caddick, Mason, W. Lowder, Blackham and Crichton, committee. Hickman, an early benefactor of the club, was, and for some years remained President.

Also on October 1 1881 the Wanderers opened their season with a match at Dudley Road against Stourbridge Standard, the team being Caddick; Baynton (capt.); Blackham, Mason, Hardiman; Hill, Cadman, Cliff, Shelton, Crichton, Whitlock. 'Nearly 200 people assembled to witness the match, and, although the scoring seemed all on one side, the spectators were treated to some really good play, only 2 goals being obtained in the first half'. The final score was 7-1 in the Wanderers' favour. 'For the first match the home team played in far better form than was expected of them, scoring 3

Wolverhampton Wanderers
FOOTBALL CLUB.

ANNUAL REPORT
SEASON 1881—1882.

President—
ALFRED HICKMAN, ESQ.

Captain and Treasurer—
MR. J. BAYNTON.

Secretary—
MR. T. CLIFF.

Committee—
MR. J. HILL, Senr,   MR. C. MASON,
MR. J. HILL, Junr,   MR. W. LOWDER,
MR. W. CADDICK,   MR. A. BLACKHAM,
MR. R. CRIGHTON.

Date.	Matches Played.	Result	Goals Won	Goals Lost
1881-2				
Oct. 1	Stourbridge Standard	Won	7	1
,, 15	Birmingham Heath	Won	5	1
,, 29	Walsall Alma Athletic (Cup Tie)	Draw	0	0
Nov. 5	Walsall Alma Athletic (Cup Tie)	Lost	2	3
,, 12	Wednesfield Rovers	Won	2	1
,, 26	Birmingham Heath	Won	0	0
Dec. 3	Darlaston All Saints	Lost	1	1
,, 10	Bloxwich	Draw	4	1
,, 17	Cannock (Cup Tie)	Won	4	1
,, 24	Wednesfield Rovers	Won	11	0
,, 31	Wednesfield Rovers	Draw	0	0
Jan. 21	Walsall Alma Athletic (Cup Tie)	Draw	1	1
Feb. 4	Walsall Alma Athletic (Cup Tie)	Won	2	4
,, 18	Aston Clifton	Won	1	0
,, 25	Wednesbury Old Athletic (B. Team)	Won	3	0
Mar. 4	Wednesbury Old Athletic (B. Team)	Lost	1	2
,, 11	Walsall White Star	Won	3	1
,, 25	Walsall Alma Athletic	Won	4	0
	Total		51	18

Number of Matches played ... 18
Matches Won ... 10
Matches Lost ... 4
Matches Drawn ... 4

Number of Goals scored by W.W.F.C.—51.
Number of Goals scored against W.W.F.C.—18.

SECOND TEAM PLAYED 7 MATCHES, WON 4 AND LOST 3.

	£	s	d
Total Receipts ...	33	0	0
Total Expenditure ...	27	13	4½
Balance in hand ...	£5	6	7½

JOHN BAYNTON, Hon. Treasurer.
WILLIAM LOWDER, } Auditors.
WILLIAM CADDICK, }

goals in the last six minutes. The passing of the forwards was at times very good, as was also the defensive game played by the backs. The Stourbridge forwards played up well, but the half-backs were rather slow, which, perhaps, accounts for the long scoring of the Wanderers'. Cliff performed a hat-trick, Hill scored 2 goals, and Crichton and Cadman one each.

There was another matter of some consequence at that time. On September 28 it was reported that R. Willcock, a solicitor of Queens Street, had purchased the Molineux grounds from McGregor for Edwin Steer, a bacon factor. The price was not disclosed, but it was known that a previous offer of £8,000 had been turned down.

When Wolverhampton F.C. played against Calthorpe on November 19, in addition to the three Addenbrookes already named in the Wolverhampton team, (T. J. played striker for Wolverhampton, and H. for Sutton Coldfield), there were also C. Addenbrooke in goal, and H. G. Addenbrooke at left back, for the opposing side.

John Addenbrooke, the Wolves secretary, was not immediately related to the other Addenbrookes named. He belonged to a working class family, although a connection with the more prosperous bearers of the same name is to be presumed.

Among accounts of more important engagements a careful reader of the *Midland Counties Express* for Monday October 17 would have noticed,

> Wanderers v Birmingham Heath — Played on Saturday, near the Dudley road. The Wanderers followed up the success of their first match by defeating the Birmingham Heath 5 goals to 1.

The season progressed, and the Wanderers made new friends by their ability to score goals. A notable achievement was the defeat of Birmingham Heath in the second match of the season by 5-1. This Birmingham team was among the better-known in the district, and among those ambitious enough to enter for the Wednesbury Football Charity Association Cup.[1]

In this same season one of the early patrons of Wolves began to play a prominent part in local affairs, and to bring influence on the development of football as a community amenity. This was Levi Johnson (1850-1937). On May 9 1881, Johnson had taken his place on the Borough Council, being welcomed by Jeremiah Mason, already a councillor, with the memorable cry: "Come on, young man!"

A native of Macclesfield, Johnson had been in Wolverhampton for five

---

[1] The other competing teams that year were Aston Unity, Athletic, Castle Blues (Shrewsbury), Elwell's (Wednesbury), Oswestry, St. George's (Birmingham), Small Heath Alliance, Spital Strollers, Wellington, West Bromwich Albion.

years, and being also engaged in the 'licensing trade', had become friendly with the landlord of the King's Arm. Mason, in fact, had persuaded Johnson into undertaking the vice-presidency and the treasurership of the St. Luke's F.C. In the Ring o' Bells, kept by Johnson, there was accommodation for dressing-rooms and this was used by the Wanderers when they first went to their Dudley Road ground. Johnson's interest was with the team wherever it went and remained with him for life. In the 1881-2 season he managed the Wanderers' finances so shrewdly that there was a profit on the year's working, of £5.6.7½d. At the end of the following season—the gate receipts totalled £80—there was cash in hand—£1.0.1.

Johnson served on the Borough Council for fifty-six years, becoming Alderman in 1900 and Mayor three years later. A J.P. for many years, and a sidesman at St. Peter's Church—where he is remembered in a memorial screen—for thirty years, he served the community well.

The 1882-3 season was one of consolidation, not least because Brodie, now a teacher at St. Peter's School, was regularly available. During this season the club challenged as many good teams as would accept challenges from relative newcomers, and entered a number of competitions. What then comprised the first team pool was—Caddick, in goal; Mason, at back; Cliff, at three-quarter back, Baynton, C. Yates, A. Davidson, at half-back; Hill, J. Waldron, Brodie, R. M. Vealy, T. Griffiths, A. Lowder, and E. Hadley[1], at forward. One of the players 'rested' from any game acted as umpire. Hadley and Griffiths had by now joined the team from Wednesfield Rovers. Of these players some began to emerge as distinct personalities of the game. Baynton, who was captain, playing either at back or half-back, was conspicuous for his energy. He was always capable of "making a run the length of the field" in freebooting style, to dismay flat-footed opponents, as he notably did in the 4-3 defeat of Dudley Town on October 10 in the first round of the Birmingham Cup. In the second round on December 16 the Wanderers defeated Derby St. Luke's by the same score.

Sometimes defeat is thought to be more encouraging than victory—to the cautious mind, at least. On October 14 the Wanderers travelled to North Staffordshire to play against Stoke, a team which only one week before had beaten Nottingham Forest. The result was much closer than any had anticipated, the home side only just scraping by with a score of 2-1. There were "many spectators" who (such was the temper of those times) were 'most impartial'. Generous in applauding the surprising technical quality of the visitors' play they were treated by the Wanderers to a kind of elegance, in that their 'passing was much better than in any previous match . . . this

[1]Hadley died in December 1929.

season'. In a return match, two days before Christmas, the Wanderers reversed the earlier result, winning 1-0.

After Christmas the Wanderers' results included wins over Handsworth Grove (twice), Walsall Alma, and St. George's, Birmingham. The extent by which interest was rising is indicated by the number of games at which the attendances were reckoned in thousands rather than in hundreds. When Walsall Swifts (occasional effective marauders in the early rounds of the F.A. Cup) came to Dudley Road on April 7 1883, there was a crowd of 2,000: but the Swifts won 1-0. On this occasion Brodie was captain.

This, however, was the season in which Wolverhampton Wanderers won their first trophy. It was a modest achievement, and not blazoned on the club's banner. Nevertheless it was a landmark. On March 24 the Handsworth Grove Cricket and Football Club organised a 6-aside competition, for which eleven clubs entered. The Wanderers were the winners, taking away the first prize of £5.

At the end of that season, on May 5, the club—now being regarded as gateworthy in a wider sphere—went to Stafford to play a match against Stafford Rangers in aid of the local Infirmary. Although playing with only ten men, and two of those from the second team, the Wanderers won with greater ease than the score of 4-1 indicated.

St. Luke's F.C. still maintained an independent life, and on March 3, 1883, on their own ground and 'before a great number of spectators' they played Springfield Rovers, but lost 2-1. The team was: E. Meecham; W. Green, W. Hodson; W. Johnson, R. Fidler, J. Badley; F. Hill, T. Johnson, W. Minshull, J. Griton, C. Leicester.

From the pastoral angle the Wanderers were still within the care of St. Luke's Church. The newly appointed Vicar—to remain at St. Luke's for six years—was J. G. Addenbrooke (1849-1922), a member of a West Midlands family with a history reaching back to Norman times and with a good sporting record, as already noticed on p. 12.

At that time the pressures on players were considerable. They were amateurs, but they were beginning to be expected to turn up entertainment of a professional quality, and to provide supporters with results satisfactory to their self-esteem. The Wanderers were finding that life nearer to the top made severe demands, and injuries became more frequent.

In the autumn of 1883, a week after a pipe-opener at Dudley Road against Oswestry on October 1 there was a severe test against Stoke. 'Between two and three thousand spectators lined the ropes to witness the present encounter, which was one of the best that has ever been played on the Dudley Road ground.' A 2-2 draw was all the more meritorious in that the goalkeeper, Caddick, was 'badly hurt' at the beginning of the match and 'rendered almost useless.' Three weeks after that was a first round F.A. Cup match against Long Eaton Rovers—undefeated for two seasons—in front of a gate of 3,000.

The team was J. Griffiths; Mason, Cliff; Davidson, Baynton, Blackham; Hill, Lowder, Brodie (capt.) Hadley, J. Griffiths. The umpire on behalf of the Wanderers was W. Dallard.

Long Eaton seemed to be every bit as good as they had been described as being. Despite their threatening attacks, however, there were no goals until the 25th minute. Then the home goal hope, Griffiths, fatally punched a ball at the feet of a Long Eaton forward. Just before half-time Brodie took ball and goalkeeper through the goal; but the goal he claimed was disallowed. After half-time the home team found their rhythm. Hill diverted the attention of the visiting goalkeeper and Griffiths took an easy chance to level the score. Stern tackling of two men by Davidson and a shrewdly placed pass to Brodie took the Wanderers ahead. By now confident, they played attractive, even bewildering, football and a neat movement between Hill and Lowder left Brodie with another chance to score. With a few minutes left Griffiths scored his second and his team's fourth goal. This was an auspicious entry into the F.A. Cup competition.

A week later the Wanderers played one team against Brownhills, winning by 8-1, and another against St. George's. That was a 3-3 draw. The same afternoon Goldthorn Villa, 'on their own ground' (which suggests that taking into account other clubs, Goldthorn Hill at that time, was almost totally dedicated to football pitches) beat Wolverhampton Swifts 4-0. J. Waldron was captain, while Arthur Worral, younger brother of George, and one A. Brodie (another familiar surname) were in the team.

On November 10 for the Wrekin Cup tie against St. Paul's (Lozells), the versatile Baynton was in goal. H. Gale came into the forward line, but was not at his best, having suffered from rheumatism for the previous six weeks. The Wanderers won 7-0. This cleared the decks for a Birmingham Cup match the following week. Castle Blues, of Shrewsbury, came to Dudley Road with misgivings and left with more. At half-time, there being no score, they registered optimism. That this was misplaced was proven within five minutes during which the Wanderers scored five goals. The final score was 10-0.

Those were vigorous days so far as Cup football was concerned. On December 1, both Stafford Road and the Wanderers were involved in the F.A. Cup; the former at home against Aston Villa; the latter at the Oval, Wednesbury, against the Old Athletic. The former was the match of the day, attracting a crowd of 3,000. But the home team and their supporters were in for a shock. 'At the outset', reported the *Evening Express*, the Stafford Road team lost the services of Sellman, their noted back, he having declined to play on account of the hard condition of the ground. The strangers having won the toss, elected to play up the field . . . And they had an easy victory, 5-0. The Stafford Road team was: Ray; Riley, Crump; Whitehead, Turton, Nicholls (capt.), Jones, Morgan, Foster, Baker, Griffiths.

At Wednesbury there were but 1,000 spectators, who saw a fairly easy win for the home side, 4-2.

Next came a Walsall cup match, on December 8, against Stafford Rangers, which was reported as having been won by the Wanderers by '3 goals and 1 disputed to nil.'

Coming up to the season of good will the Wanderers played a friendly game on Christmas Eve against Wolverhampton Town (the name now of the former Wolverhampton Association) who, having arrived only with nine players, were beaten 4-1.

A dark shadow was thrown over Christmas that year since a few days beforehand the brougham taking the Mayor and Mayoress—Alderman and Mrs. John Brotherton—to a soirée in Wednesbury overturned and both were injured. The cause of the accident was a group of itinerant Italian musicians drawing a piano along the tramway lines, to the distraction of a freshly commissioned horse, the discomfiture of the occupants of the carriage, and (according to the newspaper) the general consternation of the people of the town.

Sadder still, however, was the misfortune that struck the Wanderers on Boxing Day, when they had a home tie in the third round of the Birmingham Cup against Villa Cross, Handsworth. The team was the same as that against Long Eaton, given above. The match turned out to be a walk-over. The Wanderers pursued a relentless course and had already scored six goals when Arthur Blackham added a seventh. Tackled as he shot, he fell, and 'did not rise'. It was a broken leg, and Blackham was taken straight to the hospital. After that the Wanderers added another eight goals, making the final score 15-0.

'It is satisfactory to know that it was a pure accident, as no rough play had been indulged in'. Blackham, it was added, 'was one of the most consistent players in the team, and was always a great favourite with the spectators for his clever play'. But he never played again. Blackham's enthusiasm and experience, however, was not lost to the game. He joined the Wanderers' committee and acted for many seasons as a linesman. He kept up a close connection with the club until 1922 when his friend, of St. Luke's and the Wanderers, John Addenbrooke, died. Blackham lived on to a ripe old age, to die at the age of 85 in 1945.

On the brighter side it was remarked how the Wanderers gave a football to the Dudley Road Board School team which had defeated the St. Luke's team in a two-leg match played on the Wanderers ground (Admission—adults 2d; children 1d) on December 27 and 29. The first leg ended in a 3-3 draw; the second—'toughly fought'—in a 1-0 win for the 'Board School'. The proceeds were divided between the two schools for the benefit of the poorest children. Occasionally Wolves went in for gamesmanship. On February 23, 1884, a Birmingham Cup-tie, 4th round, with West Bromwich Albion, ended in a 1-1 draw. The Albion appealed for extra time—but while they were doing so the Wanderers quickly left the field.

That year the Wanderers won their first important trophy—the Wrekin Cup, in the Final of which they defeated the Shropshire team Hadley 11-0. But what had given more satisfaction than this was the fact that in the third round Stafford Road had been disposed of by 5-1. The Wanderers team was different from that on p. 17 only in respect of Pearson for Blackham, and Waldron for Lowder. Stafford Road, in comparison with the team given on p. 18 had Sheldon at half-back in place of Whitehead, and Whitehead for Baker in the forward line. The result of the match signified the passing of an era of glory. Stafford Road, who met the Wanderers again in the F.A. Cup in the 1885-6 season, only to lose 4-2 after having been two goals ahead, were on the way out of the top class.

In those, as they may now seem, carefree days, spectators at Dudley Road paid 3d for admission, with a further 3d due for admittance to the 'boarded reserve'. To gain some idea of what those charges represented in 'real terms', those who patronised Jessop's luncheon bar in North Street at that time bought a glass of ale with crust, cheese, and cress for 1d, a hot sausage with potatoes and bread for 3d, hot roast beef and potatoes for 5d, stewed steak for 6d, and boiled fowl and bacon for 8d.

Football had at first been carefree, with development from the centuries-old folk game gradual. It was now becoming more professional in character. The first trainer of the Wanderers was said to have been William Shipton, landlord of the Vine, at Upper Vauxhall. He supervised a training schedule that consisted chiefly of spare-time walks, as far afield as Penkridge and Rugeley. Such exercise was solemnly performed, in suits and with ties. But what the players looked forward to most of all were the mutton chops—each plateful decorated with two eggs—and the half-pint of old ale, at the Ring o' Bells, which followed night manoeuvres at Dudley Road.

In the autumn following Walsall Swifts were drawn against Stafford Road and Wanderers against Derby St. Luke's in the first round of the F.A. Cup.

Both Wolverhampton teams lost, but the Wanderers (Griffiths; Mason, Cliff; Pearson, Baynton, Davidson; Stanford, Brazier, Brodie, H. Wood, H. Deans) took Derby to a replay. Having drawn 0-0 at home, they led Derby on their ground, on Monday November 24, by 2-0 at half-time. When full-time came the score was 2-2, and in extra time the home team, staying the course better, added two more goals to their total. Also occupied in the Birmingham Cup, the Walsall Cup, and the Staffordshire Cup, the Wanderers had their work cut out to keep a consistent record. In the event they collected the Staffordshire Cup. In 35 matches that year the Wanderers scored 116 goals, with only 32 against them.

During that season football had been in a state of ferment. Professionalism in some clubs was known to be rampant; but for as long as they could the authorities shut their eyes to the facts. Among those most strongly opposed to professionalism was Charles Crump, representing at that time the Birmingham F.A. On January 19, 1885 a special meeting at the F.A. voted 112-108 against allowing professionalism. Another attempt to regularise the situation in March was unsuccessful. On July 20 of that year however, the progressives won the day. And if there was one place where it was difficult for players to maintain both the standard required by the public and their own livelihoods outside the game it was Wolverhampton.

When Addenbrooke became secretary, at a critical time in the history of the game, the foundations had been laid. For there was the nucleus of a team which within a year or two was to be spoken of with respect throughout the land. Brodie, Baynton (who once scored a goal in a cuptie from 97 yards!), Mason, Lowder, of the first generation, were a tower of strength. And they continued to provide inspiration and experience across the years that took the Wanderers to the top.

An omission from this group is Jimmy Hill. One of the most successful inside-forwards—he combined especially well with Jack Brodie when Brodie was centre-forward—Hill was approached by Stoke after he had put in a particularly good performance against them. But Jimmy was not to be persuaded away from his loyalties. He spent seven years with the Wanderers, at the end of which it seemed that he was out of the game for good with a knee injury. He was as near being heart-broken as makes no odds.

But work took him south. A sheet-metal worker he found a job at Woolwich in the Royal Arsenal Works, where another Wanderers player, Bob Crichton, had preceded him.

Both men discovered the Royal Arsenal Football Club, and having found it gave the benefit of their wisdom. Both played for the club and when Hill gave up he became a member of the first board of directors of Arsenal when that

Lake in grounds of Molineux House c. 1860.

Molineux Pleasure Grounds c. 1860.

Molineux Pleasure Grounds, 1869.

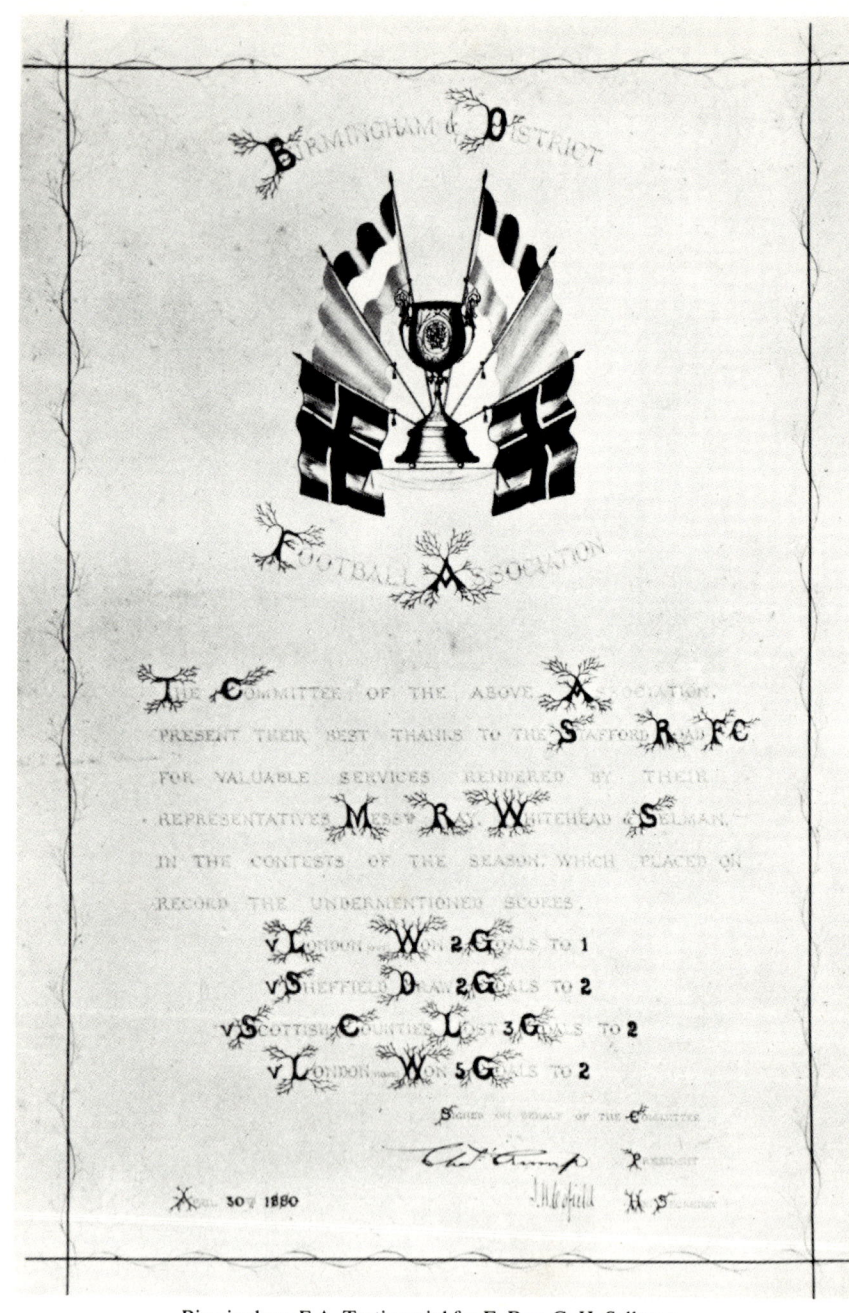

Birmingham F.A. Testimonial for E. Ray, G. H. Sellman, and J. Whitehead, 1880.

club embraced professionalism. In his later years Hill lived close to the Charlton ground in south London, and there was discovered in 1953 when the Wolves played there. A year later he was a guest of the Wolves when Charlton were visitors. In 1955, aged 93, he died, a wonderful testimony to the life-preserving force of a constant interest in football.

3

Last days at Dudley Road

'It was a great day for them and for everybody, at least in Wolverhampton'
Out of Doors, April 1 1893.

IT was clear in 1885 that if the pinnacles were to be scaled the affairs of the club must be shrewdly directed and the public made to understand their responsibility. This is why Addenbrooke was appointed secretary, with the first duty of adjusting to the professional game. There were at that time more than 75,000 people living in Wolverhampton, and gates of two or three thousand at a few pence a time were not adequate to sustain the aspirations of the zealots. The faithful wandered off to the uneven, hilly pitch at Dudley Road, where the only shelter against inclement weather—contrasting forcibly with the latter-day advertisement of 'covered accommodation for 30,000'—was a lean-to shed. They encouraged players with occasional cries of 'Come on, me little Wanderers'—but the wider vision stimulated hopes of many thousands of clustered partisans, willing and roaring their side—and their town—to supremacy.

In the 1885-6 season the Wanderers made their most extensive foray into the select, highest circles of the F.A. Cup competition. In the first round they wiped off a score that had rankled for a twelve-month by summarily disposing of Derby St. Lukes, their victors in the same round in the previous season. Their next victims were Stafford Road, and after that Walsall Swifts. In the fourth round they met their masters in West Bromwich Albion, at Stoney Lane, who, however, went on to the Final, where they forced Blackburn Rovers to a replay. And the Rovers that year were winners of the F.A. Cup for the third time in succession. Thus it can be seen that elementary calculation brought the scent of fame to the nostrils of the Wolves and their by now ardent camp-followers.

In that season two examples of enterprise captured the imagination. On March 20 the Wanderers were due to play Walsall Town in the semi-final of the Walsall Cup. The *Wolverhampton Chronicle,* this year realizing that football deserved more or less adequate notice—though visits to the town of George Grossmith, Henry Irving, Oscar Wilde, and Mr. Gladstone, and the meets of the Albrighton Hunt, would be allowed many more inches of newsprint—noted that the fixture was played at the *Molineux Grounds*. There were 4,000 spectators. That Walsall won by a single goal is less important than the success of staging the event in the acknowledged pleasure-grounds of the town. It was obviously to the general advantage to have football centrally located. A week later another match took place at Molineux, between Stafford Road and Wellington. This was a benefit match in aid of one of the Stafford Road players, Harry Turton, who was in hospital with rheumatic fever. Stafford Road played a number of matches at Molineux in the hope of retrieving their lost glory; but to no avail.

As far as the Wanderers were concerned, the idea of moving from Dudley Road was not practicable. Nevertheless, there were other avenues to explore in order to educate the community. In October 1885, the Wanderers had travelled to Preston, had played against the North End, and, as might have been expected, lost roundly by 4-0. Could a return match be staged at Dudley Road? One after another the Midland clubs had tried to cajole the 'Invincibles' out of Lancashire, and all had failed—except the Wanderers. The North End had, in fact, visited Dudley Road in the spring of 1885. On April 17, 1886, they came again.

On this occasion they were received with all ceremony, befitting their title and record: 49 wins and 3 draws (these when the team had been under strength) from 52 matches; goals for, 267, against, 49.

It was wet on April 17—which is why the North End 'did not appear in the uniforms presented by the Prince of Wales'—and there was a blustering wind. In spite of this a crowd of 6,000 turned up at Dudley Road, where the visitors gave a masterly exhibition of calculated and scientific play. They won by 4-1. The Wanderers had at least the satisfaction of raising the goals against tally to a round half-century. But this goal, the fortuitous result of a long kick, was not scored by a Wanderers player, but by a distinguished guest, George Bakewell, of Derby County. He, it was said, was 'for some years one of the most dangerous forwards to be found in football'.

The team that day was: Griffiths; Hawkins, Mason; Pearson, Baynton, Lowder; Bakewell, G. Wood, Cattell, H. Wood, Horton.

In 1887 the Wanderers followed up their Staffordshire Cup success of two years earlier. They were successful in another highly respectable competition, winning for the first time the Lord Mayor of Birmingham Charity Cup, but by default, since their opponents—Aston Villa—withdrew. We now discover the club acting as patron of the game. The lesser teams of the town—Wolverhampton Druids, Wolverhampton Albion, Wolverhampton Rangers, Wolverhampton West End, Wolverhampton Olympic, St. Andrew's F.C., and the once renowned Whitmore Reans—were playing against each other for the 'Wolverhampton Wanderers Junior Charity Cup'. The march of progress can be measured by the fact that only five years previously the Wanderers (Baynton, back and goal; Blackham and Tom Cliff, halves; Hill, Brodie, and Hadley, forwards) had been delighted to defeat Whitmore Reans F.C. in the six-a-side tournament, already referred to. (see p. 6).

The notable event of 1887 was the long drawn out contest with Aston Villa, in the third round of the F.A. Cup. In the end Villa won the tie and went on to beat West Bromwich Albion in a stirring Final. But the third round nearly proved their undoing. The had expected to win at the first attempt on their home ground at Perry Barr, but had to be content with a 2-2 draw.

On January 15, there was a high expectancy at Dudley Road. Having held the powerful Villa away from home, surely the Wanderers could now prevail? A neat stroke of publicity nearly turned the match into an all-ticket affair, for it was announced that 'reduced tickets at **4d**' were available until the evening before the match, and that 'parcels of six tickets will be forwarded to any address on receipt of stamps'. The quality would be accommodated through the 'private gate', a two-wheeled carriage being admitted for 1s., a four-wheeler for 2s 6d.

Alas! the ground was treacherous, being sheeted with ice, and both captains protested—but to no avail. The referee ordered the match to be played. It ended in a draw, each side scoring once. The second replay, for some extraordinary reason also played at Dudley Road, was no more conclusive, though on this occasion the teams shared six goals.

For the third replay, at Perry Barr, excitement had risen to explosion point. A special train left the London and North Western station at Wolverhampton with a load of supporters. Mr. George Kynoch, M.P. for Aston, took a party to the ground. The gate was 10,000, something like a record for such a match; although a match between the London and Birmingham Associations in 1883 had attracted a like number. One of the umpires was William McGregor, a figure of more than local importance at that time.

At the outset of this match it was clear that Villa had the edge. Attack after attack came in the opening minutes, generally through the astute positioning and distribution of Archie Hunter. After eight minutes Dawson, the Villa centre-half, scored. At this point the Wolves could feel sorry for themselves for Brodie was off the field with an injury, nor did he reappear until midway through the first half. But the Villa played inspiringly, the short, classical, methodical passing having the visitors' defence in continual trepidation. Another goal came before half-time. The second half was a resumption of the stalemate of the earlier rounds. There was no further score, even though, as the reporter of the Wolverhampton paper pointed out, the Wolves did everything but . . .

For this mammoth series of matches both sides had undergone strict—by the standards of those days—training, the Wanderers now under the expert guidance of Beaumont Shaw. The toughness of the players is illustrated by the fact that only one change was necessary in the composition of the teams, George Wood replacing B. Griffiths, who was injured in the last match. The teams were:

Wolves: J. Griffiths; Mason, Baugh; Lowder, Allen, Pearson; H. Wood, George Wood (B. Griffiths), Brodie, Knight, Hunter.
Villa: Warner; Coulton, Simmonds; Yates, Dawson, Burton; Brown, Davies, Hunter, Vaughton, Hodgetts.

In Easter Week an opportunity came whereby football might be used ceremonially. Queen Victoria (who had visited Wolverhampton to unveil the statue of the Prince Consort in 1866) had been on the throne for fifty years, and the loyal Wulfrunians considered that a series of 'Grand Jubilee Festival Matches' would be an appropriate commemoration. The Wanderers, therefore, invited attractive visitors in Derby County, Rotherham, and Edinburgh Hibernian.

Rotherham at that time were a powerful combination, having beaten all the leading teams in the Sheffield district. But they were no match for the local team, who trounced them by 6-0. With Hibernian it was a different matter. They came south with a proud record and were the current holders of the Scottish Cup. Nearly 3,000 people turned up to see them on Monday morning, April 18, and they were soon enthralled by the finesse of the Scots. By half-time they led the home team by 2-0. Then, however, came a characteristic revival. The Wanderers turned round in fury, tore the Hibs defence to shreds to run out winners by 3-2. Thus began an association with Edinburgh that lasted for many years.

The team which represented Wolves on this occasion was Llowarch; Mason and Baugh; Tuft, Allen, Lowder; Hunter, B. Griffiths, R. Danks, Knight, H. Wood. Llowarch, Baugh and Griffiths had previously played in the Wolverhampton Rangers. Danks, at Saltley College in Brodie's time, played first for Stafford Road. After a spell with the Wanderers he went to

Wednesbury Town, then to the Old Athletic, and finally to Port Vale as captain and secretary. He died on November 19 1929. Baugh had also been at Stafford Road, with which club he had won an international cap against Ireland. The changes from the Villa match give some idea of the reserve strength, and in the next year the reserve team played in the Dudley Charity Cup Competition. In the first round they met yet another local side, the now long since defunct Wolverhampton Town.

The quality of the 1887 Wolves is reflected in the fact that that year they lost only nine matches out of forty played, and a matter for particular satisfaction was the selection of Charlie Mason to play for England against Ireland at Sheffield. In the following season international caps came also to Allen, who played in all three fixtures, to Brodie, and to Fletcher.

In March, 1888, William McGregor of Aston Villa, and the Birmingham Football Association, canvassed prominent clubs in the midlands and north in respect of the inauguration of a League system, which would rationalize programmes and match teams of more or less even calibre on the one hand, and act as a focus for the consistent attention of the public on the other. In Sheffield McGregor met with no enthusiasm, for the Association there was averse from antagonising the F.A. In the midlands, however, there was considerable support—particularly from the Stoke, West Bromwich, Derby, and Wolverhampton clubs. The spokesman for the Wolves at the first meetings—at Anderson's Hotel, London, on March 22, and at the Royal Hotel, Manchester, on April 17, was W. Allt. The owner of a shoeshop opposite the Molineux Hotel, at 14 North Street, and another at 14 Worcester Street, whence came some of the club's boots and footballs, Allt also has claim to distinction as the father of Dr. W. Greenhouse Allt, a celebrated musician. His colleagues on the first Management Committee of the League were W. Sudell and J. J. Bentley of Preston North End, H. Lockett of Stoke, and McGregor. Allt remained on this committee for four years, during which time he had to see judgment passed on his own club—during the 1890-1 season—for attempting to poach a Preston player. That cost a fine of £50. But, as will shortly be evident, the Wanderers at that time had a good reason for such covetousness.

The first season of League football got under way, not without initial difficulty. For instance, the 'points' system, which still prevails, was not finally agreed until November 21, by which time the competition had already started. Nor were the spectators always quite considerately treated. The journal *Pastime,* for instance, about this time reported that 'at Wolverhampton, the home supporters had the gratification, if not of seeing (for the game ended in almost total darkness), of *hearing* that their men were victorious by 2 goals to 1'.

The clubs involved, in addition to the Wanderers, were Accrington, Aston Villa, Blackburn Rovers, Bolton Wanderers, Burnley, Derby County, Everton, Notts County, Preston North End, Stoke, and West Bromwich Albion. As might have been expected, the first champions,—as also in 1889-90—were Preston North End, undefeated and with 40 points out of a possible 44. Wolverhampton came third, with 28 points. During the season Brodie and Allen played for the North against the South, preparatory to their selection for the national side.

As yet the new-fangled League was of lesser importance than the by now well-established F.A. Cup, and in 1889 Wanderers progressed to the Final. On the way they defeated the finest of southern sides—Old Carthusians, Walsall Town Swifts, Sheffield Wednesday, and, after a replay, Blackburn Rovers. The defeat of the Rovers at Crewe on March 23 caught the fancy of Wulfrunians, and 'On the Wanderers' return thousands of their admirers thronged the High Level Station, and followed the team through the town, cheering lustily. The captain especially came in for an enthusiastic reception'. As for the Rovers they evinced the traditional qualities of high sportsmanship associated with the Cup competition: their president, Dr. Morley, 'speaking to a prominent member of the Wanderers, candidly admitted that the best team had won'.

The growth of general interest may be measured by the vital statistics now appearing in the *Wolverhampton Chronicle;* the average height, weight, and age of the players were 5 ft., 9 in., 11½ stone, and 24 years respectively.

And so on to the Final, on March 30. With the exception of 1873, when it took place at Lillie Bridge, the Cup Final was played at the Oval from 1872 to 1892. The other finalists in 1889 were Preston North End, and there were few who allowed the Wanderers even the remotest chance. Nevertheless, 25,000 people turned up to constitute a then record attendance. The three presiding officials were august personages. The referee was Major Francis Marindin, President of the F.A., the umpires Lord Kinnaird and J. C. Clegg; three of the greatest names in the game. The regulation of the game according to the old principles was, however, near its end, for in 1891 umpires were replaced by linesmen. Until their institution each umpire controlled one half of the field, 'referring' from time to time to the referee who was immobile, enthroned on the touch line. A goal was a goal only if ratified by referee and one of the umpires.

The team of 1889 was:

Jack Baynton, for whom it was the last match of his career; Dick

Baugh, whose son played for Wolves thirty years later, Charlie Mason; Albert Fletcher—from Willenhall Pickwick, Harry Allen, Arthur Lowder; Tom Hunter—from Walsall, David Wykes—from Walsall, Jack Brodie, Harry Wood and Tom Knight.

Preston were represented by:

Dr. R. H. Mills-Roberts;[1] R. H. Howarth, R. Holmes; G. Drummond,[2] D. Russell,[2] J. Gordon;[2] J. Graham,[2] J. Ross,[2] J. Goodall, W. Thompson, F. Dewhurst.

From the kick-off, which was at four o' clock, the Wanderers swung the ball vigorously—in contrast to the more scientific style of Preston—and had the best of the early exchanges. History might well have been different if an early shot of Knight had been inches lower. He hit the cross-bar, and thus narrowly missed the distinction of notching at least one goal against the North End who, however, kept their debit side unsullied from first round to Final. Shortly afterwards Ross did the same thing at the other end, but Dewhurst was there to pick up the ball on the rebound and to push it gently past the out-of-position Baynton. The Wanderers lodged an appeal for off-side, which was rejected. This goal gave the North End the spur they needed and they increased their lead before half-time; rather luckily, perhaps, but not really against the run of the play. Ross shot weakly and poor Jack Baynton froze in mortification as the ball slowly passed between his legs. In the second half Preston scored again, through Thompson.

The local critics advised the Wanderers in future to improve their shooting, and drew attention to the disparity between the short passing of the North End and the sometimes wild, long kicking of the Wanderers. The *Daily News* was caustic: 'Judged by their play on Saturday, the Wolverhampton Wanderers have still a good deal to learn before they can expect to cope successfully with Preston North End'. It might have been otherwise, however, if W. C. Rose, the recently signed goal-keeper, had been available. But, having already appeared for Warwick County in the competition, he was not; and Baynton's trade was not goal-keeping.

There were many who attributed defeat to supernatural intervention. The President of the Wanderers was Alfred Hickman, whose interest in the club was of long standing. On the way to the Oval his carriage met with an accident and he was injured. Thus his talismanic presence was rendered impossible.

[1] Welsh International.   [2] Scottish International.

However, the players took their disappointment well and were in good heart at the evening celebrations. Guests of the absent Alfred Hickman at the Constitutional Club, they were enthused by brave words from Charles Crump and from their captain. 'The Wanderers', said the former, with some emotion, 'were essentially a local team (hear, hear), whilst North End comprised men from England, Wales and Scotland, at least'. That 'at least' was an excellently sardonic touch.

For the captain it was an occasion full of emotion. He 'alluded to the starting of the club by himself and Mr. Baynton, and said for eleven years there had been a hard, uphill fight, but he was very proud in having at length brought his team to the Oval (cheers). They must hope for success another year (hear, hear)'.

On the Monday night following, the team were entertained at home, at the New Inn, Horseley Field, by their Chairman—Councillor A. Hollingsworth.

The season ended with a defeat in the Final of the Birmingham Cup, and with Brodie and Allen as members of the English side that lost, again at the Oval, to Scotland.

4

Molineux

'He remarked that last year he was in the South of France and one morning when bringing in the coffee the waiter spoke to him of the Wolverhampton Wanderers, observing that they were doing very well'.

C. T. Mander, Mayor, to the Town Council,
March 27 1893.

THE Local Government Act of 1888 raised the town of Wolverhampton to the rank of a County Borough, which status was officially adopted on April 1, 1889. It was not compatible with such dignity that the premier football team—which was beginning to make the rest of the world aware of the town's general importance—should continue to be indifferently accommodated at Dudley Road. There was only one fitting site: the spacious grounds that lay well below the tall, eighteenth-century Molineux House, where the Stafford Road club had staked a claim which they were unable to sustain.

Once the property of the Molineux family, the house and grounds had been taken over in the mid-nineteenth century by a Mr. Brewster, of the Prince of Wales Concert Hall, who exploited the gardens to the full.

On July 2, 1857, Jullien's Musical Fête—of which the central attraction was the ascent of Mr. Gray, aeronaut, in a balloon—was held there. On a June day of 1860 the celebrated pugilists Sayers and Heanen demonstrated their art. Somewhere during this lively period Sam Cowel gave the first performance of his celebrated ballad 'The Ratcatcher's Daughter', and in 1869 there was housed the local Exhibition of Art and Manufacture. Before footballers began to take interest in Molineux the sportsmen of the district flocked to the grounds to see professional cycling, in which the popular champion was the local rider Dicky Howell.

Not without justice the *Chronicle* wrote in 1884 that 'the grounds attached to Molineux House were the best apology that Wolverhampton could offer for Hyde Park'.

It was a considerable task to uproot flower-beds, to disperse a lake, and to prepare a surface fit for the highest class of football. And the work was hardly

Molineux Hotel
Wolverhampton
May 24/89

Councillor Hollingsworth
Chairman W.W.F.C Committee

Dear Sir

I have written to the Northampton Brewery Co & they are prepared to let Molineux Grounds to your Club for the sum of Fifty pounds per annum and also to grant your club a lease for a term of years, subject to a satisfactory arrangement of the minor details

Should this meet with the approval of your

complete by September 2 1889, on which date the first League match of the season was due to take place. Workmen, indeed, were still 'fixing and removing, digging, turfing, and levelling, while bricks, soil and the general disorder which incompleted alterations of the kind always bring were to be seen on all sides'. Spectators, who were somewhat inconvenienced by the miscellaneous debris, were, however, enchanted by the velvety sheen of the 'new patch' which '115 by 75 yards, looked as level as a billiard table'.

The opening match of the season was against Aston Villa, who had finished their first year in the League in second place, with one more point than the Wanderers. The start was fixed for 5.30, and precisely at that hour Councillor Hollingsworth kicked off. The referee was Charles Crump. The result of an even game was a one goal victory for the home side, the scorer being David Wykes.

After the match both teams were entertained to dinner, as well as music and speeches, at the Molineux Hotel which, also had been their dressing-rooms. One of the principal speakers was William McGregor of the Villa. 'He hoped', it was reported, 'the Wanderers would win every match they played, except those against Villa (laughter and applause)—and even then if, as they had done that day, they proved themselves the better team, he would be pleased to see them win (cheers)'.

But the Villa had some excuse that day—through an apparent piece of sabotage at West Bromwich. The *Birmingham Gazette* described how 'The Villa team journeyed to Wolverhampton in a brake drawn by four horses. As the brake entered West Bromwich an axle arm of the vehicle broke. The driver was thrown off his box and the players were shaken enough to give Villa supporters a valid explanation for the defeat of their team'.

The 1889-90 season brought no spectacular results in the League matches, and the Wanderers finished respectably fourth; ahead of them were Preston, Everton, and Blackburn, while level with them were West Bromwich Albion. The portent in the final figuration of points was the record of Everton.

The cup-ties of this year, however, were not without their sensational aspect. In the first round Wanderers were drawn at home against the same powerful Old Carthusians—Cup winners of 1881—whom they had only narrowly defeated twelve months before. So far as Wolverhampton were concerned this match represented the triumph of professional organization and method over inspired, skilful, but essentially recreational, amateurism. Training was in its infancy, no doubt, but those long walks, sessions with the Indian clubs, and immersion in the brine baths of Droitwich, had a toughening effect, especially valuable for ninety minutes on a heavy ground; and in the winter months of 1890 the ground at Molineux was no longer in its pristine freshness.

The Old Carthusians field three internationals—the famous brothers Walters at full-back, and C. Wreford-Brown, a fearless centre-half, in a side that otherwise contained F. C. Vogel in goal, Cowie and N. F. Shaw at wing-half, and W. H. Ainger, A. C. Nixon, E. S. Curry, E. H. Parry, and M. F. Stanbrough as forwards. In the home side were seven internationals: W. C. Rose, the amateur goalkeeper recruited from Preston, Baugh—who had won his first cap with Stafford Road—Mason, Fletcher, Allen, Lowder and Brodie. The interest aroused by the fixture was great and 13,000 spectators were present to see the Wanderers win by 2-0. The newspaper commented on the quality of the Carthusians but lamented that they did not last the pace: 'fine staying power and stamina', it prophetically added, 'are the prime features of the Wolves play'.

Small Heath (later Birmingham City) were defeated in the next round. When it came to February 15, the date of the third round match at Molineux against Stoke, the weather was dreadful. It rained and snowed by turns in the morning and by the afternoon a great part of the pitch was covered with water. 'Owing to the very heavy state of the turf the visitors lodged a protest'. The Wanderers kept silent, secure in their ability to make hay without sunshine. They revelled 'on the heavy ground, and made such an exhibition of the Stoke as the latter could never have anticipated'. Such was their supremacy that Rose, ill-disposed to cold inactivity in an unassailed goal, frequently went up-field to take part in attacks which not even the mighty defence unit of Rowley, Clare, and Underwood could withstand.

Wanderers won by 4-0, and, as the referee observed that the ground was not in such a bad condition as when the Old Carthusians came, the situation looked promising. The Stoke appeal, however, was upheld by the F.A., and the match was ordered to be replayed. The locals grumbled that it looked as though this year one would have to win the Cup twice in order to win it at all. If the first match had been an unhappy experience for the men from the Potteries, the second was a massacre. Wanderers putting on one of their higher-powered performances to win by 8-0. The semi-final, against Blackburn Rovers at Derby, looked also like running into a replay; but three minutes before full-time the Rovers scored. After which fortunate episode they went on to beat Sheffield Wednesday, 6-1, at the Oval.

In 1891 the Wanderers again found Blackburn too strong, this time in the third round, and once again the Rovers went on majestically to win the Cup—for the fifth time in eight years. Maintaining their competence in the League—fourth in 1891 and sixth in 1892, and asserting their regional eminence by winning the Birmingham Charity Cup again in 1892—the

Wolves were a definite menace to all clubs in the F.A. Cup during this period. In 1892 their progress was again only halted by one of the eventual finalists; on this occasion the Villa, who, however, lost to the Albion in one of the classic and long remembered matches. In 1891 the reserve team had won the championship of the Shropshire League.

At the beginning of the 1891-2 season the Villa directors had committed an unneighbourly act in that they had refused permission to some of their players to take part in a benefit match for Albert Fletcher. This was the more reprehensible in that Fletcher's career had ended with an injury received when playing against Villa. On October 12, however, a fine team—consisting of Roberts (Albion); Clare and Underwood (Stoke); Bayliss (Albion), Holt (Everton), Perry (Albion); Lofthouse (Blackburn), Worrall (Burton Swifts), Thomas (Everton), Wood (Walsall Town Swifts), and Pearson (Albion),— came to honour Fletcher. The visitors had the grace to lose 3-0, and were recompensed with an excellent dinner in the Molineux Hotel.

That period was otherwise notable at Molineux for the introduction of penalties, as regularized by the F.A. Council on September 1 1891. The *Birmingham Gazette* for September 15 thus noticed the match of the previous evening at Molineux, against Accrington Stanley: 'One of the Accrington half-backs acted as goalkeeper and the new rule which gives a free-kick to the attacking side with no one but the defending goalkeeper in front, was enforced. Heath took the kick and shot the ball through with a clean, hard shot'. Not only was this the first penalty scored by the Wanderers, but it seems almost certain that it was the first in English League football'![1]

In 1892 the Wanderers showed their determination to strengthen the club as a whole by appointing Henry Dallard (1858-1940), a founder member of Walsall Swifts, as manager of the reserve team, which post he occupied until the end of the war of 1914-18. From then until the time of his death Dallard represented the club on the Birmingham F.A.

The structure of the club at the top at this time was, by modern standards, somewhat top-heavy. The president was Sir Alfred (as he now was) Hickman; the Vice-President, Sir William Plowden, K.C.S.I., formerly an Indian civil servant and finally a member of the Governor-General's Legislative Council in Calcutta, until this year M.P. for Wolverhampton; the Directors were A. Hollingsworth (Chairman), T. B. Adams, W. Allt, W. Blakemore, M. Bray, S. Craddock, C. Crump (formerly of Stafford Road), C. Forder, L. Johnson, B. B. Nock, J. J. Tate, G. W. Walter; and the Players' Committee comprised, Johnson (Chairman), Allt, Craddock, Forder, Tate. This committee was in fact the selection committee.

[1] B.B.C. 'Sports Report', Angus Mackay, April 26 1958.

A PLEASANT GAME.

A SCRIMMAGE IN FRONT OF THE VILLA GOAL.

H. ALLEN CAPT^N of W.W

J. COWAN VILLA CAPT.

MR J. DUNKLEY

MR J.T. LEES.

J. LEWIS TRAINER OF THE W.W.

G. BEASLEY TRAINER OF THE VILLA

ASTON VILLA v. WOLVERHAMPTON WANDERERS, AT MOLYNEUX GROUNDS, WOLVERHAMPTON, SATURDAY, OCT. 8, 1892.

The 1892-3 season proceeded with new faces in the team, and at this time the last links with the foundation of the club were severed; for at long last John Brodie described then 'as one of the finest gentlemen players in the kingdom', was on the retired list. In 1890 he said he would only play occasionally—but now he was adamant. His experience and influence, however, were not lost to the game, as he joined Jack Baynton on the rota of referees and continued to serve his own club in other ways.

Among newcomers was George Swift, who came from St. George's F.C. near Oakengates in Shropshire—a reservoir of talent profitably tapped in subsequent years. Swift replaced Charlie Mason. At right-half was twenty-six-year-old Billy Malpass, a graduate of Wednesbury Old Athletic, who, two years later, received a testimonial to his quality from an unexpected quarter. Mr. Edward Elgar, as he was then, visited Wolverhampton frequently, and was not difficult to persuade to the Molineux Grounds, where it was, he acknowledged, the sterling displays of Malpass that particularly captivated him. Elgar indeed composed a few bars of music in honour of Malpass, which were contained in a letter to Dora Penny, daughter of the Rector of St. Peter's Church and a friend of Elgar.

George Kinsey, from Burton-on-Trent, was at left-half. In the forward line the outside-right berth was occupied by Dick Topham, a native of Ellesmere in Shropshire. Topham was a dashing player—though with somewhat nonchalant habits—who was up at Oxford. At centre-forward the accent was on youth: eighteen-year-old Joe Butcher,[1] strong and persistent, having reached that eminence after a brief apprenticeship with Wolverhampton West End. The outside-left was Alf Griffin, just twenty-one and a Walsall man. Behind the team was Billy Rose, whose enthusiam has already been noticed, and whose previous experience with the Swifts, Small Heath, and Preston North End, gave him a wide knowledge of tactics and of the psychology of his opponents.

In the League matches (there were now sixteen clubs in the competition[2]) the team was disappointing. In all, fourteen matches were lost, and the final placing was eleventh, and the lowest place yet held by the Wanderers. Early in the season, indeed, there was a threat of civil strife. On October 15 the team visited Newton Heath (later Manchester United), and on a dismally wet day lost by 10-1.

What happened afterwards reads like modern times. After censure from all the local newspapers the team committee resigned. The rest of the directors,

[1] Butcher died at the age of eighty-three in March, 1958.
[2] In 1890-1 Sunderland took the place of Stoke who, however, returned a year later with Darwen. In 1892-3 the newcomers were Nottingham Forest and Manchester United.

The Wanderers c. 1890.

Fred Leek's Share Certificate 1891.

Cup Final at Fallowfield 1893.

Wolverhampton Wanderers Football Club
Winners of English Cup 1892-3.

R. Baugh. R. Topham. W. Malpass. D. Wykes. H. Allen. J. Butcher. W.C. Rose. H. Wood. G. Kinsey. A. Griffin. G. Swift.

BLACKBURN ROVERS
V
WOLVERHAMPTON WAN:
Semi-final English Cup
S TRENT BRIDGE
NOTTINGHAM
Blackburn score their only goal (5 minutes from Kickoff)
Taylor
Going to the Station
Some straggling Excursionists
Topham & Marshall
Keep an eye
on each other
Forbes held
Butcher when
he had a clear
run.
Southworth is constantly
Shadowed by Allen.

however, behaving in the most gentlemanly fashion, refused to accept the resignation. But before the next match as the committee walked round the ground to their places they were jeered at by the crowd. This brought on another fit of resignation fever, and Councillor Hollingsworth, the Chairman of the club, announced his intention to retire. In fact a change of membership of the team committee was deferred for a year, when Councillors Levi Johnson, Hollingsworth, and Major Walker took up the reins. They were all, it was said, 'popular men in Wolverhampton'.

In 1892 the reserves won the championship of the Birmingham and District League, and in the early months of 1893 the seniors moved relentlessly on in the F.A. Cup.

They defeated Bolton Wanderers, after a replay, in the first round; Middlesbrough, then an amateur side in the Northern League, in the second; Darwen in the third; and then—a sweet revenge—Blackburn Rovers in a hard-fought semi-final at Nottingham. Meanwhile Everton, a team of many talents, were progressing also towards the Final. But they were stuck in an apparently interminable semi-final against Preston North End.

On March 18 Everton came to Molineux for a League match. Here was a piquant situation. Wanderers could measure their strength against the opposition to be expected in the Final either directly or vicariously. The odds were that they would win, for Everton were sadly exhausted by two previously drawn games with Preston, and in two days' time they had to meet the North End for the third time. Their centre-forward, Geary, was in no sanguine mood. Button-holed by a reporter he excused an anticipated debacle by saying that the Everton side to meet Wanderers that day was but a shadow of its original self—'due to the cruel way in which their side had been treated by the North End last Thursday', and that of that day's team there were only three survivors. The home team faced three fit men and eight reserves.

The gate was 10,000, and, unaware of the sad plight of the opposition, the spectators looked for a close struggle. Statistics at least pointed to this for the respective records of the teams were:

	P	W	L	D	Goals F	A	Pts.
Everton	25	12	9	4	58	46	28
Wanderers	24	11	9	4	43	49	26

The result of the match, however, was shattering to the home supporters. Their team gave its worst display for years. Long before half-time they had been completely out-tricked by an agile, viperish forward line and they turned round 3-0 down. Shortly the score was 4-0. That the team rallied at that point and pulled back to a final 4-2 was small comfort to those who hitherto had hoped for a victory that would have acted as a tonic for the last encounter. On Monday following, Everton, thus heartened, got through to the Final by beating Preston at Blackburn by 2-1.

By March 25, the day of the Final, however, pessimism was outlawed in Wolverhampton. The match this year was to be played at Fallowfield, Manchester, and even though it seemed outrageous to allow a Lancashire side to play in Lancashire, none doubted the capacity of Wolves to rise to the occasion. 'Every Wanderer was an Englishman, and most of them were reared in the neighbourhood of Wolverhampton'. Rose had previously been with Preston, Kinsey with Derby; otherwise the players were local. Everton, on the other hand, were predominantly foreign—with six Scots in the side.

Excursion trains left Wolverhampton from both stations, and there were enthusiastic scenes as the players, in groups, arrived at the G.W.R. Station. Last—immaculate and unconcerned—was Dick Topham. Each player was decorated with a fine, white camelia, 'cut from a prolific plant in the glass-house of the Molineux Grounds'. During the morning ballad sheets were on sale in the town. To the tune of 'The Opera is Over' those with voices were asked to chorus:

> Then hurrah! for the Wolves of the forest—
> The lads from the Black Country town.
> For they'll win the old Cup at the finish,
> And gain for themselves great renown.

... and so on.

Among those moved to attend at the great event was 'my Lord of Dartmouth with travelling-rug. His Lordship wore a very pretty button-hole bouquet, and what pleased everybody most, a rosette of black and gold'. It is comforting to reflect that the sporting of rosettes—thought by some to be slightly indecorous—was, in fact, beautified by a member of the House of Lords. My Lord of Dartmouth, however, was a democrat and he was happy to ride to Manchester in the 'saloon' with the team.

Arrived at Fallowfield, spectators discovered incredible, unprecedented scenes. Forty—some estimated fifty—thousand people were milling round in disorder to form a record gate, who paid the vast sum of £2,559. The authorities were caught unawares. They might have taken the hint from the fact that 'the Wolves of the Forest' had on two previous occasions broken existing records; but they did not do so. A squad of 176 policemen were helpless and before the game was due to start the slender barriers which separated the crowd from the playing pitch were shattered. Eventually some sort of discipline was created above the chaos but the necessary invasion of the fringes of the field put the whole match in jeopardy.

Among those determined to see the Final at all costs were three town councillors from Wolverhampton who, leaving their dignity below, climbed a tree to find uneasy balance on a shaking branch. Two managed to keep their seats in more agitating circumstances than any municipal election provided; the other fell off.

'Would the game reckon as a cup-tie or a friendly match?' Anxious officials thus questioned the referee, C. J. Hughes. He, inscrutable and almighty, darkly said that was his business! At half-time, however, he was understood to have ruled that this was no friendly match—but a Cup Final.

The game proceeded in a highly emotional atmosphere, which was intensified when Everton scored but had the goal disallowed. Half-time arrived with the sides level at 0-0. At that point there was a further alarming incident, as an 'Everton fire balloon ignited and nearly set the canopy of the stand ablaze.' Midway through the second half Harry Allen—in his second of three Finals—scored, thus demonstrating the virtues of an offensive half-back line.

In keeping with the fantastic atmosphere of the match it was by no means certain who had scored. Some said Malpass, some said Wykes, while others swore it was Dick Topham—who had already laid out one of the multitude of policemen with a near-miss. Others did not question the score as a gift from the gods. The heavens, indeed, played their part—as the one spectator who kept his eye on the ball and put his statement into print testified:'From near midfield Allen kicked the ball high in the air and it descended as a dropping shot towards goal. It was brilliant sunshine, and as the Everton goalkeeper looked for the ball the sun dazzled his sight so that the ball fell beside him into the net'.

A quarter of an hour from the end Everton protested about the conditions in which the match had been played and when the final whistle blew none appeared to know whether the appeal had been allowed or not. The Wolves virtuously began to look for the Cup. But harassed F.A. officials said that it was not to be handed over without Lord Kinnaird's sanction—and he had gone home! After some plain talking by Alfred Hickman, however, they capitulated, whereupon Hickman filled the hard-won trophy with champagne and passed it round his men.

The Wolves team was:

W. C. Rose; R. Baugh, G. Swift; W. Malpass, H. Allen, G. Kinsey; R. Topham, D. Wykes, J. Butcher, H. Wood, A. Griffin.

At 31 Rose was the oldest, and Butcher—a local boy making good—the youngest, member of the side. In contrast to what one would expect today no Wolves player was six foot tall, and in the Everton side only the goalkeeper barely reached that stature.

Everton was represented by:

R. Williams; R. Kelso, R. H. Howarth, R. Boyle; J. Holt, A. Stewart; A. Latta, P. Gordon, A. Maxwell, E. Chadwick, A. Milward.

On their way back to Wolverhampton the Wanderers were hailed by the G.W.R with salvoes of fog-signals, and their homecoming was marked with Handelian strains poured out by the Swan Bank Band, and by Chinese lanterns tastefully hung over the facade of the Victoria Hotel. Every man, woman, and child of Wolverhampton was out in the streets, so that the Salvation Army Band, engaged in its weekly duty, took it that a miracle of faith had transpired. So, of course, it had—but in another sense.

The Council met on the following Monday under the chairmanship of a sick mayor, Charles Tertius Mander. For the sake of his health the Cup was borne into his presence, whereat he immediately revived, and 'remarked that last year he was in the South of France, and one morning when bringing in the coffee the waiter spoke to him of the Wolverhampton Wanderers observing that they were doing very well'. Here was another landmark: the fame of the team had spread abroad. In the evening there was a Birmingham Cup match against West Bromwich Albion. There was a gate of 7,000, and 'they cheered themselves hoarse as the team stepped on to the field. Apart from the fact that George 'Spry' Woodhall, acquired from the Albion in the previous season, took Topham's place the Wolves were at full strength, and pleased their supporters by winning this game 3-1. Afterwards there was a procession through the town and a banquet.

'Naturally', wrote a correspondent in *Out of Doors*, April 1,

> The fact that all the Wanderers are Englishmen makes their victory more popular, and in one respect they have certainly created a record. Never has such a circumstance been known before as of two lads like Butcher and Griffin [21 years old, and only 5' 5"] tall to be taken from

unknown local junior clubs, played for a month or two in the first team, and then played in the final for the English Cup, and help to win the trophy. It was a great day for them and for everybody, at least in Wolverhampton.

5

Breakers Ahead

... redeemed their club from debt, and perhaps from dissolution'.
Express and Star, August 29 1896.

FAME, alas, is ephemeral, as the victorious Wolves of the 1893 Final were quickly to discover. A builder, running up terrace houses along the Dudley Road—on the site of the old ground—was enthusiastically marking Fallowfield Terrace with a symbolic stone replica of the F.A. Cup, set above Nos. 329-30[1] and christening the houses in Wanderers Avenue after the celebrated players of the team. The Canadian F.A. were asking for a photograph of the 'now world-renowned team', and expressing a hope that the Wanderers would soon be able to visit Canada. (A Canadian touring team had been beaten 9-0 by Wolves at Molineux in 1892.) But indifferent performances in the League, rising costs, the necessity for paying summer wages for the first time during the coming recess, the difficulty of replacement of players, and uninformed but loudly voiced criticism from a public voracious for perpetual success, cast clouds over many of the meetings of the faithful directors.

In 1888 the Football League had appeared as a magnificent project. Five years later the disadvantages of the scheme became more apparent. By this time also could be seen the reverse of the medal of professionalism. So far as the League was concerned club supporters were not so stoical as to accept the fact that some team must needs be at the bottom, and that the team might be their own. Nor were they so collectively generous as to admit that ill-success required their greater loyalty. A losing sequence, therefore, meant poor gates; poor gates difficulties in engaging players of adequate calibre; and they, in turn, were now often in a position to offer their services to the highest bidder.

In the early days of glory the Wolves and their supporters scorned teams

[1] On the demolition of this property in 1973 the stone replica was saved and given for safe keeping to the Wolves' Supporters Club.

whose excellence was not home-bred, but based on the 'hiring of Caledonian mercenaries'—as one writer put it. But times had changed and in the next decade Wolves experimented, not very successfully, in the importation of the ready-made. By August 1894 there were six Scotsmen on the books, Dunn, Robson, Black, Fleming, Bell and Hamilton. The transfer of Hamilton throws some light on the then attraction of football as a career, for a Scottish writer noted how 'John Hamilton, the popular half-back of the Ayr Football Club, has signed for the Wolverhampton Wanderers in consequence of the dullness of trade'.

In 1891—the year in which the colours of old gold and black were adopted[1] —the club was incorporated under the Companies' Act, with a

---

[1] Previously jerseys with blue-and-white, then red-and-white vertical stripes had been worn: the present colours are said to symbolize the Borough's motto—'Out of darkness cometh light'.

capital of £2,000 in £1 shares. In 1896 Aston Villa—who then moved to their present ground—were similarly incorporated, but in their case with a capital of £10,000 in £5 shares. Running a team in the Football League was relatively as expensive then as now—and if the directorate was working on a shoe-string there were many headaches.

The Wolves won the F.A. Cup in 1893. Their reward was a tip, in the form of a ten-pound note from the F.A., who until then, collared all the gate-money. Small wonder that Councillor Hollingsworth protested vigorously that the arrangement was hardly equitable. Thereafter the F.A. divided the proceeds between the clubs—less one-third of the total—and within a couple of years the Wolves directors were mightily thankful. An indirect, but considerable, benefit to the town, as a consequence of interest in open-air activities such as the efforts of the footballers symbolised, was the presentation to the citizens of the East Park by Sir Alfred Hickman, the club's President.

At the end of the 1893-4 season there were long faces in Wolverhampton. The best the team could manage was a half-share with West Bromwich Albion in the Birmingham Senior Cup, and having at one stage promised to be near the top of the League the final placing of ninth was a disappointment. The temper of crowds had altered with their increase in size—but vigour in expression and behaviour should be seen in its social context, and related, say, to behaviour during parliamentary elections. Sometimes there were scenes. On October 14, for instance, the directors found it necessary to post warning notices on account of the contumelious behaviour of some spectators towards T. Mitchell who had, a fortnight earlier, refereed the Sheffield United match. In January Sheffield United completed the double against Wolves, and Dick Baugh, for the first time in his life, was in the reserves. A friendly match at this time produced a new player. On New Year's Day Wolves played Ardwick (later Manchester City) in a match to celebrate the opening of the Manchester Ship Canal and, liking the look of him, persuaded Robson to sign for them.

The season ended, the directors sacked Rose, Baugh, Swift, Allen, and Kinsey. Allen retired from the game with a benefit match; Rose and Swift joined Loughborough, then a flourishing side with Second Division aspirations; and Kinsey went to the Villa. About Baugh the outcry was too great for the directors to disregard. He had, said one shareholder at the Annual General Meeting on May 31, 1894, 'to a very great extent helped to make the club and to bring it to its present position'. A later writer commented on Baugh: 'For his influence on the team his only equal of any Wolves player, past or present, was Stan Cullis'.

OUT OF DOORS

Nov. 18, 1893.]

It was a pity that the 1893-4 season was unspectacular; for on June 25, 1894, Wolverhampton celebrated its 900 years of corporate existence.

Baugh was recalled for a benefit match on October 1, in which Villa were beaten 3-0, he received £90 as a reward for his long service. This was one of the few happy incidents in a season of discontent. The season had started badly, with three defeats and only two goals scored with eleven against, and early injury had incapacited Hamilton—so that he had to stay in bed at the Pell's Arms, Peel Street, residence of J. Lewis, the trainer. There were demands for the return of the superannuated players. The chairman pointed out that there were twenty-six players on the books, that no more could be added—for there was no money, that anyone who would guarantee the club at the bank could take over his job and that of his board. Rumours spread about the town that there was tension between players and directors, and as they spread so the gates fell. Weekly income was sometimes as little as £35, while the wages bill was in the region of £70 each week.

In January, 1895, the club was carrying a deficit of £889—which ultimately was wiped out by subscriptions—and three months later only just missed the ignominy of playing in the 'test matches'—which then decided the issues of relegation. The local critic hastened to rub salt into the wound. 'The Wanderers', he wrote, 'escaped from playing test matches not because of their own merits but because of Small Heath's [later Birmingham City] demerits'. To add to the general state of insecurity there was a regular traffic in season tickets; the owner of one having entered the ground would frequently pass it over the fence to a friend!

For three years the income of the club had been going down, while the expenses hardly grew less despite careful pruning. Wages, of course, were a principal item, and in the Cup-winning season these added up to the mammoth total (as it seemed) of £2,548. In 1893 the gate receipts had totalled £3,645; a year later £3,225; in 1895 £2,592. The expenditure that year included training £338 14s. 5½d., travelling £236 18s. 7d., refreshments, hotels, etc., £127 4s. 9d., ground rent £183 17s. 6d., footballs £9 12s. 2d., clothes, shoes, etc., £52 6s. 9½d., depreciation of turnstiles, office furniture, gates, and timber £12 7s. 3d. the secretary, Addenbrooke, by now landlord of the Molineux Hotel, received a salary of £100 a year. Addenbrooke—or rather Mrs. Addenbrooke—added to the family exchequer, for in 1897 we read how 'the men are in good trim, due to Albert Fletcher[1] and Charlie Booth, and perhaps, to the joints that Mrs. Addenbrooke provides for those of the players who cannot well get home'.

Training by now was more ritualistic and the details of its processes were

[1] Appointed trainer in succession to Jack Lewis in 1896.

increasingly newsworthy. When the Wolves were drawn against West Bromwich Albion in the third round of the F.A. Cup the team (Hassall, Baugh, Dunn, Griffiths, Malpass, Wood, Wykes, Black, Butcher, Fleming, Griffin) was withdrawn from the rigours of town life and deposited at the Tettenhall Hotel, in 'one of the prettiest, and, perhaps, one of the healthiest little villages in the county'. T. H. Sidney supervised their training on behalf of the directors, while Jack Lewis superintended the technical aspects. Each day there was a 'three mile spin', followed by a 'good bath' and 'rub down'; after which all relaxed and took their pleasure 'at the green cloth'. By this the lyrical reporter of the *Midland Counties Express* meant that they played billiards. Other directors put in occasional appearances, particularly Hollingsworth, Johnson, and Brodie. Colonel Thorneycroft beneficently took the team one night to a Primrose League Entertainment in the Drill Hall in Wolverhampton.

But it was a sad time too. Harry Allen had died on February 23, at the age of 29. The directors sent a 'magnificent wreath', of violets, lilies of the valley, and orchids; the players' tribute was a wreath of arum lilies and orchids.

At the Annual General Meeting on August 16, 1895, there were those who considered training—the cost of which had risen by more than £150 over the previous season—an unnecessary investment. Why, they said, this molly-coddling? The men had nothing to do but keep themselves fit and they could do it for themselves. These same critics had been bitter also on account of the payment of summer wages: paying men, they said, for doing nothing. The directors should know better. Many Wolves players had sustained serious injury, against which the only doubtful compensation was a 'benefit' match, and an Insurance Coupon, worth £5, advertised in the *Midland Counties Express* 'to any person sustaining a Fracture of the Arm or Leg by Accident while footballing'.

That was a tragic year at Molineux. On March 2 Wolves played against West Bromwich Albion wearing black armbands for Harry Allen. During the summer Joshua Hassell, an excellent goalkeeper from Stafford, died from pneumonia, and before the new season opened David Wykes was also dead—from typhoid fever and pneumonia.

But the club had to continue. Billy Rose was persuaded back from Loughborough—whence also came Owen; Charlie Henderson was signed from Bolton for £20, and Billy Beats from Burslem Port Vale. In Beats the Vale knew they had a good man and, perpetually hard up, they held out for the prodigious fee of £70 and a benefit match. It is said that Beats, a builder's labourer, was persuaded to join Wolves when Addenbrooke found his quarry at work on a chapel roof and refused to let him down until his signature was promised. As new players came so old ones went—Swift to Loughborough, Bell to Grimsby Town, Haynes to Small Heath, and Butcher to West Bromwich Albion.

Apart from playing considerations there was a graver issue. The lease of the Molineux Grounds was due to expire in a year, and there was not a hope of purchasing it from the owners, the Northampton Brewery. In the end, however, the Molineux property was bought by other brewers, Messrs. Butler, who let the football field on generous terms for which they were rewarded by a seat on the Board.

In the early years of the club one is continually surprised by fluctuation between ancient and modern.

In the later 1890's, for instance, supporters of the Wolves were encouraged by the local paper to try to put their gifts of prophecy to account. Each season—until a court ruling declared the practice illegal—£250 was offered in prize money, the first prize each week being £2 10s. 0d., for correct forecasts of matches.

An alteration in the laws of the game in 1895 ensured that no longer could a goalkeeper be charged unless in contact with the ball. This was a blow to Wolves, whose previous successes had sprung from a native robustness, and one writer vividly recalled 'the old 'kick-and-a-rush' style of the Wolves on the Dudley Road ground, where—with John Brodie leading his forwards — they would come sweeping down the hill, and with irresistible force send backs, goalkeeper, and ball yards through the posts'.

Jack Brodie himself, for two years past a member of the club's selection committee, reminisced on the earliest days when supporting the re-election of Sir Alfred Hickman as President in August, 1895. The club', he said 'was then, as it is now—very hard up—(laughter). That is eighteen years ago. We passed Mr. Hickman's house every day in going to practice, and we didn't know what to do for funds. We heard how good he had been to other clubs, and whether it was 'like our cheek and impudence' (laughter) or not—for we were only boys of about 13 or 14—we wrote to him and asked him to become our president. He accepted and forwarded two guineas: and from that time he has been elected annually'.

A little while previously Brodie had discovered that the hazards of refereeing were, hardly less than those of playing. At Manor Field he had been in charge of the Second Division match between Arsenal and Burton Wanderers. Taking exception to his rulings and suspecting his Staffordshire loyalty to be greater than his capacity for impartiality some spectators attacked him. For this the F.A. ordered the ground to be closed for six weeks—which was about the time it took for Brodie's fractured cheek-bone to recover.

Hardly had the 1895-6 season started, however, before a similar penalty was imposed on Wolves—though for only a fortnight—for incidents during the visit of Everton. The optimism of the summer disappeared. The League programme was disastrous. A single point, gained at Sunderland on September 21, came from away matches and the crowds dropped badly at home. On Boxing Day, it is true, there was a gate of more than 20,000 for the Villa match—the crowd flocking to see Dick Topham who had been cajoled from his studies at Oxford University to make this occasional appearance—and the receipts were £434. But some of the players were dissipating their energies, so that at the beginning of January Tom Dunn, Billy Malpass, and Arthur Griffin were suspended for not taking their duties seriously.

From this point of insecurity, however, Wolves proceeded yet again to make their way to the F.A. Cup Final.

At the start of the season both players and management had been urged on to greater effort by an impassioned shareholder who asked what other team had held the Wrekin, Walsall Senior, Wednesbury Charity, Birmingham Charity, Birmingham, Staffordshire, and English Cups. The answer was none, and such stimulus was worth a goal in each round—except the Final. In the first round Wolves nearly slipped by only drawing at home with Notts County; but in the replay at Nottingham they got by, by 4-3. In the semi-final, on March 21 at Perry Barr, Wolves defeated Derby County by 2-1, despite the presence among the 'Rams' of the immortal Steve Bloomer—who was born in 1874 at Cradley Heath in the Black Country—and of the former Wolf, George Kinsey.

Before the Final it seemed that Wolves had sustained a damaging blow when Billy Rose—who was frequently in the wars—was injured. Rose recovered, but his deputy was playing so well that Rose himself asked not to be considered for selection. The new goalkeeper was the amateur (he later became a professional) W. Tennant, who came to the team by way of Willenhall Pickwick and Hart's Hill Unity. Before that he had played Rugby football for Moseley and in that code had been on the edge of representative honours.

The Final of April 18, 1896, was the second to be played in the grounds of the Crystal Palace—the only enclosure where there was provision for the vast public that was by now customary. There was a particular incentive this year. This was a new Cup, for during the year in which Villa had held it the original had been stolen from Mr. W. Shillcock's shop in Newton Row, Birmingham.

Wolves—their black-and-gold this year arranged in stripes rather than in quarters—went confidently to Crystal Palace; for every team they had defeated in the earlier rounds had much better League records than themselves, whereas the other finalists—Sheffield Wednesday—were companions in the lower half of the table. But Sheffield had their reputation as cup fighters as well. The had reached the Final in 1890, and the semi-final both in 1894 and 1895. More important, they had one match-winning forward, and a genius of a centre-half.

The Wolves team was:

W. Tennant; Dick Baugh, in his third and last Final; Tommy Dunn, who had come five years earlier from East Stirlingshire; Hill Griffiths, younger brother of John[1] and Jabez of earlier renown; W. Malpass; Billy Owen, from Dudley Road Excelsior; Joe Tonks, from Walsall Unity; Charlie Henderson, who had been with Leith Athletic, Darlington, Grimsby, as well as Bolton; Billy Beats, lately reserve for the English League; Harry Wood and David Black, another Scot who had served with Grimsby and Middlesbrough.

The captain was Harry Wood, veteran of the '93 Final and an England player both in 1890 and 1896.

Sheffield Wednesday fielded:

J. Massey; M. J. Earp, A. Langley; M. Brandon, T. H. Crawshaw, B. Petrie; A. Brash, A. Brady, L. Bell, H. Davies, F. Spikesley.

Crawshaw, later to win ten English caps, was an all-round player—fast into the attack, superb with his head, and a general on matters of strategy. Spikesley, to gain seven caps, was quick on his wing, adept at ball control, and an opportunist. In goal, Joe Massey, a native of Wolverhampton, presented an imperturbable front.

Whether plans for prompt destruction were worked out in advance in those days we cannot, perhaps, tell. But Wednesday scored their first vital goal within a few minutes of the start. Their forwards combining cleverly had the Wolves defenders frequently on the wrong foot, and when Brash and Bell moved down-field in a delicate pattern of inter-passing no one expected a last-minute long pass to the unmarked Spikesley. Yet that is what came and Spikesley scored. Eight minutes later, however, David Black, small and agile as an eel, found himself acutely angled but with a slender chance of

[1] John had the splendid record in his time of not missing a match for five years.

equalizing. This he did with a memorable hook. Another ten minutes went by, and then Spikesley scored his second, and the winning goal.[1]

Beaten, but not disgraced, the Wolves retired to dine as Sir Alfred Hickman's guests at St. Stephen's Club. The Monday following they were entertained at the Grand Theatre, Wolverhampton, to a performance of 'the farcical comedy, *The Passport*'. As for the inhabitants of the town, 'The vast concourse of people (who poured into the streets on Cup Final night) were naturally disappointed at the Wolves losing, but their good humour never for a moment gave place to vehement outbursts of passion. 'Wolverhampton', the writer proudly added, 'can take a beating as well as celebrate a victory'.

Partial success had stimulated the marginal supporters—that floating body who followed the currently successful team in the district—and gate receipts shot up that season to £4,600, leaving the club with a balance of £231. Thus the players, as a grateful director observed, had 'redeemed their club from debt, and perhaps from dissolution'. At the same time numerous philanthropists were themselves considerably poorer. Bonuses for winning or drawing were not regularized, but it was common practice for players to be given 'presents'. The benefactors, naturally, were generally the directors, who paid out as much as £2 a time. Small wonder that Councillor Hollingsworth felt impelled to preach a homily to footballers in general. 'One of the greatest drawbacks he knew to present-day football', he said, 'was the fact that as soon as a man became a professional he had an idea that he could do without work'. His counsel was that players should insure their futures by other regular employment.

In so far as it was possible to improve the players' conditions the Board did so. In the summer of 1896 they ploughed back some of their profits into new dressing rooms, with baths, and a room for the referee and linesmen. No longer need they all troop down the long incline from the Molineux Hotel. On the Waterloo Road side of the ground, where were the dressing-rooms, was one minute stand; on the opposite, Molineux Street side, another. Season tickets to the former cost £1 1s. 0d. for Gentlemen (Ladies or boys 10s. 6d.), and the latter 10s. 6d. (Ladies or boys 5s.). Admittance to the ground was 6d.—by which, and taking into account the changed value of money, present charges are hardly unreasonable.

The season of 1896-7 was yet another disappointment for once again the team, failing in the second round of the Cup, only just avoided the end-of-season 'test matches'. On December 27, however, Molineux housed its

---

[1] 'Spikesley was seventeen yards offside when he scored for Wednesday, and when David Black scored a beautiful goal for Wanderers, the referee said the ball was outside'. A somewhat partial recollection by R. Baugh, in *Sporting Star*, January 14, 1928.

The Wanderers 1907.

(Trainer)
A. Fletcher T. H. Lunn E. Juggins T. Baddeley J. Stanley R. H. Betterley
A. Baynham J. Smith W. T. Wooldridge W. Layton T. Raybould
A. James A. Hughes J. Whitehouse

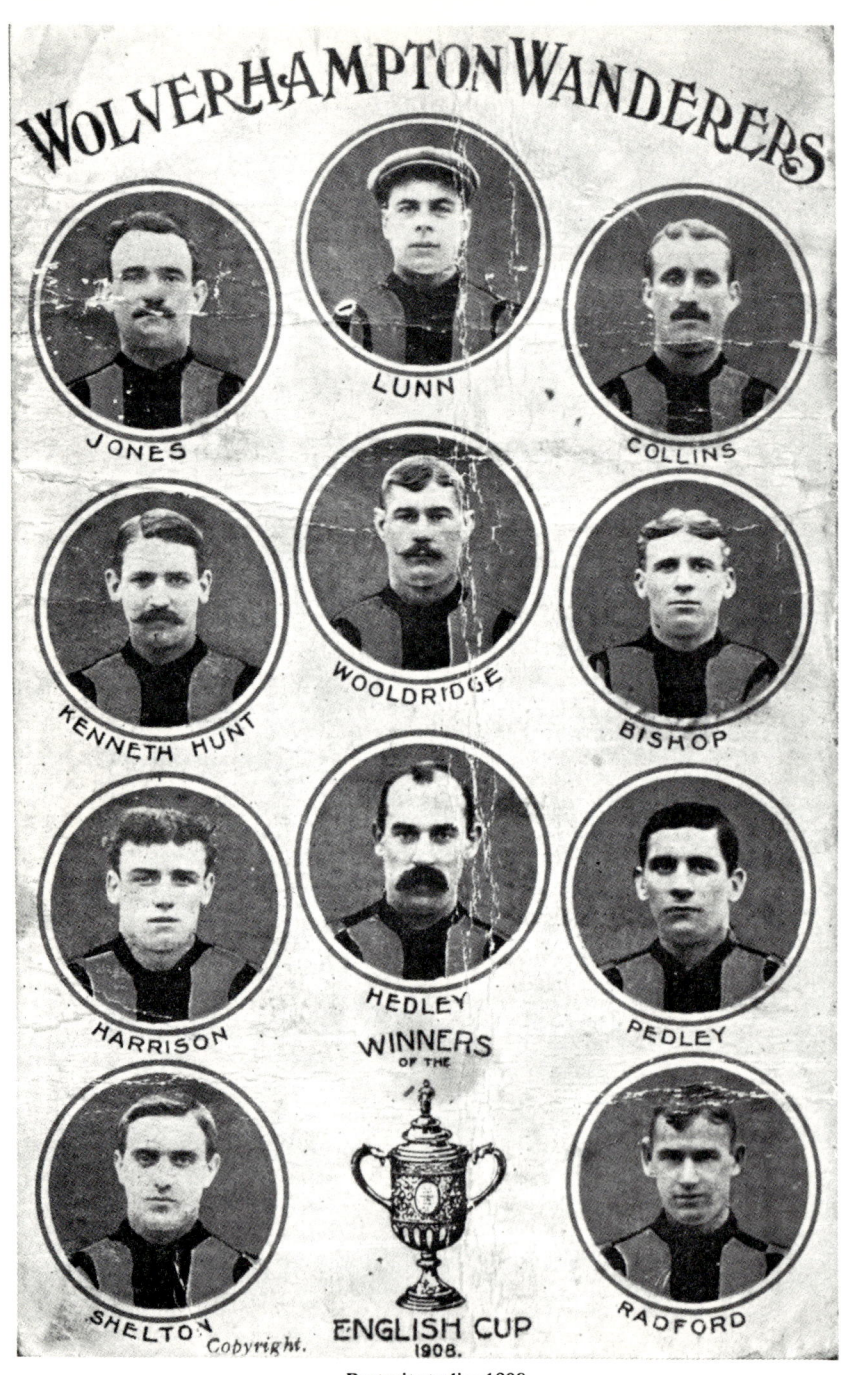

Portrait studies 1908.

Top Row.—Fletcher (*Trainer*). K. R. G. Hunt. Jones. Wooldridge (*Captain*). Lunn. Collins.
Bottom Row.—Harrison. Shelton. Hedley. Radford. Pedley. Bishop.

From the Fixture Card 1908-9.

Mr. C. Austin (Linesman).

Mr. J. Davies (Referee).

Mr. C. A. Newman (Linesman).

Cup Final Officials 1921.

largest crowd to date—27,489 (£761 7s. 6d.)—for the match with the Villa. At the end of the season interest was maintained by the prospect of winning at least one trophy. Wolves were finalists in both the Birmingham and the Staffordshire Cups. Unexpectedly they lost to Walsall by 2-1 in the former. But there were mitigating circumstances.

Crowds allowed their partisan feelings to get out of hand, and 'football hooligans', neither for the first nor the last time, appeared. A rough-house at Burnley had ended with stone-throwing. Hill Griffiths of the Wolves was hit and was required subsequently to give evidence for the prosecution in the Burnley Magistrates' Court. Unfortunately this precluded his playing in the Birmingham Cup Final.

In the Staffordshire Cup Wolves beat Stoke in a replay. The feature of this match was that Smith, at outside-left, had his 'breeches torn' during an attack. Smith was in trouble at this time for he had been sent off the field in the Walsall match for appearing to say something to the referee. As his opponents afterwards testified in an official enquiry, he neither said nor gave the impression to say anything distasteful. The referee was mistaken. Smith was cleared of obloquy.

While the senior team was making rather heavy weather of things one reporter was urging his readers to see the 'young Wolves'—the first use of a phrase later to become familiar, in later times. On April 17 the reserves had run Worcester Rovers off their feet in shocking conditions. Among the eleven names of the successful second string one leaps to the eye: that of Tom Baddeley.

6

Decline and Fall

'Wolverhampton Wanderers is another club which relies greatly upon local talent, and it is very seldom indeed you hear of the Wolves thinking of engaging a Scotsman . . . Last season they commenced with eight Staffordshire-born men and three from the adjoining county of Shropshire. The Wolves may not possess the most scientific team in the League, but they always place a trusty, go-ahead eleven on the field. I should say they look after purely locals better than any club in England. One reason probably is that they cannot afford to pay the high wages most clubs do, and always glance at their balance sheet with a vast amount of pleasure. It is one of the most economically managed clubs we have, and yet there are few more popular'.

J. J. Bentley in Football Who's Who, 1903-4.

HISTORY has its own ways of impressing its significant details on the memory. The most useful is the alliterative method, which in this instance gives us Beats and Baddeley. Tom Baddeley followed Billy Beats to Molineux from that impecunious club in the north of Staffordshire, Burslem Port Vale. Baddeley was born at Burslem and as a youth kept goal for Burslem Swifts, from which club he went to the Vale when he was 18. In 1896 he came to Wolves for a fee of £40 and in 1898 was made captain. From Wolves he eventually went to Bradford Park Avenue, but left behind him a handsome reputation, so that in 1903 (in which year Wolves again won the Birmingham Charity Cup) he was presented with a framed address by the Lord Mayor of Birmingham as a token of gratitude for his unfailing willingness to take part in charity games. When his playing days were done Tom returned to the Potteries where he died in 1946 at the age of 71.

Beats and Baddeley were for years the mainspring of the Wolves side, and both achieved national fame under not always congenial conditions. The truth is that at their coming the club entered upon an inglorious epoch: inglorious, that is, in the short view, for the policy which the directors felt obliged to adopt made early success in League and Cup problematical, to say the least.

By the end of the nineteenth century the vicious circle was complete. A club in Newcastle, or Birmingham, or Manchester, or in the newly conscious but soccer-starved region of the South, could attract large gates; and with a large turn-over inducements could be offered to the 'professors'. The stars thus assembled could compel a gate consistency that was becoming rarer in Wolverhampton.

The most talented of footballers were beginning to bargain their gifts. It was rumoured that some were making as much as £6 or £7 a week all the year round; that £4 a week and regular employment outside football were occasionally guaranteed. In 1900 we find a new phenomenon—the player-journalist, Ernest Needham of Sheffield United, and 'prince of half-backs', for instance, contributing a weekly column to a Saturday night sporting paper.

The player with the less fashionable club has no ready access to such opportunities, and the long service of so many Wolves players of the era under consideration is all the more meritorious. Baddeley nearly refused to sign on at the beginning of one season—not because he wished to leave the club, but because of the offensive remarks thrown at him by the home spectators. The reason for this, rising from frustrated hopes, will shortly become apparent. Beats, for so long kept out of the England side by the excellence of the amateur, G. O. Smith, suffered many injuries in his club career before he finally went to Bristol Rovers in 1903 after eight years of loyal service. Both he and Baddeley, however, won their England caps.

Baddeley—on the small side but gifted with an uncanny sense of anticipation and a sure pair of hands—kept goal for England for the first time in the team which defeated Ireland by 4-0 at Molineux in 1903. He won four other caps, as well as League honours, and was a sure last line of defence behind colleagues who were often outplayed. His performance against Scotland, at Sheffield in 1903, was described as 'sensational'—when that word had not yet suffered its final abasement.

As for Beats, he was by way of being an intellectual player. Small, neat, observant, he tantalized opponents by his collaboration with his fellow forwards. No bull-at-the-gate tactics for Beats; studying the general position of play he made goals by judicious passes to his wings. 'The great article in his stock-in-trade', it was written at the time, was 'his phenomenal unselfishness. With him it is a case of 'we mean to win', not 'I want to be the scorer'.' Beats played against Wales in 1901, when he was the lever of a 6-0 victory, and against Scotland in 1902. He was, therefore, present at Ibrox Park, Glasgow, when the terracing collapsed and many people were killed and injured.

In 1898—with Beats and Baddeley beginning to flower—there was a tempered optimism at Molineux. In April the club had finished third in the

League, an eminence only previously reached in the first year of the League's operation and not to be achieved again for almost fifty years. But there was writing on the wall.

Harry Wood did not re-sign. After twelve seasons he had become an institution. Whether he played on the left-wing or at inside-forward he was, it is said 'a terror to all who opposed Wolverhampton Wanderers'. His perseverance, his ardour as captain, his experience in the international field were immeasurable assets to his younger colleagues. In 1898 the directors—who had previously stood firm by a not unwise decision to forbid their players the tenancy of public-houses—let him go to 'that veritable Klondyke for professional footballers, Southampton'. Harry had not wanted to go. He said he would have stayed at Molineux could the directors offer him the terms promised at Southampton and allow him to become a publican. The directors could not pay more—that summer, the best that they could bring out of the balance sheet was the reduction of the club's liability to £224—nor would they retract from principle.

The cry was economy. There were indirect forces at work, for what with the war in South Africa, the death of Mr. Gladstone, an alarming Liberal victory in South Norfolk, and talk of reform of the House of Lords, the steady burgesses who were the Wolves directorate were more than a little timorous of the future. A year or so before they had been shaken at an Annual General Meeting when one shareholder protested that the board was too Conservative—in a political sense. No one agreed, so no damage was done. But straws blowing in the wind can darken the vision. There was, moreover, a Players' Union—which implied more expenditure in the long run—and in 1899 a Wolves Player, Hill Griffiths, joined its committee. The idea of such a body stemmed, in fact, from a proposal of W. C. Rose, captain of Wolves, as far back as 1893.

Wood went to Southampton; Owen and Eccles to Everton; Tennant to Walsall. A year later Malpass retired, and some of the younger players who did not look like making the grade were discarded. In 1900 the only Scotsman left on the staff—Fleming—went to Liverpool.

Fleming had enjoyed a benefit match at the end of the previous December. For this occasion Wolves had invited as their opponents the redoubtable Corinthians. Corinthians lived up to their reputation and won by 4-3, thanks to fine play by G. O. Smith, the England centre-forward, and L. J. Moon, who, although also a centre-forward, played that day at inside-left. Of the Corinthians three had previously been members of the 1898-9 Oxford side, which had only lost 1-0 to a complete Wolves League side. Corinthians visited Molineux again at the end of 1900, when they won more decisively by 8-3.

Such was the strength of amateur football in that period.

George Bowen, who, a year earlier had been picked out of Walsall League football and transformed into a first-class and saleable asset, accompanied Fleming to Liverpool. The Liverpool secretary congratulated himself on his own good judgment but, also observed the acumen of the Wolves board. 'I suppose', he said, 'you'll do as usual, find a couple of local juniors to take their places'.

So it was. The directors more and more found themselves obliged to recruit locally. Exceptionally they might go further afield, as when they went to Crewe Alexandra for the Welsh international centre-forward Trevor Owen. But generally Willenhall Pickwick, Wednesfield, Bridgetown Amateurs, Halesowen, Blakenhall St. Luke's (for the old name survived), and a host of other such minor centres, provided the raw material: and very raw it often was, until refined by the estimable Fletcher and the senior players.

In 1900 the playing strength of the club had diminished, there now being only twenty-five professionals on the books. But there was a unity about the fraternity that was, to put it no higher, unusual: of the players twenty-one were born in Staffordshire, the others were all natives of Shropshire. When Robotham was signed from Hunslet that year people asked, why Hunslet? The player had, in fact, been born in Wolverhampton, and his father had at one time belonged to the Wolves.

There was a fine spirit in other ways. Because the policy was against expensive signings players had to be adaptable. Whitehouse was translated from the forward to the half-back line at a time when half-backs were unavailable. Wooldridge eventually came from inside-left to centre-forward on the departure of Beats, even though it meant splitting an excellent left-wing partnership with Miller. To such extremes was versatility carried that once, through the effect of a spate of injuries, the Wolves turned out with nine players who were all bred as half-backs.

About the administration of the club there was a kind of matiness that enabled people to discuss matters of moment in a more or less relaxed manner, while the diverse interests of the people involved ensured a good network of communication. Hickman was still President. C. T. Mander was Vice-President, but also President of the Wolverhampton Rugby Football Club which functioned in Henwood Lane. The Chairman of the Board was G. W. Walker, and his fellow-members were Allt, Crump, Craddock, F. T. Langley, J. Lawrence, H. Whitworth, F. D. Taylor, Levi Johnson, A. J. Evans, and T. H. Sidney. The last three formed the players' committee. Johnson by now had added the Presidency of the Wolverhampton Bowling Club—headquarters at the Ring o' Bells—to his duties. Sidney, very much a rising star in the wider fields of football administration, was President of the Wolverhampton Nomads Cycling and Touring Club, which conveniently had its base in the Molineux Hotel. In Topham Villa, Wanderers Avenue, the Blakenhall Ladies Cycle Club, over which Lady Hickman presided, used to meet.

In retrospect those times look positively idyllic, although for most people they were quite otherwise. However, the illusion of comfort continues as, in the last three seasons of the nineteenth century we see Wolves coasting along comfortably enough in the League—though with no success in the F.A. Cup: 3rd, 8th and 4th, positions of respectability. In 1898 rising costs compelled the directors to try to raise more funds by adjusting the charges for admission. When season tickets had been fixed at 10s., it was pointed out, wages were but a third of what they had become. So on August 19 patrons paid for each match—6d for entrance to the ground, 6d extra to the Molineux stand or 'reserve', 1s. 6d. to the Waterloo Road stand—the same price for ladies; and the success of the reserve team in the Birmingham League emboldened an increase of 1d., the charge going up from 3d. to 4d. The next year season tickets were back, but, mindful of the unscrupulous behaviour of former holders, the pages of the books were numbered from 1 to 40; the appropriate page being torn out at the turnstiles.

In 1901, however, the situation was bad. Preston and West Bromwich Albion had been relegated, and—while it could be pointed out that Wolves and Everton were the only two original League clubs which had never been thus humiliated or even subjected to the indignity of competing in 'test matches'—Wolves had sunk to thirteenth in the table. The receipts for the season were £4,966 17s. 11d., expenditure £5,297 6s. 0d. No great calculation was needed to show a deficit on the year's working of £330 8s. 1d. Taking into account the red patch that had crept over the account at the bank over the previous few years the directors found themselves with a total deficiency of £1,392 12s. 3d., and a peevish bank manager.

There followed, as in 1895, a public appeal—this, it was agreed, must positively be the last—to which the response was £1,000. Of this windfall the greater part came in four individual gifts: 5,000 regular patrons could only muster £250 between them.

The 1902-3 season began with the club £800 in arrears, after the payment of summer wages. The stringent measures taken in regard to the employment of local players began, however, to pay off; for the season ended with a profit of almost £200 on the year. The playing record was also improved, the team finished eleventh in the table, which was at least better than in the two previous seasons.

There was, however, a general idea abroad that Wolves were not now what they once were. 'Time was,' wrote one columnist, 'when the name of Wolverhampton Wanderers figured frequently in the semi-final and the final stages of the [F.A. Cup] Competition.' The Midland Micawbers always expected something to turn up in this respect, but, year after year, nothing did.

In 1900 Queen's Park Rangers, an unknown side to Midland enthusiasts, had the temerity to hold the Wanderers to a draw in London and to win at Molineux; and in the first round. A year later the eventual finalists, Sheffield United, soundly beat Wolves in the third round, by 4-0. Those were the days in which the United's goal was kept by the amiable, mountainous Foulke, whose best performances were reserved for the Wolves since the day that Griffin, in a League match at Sheffield in 1895, had the inspired temerity to charge him through the goal. First round defeats followed in two succeeding seasons. But in 1904 hope stirred anew.

On February 6 Wolves played Stockton, holders of the Amateur Cup, on Tees-side. Finding a heavy ground to their own prescription, as it were, they revelled in the mud and outplayed and outgunned their lighter opponents—among whom was G. Wreford Brown, a clergyman and one of a distinguished footballing family. Wolves returned from Saltburn, where they had stayed, to discover as their next opponents Derby County. There followed a marathon. At Derby, on February 20, the match was drawn, each side scoring twice. The result after the replay on February 24, at Molineux, was the same. The second replay was at Villa Park five days later. Here Derby County just got home by 1-0, but supporters of Wolves had reason to feel aggrieved. Baddeley was chosen to play for England against Wales at Wrexham on the same day, and he could not be released. From the Derby side the great Bloomer had been selected as an English reserve, but had been let off to play in the cup-tie.

A little over a year later Wolves took their revenge for this defeat; but in such circumstances that any sort of rejoicing was impossible. One does not laugh at death-beds, even though the prospective corpse is momentarily inspired to shake a fist at the attendant wraith.

In 1905 Wolves had ended the season disastrously. In their last three matches they gave away ten goals and did not themselves score. The defence that season let through seventy-three goals in all—the most dismal record since the League started. Supporters clamoured, as usual, for new blood. Angry voices were raised against the attempts to 'muddle through'. A team was demanded which should 'at least hold its own'. In October the directors capitulated to the outcry so far as to engage the aged genius Archie Goodall to assist in their salvation; but he was past it, and his later appearance at the Empire as a trick cyclist gave more pleasure to Wolverhampton than his last remnants of football skill. By Christmas it was clear that the side was doomed, four matches only had been won and defeats had included catastrophes against Newcastle and Villa, the former winning by 8-0, the latter by 6-0. January passed disconsolately—Wolves 0, Stoke 4: Wolves 2, Manchester City 3; Wolves 2, Bolton 3: February almost equally so—Wolves 1, Woolwich Arsenal 2; Wolves 0, Middlesbrough 0; Wolves 1, Blackburn 3: March came and went—Wolves 2, Preston 3; Wolves 2, Sunderland 7; Wolves 0, Newcastle 2; Wolves 1, Sheffield United 4; Wolves 3, Birmingham 3; Wolves 4, Aston Villa 1.

At that point Wolves began to play like new men. After forcing a credible draw with Everton on April 7, they ran riot on Easter Monday and whipped Notts County by 6-1, largely thanks to a sequence of accurate centres from left-winger, Pedley.

The last match of the season was on April 21. Wolves were destined for the Second Division. The visit of Derby County, always popular guests, gave an opportunity for the club to show its gratitude to two loyal players of the bleak years—Wooldridge and Whitehouse—in a benefit match. Before this match the goals scored against Wolves totalled ninety-nine. The most that was hoped for was a goal-less draw, so that the adverse century might be avoided. The result of the match: Wolves 7, Derby County 0. With such a grand, defiant gesture, Wolves left the First Division.

7

Second Division

'The winners were always strong, relentless and cool'.
The Times, April 27 1908.

THERE is, it is stoically understood, a virtue in accommodating oneself to reduced circumstances. At the end of August 1906 the leading sporting journalist of Wolverhampton turned his note appropriately by observing that the patrons of Molineux would—or ought to—rejoice at the sight of new faces. The Second Division then embraced Leicester Fosse (later City), Grimsby Town, Chelsea, Barnsley, Lincoln City, Hull City, Stockport County, Clapton (later Leyton) Orient, Blackpool, Burslem Port Vale, Burton United, Notts Forest, Glossop, West Bromwich Albion, Leeds City, Burnley, Gainsborough Trinity, Chesterfield, Bradford City, and Wolves. The first of the newcomers to Molineux were Hull City, on September 1.

The temperature that day was so high that factories had to close down, and reporters encased in their glass-house simmered in grievous torture. The players discovered that the lower regions were warm in more senses than one, for Hull City, showing splendid form, forced a creditable draw. Since there was a clash of colours Wolves played that day in white shirts—a style that had nearly been adopted as a permanency before the familiar old gold and black in 1891.

The records show that Wolves finished that season in sixth place. A detailed analysis, however, reveals how easily they might have done much better. Their away record was dismal, with only four wins to set against twelve defeats and three draws.

On March 2 came one of those turning-points in men's careers that make poignant reading. Wolves were playing against the bottom club, Burton United—their last season in the English League as it happened—when Tom Baddeley, then captain of the team, injured his wrist and had to leave the field, Jones taking his place in goal for the remainder of the match. For the next match little Lunn, a spectacular fellow, came up from the reserves.

Baddeley never returned. At the season's end he was transferred to Bradford Park Avenue, speeded on his way with this closing tribute—'But that the celebrated little international will be a splendid sample of the conscientious professional is certain . . . a loyal servant and a gentleman.'

During the last days of the season Jack Jones was also incapacited. Between training and matches he engaged in country sports in a lordly way, which came as a surprise to many Wolves supporters, when they discovered his non-selection on April 6 was due to his having been accidentally shot while out in Shropshire with a gamekeeper! A tough customer, however, he quickly recovered—the bullet having penetrated no vital area.

The policy of the club remained as it was in First Division days. All the new signings of 1907—except for W. R. Radford who had, although previously a Wolves player, spent a year with Southampton,—were recruited from local minor leagues. In the practice matches one newcomer to senior football particularly distinguished himself. Kenneth Reginald Gurney Hunt (1884-1949), the son of Rev. R. G. Hunt, Vicar of St. Mark's Church since 1897, was an undergraduate at Queen's College, Oxford. He had won his Blue at Oxford in 1905, 1906 and 1907 (and was to play for the University yet again in 1908), had had experience with Oxford City and Wolves Reserves, and had played for the England Amateur side against Ireland and Holland. A big six-footer, quite dauntless and very fast, he was, by 1907, the equal of any professional player in the Second Division, and beyond his technical skill he had a striking personality that endeared him to other players and spectators alike.

In August, 1907, it was clear that Hunt was bound to keep the right-half position—if this occupation could be fitted into the academic chores of his last year at Oxford preparatory to his ordination.

As the season progressed, however, the supporters began to resign themselves to yet another year of disappointment. The defence played well enough, but the forwards struck no sort of form. Twenty matches went by and only sixteen goals were scored. The first round of the Cup was imminent and prospects seemed far from bright. Wolves were drawn against Glossop on January 4. 'The selected of the Wanderers players' reported the newspaper. 'will enter into residence at Molineux Hotel . . . and the usual regime *(sic)* of health-giving country walks and lung-expanding exercises at the grounds will be indulged in'. Excepting, that is, Kenneth Hunt, who was at Oxford from each Monday to Friday and properly immersed in his studies in the Early Fathers, and the other amateur, P. B. Corbett, an old boy of Wolverhampton Grammar School. The preparation was effective, Glossop being defeated by 5-0.

Next came a more difficult proposition. Bradford City, destined to head the Second Division that season, had trounced Wolves in a cup-tie only two years previously; and now Wolves were to play them at Bradford on January 11. Taking heart from a draw, 1-1, Wolves prepared for a replay four days later. This again was a close affair, but Hedley, at centre-forward, emboldened by an adamantine defence took the one opportunity that came his way. His one goal was sufficient. Spectators remarked on the sterling play of Kenneth Hunt 'the pick of the halves', and neutral observers on the 'Wolves' grit'. 'Now', said someone in Wolverhampton 'we are ready for the other B's—they of Bury'.

On February 1, the sporting edition of the *Express and Star* headlined 'victorious Wolves'. A huge crowd of 27,127 had seen Wolves triumph 2-0. After Bury came Swindon Town, a forceful side in the Southern League. In order to play for his own club side Kenneth Hunt had that day to sacrifice an amateur cap, for he had been selected to play against Wales.

Remembering that Wolverhampton too was a railway town it is not surprising that there was a dual interest in the visitors from Swindon, especially when it was reported (falsely, in fact) that the team would be drawn by the 'Great Bear' locomotive, newly built at the Swindon works. The match itself was an absorbing struggle, grim and rentless, man-to-man warfare with quarter neither asked nor given. Neither side could score, and Wolves seemed at a disadvantage when Wooldridge, the captain, was injured and removed from the field. Into his place came Hunt, who played as one inspired. Twice, he was laid out; but 'there were times when he appeared to be playing all Swindon by himself. Over and over again he beat two and three men, and then taking in the situation at a glance, placed the ball either to the wings or to the inside men, so that he kept the whole team moving like a flywheel setting all the machinery in motion . . .' In the last two minutes Harrison, formerly of Crewe Alexandra, and Hedley scored goals that sent the home crowd delirious. On Monday morning the *Morning Leader, Daily Mail, Daily News,* and *Athletic News,* became ecstatic at the match-winning display of Hunt. He, for his part, paid a second visit to the Hospital to enquire after the progress of Swindon's Chambers—who had suffered much damage in an attempt to contain the irresistible undergraduate—and then caught the train to Oxford.

By now the team was ablaze with determination and after visiting Stoke—where the gate was 31,800—on March 7, the headlines read 'Still onward: Black-and-gold in the Ascendant'. A 1-0 victory but more convincing than the score suggests, for the side was 'aggressive' from start to finish. The semi-final was at Stamford Bridge, on March 28, against

Southampton. There had been a previous cup-meeting between the two sides in 1905, of which the only Wolves survivors were Jones and Wooldridge. Radford scored before half-time; Hedley midway through the second half; Wolves were in the Final again.

As the match was played before 45,000 spectators in London, Queen Street, Wolverhampton, was thronged with anxious citizens including Rev. R. G. Hunt, dependent on up-to-the-minute news from the office of the *Express and Star*.

April 25, the date of the Final, drew near, and Wolves prepared themselves for the encounter with Newcastle United by going to Matlock. During the last week of preparation the town of Wolverhampton was in ferment. Not only was there a Cup Final to contend with, but also a by-election, caused by the elevation of Sir Henry Fowler, member for Wolverhampton East, to the peerage. The two contests became ludicrously intertwined—particularly since Alfred Hickman, still President of the Wolves, and Levi Johnson were vigorously campaigning on behalf of the Unionist candidate, L. S. Amery. As for Amery he was among those who saw the team off to the Crystal Palace, hoping thereby to show that his politics were as sound as his sympathies.

The teams were as follows:

Wolves: Lunn; Jones, Collins; K. R. G. Hunt, Wooldridge, Bishop; Harrison, Shelton, Hedley, Radford,[1] Pedley.

Newcastle United: Lawrence; McCracken, Pudan; Gardner, Veitch, McWilliam; Rutherford, Howie, Appleyard, Speedie, Wilson.

Newcastle, studded with English, Scottish, and Irish internationals, with six of their Cup Final side of 1906, and First Division champions, were favourites. Wolves were not given a chance, save by their fellow-townsmen, but the world in general was on their side. Besides, once again, they were an English side. Lunn was a native of Spennymoor, Co. Durham; Hedley of South Bank, Middlesbrough; Radford of Pinxton, Derbyshire: the remainder came from the neighbourhood of Wolverhampton.

Prior to the match a reporter asked Kenneth Hunt how he thought Wolves would deal with the situation. 'We shall', he said, 'hustle them off their game'.

A dismally wet day kept the attendance down to 74,000. The rain ceased

[1] Radford came in for Corbett against Bury, and this was the only change in the side in the course of the competition.

before the kick-off, but it remained cold and miserable. Such was the temper of the game, however, that the spectators quite forgot their discomfort. For half an hour Newcastle, the current masters of scientific, closely woven style, pressed; but they could find no way through a defence that had perfected the art of coverage. The Newcastle forwards needed time, which they were never given, to complete their attacks, and, forced into making quick shots at goal, were put off balance. As time went by the Wolves half-backs grew dominant, and even adventurous.

After the initial supremacy of Newcastle had faded the Wolves attack began to threaten. At one moment Hedley sent a long pass out to Harrison on the wing. The outside-right returned the ball to the centre where it ran loose for a moment until collected by Hunt. Although still far from goal, Hunt chanced a long shot. As though surprised Lawrence fumbled, and the still rising ball was in the net. The barriers were down, and almost immediately Hedley, refusing to be harried by McCracken, added a second goal.

In the second half Howie scored for Newcastle, but Harrison, now at his best and putting the ball, time after time, round the opposing half-back, added yet another for Wolves—after taking the ball half the length of the field.

Only once before, in 1894, had a Second Division side won the Cup.

The presentation was made by the Lord Mayor of London, who noted the Englishness of the winners and commended the game of football in general: 'so healthy a game as football', he said, 'must benefit the body and also the mind, and so must help to give the country men fitted to represent the nation in any sphere of life'. Lord Kinnaird also spoke, and with tours of the time in mind, warned his listeners that England's football supremacy might soon be threatened by foreign countries.

While the Cup Final was taking place the *Express and Star* who had, at great cost, installed a telephone box at the Crystal Palace, relayed information from their observer on the spot. And such were the wonders of science that on the Monday following a notice went up outside the Empire Palace: *See your own team before they arrive: See how they scored the goals.* A film was available and as the bioscope threw shadows on the screen, packed audiences persuaded themselves that what they saw was as good as the real thing, and 'every point made by the Wolves was lustily cheered'.

Cup Final or no Cup Final, politics must go on. As Amery sanguinely moved about the town—for what with the death of the Premier, Campbell-Bannerman, the defeat of Winston Churchill in Manchester, and the new Licensing Act, Unionist hopes ran high—he sought to instruct his prospective constituents in a language they understood: 'an election and the final of a cup were, in the long run, very like each other, because it was the best style of play that won . . .' and 'My dear Winston . . . was always off-side'. But the Liberals were not to be outdone, and Alderman Lewis issued a stirring exhortation on behalf of the local candidate, Mr. Thorne: 'Emulate the Wolves. Get to work at once. Poll early. Gain goals. Secure your majority before half-time, and then work unceasingly to increase your lead until the whistle goes for full-time, and Thorne will be in with the numbers he deserves'.

On Monday *The Times* lamented the dislocation of the hustings.[1]

> It is feared that public meetings fixed for tonight will be deserted, as the Wolverhampton Wanderers team come home at half-past 7 o'clock with the Association Cup. Arrangements are made for an enthusiastic welcome and a parade of the town with the Cup, brass bands and banners. It is expected that for two hours the town will be given up to demonstration.

And a remarkable demonstration it was. One of the points of call—the Cup team of those days perambulated like a set of medieval mystery players—was the entrance to St. Mark's Vicarage. The Rev. R. G. Hunt had cakes and cocoa for the victors; but such was the crush that safety decreed a postponement of this clerical entertainment. As for the son of the Vicarage he found himself among the F.A. party selected to tour in Austria, Hungary, and Bohemia, and then to play for Great Britain in the Olympic Games. During this same year he was ordained deacon in the Church of England.

New names had by now appeared among the directorate—notably E. Barker, W. Fleming, A. G. Jeffs, W. Shepherd, and T. Addenbrooke. The last-named was a link with older times.

On May 30 the Annual General Meeting of the Football Association was held at the Holborn Restaurant. Lord Kinnaird being absent, Charles Crump, as senior Vice-President, took the chair. It was an important meeting, for Mr. Clegg was to propose the abolition of any restriction on wages and bonuses. The existing regulations, he said, were being flouted. But 'Mr. Sidney',[2] of the Wolverhampton Wanderers, opposed the suggestion. 'The present rule', he argued, 'worked excellently, and they had no trouble in re-signing their players. Everything in football must not be sacrificed to money, and clubs with little money, but any amount of enthusiasm, must

---

[1] The result of the by-election, declared on May 6, was—Thorne, 4,514; Amercy, 4,506: as narrow a margin as in the Wolves balance sheet of that period.

[2] T. H. Sidney had been a member of the League Management Committee from 1897 to 1905.

have a chance to carry off the highest honours of the football field.' Supported by the representative of Preston North End Mr. Sidney carried the meeting with him, and the motion was defeated.

Sidney, the effect of whose views was to be felt in football for half-a-century at least—was the Wolves share in that year's Cup takings represented great riches, the result of hard graft and relentless endeavour, of scrupulously economic management, of local pride and faith.

In all the profit on that season was £3,427 9s. 11d. Against that figure should be set the receipts, which amounted to a little over £9,000, and the fact that only one club in the League—Chelsea—could show a larger profit. Chelsea, their total receipts being £24,411, made £3,626 15s. 3d., from which it may be deduced that the Wolves directors managed their budget rather more efficiently. With the reserves thus accumulated, and with a continuation of the same close economy, the club maintained its solvency until the end of the season of 1914-15.

The echoes of the 1908 Final were long in dying—if indeed they can be said ever to have died. At the beginning of the 1908-9 season the now Rev. K. R. G. Hunt, whose photograph made a splendid frontispiece to the *Athletic News Football Annual,* was appointed to the staff of Highgate School in North London—whence he emerged at holiday times to take his place in the Wolves side. George Hedley joined the ranks of footballer journalists and in an article of September 5, 1909, entitled *The Open Game,* protested his, and his club's, dislike of studied, formalized football—such as Newcastle United had unsuccessfully set against this robustness. The article links the old and the new and emphasizes the essentially romantic style which, with variations and adaptation, has characterized the club's tradition.

By now the Football League had been in existence for 21 years. To mark this milestone Addenbrooke and his friend G. S. Ramsey, the Villa secretary, were presented with long-service medals by the League.

The Edwardian period passed. Irish Home Rule and the question of the House of Lords engaged the attention of immigrant Irishmen and native Radicals. The clouds of war began to gather in the Balkans. The death of Florence Nightingale caught the eye of the reader of the sports edition one night in August, 1910. Football in Wolverhampton settled down to a provincial jog-trot. Lunn went to Tottenham, being replaced by Boxley of Cradley Heath; Wooldridge to Croydon Common; A. J. Walker, Harry Jones and Shelton to Port Vale; Jack Jones to Wellington Town, 'where he settled down in the licensing trade'. The departure of old players was regretted, for 'there are few club managers who persevere with the men whom they have once placed their trust with the same persistency as the directors of the

Wanderers do'.

Among the players who came to the club were the Rev. W. C. Jordan,[1] formerly with Everton, whose short stay during the 1911-12 season gave Wolves the spiritual satisfaction of two clerks in holy orders on the books at the same time. Another bird of passage was the Irish international W. Halligan, who had played for Derby County and Leeds City and was to go to Hull, after two years at Molineux, in 1913. More notable signings were E. J. Peers, a Welsh goalkeeper, who represented his country both before and after the war, and Sammy Brooks, a diminutive outside-left (5 ft. 2 in.) from Brierley Hill.

In 1911-12 Wolves were fifth in the final table, the highest position yet attained in the Second Division. To the discomfiture of their supporters the team lost far too many home matches ever to threaten the eventual supremacy of Derby County and Chelsea. Three years later the record of the club was still better, but it mattered little to anyone in April, 1915, what was the state of the English League. For, for a long time, this was the end. A war-time League Emergency Competition was instituted, but the Wolves took no part, and the majority of the players joined the engineering firms of the town and neighbourhood.

---

[1] A graduate in Natural Sciences at Cambridge, Jordan was ordained in 1907 and at this time was curate at St. Clement's Church, Nechells, Birmingham.

Team of 1922.
Top Row.—R. Baugh, J. Hodnett, N. George, V. Gregory, A. Riley, G. H. Marshall.
Bottom Row.—T. Lea, F. Burrill, G. Edmonds, A. Potts, S. Brooks.

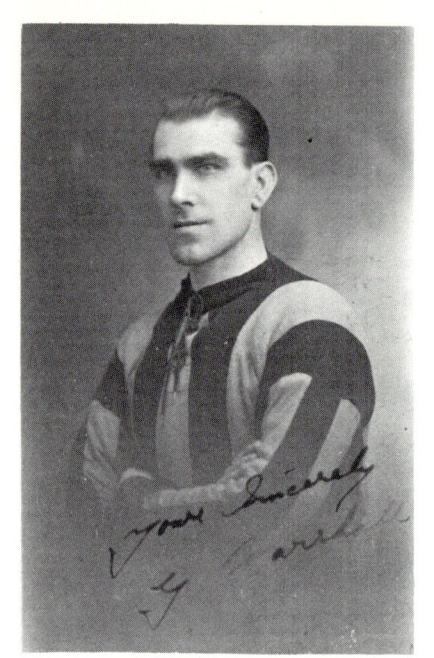

G. H. Marshall

A. Riley

S. Brooks.

E. J. Peers

N. George

A. Potts

J. E. Hodnett

G. Brewster

T. Lea

8

Hard Times

'It was next decided that the directors be asked to receive a deputation.
   "How many shall it consist of?" inquired the chairman.
   A voice: "Sixteen thousand."
   Another: "Let us all go" '. (Exeunt omnes.)
                    Report of a public meeting, November 29 1919.

THE social consequences of the immediate post-war period were reflected in the football field—which holds up the mirror to nature as effectively as any other medium, and the directors of Wolves found new situations to face and problems to solve.

Starved of entertainment for so long the public was avid for football. But the same public was less tolerant than formerly. The Molineux Grounds, they said, were below standard. If there was a large gate—and now there generally was—half the spectators could not see what was going on. Those who stood on the Molineux Street side complained that the sloping bank made their feet ache. Those who were past standing urged the erection of a new stand on the Waterloo Road side. Once—it was pointed out—international matches were staged at Molineux, but without adequate amenities these would be placed elsewhere. If the directors of Rotherham, for instance, could launch out in ground improvement why not those of Wolves? And then there was the team. The dignity of Wolverhampton demanded a first-class side, which should be in the First Division. Thus ran the critical thoughts of the supporters of the club.

The players were eager to be back; but they too had a fresh approach, rooted in industrial experience. Living costs were up; therefore wages should be brought into line. Thus the rate for the top-line players was settled at £8 a week.

Then there was the government. Entertainment tax, the thoughtless imposition that long continued to cripple many forms of endeavour, laid a further burden on the football administrators.

Immediately, the price of admission to League matches at Molineux was raised from 6d. to 1s. Since players' wages were up by 50 per cent over the pre-war rate, and since half the increase was allocated to entertainment tax it can be seen that the club could only benefit by a substantial increase in the average gate. This, in fact, happened and the weekly attendance fluctuated between 12,000 and 19,000.

The first match of the new era was at Leicester—where the team previously called the Fosse was now known as the City—and Wolves did well enough by beating a young side by 2-1. The team that day was:

> Peers; Jones, Garratly; Price, Groves, Bishop; Harrison, Howell (a Warwickshire cricketer), Bate, Needham, and Brooks.

Eight of that side had played in the last pre-war matches while Bishop, who was captain, and Harrison were veterans of the 1908 Final. Garratly was almost as venerable, having been with the club since 1909. The more loud-mouthed among the spectators might well comment on the veteran aspect, and urge the infusion of new blood.

As the opening matches went by, the Leicester victory proved a false omen, and aspirations towards Division I were gradually ousted by forebodings regarding the new Division III. Tempers rose easily on the cindered banks and on October 18 there was almost civil war. On that day—when Vizard, later to become known in another capacity at Molineux, was playing for Wales in a so-called Victory international at Stoke—Wolves were entertaining Bury. Five minutes before full-time, Bury leading 1-0, the referee awarded a penalty to the visitors. Not content merely with voicing disapproval hordes of spectators invaded the field and made threateningly for the referee—behaviour of a kind often thought to belong only to the present.

> The referee was surrounded, and he considered flight the best course to pursue. He dashed off at top speed in the direction of the dressing-rooms, but near the halfway line he slipped and came a cropper.

Despite the efforts of the players to protect him, and the exhortations of Jack Brodie—who by now had reached the rank of headmaster—the crowd continued to harass the fallen referee. Police reinforcements were summoned, and the Chief Constable superintended rescue operations. The referee was taken to sanctuary, where he remained until he could be smuggled away. Meanwhile—'for a long period people assembled in the street, and called for the referee, but,' the *Express and Star* engagingly concluded, 'they were not accommodated'.

The players and the club officials came out of this with honour. For the irresponsibility of some of their clients, however, they were heavily penalized. The ground was closed by the F.A. and for some time home matches were transferred to the Hawthorns, the Albion having thus generously come to the aid of their troubled neighbours. It was estimated that this interruption cost the club not less that £1,000.

The winter came, and by November 22 Wolves could only look back on one victory since September 8. With 11 points from 15 matches they were fourth from bottom of the table. It was announced that 'the directors of Wolverhampton are seeking for material to strengthen the vital parts'; but disgruntled citizens were convinced that whatever action the present directors took would be wrong. Accordingly a public meeting was called, and was held on November 28 at the Newhampton Road Schools.

At this meeting was enacted the playlet set out at the head of this chapter. There was also anger at the lack of supervision of promising schoolboys who had left the town to join other clubs Wilding of Chelsea and Bowyer of Clapton Orient, both of whom had shown marked ability in local school football. Lately Stoke had signed R. Whittingham from Chelsea—a worthy player who gained an International cap with Stoke—but only because of the dilatoriness of the Wolves board.[1] This was another cause of anger.

The first match played at the Hawthorns was against Barnsley. Not only did Wolves lose, but Peers and Harrison were both injured and carried off. After the Christmas matches—the climax being a never-to-be-forgotten 10-3 defeat at Hull—the League position was the same—fourth from the bottom, with only 5 wins from 21 matches. On February 14, 1920, the directors, who had been driven to the ignominy of appealing to neighbouring clubs for any superfluous players who might be of assistance,[2] refused Peers and Richards (the only Welshman and the only International on the books) permission to play for Wales. On Easter Monday a statistical milestone was passed when the 30,425 crowd who came to see the Spurs at Molineux established a record for a midweek fixture.

On April 26, sentiment brought 15,000 people to Molineux to see Rev. K.

[1] A. G. Jeffs (Chairman), Major A. J. Holloway, E. Barker, W. T. Cattell, F. T. Hollins, B. Mathews, F. L. Hill, J. B. Brodie.

[2] Albion and Villa transferred A. F. Wright and B. Smart respectively, while Eric Cutler of Wolverhampton Amateurs, and captain of the English Schoolboys in 1914, played in thirteen matches.

R. G. Hunt play his last match for Wolves in a local Derby against Stoke. (He was still a member of the England amateur side.) Hunt was at right-half, Bishop at left-half, and Harrison, who had played with Stoke during the war, at outside-right. The three players, reviving the spirit and assurance that belonged to the dim and glorious days of 1908, gave a memorable exhibition. Wolves won by 4-0. A feature of the side that day was the distribution of the half-backs, among whom was now Woodward, a splendid player from the north.

But the pleasures of the afternoon were subdued by an acrimonious meeting in the Market Place at night. F. J. Somerville, who had taken the chair at the public meeting of the previous November, led the dissidents in demanding the transformation of the Club into a Limited Liability Company, and in adopting the slogan, 'Up with the Wanderers Football Club and down with the present directors'. That, he stated, was the policy of the newly formed Wanderers Supporters' Club.

At least the team could hardly be accused of inconsistency. At the season's conclusion they were still fourth from bottom.

That the next season would bring them to yet another Cup Final was beyond all reasonable expectation. Yet that is what happened.

In 1920 Albert Fletcher at long last retired, and another link with the far past was broken. In his place came Elijah Morse, from Spurs, with new ideas. The keen-eyed reporter of the *Sporting Star* joyfully noted in September that the members of the team were yards faster and that 'their power of endurance had been intensified'. A new training regime was working wonders. So much so that on September 23 George Edmonds, the centre-forward who had joined the side during the previous season from Watford, sent a shot of such velocity into the Bristol City goal that it broke the net. The referee, bewildered by such happenings, refused to agree that a goal had been scored, and the match, unfortunately for Wolves, ended, for the record, as a goalless draw. On October 16 Billy Harrison—almost within sight of another Cup Final—played his last match for Wolves before his transfer to Manchester United.

Those were difficult times, as is shown by the Charity Match played at Molineux on Christmas Day morning between the Old Wulfrunians and the (St. Peter's) Amateurs for the Benefit of the *Express and Star* Unemployment Fund, and by the requests for collections to be taken on Boxing Day for the Discharged Soldiers' and Sailors' Fund. The Wolves' programmes from then and for some years drew attention to the Chief Constable's Boot Fund, the Mayor's Distress Fund, and the Kingswood Camp, all of which were evidence of widespread suffering and want.

By now the spectators at Molineux were, however, somewhat better accommodated, and there was banking all around the enclosure. Plans for a new stand were also beginning slowly to mature. The want of adequate seating was particularly noticed on January 8, 1921, when Stoke were due for the first round of the F.A. Cup. A local Derby within Staffordshire used to be of a totally individual kind, with the rivalry of an almost unendurable intensity. On this occasion there was a gate of 35,000, and Wolves just got home by the odd goal in five.

Old opponents in Cup battles of many years before—Derby County—were hosts in the next round, on January 29; and the record crowd of 25,184 which filled the Baseball Ground to overflowing, saw a 1-1 draw. In the replay Wolves took revenge for that close defeat in a second replay in 1904, winning by the narrow margin of 1-0. For this they were largely indebted to Noel George, a Hednesford boy, who had come in Peers's place but whose performance ensured his retention in the first team. Derby had other worries at the time, being, yet again, well on the way to relegation from Division I.

Then came a visit to Fulham. This match was looked forward to with some apprehension. Although in the Second Division the London Club were a skilful combination, and in splendid form at Craven Cottage. Moreover the Wolves half-back line, which had developed into a sturdy force in the best tradition of the club, was without Val Gregory, who had by now succeeded Harrison as captain. Gregory—a fellow-traveller from Watford with Edmonds—had broken his nose when playing against Coventry a week previously.

A stern defence kept Fulham at bay and a sudden second half thrust by the Wolves left-wing, Potts and Brooks, brought a goal that, on the whole, was against the run of the play. The most ardent Wolves supporters found that in honesty they must reckon Fulham as unlucky losers. By now the fighting spirit of Wolves was fully roused. Everton were to be met in the fourth round, and that they were fourth in the First Division acted as a spur to further effort. On March 5 thousands of Wolves supporters invaded Liverpool, confident of victory, and 12,000 who had been left at home went to Molineux where, at the Reserve match, the score at Everton was posted every quarter of an hour. At Goodison Park 53,000 people saw the home side thoroughly over-powered, even though the final score was only 1-0 in Wolves favour.

Thus Wolves were in their sixth semi-final—this time drawn with Cardiff City, who were to win promotion at the end of the Season. For this match Wolves again were required to travel to Liverpool—to Anfield—where their gallant display against Everton had won for them many admirers. Defences were well on top yet again and neither side scored. During the interval both teams were presented to King George V, who had taken the opportunity to mingle pleasure with business while in Merseyside. In the replay, at Manchester, the Wolves forward line realized its potential—which then it too rarely did—and Cardiff were well and truly beaten by 3-1.

Among those who had some part in Wolves' success during this campaign were Peers, the goalkeeper, who played against Stoke and Derby, R. W. Richards, outside-left, whose goal put Derby out of the Cup, and Baugh—son of Dick Baugh—right-back. Richards, although deputy to Sammy Brooks, was a Welsh international, and on April 9 he joined Peers in the Welsh team that defeated Ireland by 2-1 at Swansea. Neither, however, was selected for the Cup Final team. Peers was unable to win back his place from George; Baugh, whose promise was considerable, was declared unfit, and his substitute was Woodward. That the 'auburn-haired little warrior Baugh' should be denied the opportunity of adding to the family collection of Cup Final medals was a source of regret to all traditionalists; while any analyst of the match itself must come to the conclusion that had he been playing Wolves conceivably might have won.

Their task was difficult. Their opponents on April 23 were Tottenham Hotspur—only the third London club to reach the Final in forty years—with a team as great as any to have represented that distinguished club; and the Final—as in the previous year—was staged in London at Stamford Bridge.

The Wolves approach to the game was much as it had been in the Final of 1908. George Edmonds thus expressed it in the *Sporting Star*. 'I have', he wrote, 'heard it said that we do not play a very clever type of football, but at least it produces goals.' So far there was, perhaps, a little wishful thinking; for goals had not been very plentiful. The next sentences are more apt; 'Our play is plain and straightforward. It is fast and resolute, and it is marked by a boldness that commands respect'.

In pouring rain the teams were presented to King George V, who was accompanied by the Prince of Wales. Also among the spectators was the newly arrived party of Australian cricketers. The finalists lined up as follows:-

Wolves: N. George; M. Woodward, G. H. Marshall; V. Gregory, J. Hodnett, A. Riley; T. Lea, F. Burrill, G. Edmonds, A. Potts, S. Brooks.
Of this team, six were local products.

Tottenham: A. C. Hunter; T. Clay,[1] R. McDonald; B. Smith,[1] C. Walters, A. Grimsdell;[1] J. Banks, J. Seed, J. Cantrell, B. Bliss,[1] J. Dimmock.

[1] English internationals at that time. Seed was to win his first cap two years later.

STAMFORD BRIDGE S.W.

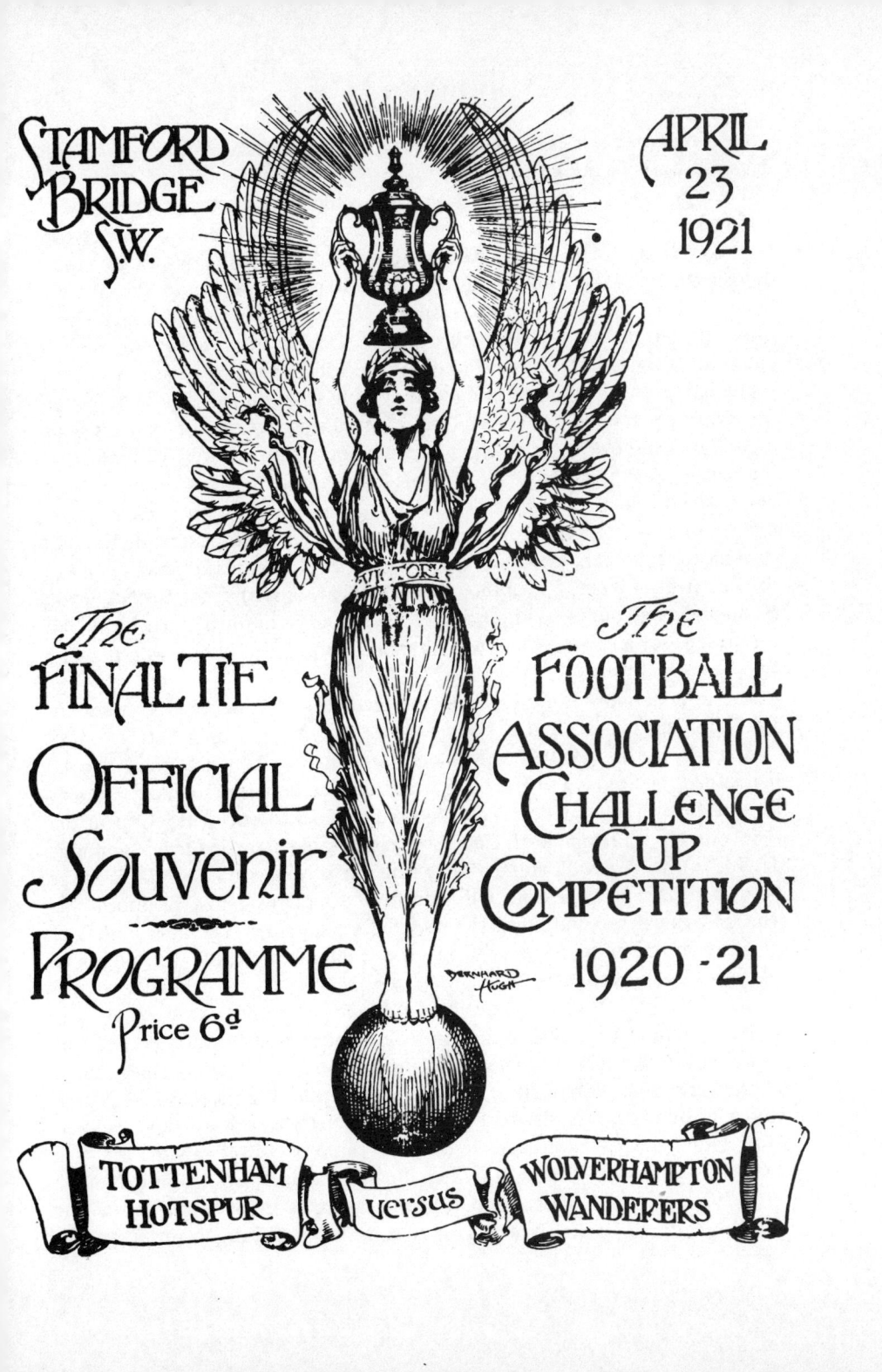

APRIL 23 1921

The FINAL TIE OFFICIAL Souvenir PROGRAMME
Price 6d

The FOOTBALL ASSOCIATION CHALLENGE CUP COMPETITION 1920-21

TOTTENHAM HOTSPUR versus WOLVERHAMPTON WANDERERS

Missing from this team was the popular idol 'Fanny' Walden, who was declared unfit at the last moment.

The Spurs won the toss and both sides could have been pardoned if they had forsaken all football finesse on the treacherous turf. But, to their credit, neither side did. The Spurs led frequently with a 'southpaw' attack, their dangerous left-wing looking always more likely to penetrate the Wolves defence. But the defence was resolute, George especially distinguishing himself: and half-time came with no score. During the interval the Wolves changed their shirts. The clean ones in which they reappeared, albeit symbolizing the civic motto of light appearing from out of darkness, lacked the borough coat-of-arms. This omission disheartened the superstitious among their followers. After eight minutes there was disaster. Dimmock on the Spurs left-wing attempted to dribble his way past Woodward, but lost the ball to the full-back. Woodward, for one crucial instant losing concentration, made a half-hearted attempt to clear, but only succeeded in sending the ball straight to Dimmock, who, now unembarrassed, shot hard and low. That was the decisive moment; for, although McDonald cleared from Brooks when Hunter was well out of position, and Hunter once fortuitously turned the ball off his legs for a corner, there was no more scoring. Spurs had won the Cup for the second time.

The attendance was 72,805, and the receipts—of which £2,842 went in entertainment tax—£13,414.

A year later the position at Molineux was again gloomy. By now Brooks had joined the Spurs, and Harrison and Peers had departed to that repository for ancient warriors at Port Vale. Although knocked out of the Cup in the first round by Preston North End the League table showed further ominous decline in the Wolves fortunes. They finished seventeenth, two places lower than in the previous season. On March 11 a match against Bradford was won, but there were no more victories for a long time. The only crumb of satisfaction was in the respectable placing of the reserves, who were eighth in the new Central League.

On June 25 Dr. Wolverson declared Addenbrooke unfit for work. He was allowed six months' sick leave, but on September 7 he died. A. H. Hoskins took over the Secretarial function and George Jobey came as manager-coach. There was also a new trainer at the start of that 1922-3 season—George Holley of Sunderland, who had toured South Africa with an F.A. team in 1910. On October 7 Wolves defeated Rotherham by 3-2. It was the first win since the preceding March 11, and during the intervening period not a Wolves forward had scored a goal. Such scoring as there had been was the work of the half-backs. It was a sorry state when visiting teams began to

"JACKERY" JONES,
THE TRAINER.

E'er my playing days were done, with Pat and Bish and Lunn,
  I gambolled on the turf at Molineux,
Now I mend the hocks and noses, broken knees and damaged
        toeses,
  Of the other chaps, and tell 'em what to do.

JUST as there is only one "Jackery" in the great Jones family, so it can be safely asserted that among the well-wishers of the good old Club, no one could have been more loyal in season and out of season than the Club's new Trainer, who is fittingly placed at the head of this biographical series. On him will devolve a good deal of responsibility in what may be a momentous season, and though "Jackery" Jones has never trained a football team before, he possesses the knowledge and necessary capabilities for the post, and we have every confidence in his ability to handle his charges with credit to himself and to them. The "happy family" spirit already exists.

excuse themselves for winning at Molineux. Yet this appeared in one of the programmes of Manchester United, after a 1-0 win at Molineux: 'We came back with a point more than we can truly be said to have earned. The chief factors in such a result were the wretched finishing of the home team—which was their fault, not ours—and the inept display of our own front-rankers'. Manchester United provided a new signing for Wolves in George Bisset, who for a time was the only Scotsman at Molineux.

Fazackerley and Brewster—a Scottish international—were signed from Everton in November, but the attack maintained a dismal incompetence while the defence broke down under an overpowering weight of responsibility. A victory over Merthyr Town, by 1-0 in the first round of the Cup was hardly won, and a gate of 40,079 came to Molineux to see Liverpool triumph, by 2-0, in the second round. In that year Jackery Jones, a player with Wolves 20 years previously, joined the training staff.

On September 3 the programme deplored the hooligan behaviour of young supporters, whose chief pleasure was in throwing cinders at all and sundry, and from which exercise their elders made no attempt to dissuade them. To keep the players happy at that time a motor charabanc was hired to take them on a day trip to Stourport for a river picnic.

A month later doom was inescapable. The season was played out cheerlessly and not without incident—for in April the ground was again closed on account of some episode in the Leicester City match which caught the disapproval of the referee and also of the F.A. During this month the club was transferred into a new Limited Liability Company. But the prospect of Third Division football overshadowed any such reorganization, and the oldest supporters were hard put to it to restrain cynical observation. The financial loss on that season's working was £3,885. Nevertheless instructions were given to proceed with the purchase of the freehold of the land for not more than £6,000.

| F. A. GILL'S **Famous Sausages,** DUDLEY RD. & CHAPEL ASH, WOLVERHAMPTON. Wholesale and Retail. Telephone 1254. | "For Aim and Tone, They Stand Alone." **SUNRIPE** The EXTRA SIZE Fine Golden Virginia **CIGARETTES** **10 for 6ᴅ**   20 for 1/- Also 50's | **CONDITION** was one of the main factors which got the "Wolves" into the Final of the English Cup. Good Food is essential in order to get into the necessary condition. **THE FISH and POULTRY** Supplied by me to feed the Wolves' Club during their period of training was always Fresh and of the very Best Quality You can get as fit as the "Wolves" by ordering your supplies of FISH, GAME and POULTRY, from **W. G. SMITH,** 42, Queen Street, Wolverhampton. Telephone No. 1415. |

Hark to that call of Co-oo-ue.

EVERY DAY AND IN EVERY WAY WE ARE PLAYING BETTER AND BETTER

THE WOLVES:—" Auto-suggestion means that you persuade yourself you can achieve that which seems impossible. If hard training, hard work, and hard play can't change our rotten-luck, jiggered if hard thinking can."

| **WALTER EDWARDS,** 50, Lichfield Street, Hatter, Hosier, Glover Large Stock of All-Wool Winter Shirts and Gents' Underwear. **NECKWEAR!** SOMETHING NEW CAN ALWAYS BE HAD HERE | *Do You Want a* Suit, Overcoat, or Boots, FOR CASH OR WEEKLY, If so, Call or Write to— 40½, Bilston Rd., Wolverhampton. LADIES' AND GENTS' CLOTHIER, Ready-made or to Measure. Good Fit Guaranteed From 40/- FUNERAL ORDERS IN 24 HOURS. | **GEORGE & MATTHEWS,** COAL MERCHANTS, General Hauliers and Steerers. HAULAGE BY HORSES OR MOTOR LORRIES CONTRACTED FOR. Enquiries to:— **METROPOLITAN CHAMBERS**, LICHFIELD ST., WOLVERHAMPTON. 'Phone 804. |

9

Return Journey

'Everybody who knows anything of football needs no reminder that a football game is not a children's tea party, nor yet a Band of Hope meeting, and further that a football crowd is not composed of mealy-mouthed innocents.'

Programme, February 11 1922.

'As Major Buckley, our enthusiastic Secretary-Manger, said at the dinner held recently at the Molineux Hotel, words get us nowhere. Football is like war. Battles have to be won and I have never heard a matter of this kind summed up more concisely or more accurately'.

ibid., August 27 1927.

IN retrospect, the Division III period of the Wolves saga was not without its benefits; for it enabled one record to be established—that of being the only club to date to have been champions of three Divisions. Somewhat oddly, considering the age of the club and its proud Cup record, the order of these triumphs is from the bottom upwards.

In August 1923, however, the immediate objective was to make good the cartoonist's claim that residence in the lowest department would be of the minimum duration. The general Third Division standard—there being at that time, as ever since, a number of marginal teams—might be uneven, but fierce competition could be expected from a select handful. Neighbours at Walsall had only been five points short of promotion at the end of last season; Wigan Borough were firm and resourceful; Bradford Park Avenue, smarting under the indignity of relegation in 1922, were anxious to rejoin Bradford City; Accrington Stanley, conscious of their dignity of founder-membership of the league, were a resolute combination; and Chesterfield were also making strenuous and not entirely discouraging attempts to build up a team worthy of better company. In the event, however, it was none of these, but Rochdale, who acted as pace-makers in chief. This was surprising as Rochdale had hitherto unostentatiously filled a modest place in the lower half of the table.

On August 25 Wolves made their debut in Division III, and attracted a crowd of 13,000 to the Recreation Ground, Chesterfield.

AUGUST OPTIMISM.

The Landlady: 'And how long shall you be staying, sir?'
The Wolf: 'Oh, only this season.'
The Landlady: 'That's what they all say when they come here, but they mostly stay longer.'

The team comprised:

George; Watson, Shaw; Getgood, Caddick, Kay; Harrington, Fazackerley, Legge, Lees, Edwards.

Comparing this with the list of the Cup Final players of 1921 it is apparent that the old order had changed: the only survivor was George. George, indeed, was a striking figure at Chesterfield, for he was dressed all in white, while the rest of the team wore 'new jerseys of striking design'.[1]

The Chesterfield match, hard-fought, was a victory for the defences, and ended in a goal-less draw.

It is salutary to see ourselves as others see us. In this way the *Derbyshire Times* summarized this match and in so doing implied some of the virtues necessary in Third Division football.

[1] Gold, with black V at neck and black cuffs, in place of the former stripes.

Judged by the figures published in a sports paper the Wolves appeared to be the smallest and lightest side in the Northern Section but the very reverse proved to be the case. Heavier and taller than last year's lot as are the Chesterfield players, they were put in the shade by the Wolves, and if physique counts for anything in battle the Wanderers should have won comfortably. The match was very easy to sum up—the defence on both sides dominated the attack. The home forwards have come in for a lot of adverse criticism, but it should be remembered that they can only play as well at their opponents will let them. Every one of the Chesterfield forwards did infinitely better that Stanley Fazackerly, who, beyond a few clever touches and a great drive over the bar . . . was absolutely blotted out. Legge was no better than Shaw, and Lees was not so good as Lane, indifferent though the ex-Burnley player's display was. We know the Chesterfield forwards can play better than they did, but the opposing defence never allowed them to settle down. The Wanderers did a surprising amount of pushing, and we cannot recollect them being once pulled up for it. Play was of a fast description . . .

In the phrase 'never allowed them to settle down' is the key to one side of the Wolves character to be discerned at almost any time.

In the return match at Molineux on September 1, Wolves won by 2-1.

A week later the defence gave another excellent performance, but, the attack proving tantalizingly indifferent to the necessity for finishing their job, Crewe Alexandra were able to share the points in another goalless draw. By September 15, by which time Molineux had a new flag, six matches had been played. Three had been won three drawn, and there were only two goals in the opponents' column. There were, on the other hand, only seven goals scored by Wolves, which promised an insufficient margin for the day on which the defenders should relax their vigilance. This was on September 22, when Accrington on their mountainous pitch at Peel Park—a difficult ground for visitors—inflicted the first defeat—by 1-0.

As it transpired Wolves were to be beaten only twice more—away from home—during the season; at Grimsby by 2-0, on November 10, and at Walsall, by 2-1, on April 7.

During the Autumn the directors had fallen victims to nervous tension and, overstepping the limits of propriety, were ordered to pay a fine of £10 10s. 0d., by the League Management Committee for disbursing more bonus money in respect of wins and draws than was allowed. At the same time, recognizing the needs both of that day and the next, they went ahead with the project for a new stand and new lavatories, for which the Town Council approved plans on December 3.

Two days earlier the management could not but have been moved by the literary welcome accorded to the team at New Brighton. 'Our best wish', it was printed in the programme, 'is that this good old club may return at an early date to the company it has done credit to in past years, and may the dear old Dame Fortune cast her favourable glance round Molineux way'.

After Christmas Dame Fortune took a step in the right direction by exerting her influence on Swindon Town, to transfer a free-scoring centre-forward, Tom Phillipson, to Wolves. In the next few years Phillipson, a native of the north-east and a former brilliant schoolboy footballer, was to achieve many notable feats for his new club. In three successive seasons he was top scorer; with 17 goals in 1924-5, 36 in 1925-6 and 32 in 1926-7. On January 16, 1926, he scored a hat-trick against Middlesbrough. On April 26, 4 goals in a 7-1 win against Barnsley, and on Christmas day in that same year 5 goals in the 7-2 defeat of Bradford City.

In the 3rd round of the cup Wolves were drawn against the Albion. At the Hawthorns there was a 1-1 draw, but in the replay on February 27 Wolves lost 0-2. There was consolation in the gate of 40,083 and the takings of £2,455 17s. 6d.—both a record up to that point.

April found Wolves, as had been hoped, at the head of Division III, a short head in front of Rochdale.

From the records (see p. 174) it will be seen that both teams had strong defences but that Wolves, who had settled down to play with a sense of style above their temporary station, had achieved in the end a more forceful attack, Lees being top goal-scorer, and Fazackerley and Phillipson making more than useful contributions.

Back in Division II Wolves pursued a successful, if unspectacular course for two seasons. Barber was now Chairman, and A. H. Oakley Vice-Chairman of a board from which Brodie was now absent. In 1924-5 they finished sixth behind Leicester City, Manchester United, Derby County, Portsmouth and Chelsea. In 1925-6 they were two places higher, in the wake of Sheffield Wednesday, Derby County, and Chelsea. During this period neat, concise football, marked by splendid teamsmanship, sometimes burst into the category of meteoric. Gates, therefore, improved, and on Boxing Day 1924, a new record was established for the visit of Chelsea. There were 32,264 spectators, the largest midweek attendance at Molineux to date.

The team was much as had served in the Third Division, with Noel George, Harold Shaw, Ben Timmis—from Walsall, and Bradford, conspicuous in defence—and 'Blog' Edwards and Harrington ably feeding the inside-forwards from their wings, and with Phillipson normally quick to complete the attacking moves. Notable signings were few, an exception being that of the right-half Jack Mitton who came from Sunderland.

The ground itself was beginning to acquire the facilities of a first-class enclosure as then expected. During the latter part of 1924 the Waterloo Road stand, with dressing-rooms below, was completed, the old covering—a section 200 feet long—being transferred to the Molineux Street side to make room for it. The dignities were enhanced by the presence at every match of the Borough Silver Band, which played two-steps and tangos, fox-trots and marches, and slices from Elgar (an old Wolves fan) and Sullivan (once a notable race-horse owner). New Year's day came in blusterously in 1925, and, while Hobbs and Sutcliffe were making a massive reply to Australia at Melbourne, gales swept over Britain. The result was seen in Wolverhampton on Sunday, January 4, when the once uprooted shed suffered a second transition; this time a wind from the north-west lifted it, together with the new and private telephone box of the *Express and Star*, out of the enclosure and into Molineux Street, where it effectively blocked the way to traffic for several hours.

As for the new stand on the opposite side it survived trial by tempest and was officially opened by Mr. J. McKenna, President of the Football League, on August 29. Alive to the needs of such an occasion Wolves trounced Portsmouth by 4-1.

In 1925 Arsenal, now managed by Herbert Chapman, were on the verge of the most notable period in their history and when the New Year came they were at the head of the First Division. Wolves—whose supporters were sanguine of promotion that season—drew Arsenal at Molineux in the third round of the Cup. Here indeed was a yardstick by which to measure the potential of the team. On January 9 a new ground record was established with a gate of 42,083 and receipts of £3,008. The attendance was greater by 2,000 than that at the third round tie with Albion two years before. The Arsenal were represented that day by:

> Harper; Mackie, John; Baker, Butler, Blyth; Hoar, Buchan, Brain, Neil, Haden;

Wolves by:

> George; Watson, Fox; Mitton, Charnley, Bradford; Harrington, Scott, Phillipson, Meek, Price.

After twenty-five minutes Arsenal scored and they held a one-goal lead until half-time. Wolves, forsaking the free improvisatory style, attempted close play which came to grief against a stout defence. Five minutes of the

E. Morse

R. W. Richards

G. W. Edmonds

W. Hann

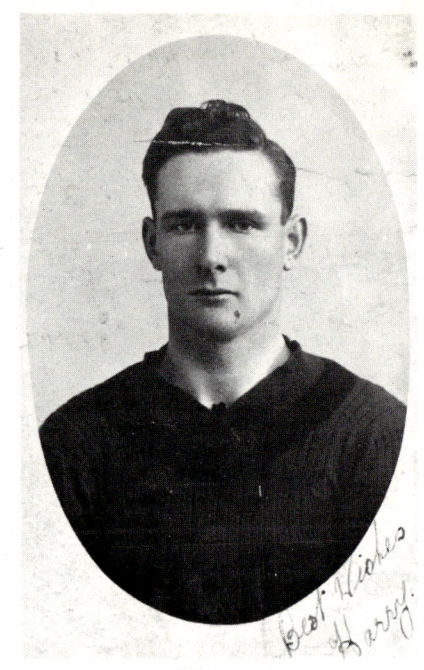

H. Scott

A. Canavon

M. Woodward

F.A. Cup-tie, Wolves v Wrexham, at Molineux 1931.

T. Smalley

C. Phillips

A. Tootill

MR PRESIDENT
ASSISTED BY
HIS WORSHIP THE MAYOR
WELL AND TRULY - OPENED THE STAND —
HINGLEY 1935.
TOMMY BOWEN OPENED THE SCORE
GOAL
STILL
ANOTHER OPENING
KERR — KEETLEY - AND PRICE
FOUND OPENINGS —
THUS SUCCESSFULLY ENDED ONE OF THE BEST GAMES WE HAVE SEEN FOR SOME TIME
I NOTICE — PORTSMOUTH WERE NOT GREETED AS PRESTON WITH MUSICAL HONOURS
WHY NOT 'A LIFE ON THE OCEAN WAVE' - WE MAY THEN HAVE WON THE 'TOSS'
I'M GOING TO EXPOUND MY IDEA OF WHAT A BAND PROGRAMME SHOULD BE LIKE ONE OF THESE WEEKS
LOOK OUT FOR NEW FEATURES — I SHALL IN ALL PROBABILITY WANT TO WHEN THE BANDMASTER SEES ME —

second half had gone when Phillipson seized his one opportunity to equalise with a brilliant, calculated goal. Apart from isolated sorties, during one of which Harrington missed an open goal, it was heavy Arsenal pressure to the end; but the defence, despite injuries to both full-backs, remained resolute.

The following Wednesday the replay took place at Highbury before 42,823. On a wet, miserable day the pattern was as before; except that Arsenal managed to win by a single goal—a result of a defensive misunderstanding, when Fox deflected the ball past the unfortunate George.

In the following season came another encounter with Arsenal, but under less propitious circumstances. At the beginning of the season Wolves played without luck, sometimes without judgment, and under the disadvantage of too many team and positional changes. Scotchbrook, the secretary-manager appointed in March 1926[1], was disheartened at the whimsical variation imposed on him by the board and also by the financial strategy which made excursions into the transfer market so frequently pointless. After a bad defeat at Blackpool in November 1925, the programme writer complained, 'Get new men. There is no mention made of where they are to be obtained'. There was, however, one important signing to come in the not too distant future, of W. Weaver, an outside-left from Everton. The story of Weaver's signing was told by Scotchbrook at a later date, and it emphasizes—as it was meant to do—the necessity for complete confidence in the technical capacity of the club's chief officer.

'I signed Weaver', said Scotchbrook to an Annual General Meeting on June 27, 1927, 'one Friday morning. On Friday night at Crewe there were three directors. One said he did not think he was any good (ironical laughter), the second said he was too frail, and the other said he liked him but that the money was too much'.

Weaver celebrated his transfer on October 16, 1926, by helping Wolves to their first win of the season, against Blackpool. This was a good win. It was Blackpool's first defeat at home. Phillipson missed a penalty, and Wolves were 0-2 down at half-time, yet turned the score into a final 3-2. Despite this effort, however, the situation needed much redemption, for with 5 points the team was ominously placed next to bottom in the table. The League position appreciated slightly after Chadwick (once with Everton) had come from Leeds City to renew partnership with Weaver; but fear of relegation hung heavily. The eventual placing was fifteenth—a sad decline from the previous season.

[1] Scotchbrook had graduated from the Gymnasium F.C., Horwich and Horwich F.C., to Bolton Wanderers, for whom he played and later acted as coach, before managing Stockport County, which he left for Wolves.

No. 39.

WOLVES v. BURNLEY RES.

At Molineux Grounds. Apr. 19. Kick-off 6-30.

THE WOLVERHAMPTON WANDERERS
OFFICIAL PROGRAMME AND CLUB'S RECORD
PUBLISHED BY AUTHORITY

Names and Positions of Players.

WOLVES

Colours—Gold Body with Black V shape back & front, Black Cuffs.

	RIGHT		CANAVON (1)		LEFT	
		TYLER (2)		FOX (3)		
	HIGHAM (4)		BURNS (5)		BOSWELL (6)	
HARRINGTON (7)	LEGGE (8)		KERR (9)		BOWEN (10)	BRADLEY (11)

Referee—
Mr. J. H. ROPER
(Birmingham).

Linesmen
Mr. E. C. Broughton (Derby)
White Flag, Black Stripe
Mr. H. Kinsey (West Bromwich)
White Flag, Gold Stripe

LANCASTER (12)	BEEL (13)	RICHARDS (14)	DEVINE (15)	POLLARD (16)
	HUGHES (17)	SPARGO (18)	BASNETT (19)	
		HEAP (20)	FERGUS (21)	
LEFT		ASHCROFT (22)		RIGHT

BURNLEY (Reserves).

Colours—Shirts, Claret and Light Blue. Knickers, White.

The teams are subject to alterations. Changes will be shown on Score Board.

RETAILERS v. WHOLESALERS

SPECIAL EFFORT BY THE WOLVERHAMPTON BUTCHERS' ASSOCIATION

FOR THE
Poor Children's Holiday Camp & Chief Constable Boot Funds

Charity Football Match at Molineux Grounds
THURSDAY, APRIL 29th.
KICK OFF 3 P.M

ADMISSION
Stand 1-
Ground 6d.

His Worship the Mayor,
Ald. F. A. Willcock, J.P., has consented to kick off

OUTFITTING KINDLY LENT BY MR. F. C. PYNER,
DUDLEY ROAD

ONE PENNY.

During the first half of the season Molineux was put at the disposal of the Wolverhampton Rugby Football Club, who celebrated their Jubilee (in the wrong year if the centenary celebrated in 1975 is correct) with a match against Commander W. J. A. Davies' XV. On November 15 a landmark in regional football history was commemorated at Molineux, when the Jubilee of the Staffordshire F.A. brought these two interesting sides in opposition:

Staffs. F.A.: Wait (Walsall); Baugh (Albion[1]), Shaw (Wolves); Magee (Albion), Mitton (Wolves), Dale (Birmingham); Low (Port Vale), Davies (Stoke), Briggs (Birmingham), Walker (Villa), Dorrell (Villa).

F.A.: Brown (Sheffield Wednesday); Goodall (Huddersfield), Wadsworth (Huddersfield); Edwards (Leeds United), Kean (Sheffield Wednesday), Green (Sheffield United), Spence (Manchester United), Brown (Huddersfield), Dean (Everton), Kelly (Sunderland), Ruffell (West Ham).

As might have been expected the visiting team—whose composition was a compliment to the County Association—were too strong and won comfortably.

In the third round of the Cup Wolves travelled north, to Carlisle, where two goals by Weaver put them one stage further. The next opponents were Nottingham Forest, who were beaten, also by 2-0, at Molineux on January 29, 1927. A social feature of this, and subsequent ties this season, was the community singing organized by the *Express and Star* and directed by that excellent Black Country musician Joseph Lewis: this part of the match was, in fact, solemnly written up in the evening newspaper by the music critic. Not even a 'flu epidemic could dampen either local ardour or the Wolves' fighting spirit at this juncture. For on February 19 Hull City joined the Forest in the ranks of the defeated. The 1924 gate record was broken, for on this occasion 48,949 spectators, who paid £3,589, packed the ground.

And so to March 5, to Highbury, where Arsenal, eleventh in Division I, provided the next, and, as transpired, the last opposition in the competition. On this day there was an attendance of 52,821. The teams were:

Arsenal: Lewis; Parker, John; Baker, Butler, Barley; Hulme, Buchan, Brain, Blyth, Hoar.

Wolves'; George; Watson, Shaw; Higham, Mitton, Kay; Harrington, Bowen, Phillipson, Chadwick, Weaver.

The Arsenal team of that day had sufficient distinction to make Wolves

[1] The former Wolves player.

chances look pretty poor: but after twelve minutes the visitors took the lead. Harrington was fouled and, taking the free kick himself, found Phillipson, who headed the ball, deftly and accurately, into the goal. Sixteen minutes later Arsenal equalized, through their inside-left. After thirteen minutes of the second half Butler scored what proved to be the winning goal, with a sensational header from outside the penalty area. Phillipson put the ball into the net and there were long post-mortem discussions as to whether the referee's decision of off-side was just or not. Whether or not it was, however, was not relevant since the score was unaltered.

Not even the keenest partisans, however, disputed the general superiority of Arsenal, particularly in defensive strategy—which employed the off-side trap to the frequent confusion of the Wolves forwards. Scotchbrook put the defeat down to the obduracy of his board. 'We should', he said, 'have reached the Final if we could have bought a centre-half'.

The club took a benevolent, if not active, interest in the semi-final for the match between Reading and Cardiff City was played at Molineux on March 26. Semi-finals had previously been played there in 1892, 1898, 1899, and 1904. On April 16 the attractive fixture against Portsmouth, who won promotion, was set apart as a benefit match for Watson, the right full-back, who had joined the club from Pontypridd in 1921. On this occasion Portsmouth won by 1-0, and the season came to an end with exactly half the League matches lost.

Vacillating fortunes in the football field play havoc with the nervous system. In the summer of 1927 the crisis in the boardroom led to the termination of the manager's contract, while influential citizens not members of the board instituted a Shareholders' Club[1] to stimulate the club's finances and also to oversee, so far as was possible, the general policy. The background showed discouraging and inescapable facts.

The nominal capital of the 1923 Company was £30,000; the subscribed capital was £8,402. This left on paper, therefore, a balance available of £22,000. The overdraft at the bank was £14,783 12s. 0d. In 1924 the profits had been £499 14s. 9d., and in 1925 £3,502 16s. 1d. In the two succeeding seasons indifferent performances on the field were reflected in losses of £662 6s. 9d. and £1,557 7s. 7d. respectively. The account of transfer fees for 1926-7 tells its own story: £3,325 was expended against income of £700. Finally, the wages bill was in the region of £12,000 a year: a sum which absorbed practically the whole of the gate money. Clearly the position was unpromising, and it would take time and patience to improve it. But the management at that point made an appointment of historic importance—not

[1] Inaugurated on May 11.

only to Wolves but to English football in general.

'The directors', said a statement issued by the Shareholders' Club, 'have the assistance of a thoroughly capable man in Major F. C. Buckley, and he is concentrating on putting into the field only those players who are capable and fit to do themselves and the club justice'.

One reads between the lines to understand the intention of discipline. Buckley, appointed for three years in the first place, welcomed his playing staff on July 27 without superfluous ceremony; he immediately instructed them as to routine, issued each with a printed list of rules, emphasized that these were strictly to be observed, and demonstrated the 'rowing machine', the latest addition to the training apparatus. The manager was unequivocal, progressive, ambitious, and voluble. His ideas were freely communicated to the newspapers. On August 8 he pronounced himself as against the use of a white ball, such as had lately been the subject of experiment at Cowdenbeath. On the other hand he advocated the numbering of players for the enlightenment of spectators.

THAT UNWELCOME APPARITION.

THE SUPPORTER TO THE WOLF.—" I hope you haven't partaken of any of that Relegation Pudding during the Xmas, and if you can get through to-day, you shall have a real bust-up to-morrow."

At a dinner at the Molineux Hotel he propounded a practical philosophy: 'Football', he said, 'was a business, a prestige had to be maintained. A football club in a town was an asset. It brought people to it and benefited the Corporation through patronage of tramcars and increased business for tradespeople . . .'

He had no illusions in coming to Wolverhampton. He had been connected with football too long to know that talking got a club nowhere. There was only one test. That was the acid test. Football was like war. They had got to win matches.

He made no promises, but they might get back to the First Division soccer sooner than they thought.

As he looked at his staff of thirty players—of whom but five were local—Buckley must have been conscious of the magnitude of his task. But he buried pessimism, dressed the team in yet another strip—shirts with black and gold vertical stripes and black knickers and stockings—and commenced the season with a 2-2 draw with Manchester City at Molineux. Thus the curtain rose on the new season.

About this time audiences at the Hippodrome were entertained by an actor who chose to cloak his identity beneath the intriguing title of 'The Stranger'. 'The Stranger' did training stints at Molineux and, when interrogated about this untoward preparation for a twice-nightly said that he had formerly been a footballer and had played with Major Buckley. Nor was this his first acquaintance with the ground. He had had a part in a British film *The Winning Goal*, of which some scenes had been shot at Molineux. The shape of things to come.

10

The Buckley Era

'Wolverhampton has seen high-class football this season and we hope that now we have got into the First Division we will stay there'.

Major F. C. Buckley, April 23 1932.

BUCKLEY was one of two great managers of his era; the other was Herbert Chapman of Arsenal. Each inherited a lamentable situation, and each proved himself by a combination of technical skill, business acumen, and personal magnetism. It would be invidious to attempt to balance the final achievement of the one against the other; but it should be remembered that Buckley, in charge of a then not conspicuous provincial club, had none of the resources that were available to his counterpart at Highbury. He could not buy fine players (in two years Chapman had spent £25,000 in transfer fees), but only look for promise which, properly nurtured, would mature in the future.

A Lancastrian by birth, Buckley had enlisted in the army at the age of sixteen at the beginning of the Boer War. While serving in Ireland his commanding officer noted his talent as a footballer and it was not long before young Buckley was on the staff of Aston Villa. His first match in the first team was in the 1902-3 season, a Staffordshire Senior Cup-tie—against Wolves. From Birmingham, he moved to Derby, for whom he played sturdily at centre-half. He gained an international cap against Ireland in 1914. During the 1914-18 war he served with the 17th Middlesex Regiment ('Footballers' Battalion) and rose to the rank of major. Demobilized he went into management, first with Norwich City and then with Blackpool, with whom he was for four years before taking up his three-year contract with Wolves.

In 1930 Blackpool were promoted to the First Division. The credit for this success was generally ascribed to their former manager, 'Good judges of the game are saying', it was written at the time, 'that Major Frank Buckley really built up the Blackpool team that won promotion last season and that his efforts at Wolverhampton will bear the closest scrutiny'.

A realist, Buckley knew at the outset that he needed time. The question was whether he would be allowed time in which his plans might mature. After the 1926-7 season and its relegation scares the supporters of Wolves were not likely to bear indefinitely the anguish of deferred hope. Nor were they likely to remain silent when the manager went against their sentimental inclinations.

One by one familiar figures passed out of sight. On November 5, 1927, Noel George played his last match for Wolves against Bristol City at Ashton Gate. The City won by 4-1, in some measure assisted by the fallibility of the visiting goalkeeper, which was caused by the onset of the rheumatoid arthritis which was to end his life only two years later. At the time Buckley had three other goalkeepers on the books—Botto, Canavon, and Bryce. In the following February Tom Phillipson, captain, went. In this case an offer for his services came from the directors of Sheffield United, who had beaten Wolves in the fourth round of the F.A. Cup, and Buckley had no hesitation in accepting the offer. For, in addition to five other centre-forwards, he had a brilliant prospect in Reg Weaver, not long signed from Newport County. He had also signed Lewis, a player of some promise from Sunbeam F.C. to which went a donation of ten guineas. More interesting, perhaps, was the fact that St. Luke's Blakenhall F.C. were recipients of five guineas since Lewis had sharpened his earliest skills with that old foundation.

On March 2, 1929, Ted Watson, now too slow for the intended pattern of quicksilver play, lost his place. A week later Reg Weaver, in whom Manchester City and Spurs had also been interested, went to Chelsea. This was beyond the understanding of the shilling patrons at Molineux, who saw their team consistent in staying within easy reach of relegation. But Buckley by this move enriched his club by £5,000—the largest transfer fee so far paid to Wolves—without which the end-of-season balance sheet would have presented a forlorn appearance.

A year later there was near-revolt at another daring transfer transaction. In February, 1930, the Major, always with an eye for the newsworthy detail, completed the transfer of Harold Shaw to Sunderland in a train from Nottingham. Shaw, who played 234 matches for Wolves, was a fine defender, cool and self-possessed, and with a neat sense of distribution. In 1929 he had been considered good enough to take part in an international trial match at Tottenham. His loss, by any judgment except that of Buckley, was a sad one, as his subsequent brave displays for relegation-haunted Sunderland seemed to emphasize. A month after Shaw's departure Harry Marshall was placed on the transfer list. 'Another bombshell' reported the *Sporting Star*.

But there was another side to the picture. Buckley was ever on the move. At one time his absence from Wolverhampton was explained by his pursuit of 'an extensive campaign . . . covering many miles of country'. His directors were kept in motion, too, sometimes repining when their tours of inspection kept them in remote places until unfamiliar hours of the night. Beside Reg Weaver, Newport produced a possible centre-half in Pritchard.[1] Another Welsh recruit, to serve the club well in the future, was Dai Richards from Merthyr. Tootill, a goalkeeper of considerable brilliance, was brought from Accrington Stanley. In 1929-30 Lowton, Lax, Bellis came to strengthen the defence, while the forward line took in Mark Crook from Blackpool, Charlie Phillips a future Welsh international, and Jimmy Deacon of Darlington. The following season saw the acquisition of Lumberg, already a Welsh international left-back, from Wrexham, Walter Bottrill, inside-right, who had been with York and Middlesbrough, and Tudor Martin, centre-forward, from Newport County. In a cup-tie at Barnsley on February 14, 1931, Wolves had so far changed their ancient tradition as to show seven Yorkshiremen in the team—Whittaker (goal), Hatfield (right-back), Kay (left-back), Lax (right-half), Hollingworth (centre-half), Bottrill, and Barraclough (outside-left).

There were many changes, but Buckley inspired those who were given responsibility which they were willing to accept. And the critics began to see some method in his conduct of affairs. Reg. Hollingsworth played his first match as centre-half on November 10, 1928. Wolves beat Albion by 2-0 and Hollingsworth was reported as having made 'a very satisfactory debut as pivot'. When Weaver went to Chelsea Billy Hartill—a local boy—came in his place and showed his quality dramatically by outshining Weaver at Stamford Bridge only a few days after the change.

Making the centre-forward position his own Hartill went on to establish himself as at least, one of the most opportunist among Second Division leaders. During the 1929-30 season he promised to eclipse Phillipson's record of four years earlier; but his total of 34 goals, in the end, was two short of that record. Hartill had his irresistible days; thus in 1930 he achieved three hat-tricks—one of them in the third round cup-tie against Wrexham, which Wolves won by 9-1; while in the following year he went one better in respect of hat-tricks!

Among others who made a promising first appearance should be noted Dicky Rhodes, a former Wolverhampton schoolboy, who had been on loan with a minor club in Worcestershire and had been honoured with a cap, for the Birmingham F.A. Junior side, against the Scottish juniors. Coming in as reserve for Harry Marshall at inside-right Rhodes scored his side's only goal

[1] Later transfered to Charlton and broke a leg against Wolves on Boxing Day, 1929.

at Stamford Bridge on November 23, 1929, to turn what had seemed certain defeat into an honourable draw.

In the first match of the 1929-30 season Buckley introduced five new players—Lowton (right-back), Lax (right-half), Bellis (centre-half), Forshaw (inside-right), and Roy Davies (outside-right). Of these, Lowton, Lax and Bellis made the grade, appearing during that season on 40, 40 and 23 occasions respectively.

The battle for restoring Wolves to their former eminence was necessarily waged on several fronts. After one year of Buckley's management the majority of supporters could only see that the team's League position had deteriorated. They were one place nearer the bottom of the table, and with a shocking number of goals against. The Central League side were forced to apply for re-election. On the other hand first team attendances were up; there was a profit of £2,076 10s. 8d (from which was deducted the loss of £300 on the previous season); and the overdraft at the bank now stood at £10,000—a reduction on that shown on the previous balance sheet. An interesting feature of this balance sheet relates to transfer fees; in respect of these the income was £4,275 and the expenditure £4,500. A year later there was again a generally satisfactory balance sheet, with a profit of £2,977 10s. 8d. and a further reduction of the overdraft to £8,000. But this year £2,400 was expended on transfer fees, as against receipts of £6,400. The playing record, however, was even worse! Wolves ended the season only four places clear of the relegation zone.

The most dismal day in the 1928-9 season was the cuptie with Mansfield Town. Mansfield, a Midland League team, were not given a chance by the prophets. Yet, sustained on a week's diet of milk, and fresh eggs (total expenses of special training amounted to 19s.) they won by 1-0. 'Kick and rush', reported the *Sporting Star* 'aptly describes the style of play adopted by both sides, but Mansfield exploited it better than the Wanderers. Mansfield set off with the express purpose of winning and played like a winning team all through. They never permitted the Wanderers to settle down . . .' Forty-six years later Mansfield again defied logic, by the same score, defeating Wolves in the fourth round of the Football League Cup.

The 1929-30 season opened sadly. Richard Baugh, senior, and Noel George died, the latter after a match at Bristol. 'It was', it was written in the programme of October 12, 'a sad coincidence that we heard of the death of Noel immediately after the game. It was at Bristol, two years ago, when we lost 0-4 that the first indication of serious malady that took him showed itself. It was Noel's last appearance on the football field, and although he battled bravely to overcome the terrible affliction, he gradually became bed-ridden...'

By the following autumn Wolves, now in gold shirts and black knickers, had settled down, and in mid-October, having lost only two matches out of twelve, they were top of the table. The forward line of Crook, Marshall, Hartill, Deacon and Barraclough was playing with ease and brilliance; and 'the speed at which Wolves carry out sweeping attacks' was noted with respect throughout the country. It was too good to last. Injuries and a disconcerting tendency to do anything but score when goals were badly needed led to an unhappy Christmas holiday, during which damaging defeats were suffered from West Bromwich Albion and, twice, from Charlton. Promotion was not the prize in 1930. But to finish ninth was a distinct improvement.

THE FAIRY TALE.   The Wolf: "Come off it Kate, that Grandmama story won't wash here, besides your Grandma don't live in Wolverhampton."

SCORE BOARD FOR X-MAS DAY MATCHES.

A Aston Villa / M'chester C	**B** Blackburn / Sunderland	**C** Bolton W / Burnley	**D** Everton / Sheffield W.	**E** Grimsby / Leicester C.	**F** Leeds U / Derby C
G M'chester U / Birmingham	**H** Newcastle U. / Middlesboro'	**J** Portsmouth / Arsenal	**K** Sheffield U. / Liverpool	**L** West Ham / Huddersfield	**M** Blackpool / Chelsea
N Bradford C / Reading	**O** Bristol City / Cardiff	**P** Bury / Preston N.E.	**R** Hull City / Stoke City	**S** Millwall / W. Bromwich	**T** Derby R / Wolves R

QUEEN'S PICTURE HOUSE   TO-DAY—WALLACE BEERY in "CHINATOWN NIGHTS"

It was, however, another bad Cup year. The Wolves neither for the first nor the last time were palpably robbed. It was not only the Wolves party who said so, but that famous old player Charlie Roberts who wrote in the *Manchester Evening Chronicle* about the match played at Oldham on January 11:

> Two minutes from time Hetherington, the Wolves outside-left, beat Adlam and Ivill, and cutting in towards goal, sent in a shot which would certainly have counted had it not been for a superhuman save by Hacking, who sprang at the ball and just touched it over the bar.
> To the surprise of everybody, the referee gave a goal-kick, when undoubtedly it should have been a corner.

From the goal-kick Oldham broke away and scored.

"This Season's 'IT'"

THE WOLF.—" Pipe it up lads, I love those inspiring words."
(I'll do the playing, carry on).

Owing to pressure of space, the Ringed-head Photos taken at Monday's Match will appear in Monday Evening's Programme.

QUEEN'S PICTURE HOUSE | Monday Next—RALPH INCE in "WALL STREET."
ALL TALKING.

The match which the Wolves programme-writer mourned a week later and which he described as one that would be long remembered was, of course, soon forgotten. One detail worth recalling are the comforts afforded to supporters who went to away games. Writing from the Trocadero, Queen Street, Arch Wilson, to outbid Lazenby; Travel Agency, thus offered a cut price outing,

> A trip is being arranged in connection with the Wanderers away match at Oldham.
> The fare will include Rail Saloon, Luncheon, and Stand ticket at 12/-.
> If desired, Tea may be ordered after the match at an extra cost of 2/6. Supporters who patronized the Chelsea trip were very pleased with the Hot Meat Tea after the match, and there is no reason why the same arrangements should not apply to this trip.
> It is necessary for intending travellers to book early if they would enjoy the comforts of collectively booking.

Those, one might say, were the 'good old days'!

A pleasant end of season diversion was provided by the visit of St. Mirren —winners of the Scottish F.A. Cup in 1926—in a charity match. Playing what then was regarded as traditional Scottish Football, St. Mirren were too good for Wolves, winning by 2-0 and taking home a special cup given for the occasion.

The improvement in the team that season is reflected in the profit of £5,052.

Wolves went nearer to their main objective in 1930-31. They were finally fourth in the table, the teams promoted being Everton and West Bromwich Albion. In a season of free scoring the Wolves forwards could not match the records of Everton who—led by Dean—amassed 121 goals, of Bradford, of Tottenham, who scored 97 and 88 goals respectively. Nor could they quite compete with the defensive discipline of West Bromwich. As it happened the sensational matches of that season were against Albion in the sixth round of the Cup. The sixth round was at the Hawthorns on February 21, before a crowd of 52,300. W. G. Richardson, one of the greatest players of that day, scored an early goal to put Albion in the lead; but one minute before half-time an own goal by their right full-back made the score 1-1. And so it remained. The replay was on the following Wednesday—despite vigorous protests from the Wolverhampton shopkeepers for whom Thursday was the half-day—and 46,800 people saw Albion gain a narrow victory by 2-1. On

OUR ARTIST SEES MANY PLAYERS

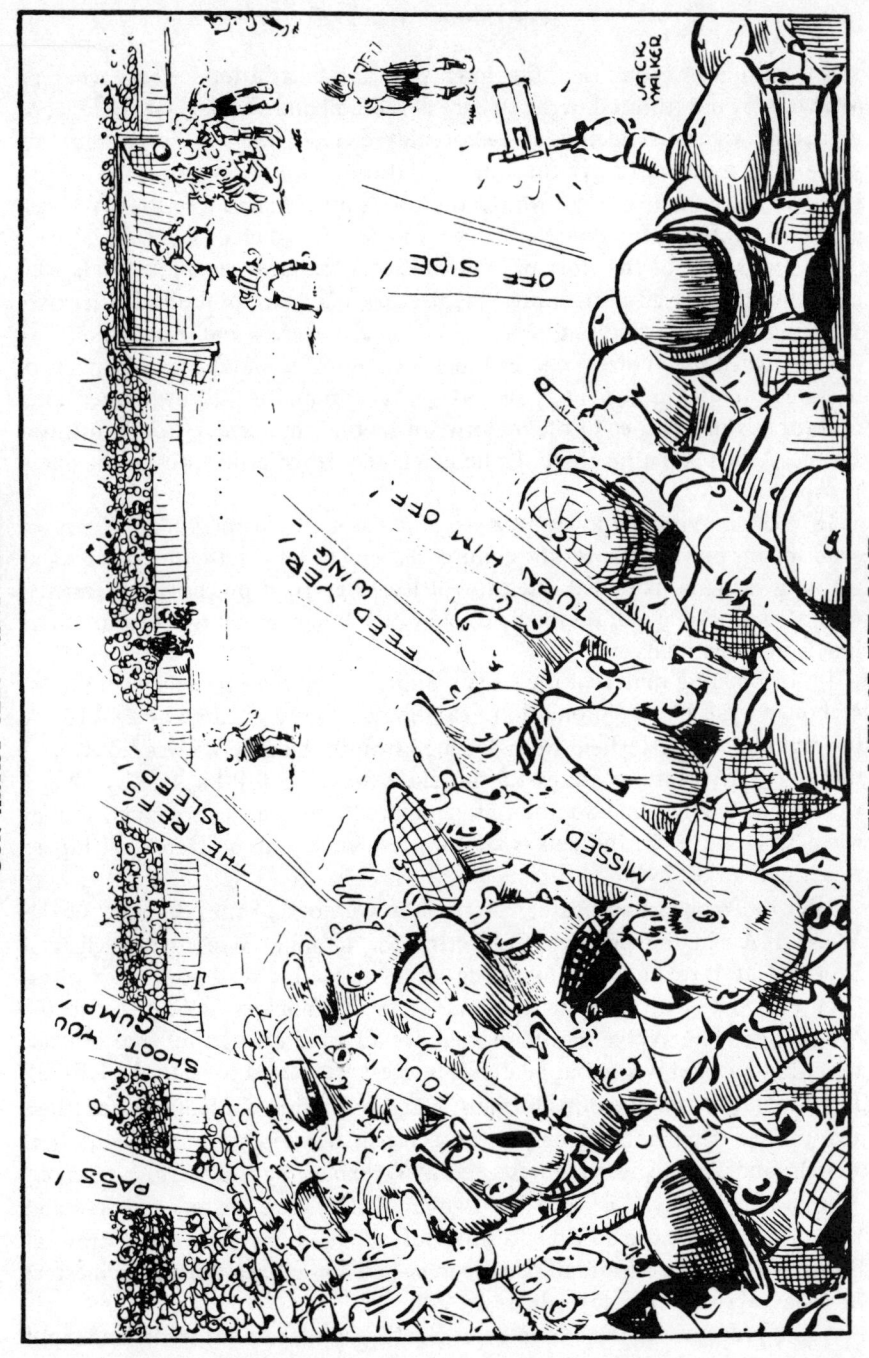

LAW 1.—The Game shall be played by not more than Eleven Players on each Side.

this occasion Albion used the long pass to devastating effect, whereas Wolves—by now tutored in the science of football and no longer adherents of a merely 'vigorous' technique—kept play close. That was truly Albion's year—they went on to win the Cup and also to gain promotion to the First Division, an incentive to all Midland clubs, but to none more than Wolves whose amiable rivalry with the Albion was of such ancient standing.

The first part of the story of Wolves is of a fraternity of individuals who sometimes contrived to rise above themselves. The mark of the early successes was fervour—a quality suitable to a Romantic era—and one which has distinguished the Wolves in later times also. Buckley—and this is implicit in his statements quoted on page 91—was a man of his own age, and accordingly in advance of the majority of football managers. Football was a business, the team a machine. If the machine worked efficiently the business prospered.

In 1931-2 Wolves did appear as efficient and business-like. Years of scouting for players all over the country, insistence on precise time-keeping at training sessions, personal integrity (at least one good player was dismissed for unseemly behaviour on the field), and on a balanced budget began to pay handsome dividends.

In the opening match of the season Spurs—as in the previous year—to be reckoned as likely promotion candidates—were beaten by 4-0. A fortnight later Chesterfield were defeated by 6-0, the only Wolves survivor of the Third Division meetings of the clubs was the full-back, Kay. Away victories at Burnley and Southampton augured well. Gates were good, so that when Stoke came to Molineux (snatching a surprise win) on October 10 there was a gate of 30,794.

After the Wolves had beaten Swansea on October 24 the Secretary of the Welsh F.A., in the process of selecting the national side to play against Scotland at Wrexham the following week, paid this testimony to Wolves. 'You may take it that at any rate one of the Wanderers will appear in the Welsh side. The Wolverhampton men are all good enough for me, but one never knows what might happen'. His interest was stated to be in the left-half Dai Richards, and the outside-right, Charlie Phillips. As it happened these two players were not chosen for the Scottish but for the subsequent Irish match, and Wolves were represented at Wrexham by Lumberg, a reserve.

It was, perhaps, as well for while Wales were losing to Scotland Wolverhampton were having to pull out all the stops to force a draw at Barnsley. This was a characteristic second-half come-back, for at the interval Barnsley were comfortably ahead by 2-0.

A fine progress during November—Hartill scored two hat-tricks and eight

M. S. Crook

W. G. Lowton

D. Richards

Molineux Grounds c. 1925.

Relaxing at Nice 1933.

Pre-Match Courtesies, Nice 1933.

F. C. Buckley

Cup Final memories, 1908, 1939.

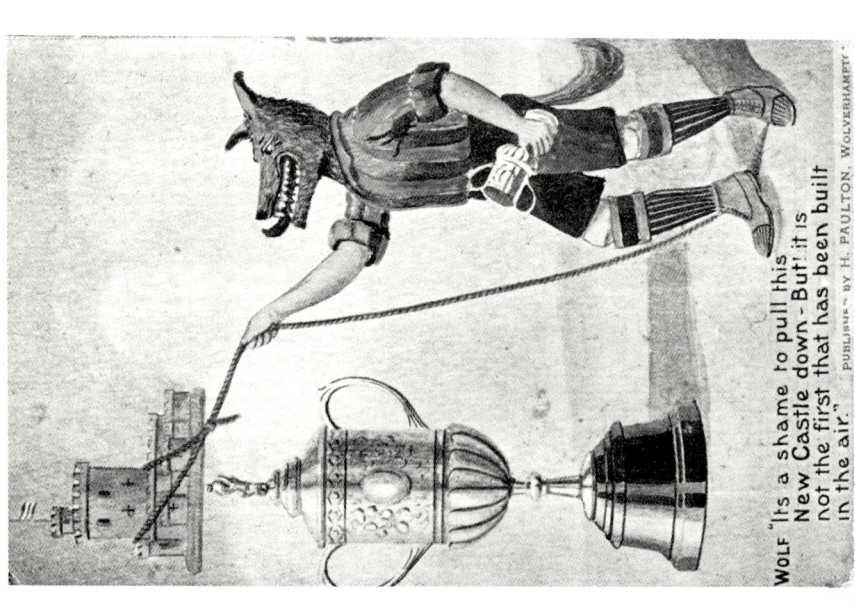

goals in three games—brought Wolves into second place in the table with 23 points as against the 27 of Leeds United. In December came some more feats of high scoring; 6 goals against Bury, 7 against Port Vale, and 7 against Manchester United before a Boxing Day crowd of 37,247—the season's best gate. At the end of the year the gap had narrowed. From 22 games Leeds had 32 points, from 21, Wolves 31; and the Molineux half-back line—regarded traditionally as the power-house of a team—was acclaimed generally as the best in the Second Division.

By the end of January, 1932, having passed out of the Cup in the fourth round at Preston, Wolves were top of the table. During February it was a see-saw between them and Leeds, and on March 17 Wolves were top only on goal average. There was a certain and understandable nervousness apparent. The free-scoring tendencies were temporarily curbed and Lowton, usually a master of the art, was missing penalty kicks: one of these errors might have proved expensive, for it occurred during a drawn game with Leeds.

The earlier irresistibility, however, re-established itself and there was a run of victories from mid-March until mid-April. On April 2 Wolves were away to Bristol City and won by 4-0. A week later they scored 7 goals against 1 from Oldham. And at this point, 3 points ahead of Leeds and 7 ahead of Stoke City and Bradford, only 1 point was needed to ensure promotion.

Some of the London papers had been taking exception to Wolves play, scaring their readers with lurid references to 'kick and rush', 'extreme vigour', 'unscientific tactics'. Neither for the first nor the last time was there a metropolitan dash of sour grapes. The local critic answered back; 'Let London notice . . . that Wolves do not run a third back. That is why the first team have got 110 goals and the reserves 118'. Again a cardinal point of tradition appears: Wolves were, and have tended to remain, essentially an attacking side, intent on breaching alien defences rather than remaining content to exploit the occasional break-out from siege.

Losing to Bury on April 16 Wolves had to postpone their celebration of promotion until a week later. But for the supporters that was a convenience: for it is a stirring thing to be present at a climactic match. Port Vale were the visitors, who were comfortably beaten in a sporting encounter by two goals by Hartill, and of the gate of 28,744 the majority were Wolves supporters. At the end of the match they streamed across the field until the team was produced in the Directors' Box and speeches were made.

The team was:

>Tootill; Lowton, Cecil Shaw; Rhodes, Bellis, Richards; Phillips, Bottrill, Hartill, Deacon, Barraclough.

FIRST-HALF.

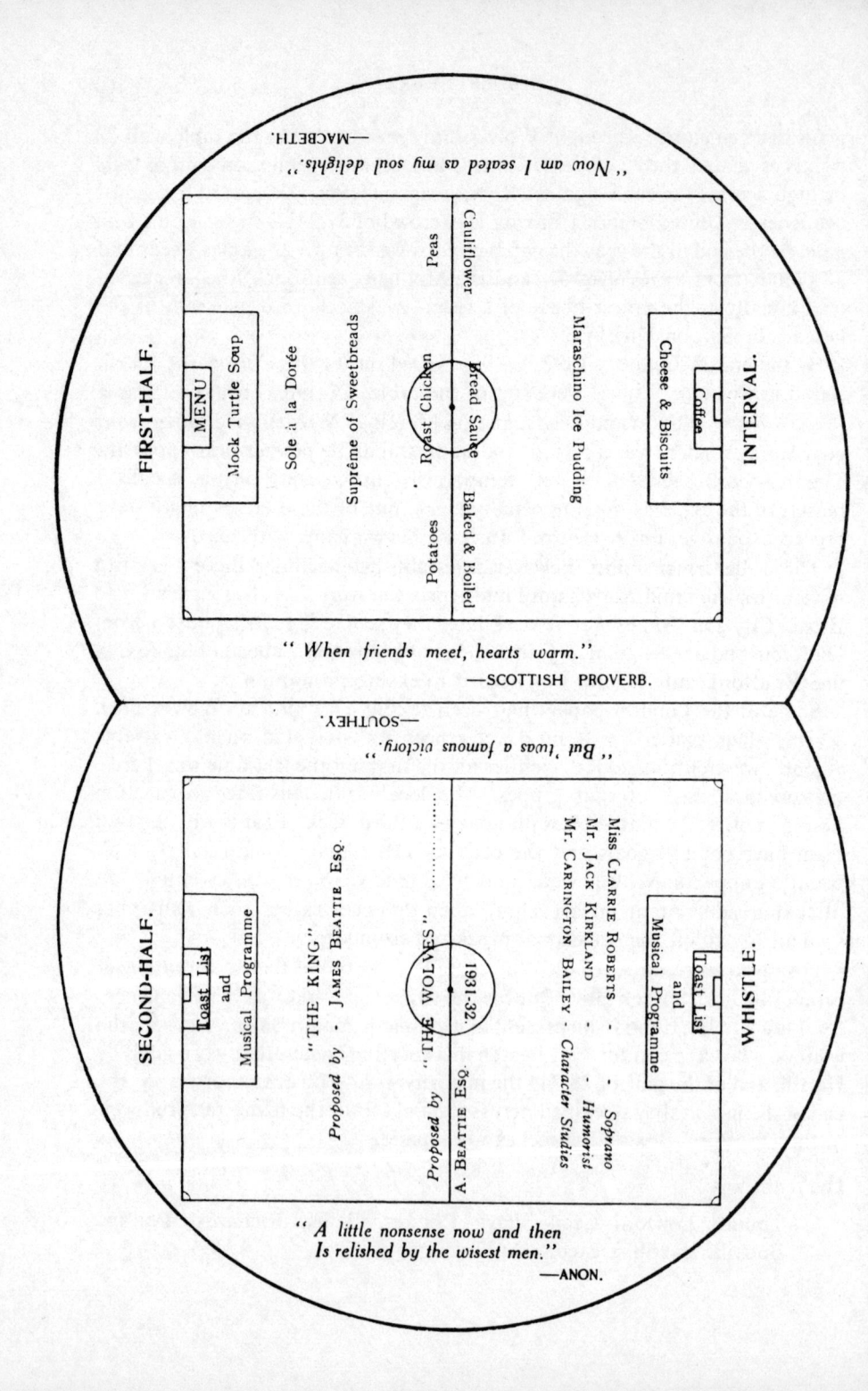

"Now am I seated as my soul delights."
—MACBETH.

MENU

Mock Turtle Soup

Sole à la Dorée

Suprême of Sweetbreads

Cauliflower — Peas

Roast Chicken
Bread Sauce

Maraschino Ice Pudding

Potatoes
Baked & Boiled

INTERVAL.

Cheese & Biscuits

Coffee

"When friends meet, hearts warm."
—SCOTTISH PROVERB.

SECOND-HALF.

"But 'twas a famous victory."
—SOUTHEY.

Toast List and Musical Programme

"THE KING"
Proposed by - JAMES BEATTIE ESQ.

"THE WOLVES"
1931-32.
Proposed by .... A. BEATTIE ESQ.

Miss CLARRIE ROBERTS   -   -   Soprano
Mr. JACK KIRKLAND   -   -   Humorist
Mr. CARRINGTON BAILEY - Character Studies

WHISTLE.

Toast List and Musical Programme

"A little nonsense now and then
Is relished by the wisest men."
—ANON.

Of that team Richards and Phillips were by now internationals. Lumberg, of the reserves, had also won another international cap to add to those he had acquired while with Wrexham. Hollingworth, still incapacitated through injury, had lost the chance of an international trial when he was hurt at Barnsley; and Hartill was generally considered unfortunate not to have received wider recognition of his skill. It was like old times to have internationals and potential internationals at Molineux.

The League success of any club depends almost as much on the reserves as the first team. In that season any reserve who came up temporarily into the senior side fitted adequately—sometimes more than adequately—into the scheme. Shaw could take Kay's place at left-back, while Tom Smalley, from South Kirkby Colliery, and Arthur Buttery, a local boy, were young inside-forwards patently with a future. In fact, the only discordant note in a cheerful summer sounded when Buckley transferred Buttery to Bury. Councillor Smithies hoped that Buckley would henceforth refrain from getting rid of good players . . .'

The Wolves won promotion and their reserves the championship of the Central League. Congratulations poured in from all the Midland clubs, from Arsenal, from the President and the Secretary of the F.A., from George Jobey, now managing Derby County, from the aged Alderman Levi Johnson, from Jack Pedley, outside-left of the 1906 team that had dropped from the First Division, from F. J. Somerville, the promoter of the Supporters' Club in less happy days, and from overseas followers of the Wolves. The Major organised a Presentation Fund. The overdraft at the bank was extinguished, after a profit of £4,123 17s. 3p. on the season, and on June 2 there was a Complimentary Dinner at the Victoria Hotel, at which the Alderman Levi Johnson was one of the speakers.

But there was the future to look to. The directors, therefore, putting their faith in Buckley and the team's capacity, went ahead with general improvements, and during the close season the new stand was erected on the Molineux Street side of the enclosure.

Buckley's energy and determination had produced a good Second Division side, but one which lacked genuine craftsmen and outstanding personalities. The first year back in the First Division nearly ended in disaster, but fortunately disaster was averted. During the next period of Buckley's reign the craftsmen came—usually before they were aware of their own potentialities—and some of them became the dominant influences of their generation. As this transformation took place the Wolves emerged as a power in the land, and their manager was hailed as a genius. Perhaps he was.

By Christmas 1932, however, it was clear that his skills were being

Complimentary Dinner

TO

WOLVERHAMPTON WANDERERS
FOOTBALL CLUB

Winners of League Championship
Division II
1931–1932

Mr. W. Lowton.

AUTOGRAPHS

B. L. Crichton
Bert Allen
John Morris
Cyr Hollins
J. A. Wilson
Roy Matthews
Cullis
W. Barrett
Paul W. Round
Joseph Hadcock
Ernest Barker
A. Mungrell
Alfred J. Pipp

subjected to a severe test. Wolves were at the bottom of the Division, with disheartening defeats from Chelsea—Gallacher being the architect of that debacle—West Bromwich Albion—the clubs' first First Division meeting for twenty-nine years—and Arsenal, of whose 7 goals Jack was responsible for 3, and Bastin 2. For a large part of the first half of that season, Wolves carried fewer points than any team in any of the four divisions; the defence was as effective as a large-mesh sieve; and Hartill particularly, seemed to have lost his old effectiveness.

Changes were made in the composition of the side and there were fresh signings. A new goalkeeper, Wildman, came from South Kirkby, a colliery village in Yorkshire, Ivill, a left full-back, was transferred from Oldham. As some came others went; Bellis to Burnley, and Hetherington—after five years' service, though only one appearance in the promotion season—to Rotherham. After Christmas the tide turned. Wolves went out of the Cup, in the third round (in which their modest neighbours at Walsall won everlasting glory by humiliating Arsenal at Fellows Park), which left them fortunately with but a single objective. They progressed for three months losing only three matches—to Chelsea, Sheffield Wednesday, and Manchester City—and marking notable victories against Huddersfield, Arsenal, Sunderland, and Birmingham. In each case the chief credit went to Hartill, who scored the vital goal in each match.

Nevertheless, when the last day of the season, May 6, arrived it was still necessary for Wolves to win if they were to escape relegation on goal average, in the event of Blackpool (who ultimately went down with Bolton Wanderers) winning. And Wolves' opponents at Molineux were Everton, who had won the F.A. Cup on the previous Saturday.

'The visitors', noted the *Sporting Star*, 'played in their Cup Final colours—black knickers and with a white shirt—and on the back of each player was a number from 1-11, starting with the goalkeeper. This was the first occasion on which numbered players had taken part in a game at Molineux.' But neither their auspicious strip, nor the parade of the F.A. Cup which Everton had brought to awe their hosts, were of avail. Playing quite beautifully Wolves ran out comfortable winners by 4-2, thereby earning their domicile in the First Division for another year, and a close season tour of France; with matches against the Racing Club de Paris, and the club sides of Marseilles, Nice[1], and Nîmes.

---

[1] The match at Nice was a fiery affair, culminating in such civil disturbance that Buckley took his players off the field and only returned them when extra gendarmerie had been drafted in. 'I have brought my team here to play football', he said, 'not to be slaughtered'. *Express and Star*, May 26, 1933.

In the following season Nice visited Molineux; and so began a contact with the Continent which subsequently grew much more intimate. Now that the world has become so much more contracted it is odd to look back on the earlier encounters with foreign sides and to reflect on the little stir they created. On November 27, 1936, for instance, the Jugoslav team Pavi Kavatski Gradjanski Sportski Klub were in Britain. Having taken on Liverpool and Hearts they came to Wolverhampton, where they lost by 4-2. The attendance was 646. It is true that the game was played in a fog, but not even that would nowadays deter a more than normal First Division gate.

Despite the vacillating fortunes of 1932-3 the directors were able to show a profit of £7,610, and they could proudly point to the new Molineux stand—which cost £20,487—and other improvements on the North and South Banks as emblems of their faith in the future. Behind the scenes Dick Bradford, masseur, was busy establishing his therapeutic equipment which, in due course, paid off handsomely in curtailing absenteeism through injury.

In September, 1933, Cyril Spiers came from Spurs as understudy to the goal-keeper Wildman, and Jack Beattie, an inside-right from Aberdeen, arrived to add power and incisiveness to the forward line. His debut for his new club was unpromising, for on September 9 Wolves gave one of their less resolute displays and conceded six goals to Sunderland.

On November 4 Buckley brought to Molineux a shy boy, who had once worked in a pit at Merthyr Tydvil. His name was Jones—Bryn Jones, brother to Ivor Jones, of Swansea, West Bromwich Albion, and Wales, and of Emlyn Jones, of Southend. Young Jones played for Merthyr Amateurs, and for Plymouth United—in the Merthyr and District League. He had had a trial with Southend, who had not kept him, had spent a season with the Belfast Club, Glenavon, and had lately been with Aberaman.

Bryn Jones came into the Wolves side on November 18—on which day his compatriots Richards and Phillips were ensuring the international championship for Wales for the second successive year. (Richards played in the national side every match those two years, while Phillips was ever present in 1933-4). Without these stalwarts Wolves nonetheless were able to defeat Everton at Goodison Park. Jones, at inside-right, was marked down as 'a promising recruit'. But on December 9 the report was less formal. 'The most pleasing player on the field was young Jones, whose speed when in possession was remarkable and who on a tricky ground showed wonderful ball control'. Jones, lithe, intelligent, co-operative, elusive, perplexed the Newcastle defence that day and collaborated happily with a new centre-forward, Goddard, who was a complementary player of a fearless and robust type. Goddard, recruited from Queen's Park Rangers, was that day taking the place of Billy Hartill, who was taking a well-earned rest after fifty-nine consecutive appearances. A fortnight later Jones showed himself in the role of goal-taker as well as goal-maker, claiming 2 out of the bag of 8 collected from Manchester City.

After Christmas fortune was less kind and for two months not a League match was won. Two matches stood out. On January 6, 1934, a vigorous encounter with Chelsea culminated in the players of both sides—except for the goalkeepers—being lined up around the centre circle to be lectured by the referee. On February 10 Stoke City defeated Wolves by 2-0. On the Stoke right-wing was a young player—appearing for the first time in a First Division match at Molineux—named Stanley Matthews. On the other wing was Johnson, in due course to accompany his opposite number into the England team. 'The Stoke City wingers were always dangerous and severely tested the Wolves defence'. Matthews tested the defence in all ways for his shooting was fierce and accurate. (A week later he scored the two goals that put Chelsea out of the Cup).

The season ended without any more satisfaction than could be derived from occupying the fifteenth place in the table. For the second year running the last visitors to Molineux were the new Cup-holders; this time Manchester City, who lived up to their status by winning by 4-0. But Wolves established one record, and one of which they were justifiably proud. On April 27 Lowton, Hartill, Barraclough, Rhodes, reserve for the Football League in Belfast in 1932, and Deacon and Hollingworth, each received a benefit of £400. No other club, claimed Sir Charles Mander, President since 1932, had given so many as six in one season. Mr. Oakley, underlining the policy of the directorate, emphasized that the majority of those long-serving and loyal players had graduated from the 'A' team; and Major Buckley seized the opportunity to proclaim the ascetic virtues, practised by the beneficiaries, of 'application, concentration, and self-denial'.

This, however, was a transitional period, and security of tenure at Molineux became possible only for the above average. So that in November, 1936, there could only be found seven out of thirty-four professionals who had been with the club for three or more years. Major Buckley was here, there, and everywhere. Recruits came to his playing staff in droves; and as quickly as some players came so others left. In December, 1934, Buckley went to Ireland—'to get a right-back irrespective of cost'. He came back with a centre-forward, an inside-forward, and a goalkeeper, in 'Boy' Martin, an international player, and Jackie Brown, both from Belfast Celtic, and Utterson, from Glenavon. These represented the Major's extravagances, for the great majority of his newcomers cost virtually nothing, and among these were names destined for greatness.

Joe Gardiner had joined the staff from obscurity in County Durham as long ago as December, 1932. Fourteen months later a youth came from Ellesmere Port Wednesday. His name was Cullis. Shortly after Cullis, Tom Galley was recruited.

Galley, Cullis, Gardiner: four years later that represented one of the strongest half-back lines in the history of the club.

When these youngsters came, their arrival was almost unnoticed. On the other hand exits were much more prominent.

In 1935 Hartill (who that year was chosen as inside-right for a Midland team which played West Bromwich Albion) ended his not undistinguished career. In 1936 Cecil Shaw—who missed no match for Wolves between 1931 and 1935—went to West Bromwich; Jackie Brown went to Coventry City; Weaver to West Ham; Waring, who had been with Villa, to Tranmere; Laking to Middlesbrough; Iverson to Villa; Wrigglesworth to Manchester United. A year later Jones (E.) and Wharton were conferred on Portsmouth, Clayton on Villa, and Ashall on Coventry City . . . The end of season at Molineux was like a university college after Degree Day.

The crowd at Molineux had its own views in the matter. It was a conservative body which shifted loyalty slowly, and it began to think the Major of a restless disposition. Matters came to a head on November 7, 1936. It is almost axiomatic at Molineux that if a sensation is required then Chelsea are a necessary ingredient. This is no reflection on Chelsea, who seem to have been not infrequently the victims of coincidence.

There, in any case, on November 7, were Chelsea. Wolves were third from the bottom of the table, having won only 4 out of 13 matches. This match did not improve the record: Chelsea scored two goals, both by Mills, while Wolves could only reply with one, by Wrigglesworth from a pass by Bryn Jones. Some points of refereeing caught critical attention and a score of excited fans climbed on to the pitch from the Hotel end. There were visions of a repetition of the episode of October 18, 1919, and police hastily put the referee into a place of safety. By now, however, some 2,000 persons were on the field. There followed a disorderly procession to the players' entrance. Extra police were rushed to the scene to form a 'human wall between the crowd and the players' entrance.

Officials attempted to address the crowd, but to no avail. What the incensed supporters wanted, it transpired, was the manager and the directors. Why they wanted them was to impress their views regarding the spate of transfers. While this continued, it was inferred, only disaster could transpire. Due emphasis was given to this opinion by those strong-armed individuals who partially uprooted a goal-post, leaving it swaying to and fro like a drunken man. The episode duly earned a strong reprimand from the F.A. In view of modern attitudes and behavioural problems one wonders what those who then uprooted goal-posts (and worse) have to say now.

Yet the club could point to spectacular results. That very season showed a profit of £17,790; the next season topped £18,000; and over a four-year period from 1935-1939 the income from transferred players was no less than £110,658. Of this prodigious sum £14,000 is a small fraction; but precisely this sum created more notoriety for Wolverhampton than anything in modern times.

Bryn Jones came to Molineux at the end of 1933. Within a few months of his arrival that astute assessor of football skill George Allison, the great Arsenal manager, discerned his genius, recognizing that it might be used profitably at Highbury. Allison saw Jones play for Wolves. Indeed, he viewed Wolves with frequency 'Has he,' asked the *Express and Star* 'ever heard of a player named Bryn Jones?' Mr. Oakley answered Allison's questions before it was asked: 'Arsenal have not enough money to buy Jones'.

Allison, however, persisted and by July, 1938, frantic for an inside-forward of real distinction since the end of Alex James's career, was importunate to the point of bidding in, for those days, astronomical terms. £10,000 had been mentioned. Tottenham Hotspur having stepped in, it went up to £12,000. Back came Allison with £14,000—a then world record for a transfer fee. The Wolves directors agreed; but the player himself was indeterminate. He hovered for days unhappy as the publicity blew about his head. And the more he hesitated the greater the publicity. The newspapers issued daily bulletins on Jones's private thoughts, and anxious groups assembled outside the Wolves headquarters. Finally, on August 4, Jones agreed to go to London.

The *Express and Star* carried a leading article, centred on the text 'Is he going?' Thus it commented; in words which have a distinctly historical ring about them:

> ... A visitor from another planet might have thought that they were discussing the possible departure of this Dictator or that. But no—it wasn't Benito, it wasn't Adolf. It was Bryn, Welsh wizard of the football field ...
>
> Now we know where we are. Bryn is really going. And we are left to ponder the curious mentality of the British, who make more of their footballers than ever the Romans did of their gladiators. This may denote lack of proportion, but, at any rate, there is some likelihood that the sport craze is a healthy counterbalance to the perplexing problems of a harassed world.

The Jones story concluded at Wolverhampton on the afternoon of September 17, 1938, on which day Arsenal came to Molineux. As Bryn Jones appeared with his new colleagues the crowd rose to give him 'the biggest reception a visiting player has ever had . . . and the cheers were renewed when the Welshman and Cullis were photographed together with hands clasped'.

Less sure of himself than formerly,[1] the Arsenal inside-right nonetheless controlled a largely experimental forward line and enabled his compatriot Cummer to go through to score a decisive goal. Wolves still suffered from a malady not uncommon in that era—from 'Arsenalitis'—and generally did themselves less than justice. All except one; for 'time after time the ground rang with cheers for Cullis's superlative play at centre-half'—which left the normally ebullient Ted Drake unplugged, isolated, and frustrated.

The king is dead. Long live the king. With the departure of Jones the value of Cullis was enhanced and the quality of his play and his dominance over the team stood out unmistakably. At this time Buckley—with grandiose observation that 'the sky was our limit'—would have brought Matthews down from Stoke. But he reckoned without the resistance of the Stoke board.

We may return to February 16, 1935. On that day Stanley Cullis played at right-half in the first team against Huddersfield Town, at Molineux. Wolves, fifth from the bottom of the Division, were out-classed—Martin the new leader was uninspiring—and lost by 3-2. But 'Cullis opened well and showed promise occasionally'. In further outings Cullis was moved to left-half.

When the new season opened he was back in the reserves, Morris being then at centre-half. But on October 1, some re-arrangement was necessary, for Laking, the left-back, was injured. Accordingly Morris was moved to Laking's position and Cullis instated at centre-half. With abundant energy he opposed the Everton centre-forward Dean, and the resultant clash of contrasting temperaments called for some friendly advice to both players from the referee. Everton won, but that the score was kept to 1-0 was in large measure due to the tenacity with which Dean was policed.

At this early stage of his career Cullis was prominent because he saw the general implications of a match; while defending his own section he could anticipate what was likely to happen elsewhere. So it was that on November 28 a lively Grimsby forward line disappointed its supporters: its 'attacks petered out because Cullis was so alert'. During that season Cullis's stature grew apace. It was a vigorous initiation, for play in general was of a vigorous character and injuries were commonplace. At Molineux, however, players were quickly restored to health, through the provision of the most modern

[1] Bernard Joy described the temperamental difficulties which beset Jones after his transfer. See *Forward Arsenal*. 1952, pp 119-123.

means of treatment. In 1935, for instance, the directors had installed such novelties as a 'therapeutic diathermy machine', and a 'universal machine for galvanism, sumsoidal and paradic treatments, and ultra-violet rays for irradiation'.

If Wolves players need such aids to recovery it is clear that other clubs may well have envied their recuperative opportunities; for Wolves certainly gave as good as they got. An incident at the end of the 1936-7 season indicated that possibly they gave even better. There was to have been a close season tour of Central Europe. But on April 30 a bombshell came: the F.A. wrote to Buckley:

> 'In view of the numerous reports of misconduct by players of the Wolverhampton Wanderers Club during the past two seasons, the F.A. Council, meeting in London today, decided that the application of the club for permission to play matches on the Continent during the coming close season be not granted'.

It was admitted that Wolves players had received numerous cautions, but, as the President, Sir Charles Mander, said, these were generally on account of arguments with the referee! And that the F.A. should, as they did, suggest that Buckley was encouraging unethical play was particularly resented.

Four days after the F.A. wrote, a reply went from Molineux. Neither directors nor manager knew of this. The players reacted spontaneously. Led by Stanley Cullis they replied:

> 'We should like to state that, far from advocating the rough play we are accused of, Major Buckley is constantly reminding us of the importance of playing good, clean and honest football, and we, as a team, consider you have been most unjust in administering this caution to our manager'.

It was typical of Cullis that he should thus show loyalty in an unequivocal manner. Another man might well have considered such action as likely to jeopardize his career; particularly when his international prospects were beginning to be discussed. For on February 13 Cullis's future eminence had been prophesied. On that day Everton came to Molineux, in their ranks Tommy Lawton making his debut. There were 'lively duels between the seventeen-year-old Lawton and Cullis, Wolves nineteen-year-old centre-half and captain, considered a future England player'. Wolves put on one of their devastating performances, winning by 7-2. Lawton scored the second Everton goal from a penalty.

In September a newspaper headline gave prominence to 'Wolves new lead in football tactics'. Morris was launching attacks from full-back, and Cullis was 'much more of an attacking half-back than he has ever been before . . . as an attacker he makes a heap of difference to the forward line'.

Together with Ashall and Galley, Cullis was chosen for the English League team that played the Scottish League in Glasgow in September. He came in for the Huddersfield player Young, who was injured. It remained to be seen whether Cullis would be chosen in preference to Young for the national side a month later. Would the selectors opt for enterprise or for safety? 'As footballer and tactician', wrote the *Sporting Star,* 'Cullis is out on his own . . . while as a stay-at-home, hard-tackling, big-kicking player, the Huddersfield man is better than most'. In the event Young was chosen but had to withdraw once again through injury. Thus Cullis came into his own; the first centre-half supplied to England by Wolves since 1889, when Harry Allen filled the berth.

During the Bryn Jones-Stanley Cullis era Wolves became the most discussed team in the country. This was due on the one hand to the compelling verve of their play and, on the other, to the methods and aspirations of Buckley.

A team which shows impressive results must have certain qualities among which competence and team spirit are conspicuous. In Cullis's early years both were exemplified by Cecil Shaw, ever present for two seasons. Shaw played for the English against the Irish League on September 23, 1936. Then there was Tom Smalley who in the same season appeared at right-half for England against Wales at Swansea. Scott, eminently safe custodian—known also as a baseball player in his native Liverpool—brought a secure style of goalkeeping to Molineux which was to be of inestimable value in the years preceding the Second World War. Denis Westcott, a native of New Invention, a schoolboy international, and with some kind of experience with West Ham, came into the forward line (at first as outside-right) to add punch and shooting power. In 1938 the half-backs comprised Smalley, Cullis, Gardiner, Galley, Dorsett, the reserves being able to take the places of first team players—as again in the 1950's—without the rhythm of the side being upset. Dorsett, of course, eventually settled down to inside-left.

In 1935-6 Wolves were fifteenth in the League table. A year later they were fifth. The next season ended with them as runners-up. Not for the first time the final placing depended on the last match of the programme. Having lately defeated Leicester City by 10-1, Wolves went to Roker Park confident of being able to beat Sunderland. But it was to be otherwise. Sunderland, determined to continue the supremacy established in the classic, twice replayed, sixth round F.A. Cup round of the previous season, set up all their defences against the rampageous Wolves forwards. A goal by Lester gave them victory, and Wolves second place in the Championship to the Arsenal side that had lately ended Wolves 1938 Cup progress in the fourth round.

During that season 651,532 spectators watched the twenty-one home matches at Molineux, an average of 31,025 per match, and there was a total increase on the previous season of 152,866; remarkable figures for a moderately sized town with other first-class clubs within easy access. The largest gate, however, was for a cup-tie; that against Arsenal when the attendance was 61,267. Not even this was allowed to stand long as a record, for on February 11, 1939, 61,315 people were packed into the enclosure on the occasion of the fifth round tie with Liverpool. And that—since in postwar years a limit of about 55,000 was decreed by the police—still stands as the record.

The end of the last pre-war season approached with Wolves in sight of the double. As they rode on the crest of the wave with the League championship within their grasp they ran through Bradford, Leicester, Liverpool, Everton and Grimsby[1] to reach the Cup Final, having scored 19 goals against 3. Alas! the Final, against Portsmouth, fell below standard. Wolves—their main weakness being in the wing-forward positions—never moved with their characteristic assurance, and Portsmouth took the lead in half an hour. It was a sort of Nemesis, the goal scorer was Barlow who had previously been a Wolves player. There was also another previous Molineux protégé in the Portsmouth side in Wharton. Just before half-time the score was 3-0. Dorsett scored a consolation goal for Wolves, but Portsmouth—the least fancied side ever to reach Wembley—regained their three-goal margin when Porter scored their fourth. The teams were;

Wolves: Scott; Morris, Taylor; Galley, Cullis, Gardiner; Burton, McIntosh, Westcott, Dorsett, Maguire.

Portsmouth: Walker; Morgan, Rochford; Guthrie, Rowe, Wharton, Worrall, McAlinden, Anderson, Barlow, Parker.

In some degree of exasperation the local newspaper summed up that season: 'Surely this succession of honours just missed cannot go on. In two successive seasons the club have finished second in the table, while this time they failed at the last jump in the cup'. But still Wolves were the first club ever to be runners-up both in Cup and League.

[1] At Old Trafford on March 25, where the record attendance was 76,962.

As that climacteric inexorably approached Wolves were in the public eye for many reasons, not least because of Buckley's temerity in introducing boys in their teens to the full rigours of First Division football. In later time the cult of youth teams made such introductions less remarkable, and now the whole emphasis is on youth. But it should be remembered that it was Buckley who showed how a team should be built—from promising materials nurtured under the club tradition and fitted for the club style.

Cullis came to flower early. In 1939 two other prodigies appeared: Alan Steen, at outside-right, and Jimmy Mullen, at outside-left. Mullen's first appearance in the first team was on February 18, when Wolves beat Leeds United by 4-1. Mullen—who also played in the semi-final against Grimsby—was sixteen years of age; so was Steen; so also was Goddard who played at left-half that day. And in the back room was another boy—whose chief memory of 1939 was of helping to pack the team's equipment before it left for Wembley: William Ambrose Wright, who had recently come to the Molineux ground staff from Ironbridge in Shropshire.

Thus arrived at the last, and, in some way, most remarkable example of Major Buckley's contribution to Molineux we may summarize his achievements in twelve years.

There is no doubt that Buckley was an outstanding character. In assessing potential genius he was without rival at that time, and his knowledge of tactical and pyschological issues seemed immense. In part this was the result of experience, but there was a considerable element of intuition. That is to say, he had the feel of the game.

Buckley also had a flair for relating the game to its players on the one hand—he was especially good in looking after the welfare of his youngsters—and to the public on the other. Thus in 1938 he took steps towards acquiring property to be turned into a hostel for players—a wholly admirable scheme, intended to have recreation rooms, small infirmary and gardens on the material side, and on the intellectual, provision for further education, a secular variant on a monastic theme.

When the last of his improvements at Molineux were completed in 1935 Buckley turned his mind to the future of the ground. Two years later it was his ambition to provide covered accommodation for 70,000 spectators at an admission fee of 1s. Since he had made the club to 'rank with the richest clubs in the country' no one thought this an extravagant vision. In a year's time he returned to his project. But now he dreamed of a stadium large enough to hold 100,000 spectators. And he began immediately to prospect for the erection of a new double-decker stand at the north end of the ground. Town planning and a war put insuperable obstacles in the way of fulfilment, and now one wonders if Buckley's dreams will ever come true.

What would have happened but for the cessation of football, and private involvements that lie outside this story, is anybody's guess; for in 1938 Buckley's contract was renewed—for ten years.

Buckley brought Wolves to a pinnacle of fame which none could have foreseen when he chose Molineux rather than Roker Park. But his greatest successes, looked at from another angle, were failures. His team, for all its brilliance and fire, won neither Cup nor League.

The reason would seem to be Buckley's restless disposition. He knew little of the need for personal relaxation—the portraits show him as one conscious of his dramatic role. Discipline, fitness, speed, determination, pride; these were the desirable qualities and to be engendered at all costs.

Fitness depends on freedom from injury. Injuries were more often than not caused by falls on hard grounds. Buckley gave orders that the field at Molineux was to be watered. It was easy to say, as some did, that the practice 'gave an advantage to the speed and stamina of the Wolves young players', but that was not, in the first place, the intention. However, in 1939 the Football League banned the watering of grounds between November and February—and it looked as though Buckley had been trying to pull a fast one.

In 1935 Buckley's attention was drawn to the salutary effects on human glands of intravenous injections of animal secretions—that was the age of the Serge Voronoff glandular mumbo-jumbo. Always alive to the need for seizing the scientific forelock he considered the possible advantages that might accrue from investment in a number of hypodermic syringes, and the fortification of his players by the injection of ape properties. In due course the Press discovered another Buckley headline. In 1938 the F.A. 'held an inquiry into the idea of pumping an extract of the glands of oxen into footballers', and announced that footballers were at liberty to decide for themselves whether or not they underwent such treatment. Before the 1939 Final Mr. Montague Lyons, K.C., M.P. for East Leicester (actuated, perhaps, by the Wolves summary dismissal of Leicester City in the fourth round), addressed a question to the Minister of Health as to 'whether his attention has been directed to statements that gland extracts from animals are being administered to football players . . . whether he will order an investigation into these allegations, and whether he regards this practice as desirable in the interests of national health'.

In the meantime the Major claimed that by such means some of his players had put on weight, and others height. But neither Cup nor League were won—and the value of biochemical assistance was obviously questionable.

But there were other branches of science. The collective shadow of Freud, Jung, and Alder suspended itself above the Major's office and psychology was noted as an impressive word. There is a limit to the number of bees that may buzz in a bonnet. This latest was christened by the players the 'psychological riddle-me-ree'. When a player who had been thus guinea-pigged went to a new club the subject was brought up by the curious. He was asked how many times he had been to the psychologist. His answer was: 'Five, I've only to go once more and then I shall have cured him'.

S. Cullis in defence, v Arsenal 1936.

R. Dorsett in attack, v Stoke 1938.

Team, Lady Day 1893.

Cup Final procession 1939.

S. Cullis with C. Chataway.

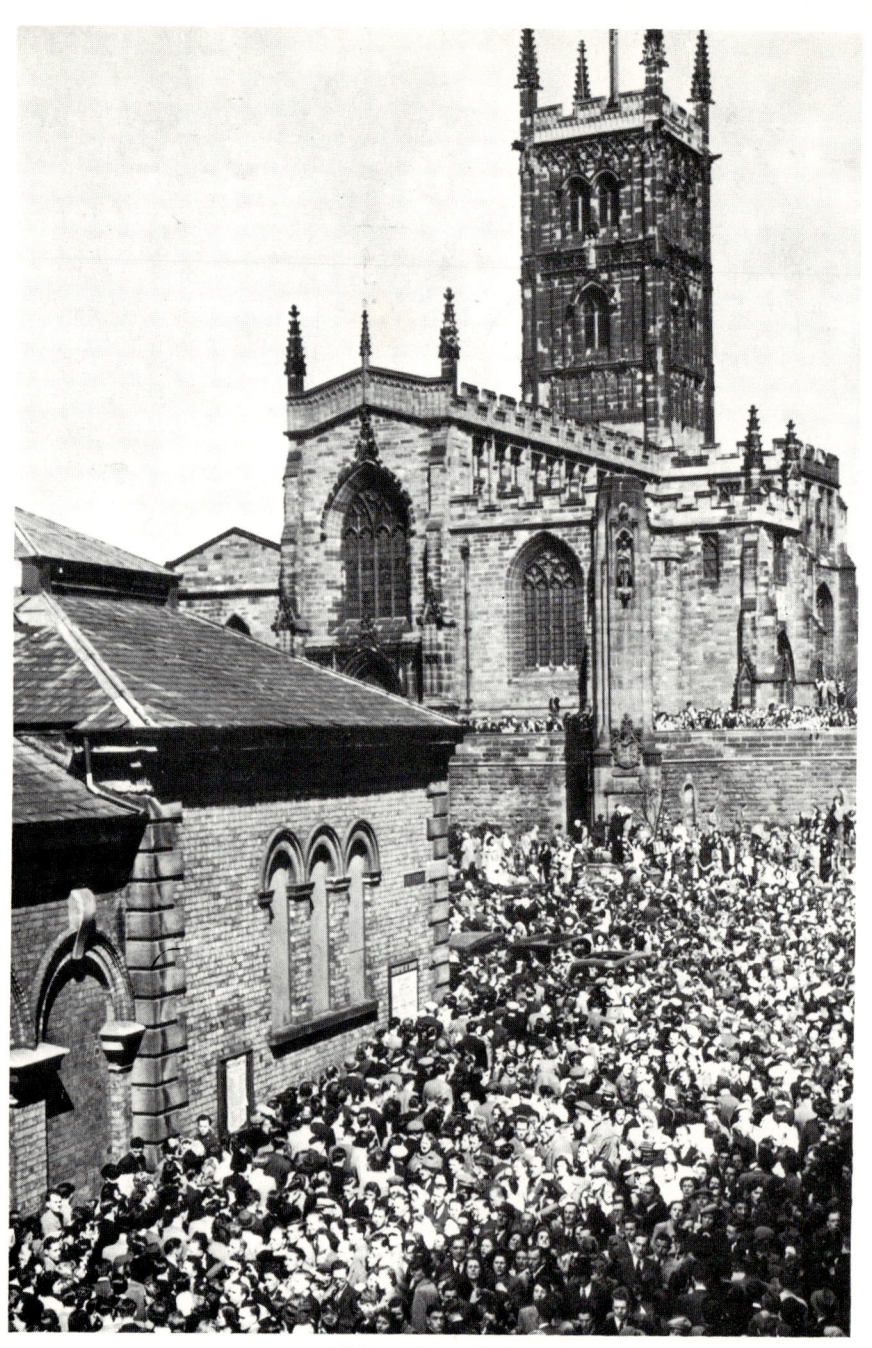

Welcome home 1949.

11

War and Peace

... and the manner in which Wolves took their most severe blow was most praiseworthy'.
Liverpool Echo, May 31 1947.

BEFORE the season of 1938-9 was ended the shape of things to come was apparent and Major Buckley 'stated that he would be very pleased for any of his players who desired to join the Territorial Army'. The first to do so was Stanley Cullis. In September when war was actual the country was prepared for a complete close-down of all that was considered inessential. Molineux was lent to the municipality as a headquarters for Air Raid Precautions, the records and apparatus of the club were removed, and the boys on the ground staff were sent home, their seniors in the meantime disappearing into the ranks of the armed forces or into industry.

It was not long, however, before the morale-boosting properties of competitive football were recognized by the government and extempore measures brought into being regional leagues. The Midland Region group comprised Wolves, Albion, Walsall, Birmingham, Stoke, Leicester, Nottingham Forest, Notts County, Crewe, Northampton; strangely assorted bedfellows—but in such abnormal times abnormal standards prevailed. To contrive a team for any fixture was, of course, a nightmare for any manager, and guest players—often servicemen stationed locally—frequently helped out.

The first season of war-time football cost Wolves £17,717, a liability which it seemed injudicious to increase. So for one year all activity ceased. In the meantime, however—in July, 1940—the directors made a patriotic gesture by lending the government £5,000 free of interest; and Major Buckley volunteered for military service. In fact, Buckley then being in the middle fifties, this offer was not accepted and he stayed where he was.

The directors at that time were A. H. Oakley (Chairman), who had had considerable experience as a referee, R. H. Archer, J. S. Baker, J. Evans, B. Matthews, and J. C. Tildesley.

Visitors to Molineux—there were very few—during the first year of the war were rewarded by some promising displays by the boys whom Buckley had been able to recall. They were the mainstay of the then Wolves team, and among them the most conspicious was the fair-haired, fifteen-year-old Wright, who might have been found anywhere in the forward or half-back line, but most frequently at inside-left. A year later, during the sabbatical period, Wright and Mullen assisted Leicester City and were able to make a substantial contribution to Leicester's winning of the Midland War Cup. Between them they scored twenty-three goals.[1]

In 1941-2 Wolves—having lost more than £4,000 in the season when no football was played—resumed activity in the temporary Football League South. If they had not done so the players on the books would have been released and the club in a physical sense would have been bankrupt. Some success was achieved that year in that the club, captained by Tom Galley, went on to win the Football League War Cup, which was based on the two-leg principle. In the first round Wolves were drawn against Manchester United and the second leg, at Molineux, drew a large crowd for those days, of 12,341. This match went on into extra time and Wolves one stage further through the goal scored by Denis Westcott in the ninety-sixth minute which gave them the tie by a 6-5 aggregate. After the United Wolves disposed of the City, also in extra time and by a goal from Denis Westcott—laid on by Billy Wright. Wright was now playing at right-half behind Frank Broome.

A first semi-final win over the Albion at the Hawthorns by 3-0 left Wolves evident finalists and in the return match on May 16 that verdict of superiority was confirmed by a 4-0 win. It was on this day, however, that Billy Wright received the most serious injury of his career—a fractured ankle. This prevented him from appearing for the club in his first Cup Final, against Sunderland. Having won this trophy, by 6-3[2] —before an aggregate of 75,000 spectators at Roker Park and Molineux—Wolves went up to London to play against Brentford, winners of the London Cup. This ended in a 1-1 draw.

Among the prominent players during that season was Cyril Sidlow, formerly Scott's understudy as goalkeeper. His sterling displays won him recognition both during and after the war by the Welsh selectors: but, for reasons which will shortly become apparent, his career with Wolves was of brief duration. Denis Westcott, was another who was at his best during the war years, when his potential in the international field was partly signified by his selection for *ad hoc* 'international' sides of the time.

[1] See Billy Wright, *Captain of England* (Stanley Paul, 1950), pp 21-30.
[2] 2-2 at Sunderland, 4-1 at Wolverhampton.

As the war went on, new names appeared on the books. There would, perhaps, be a future to look forward to; football would appreciate as it had after the 1914-18 recess; and Wolves would be expected to maintain, or, indeed, improve, on their pre-war record. In 1942 Roy Pritchard, Angus McLean, Billy Crook, Leslie Jones, Jimmy Dunn—son of the famous Everton, Hibernian, and Scotland player—joined the club. By 1944 Denis Wilshaw, a native of North Staffordshire, had appeared occasionally to lead the attack. There were other players in the neighbouring clubs who were causing speculation, especially Bert Williams, who gave a striking display for the R.A.F. against Wolves in the spring of 1944, and Johnny Hancocks, a diminutive outside-right of quixotic habits on the field of play. Both players were with Walsall, a club whose straightened circumstances have at all times militated against their retention of talent. When football was resumed after the war Williams immediately came to Molineux, and Hancocks not long after.

Unexpected things happened during the war. One day in 1944 Tom Smalley, then on the books of Northampton Town, walked into Molineux to watch his old team. But instead of remaining a spectator he was pressed into service and delighted his old friends on the terraces by a worthy reappearance. Westcott was in Bremen one day and playing for Wolves the next, while Alec McIntosh came back to the team at the end of the 1944-5 season from a prisoner-of-war camp. There were vivid memories of a superlative display, for an R.A.F. side, of Peter Doherty. And Freddie Steele of Stoke City, later manager of Port Vale, wrote his name in the Molineux annals by producing three hat-tricks against Wolves, the last for Leicester City. The first two belonged to one match—one in each half, when Stoke City defeated Wolves by 9-3. The most unexpected happening, however, was the departure of Major Buckley.

In 1938 Buckley's contract had been renewed for ten years and it had been expected that he would complete his career in honour and dignity with the club who had made his name and whose reputation he had rebuilt. But, after the beginning of 1944, he left the club 'for private and personal reasons'.[1] Soon he joined Notts County, whence, in a short time, he passed to Hull City, and then to Leeds, and finally to Walsall. At the time of his going there was a change also in the Chairmanship of the Wolves Board, J. S. Baker succeeding Ben Mathews. In the municipal year then begun the office of Mayor was filled by Tom Phillipson, one-time Wolves player and now totally reliable pillar of the civic establishment.

From the 100 applicants for the managership of Wolves, Ted Vizard,

[1] Letter from Buckley to the Directors, published in *Express and Star*, July 7, 1944.

manager of Queen's Park Rangers, was selected on April 5, 1944. Vizard had enjoyed a distinguished career as player, and within three months of joining Bolton Wanderers in 1910 had been chosen to play for Wales. He remained with Bolton for twenty-three years, taking part in that memorable sequence of between-the-wars Cup Final successes and winning twenty-three caps for Wales. He had been chosen by the Welsh selectors on forty occasions, but his club was unwilling to release him for internationals played on Saturday. Vizard had many of the qualities for management, but, of a somewhat retiring disposition, he lacked the drive and palpable energy to which Wolves, both players and directors, had grown accustomed. His tenure of office was brief, but he creditably accomplished the hazardous operation of starting the post-war Wolves on their new course.

As the Wolves were putting themselves under Vizard's tutelage and envisaging the future a voice spoke up from the past; for at the end of April 1944, the finalists in two Junior Cup Competitions were . . . Blakenhall St. Luke's.

After Vizard's appointment the seers saw a happy augury in three successive victories, and Billy Wright was described, with somewhat monotonous regularity, as 'the outstanding player on the field'. He was now at inside-left again, though in representative teams he was more often at wing-half.

The war ended and the transitional season 1945-6 (there was no proper League football and the F.A. Cup operated according to the 2-leg system) commenced Wolves, because team-building had continued, were able to dispense with guest-players and to win some convincing victories—notably over Spurs and Chelsea. This latter match, at Stamford Bridge on September 24, was 'a personal triumph for Bert Williams, making his first appearance for Wolves following his transfer from Walsall'. Such grace, poise, agility, and daring had not, perhaps, heretofore been seen; not, that is, so combined with modesty and integrity both on and off the field. Williams, Mullen, and Wright played for England in various 'Victory' internationals during that season, and Sidlow was in the Welsh side. Wolves finished sixth in the League South.

In the autumn of 1946 League Football was back and Wolves started where they had left off in 1939. J. S. Baker was now Chairman of the club, while Archer and Tildesley were no longer directors, C. H. Hunter serving in their stead. On August 31 Arsenal came to Molineux and, before a huge gate of 50,845, were thoroughly defeated by 6-1. The Wolves team that day was:

> Williams, Morris—capped against Rumania in 1939, McLean; Galley, Cullis, Wright; Hancocks, Pye, Westcott, Ramscar, Mullen.

For Pye and Hancocks this was their initiation at home, though both had played in the Wolves close-season tour of Sweden. Pye, a skilful, scheming player, had served in the Royal Engineers during the war. A native of Yorkshire and sometime on the books of Sheffield United he had come into prominence with Notts County in 1945, and had played against Belgium in the 'Victory' international of 1946. Wright, it will be noticed, is by now at wing-half, on which the comment of the *Sporting Star* of September 28, 1946, was 'Wright is one of the best utility players Wolves have had for seasons. His real position is left-half, the English selectors prefer him at right-half, and on many occasions he has played inside-forward'.

Despite the sensational opening victory against Arsenal the first month of the season was unprofitable, for four defeats followed; and these were the vital matches which affected the issue of the Championship. One of these matches was at Grimsby, where Buckley turned up, talking of a prospective enclosure at Hull to accommodate 90,000 spectators, and with the manager's residence within the compound.

After the fluctuating fortunes of the early season Wolves marched imperiously onward, so that by December 7 they were at the head of the First Division, having won 12 and drawn 2 out of 19 matches. On the morning of that day Liverpool had been league leaders. In the late afternoon the Kop at Anfield was mute, and aghast. A miracle had occured, the home team having lost to Wolves by 5-1. Westcott scored all his team's goals except one which was contributed by Mullen. A week later, at Molineux, Westcott scored four more goals, against Bolton. On December 21 he would, no doubt, have scored four more if he had not "missed the train through traffic difficulties", and had arrived at Stamford Bridge without him, however, Wolves beat Chelsea, 2-1.

As had been anticipated gates were high. In the first 17 League matches of the season Wolves attracted crowds amounting to 630,000; of these 373,500 attended nine home fixtures—an average gate, therefore, of 41,000.

As 1947 came in Wolves were, not for the first, nor for the last time, described as 'the hottest Cup favourites for years'. But that story was soon over. After an easy win over Rotherham in the third round they went out, in a replay to Sheffield United, at Sheffield. On March 1, however, despite this setback, and the chagrin of surrendering a seasonal total of four points to Brentford at Griffin Park, Wolves were still at the head of the Division. Foul weather caused the cancellation of numerous matches this year and by the end of March Wolves were four games behind most other teams. (It was an uncertain period in other respects, for—as after the first war—players were claiming for better conditions and higher wages. This time there being more organization, there was even threat of a strike unless, said the Players' Union, the Ministry of Labour promised arbitration. As a consequence of the intervention of the National Arbitration Tribunal there was some improvement in wages and a joint standing committee was set up.

On March 29 the leading places in the Championship were thus occupied:

	P.	W.	L.	D.	F.	A.	Pts.
Wolves	32	21	7	4	72	36	46
Blackpool	36	20	12	4	65	61	44
Liverpool	32	18	9	5	67	44	41

(F. and A. columns under heading "Goals")

One would have taken it as certain at that point that the Championship would, for the first time, come to Wolverhampton. The large number of goals scored was primarily due to Westcott, whose thrustful play brought him on the frontiers at least of the England team—from which he was kept by the greater footballing talent of Lawton. On May 10 Westcott scored his thirty-seventh League goal, which took him past Phillipson's record of twenty years before.

At the crucial point of the season—which was long-drawn-out on account of the earlier postponements and also of the Government's refusal to sanction midweek fixtures during a continuing time of 'national emergency'—Westcott was injured. This misfortune occured on May 17 against Blackburn Rovers, to whom he was transferred soon afterwards. Later he played for Manchester City, Chesterfield and Stafford Rangers.

On May 13 whether or not Wolves won the Championship depended on their last match, at home, against Liverpool. It was a poignant occasion. Before the match it was announced that this was to be Stanley Cullis's last match; but that he should lead his club to its first Championship success was the fervent hope of every supporter present. Throughout the season, he had guided his side with uncanny judgement. The value of his play is directly reflected in the low tally of goals scored against the Wolves. But this is but an indifferent monument to one whose genius allowed him the luxury of economizing movement; so astute was his eye for the next pattern but one of his opponents' play that he was ever in the right place at the right time—which, in another context, is the true definition of style. It seemed that he was magnetic; that he attracted the opposing attack to him, where it foundered on the certain and immaculately timed tackle, and whence, with a short push forward, a counter-attack was launched.

On that brilliant day of summer it seemed that the issue was beyond question. So much so that a special edition of the evening newspaper, pink giving way to the ceremonial 'gold' employed for festive occasions, was printed: all but the space reserved for the account of the match. Yet before half-time Liverpool were two goals ahead, the one by Balmer from a pass from the enduring Liddle, the other—a break-away goal such has often shaken the Molineux complacency—by centre-forward Stubbins. A second-half goal by Jimmy Dunn brought the best out of Wolves towards the end of the match; but Sidlow—who still trained at Molineux—was unbeatable.

That match, like others of similar importance, was below standard, for the Wolves players appeared over-anxious and so were not at the peak of form. Nevertheless the *Liverpool Echo*, echoing and answering the criticisms of the immediate pre-war period, paid a handsome tribute:

> There was a time when the name of the Wolves at football was linked up with a suggestion that they could rough it with the best. Liverpool do not subscribe to this: in the latest epoch-making game both sides revelled in sportsmanship and the manner in which Wolves took their severe blow was most praiseworthy.

Although Wolves were out of the reckoning, and Liverpool had finished their programme, there was still a chance that they might be beaten out of first place, if Stoke City could win their remaining match against Sheffield United at Bramall Lane. They could not, which left them in fourth position behind Liverpool, Manchester United, and Wolves, whose records were:

	P.	W.	L.	D.	Goals F.	Goals A.	Pts.
Liverpool	42	25	10	7	84	52	57
Manchester U.	42	22	8	12	95	54	56
Wolves	42	25	11	6	98	56	56

By comparing these figures with those of March 29 it will be seen that the defence conceded in the last part of the season more goals than it should have done. In that season more than a million spectators watched the home matches at Molineux—a tribute to daring, colourful, stylish play.

In the 1947-8 season Wolves, for whom Brice from Luton, Shorthouse, a native of the Black Country, and Smyth, formerly an Irish Amateur International with Linfield, made their first appearances, once again failed to match the expectations of their most critical supporters. Once again they resigned interest in the F.A. Cup after a replay, with Everton, in the fourth round, and the final League placing was fifth. Good enough one would have thought; but not for Molineux. Reputation had bred responsibility. It was, as Mr. Vizard had said at the beginning of the season on August 23, 1947: 'It appears we have taken over the Arsenal's position regarding popularity for pulling in the crowds, and we mean to keep it that way'.

The retirement of Cullis had made two vacancies in the team, at captain and at centre-half. Wright, experienced beyond his twenty-three years and by now well seasoned in the international sphere, took over the captaincy. At centre-half it was less easy. Brice and Chatham had appeared the most likely candidates, but in the end it was Shorthouse who came to fill the berth, and the most settled combination of the season was Williams; McLean, Pritchard; Crook, Shorthouse, Wright; Hancocks, Dunn, Forbes, Smyth, Mullen.

Behind the scenes, however, was still the presence of Cullis, who having retired as a player, was still at Molineux as assistant manager. Some foreshadowing of his quality in the new role was shown in the progress of the Central League team, which rose to third place in the Central League.

12

Rise and Fall

> 'Wolves are the best English team in Vienna since the war'
> Kurt Schmied, August 15, 1954.
>
> 'Leccio teorica de futhol de los Ingles.'[1]
> Spanish newspaper after Wolves visit to Valencia,
> March 19, 1957.

IN 1948 Wolverhampton celebrated the centenary of its incorporation as a borough. All the junketings and fanfares over, the citizens settled down to begin to implement the hopes for the future that had been expressed with piety and through poetry. By accident rather than design the Wolves, a venerable institution, (within the limits of the hundred years under consideration) also took stock of future prospects; for a new era opened under a new ruler.

During the early part of the summer the team were abroad, in Holland and France—the first English side, indeed, to play in Holland (with which country Wolverhampton had had close war-time associations). On their return Vizard (whose death on December 26, 1973 passed almost unnoticed) resigned. His decision, based so it was reported, on a disagreement with the directors 'over policy', was made public on June 12. Eleven days later the Chairman, J. S. Baker, announced that the new manager would be Stanley Cullis. To enable him to devote his full attention to technical matters Jack Howley was promoted secretary. Arrived at Molineux as a junior in the office in the summer of 1923, Jack stayed there for the rest of his working life and until the arrival of Bill McGarry as Manager at the end of 1968. He was for twenty years Secretary, with which for the last five he combined the title of General Manager. Jack died on 23 March, 1971.

Cullis inherited a good side. He made it into a great side. Bred up in the tradition of the club he revivified that tradition. The outstanding centre-half of his own generation, he imbued his players with something of his own style.

---

[1] 'A demonstration of the theory of football by the English'.

Tenacity and courage blended with shrewdness and perception, loyalty with ambition, individual talent with a conspicuous devotion to the welfare of the team: these became a latter-day quality of the Wolves, which may be seen to have blossomed from the seeds sown in the 1870's and tended by a sequence of directors for whom the football team was the focal point of personal and civic pride.

Within six years Wolves were to win the major national prizes of the game. Over a longer stretch the tally of success included two successful Cup Finals (1949 and 1960) and three League Championships (1954, 1958, 1959). Not only this, they were to uphold the prestige of English football in a sequence of remarkable encounters with foreign rivals.

At the end of his first year of management Cullis justified his appointment in that, after a lapse of forty years, the F.A. Cup again came to Molineux. As oftens happens the winning of the Cup depends less on the Final itself than on some antecedent round. In that year of 1949 Wolves established their right to the trophy by beating Manchester United in the replayed semi-final at Goodison Park; or, perhaps, rather more truthfully by holding the United to a draw in the first match at Hillsborough. That match was maintained by nine fit players. After six minutes the left-back Pritchard was severely injured and compelled to wander thereafter on the left-wing. At a later stage the other back, Kelly, was taken off the field on a stretcher. And Pye, the centre-forward, was barely recovered from a recent bout of influenza. When the replay came Cullis was harassed by the injuries to his full-backs and forced to bring back Springthorpe, who had not played in the first team since the previous September, and Alf Crook, elder brother of the right-half, who had hitherto risen no higher than the reserves.

Nor was it an easy road to the semi-final. The opposition comprised Chesterfield, Sheffield United, Liverpool, and West Bromwich Albion. For the Liverpool match, played in the week in which the famous Merseyside administrator, W. C. Cuff, President of the Football League, died, the gate was 54,983, the receipts £5,922. An even larger crowd—of 55,684, paying £6,362, was present a fortnight later, on February 26, for the Albion match. Previously Wolves had played Albion five times in cup matches, losing every time. This occasion differed from the others by the goal scored by the immaculate Mullen almost exactly after one hour's play. Until the replayed semi-final these were the players who represented Wolves:

> Williams; Kelly, Pritchard; Crook (W), Shorthouse, Wright; Hancocks, Smyth, Pye, Dunn, Mullen.

Williams, Hancocks, Smyth, and Pye were of the brief Vizard generation, having been signed by him.

In the early part of the season Smyth played at inside-left, and Dunn at inside-right. On January 1 Cullis, whose tactical conferences embraced the views of his trainers—Jack Davies, Jack Nelson, and Joe Gardiner—switched his inside-forwards so that the faster Dunn could pair with the electric Mullen, the slower but imaginative Irishman with the incalculable Hancocks.

As before, a Cup Final roused the whole Black Country to a high pitch of emotion. That the spirit of folk-song and ballad still lived on was shown by the publication of a number of lively effusions conspicuous for enthusiasm rather than for discretion of artistic sensibility, and properly wrapped in anonymity. A supporter from Sedgeley directed that

> Team of hope and glory
> Up to win the Cup:
> See them kick for victory
> Beating opponents up . . .

should be sung to the tune of 'Land of Hope and Glory', while a 'Wolverhampton Housewife' provided for the tune of the wartime favourite, 'Roll Out the Barrel':

> We're off to Wembley
> To give the Wolves a good cheer,
> We're off to Wembley
> We've got the team of the year!
> Play up the Wanderers
> You're on the up and up!
> So give the Wolves a cheer at Wembley
> And see them win the Cup!

Quick tackling, penetrating wing play, industrious and clever work by the inside-forwards, and the commanding presence of Wright, proved more than adequate for the Second Division opposition from Leicester City. Wolves were two goals up at half-time, and although Mel Griffiths, the Welsh international, scored for Leicester early in the second half, a final, brilliant goal by Smyth left the final margin a fair reflection of undisputed superiority.

The teams were:

Wolves: Williams; Pritchard, Springthorpe; Crook (W), Shorthouse,

Wright; Hancocks, Smyth, Pye, Dunn, Mullen.

Leicester City: Bradley; Jolly, Scott; Harrison (W), Plummer, King; Griffiths, Lee, Harrison (J), Chisholm, Adam.

In the League, Wolves did well enough, finishing sixth.

In the following year Wolves went to the fifth round of the Cup, and came again within a hairsbreadth of winning the elusive League Championship. The season had started with a phenomenal burst of success. Twelve matches went without defeat. But between October 8 and December 26 no victory was registered, partly, perhaps, because Wright and Williams were injured in the international match with Wales on October 15, and Dunn shortly afterwards, but more particularly because no one could be found satisfactorily to fill the centre-forward position. At one stage during the season Angus McLean, an energetic full-back, was tried in that situation. The last third of the season, however, was more rewarding and the Championship became a distinct possibility. But eventually it was surrendered to Portsmouth—on goal average. The final figures showed:

	P	W	L	D	Goals F	A	Pts.
Portsmouth	42	22	11	9	74	38	53
Wolves	42	20	9	13	76	49	53

During the season Chatham established himself as a neat and resourceful centre-half and Shorthouse dropped back to fill the left-back position with great distinction. Among the new players one began particularly to notice young Swinbourne, a centre-forward of uncommon grace and precision, tutored by Mark Crook at the Yorkshire 'nursery club', Wath Wanderers. His promise was terminated by intractable injury some five years later. The esteem in which Wolves were held by the higher authorities was reflected in the selection of six players from the club twice to accompany F.A. sides on overseas tours. From 1949 until his international days ended Wright was captain of England and at various times of the 1949 side had as colleagues in the national team Hancocks, Mullen, Pye, and Williams; while Sammy Smyth had played for Northern Ireland eight times.

Riding thus on the crest of the wave it was, then, a shock to come across two fallow seasons, during which the League record was hardly better than the doubtful years of the early 1930's. In the 1950-1 season the final placing was fourteenth, accounted for by a dismal run-in when seventeen games brought thirteen defeats and two draws. This was in part due to exertions in the F.A. Cup when Wolves went to the semi-final, to be beaten by the eventual Cup-winners. On the way they had battled resolutely with a fine Sunderland side, in which Shackleton and Ford were at their best, defeating them 3-1 in a replay in the sixth round. The semi-final also needed a replay. After a goal-less draw at Hillsborough Newcastle United won the replay at Huddersfield by the narrow margin of 2-1.

There were, however, portents for the future. In February, 1951, Peter Broadbent was signed from Brentford, and towards the season's end he showed the quality of his footwork in no uncertain manner. And the reserves won the Championship of the Central League for the second time.

A year later the reserves—among whom Norman Deeley, an erstwhile half-back, was marauding to some effect on the right-wing—won the Central League again. But the first team, deprived for some time of Dunn and Williams by injury and handicapped by Swinbourne's relatively indifferent performances, went down to sixteenth. Smyth, whose talent was spasmodic, was transferred to Stoke City. On the national level, however, the reputaution of Wolves was sustained by Wright, who was elected 'Footballer of the Year'.

The genuine supporters of football are those whose interest lies deeper than the spectacular. For them, in 1952-3, there was much happening at Molineux to inspire fervour. Once again the Central League team were carrying all before them to capture the Championship for the third time in succession. On October 3, 1953, after a celebratory luncheon given by the Central League, there was a match between Wolves Reserves and the Rest of the League which was won by Wolves 3-2. The match drew an appreciative crowd of 9,442. Those were the days, it might be thought!

And then there was the youth team, in which could be found such notabilities of the future as Eddie Clamp and Colin Booth. The policy of Cullis was to allow the young player time to mature, and teenagers were not hurled into the rigours of the First Division as had been the case with Buckley. In 1953 the Wolves youth team reached the first Final of the F.A. Youth Cup, to be defeated, however, by that of Manchester United on an aggregate on two legs of 8-4.

Meanwhile the senior team made up leeway. Taylor came from Luton in exchange for Pye, and Slater, formerly a Cup Finalist with Blackpool and a member of the Olympic Games team in Finland, signed amateur forms. Flowers and Stockin made occasional appearances and Sims took William's place in nine games. The forward line was not yet adequately balanced, the inside-forwards particularly being to frequently incoherent. But Wilshaw's conversion to inside-left added penetrative power and his 17 goals in 29 matches were a true reward for a striking capacity for seizing opportunity.

The class of Slater stood out, for here was a complete footballer, even if as yet somewhat deliberate in manner. 'Slater,' wrote the leading local critic, 'has probably made a bigger impression on a Wolves crowd than any newcomer for seasons' Sims (who subsequently served Aston Villa with notable success) looked Williams's natural successor; for Williams, out of sorts and form would appear to have ended his career. His fight back from injury and from depression was, however, a striking episode in his career, and he was able to complete his service with the club in due course on a high note.

Changes in the Wolves team under Cullis's direction were gradual; almost imperceptible. The principal players of the 1953-4 season were Williams, Short, Stuart, Pritchard, Slater, Flowers, Shorthouse, Wright, Hancocks, Broadbent, Swinbourne, Wilshaw, Mullen; of whom Williams, Pritchard, Shorthouse, Wright, Hancocks and Mullen were veterans of the Cup Final side of 1949.

In 1954 Wolves laid several bogies. They enjoyed their first win at Newcastle for fifty years, at the Hawthorns for nineteen years, and—best of all—at Highbury for twenty-one years. This latter match was remarkable in that the winning goal, two minutes from full time, was headed in by Hancocks, who in that respect was considered a total abstainer. The season started triumphantly with a long run, from August 28 to December 12, without defeat. Broadbent came into the side after three matches, displacing Stockin, who eventually joined Cardiff City, and giving displays of football skill that were exceptional. Moreover the forwards were in accurate, as well as militant, mood. Wilshaw, Hancocks, and Swinbourne all scored hat-tricks. The wingers collected 31 goals between them, and the three inside-forwards 63.

It was a season in which adventurous play, prompted by a mobile, offensive, quick-recovering defence, was the order of the day at Molineux. And Hancocks and Mullen were at their best. 'Probably no two wingers are closer in touch with the other during a game than Hancocks and Mullen; their wing to wing movements, combined with a long diagonal passes that quickly change the point of attack, have throughout constituted a dangerous threat to opponents . . .'[1]

It was thus that the Football League Championship came to Wolverhampton for the first time. 'They have', it was written in 1904, 'never won the League Championship and they never expect to win it'.[2] It took fifty years to controvert the prophecy—fifty years of effort, patience, and determination. And once again the most junior team reached the Final of the Youth Cup, to be defeated once more by Manchester United by the closest of

[1] *F.A. Year Book*, 1954-5, P.51.
[2] A. Gibson and W. Pickford, *Association Football*, Vol. II, p.93.

margins (4-4; 0-1). At Manchester this was watched by 18,000, at Molineux by 28,000 spectators.

In the following season, during which Wolves went to the sixth round of the Cup, the Championship was handed over to Chelsea. Appropriately enough the match that virtually decided the issue was that between the two teams at Stamford Bridge. Three-quarters of an hour before the kick-off the gates had been closed; 75,000 people packed the ground and many thousands more were excluded. One of the most thrilling matches ever seen at Stamford Bridge ended with Chelsea victors—by a penalty goal. A quarter of an hour from the end Seamus O'Connell drove hard and high for the goal. Williams, whose earlier performance in the game 'was stamped world-class',[1] was out of range; but Wright, ever ready to cover any gap, was not. He leapt to the ball and by a reflex action made yet another save of world-class. Alas! he was not the goalkeeper. So quick was the action that the referee at first awarded a corner, only reversing his decision after an agitated case had been presented by the Chelsea players and supported by the linesman. Sillett scored. Even so Wolves were still menacing, and Hancocks, now at centre-forward for the injured Swinbourne, twice brought Chelsea hearts near to failure.

During this season Wright was moved to centre-half, and Shorthouse to left-back. Slater played for England against Wales and Germany. Flowers played in the England 'B' team, and then won a full cap on the Continental tour against France, while Wilshaw playing against Scotland at Wembley set up a record by scoring 4 goals in a 7-2 win.

If Shorthouse had not been injured on March 12 at Sunderland . . . About such 'ifs' debate is eternal, and generally inconclusive. But at the end of 1955 the injury that ended Swinbourne's career almost certainly destroyed the team's Championship hopes that season; for at the beginning Swinbourne was in scintillating form, with 17 goals in 12 games, and after his retirement the old question of suitability at centre-forward recurred. Jimmy Murray came into the team, and showing promise of future dependability, scored ten goals. The most popular goals scored at Molineux that season, however, was by Shorthouse against Charlton, shortly before his translation to a coaching post on the Wolves staff.

Finishing third in the League, Wolves qualified for talent money for the sixth time since the war.

A young man whose signature many managers were anxious for at that time was Harry Hooper, son of the old Sheffield United player, who had often stopped the Wolves of yesteryear. As outside-right for West Ham, Harry was

[1] Albert Sewell, *Chelsea, Champions!*, 1955, p.126.

above the class in which he was playing. He came to Wolves at the end of the 1955-6 season and represented the club's largest investment to date—in the region of £20,000. Never quite settling down he proved the wisdom of the club's normal practice; after a somewhat frustrating year he lost his place to the home-grown Norman Deeley and went to Birmingham City.

That season of 1956-7 was a transitional period. The centre-forward position was shared between Wilshaw (soon to go to Stoke City), Bonson (who joined Cardiff City), and Murray. It was, as has already been stated, Swinbourne's last season; also Shorthouse's. Williams, at the peak of form, wisely decided to leave the game at that stage. Swinbourne had played in 211 League and 18 Cup games; Shorthouse in 344 and 30; and Williams in 381 and 34. Cup-ties were not to be mentioned for some time after January 26, 1957, for on that day Bournemouth came to Molineux to win the fourth round match by 1-0. During the game, at the thought of such improbable *denouément,* one of the goal-posts collapsed.

One looks back to a period in which many of the tensions that have dominated modern football had not made themselves evident. For better or for worse—and mostly it seemed for better—the paternalist system (as it would now be described) worked. There really was a family feeling and an interlude of tranquillity. At the beginning of the 1950 season no fewer than twelve players—Baxter, Chatham, Crook, Dunn, Kelly, McLean, Parsons, Pritchard, Shorthouse, Smith, Springthorpe, and Williams—were given maximum benefits of £750 each. They were not all regular first-team men. Five years later Williams, Shorthouse, and Smith (later transferred to Aston Villa) received benefits, thus joining similar beneficiaries in Mullen and Wright. In 1952-3 Stuart, only lately joined the club from South Africa, was seriously ill. The infection from which he suffered, and which put his life in jeopardy, defied diagnosis by numerous doctors. The directors spared no expense in referring the case to the most eminent authorities, nor in bringing the player's mother to England from South Africa. In the 'human relationship' side of the football industry, Wolves have had considerable cause for quiet satisfaction.

During the first years of Cullis's management two developments should be noted; the one of importance primarily to the players, the other to the spectators. In 1952-3 a new practice ground was acquired in more or less rural surroundings at Castlecroft, some two miles from Molineux.

The other major development, of course, was the installation of floodlights at Molineux. These first appeared in 1953. The floodlights—all 60 lamps—were said to have been designed after the pattern used in the Yankee Stadium, New York. "I hope," observed Billy Wright, "we shall enjoy the

S. Smyth in action, Cup Final 1949.

B. F. Williams with T. Phillipson.

WOLVERHAMPTON WANDERERS. F.C.   F.A. CUP WINNERS 1949

W. Crook   R. Pritchard   B. Williams   N. Shorthouse   T. Springthorpe
J. Hancocks   S. Smyth   S. Cullis (Manager)   W. Wright (Captain)   J. Pye   J. Dunn   J. Mullen

The Wolves, 1949 and 1951.

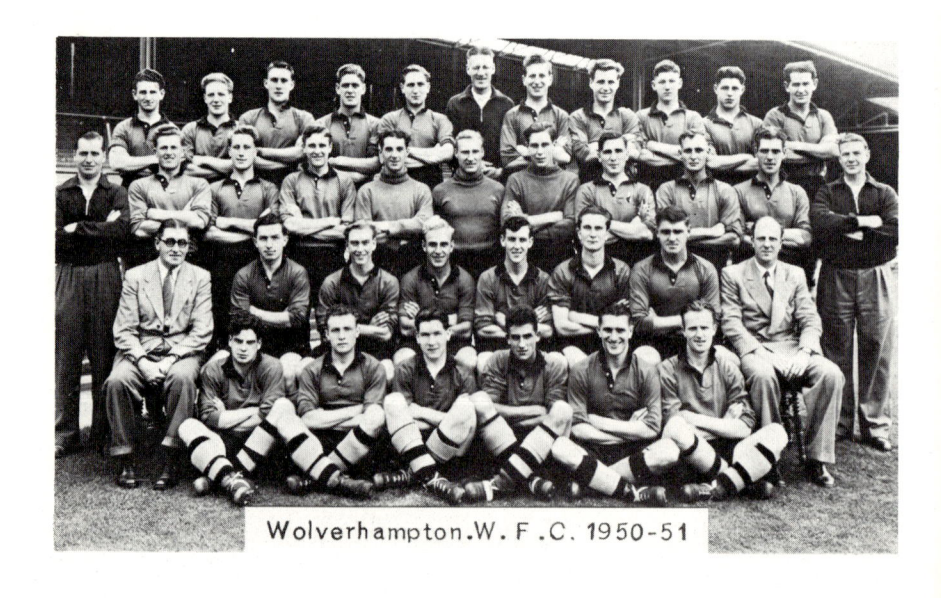

Wolverhampton.W.F.C. 1950-51

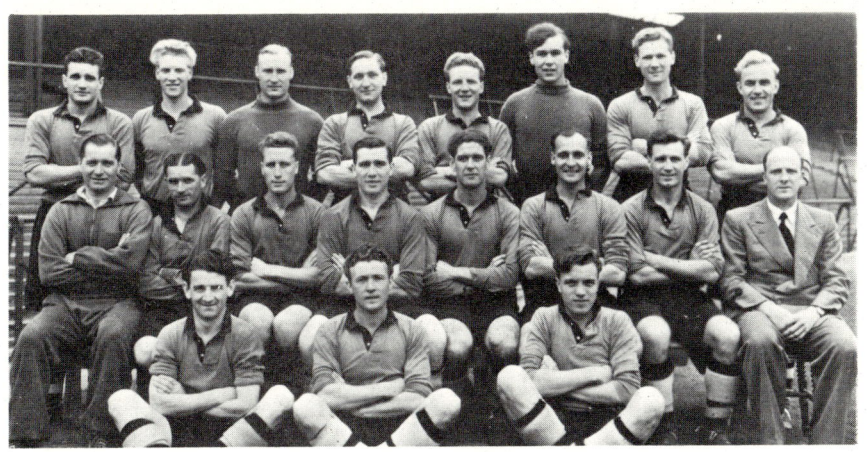

Football League Division 1. WOLVERHAMPTON WANDERERS, F.C. 1953-4
J. Taylor R. Flowers B. Williams R. Chatham L. Gibbons N. Sims W. J. Slater W. Wright
J. Gardiner J. Hancocks R. Swinbourne W. Shorthouse J. Short D. Wilshaw J. Mullen
(Trainer)   Manager S. Cullis
R. Pritchard L. Smith R. Stockin

The Wolves 1954.

v Spartak, Moscow 1955.

Voraussichtliche Aufstellungen

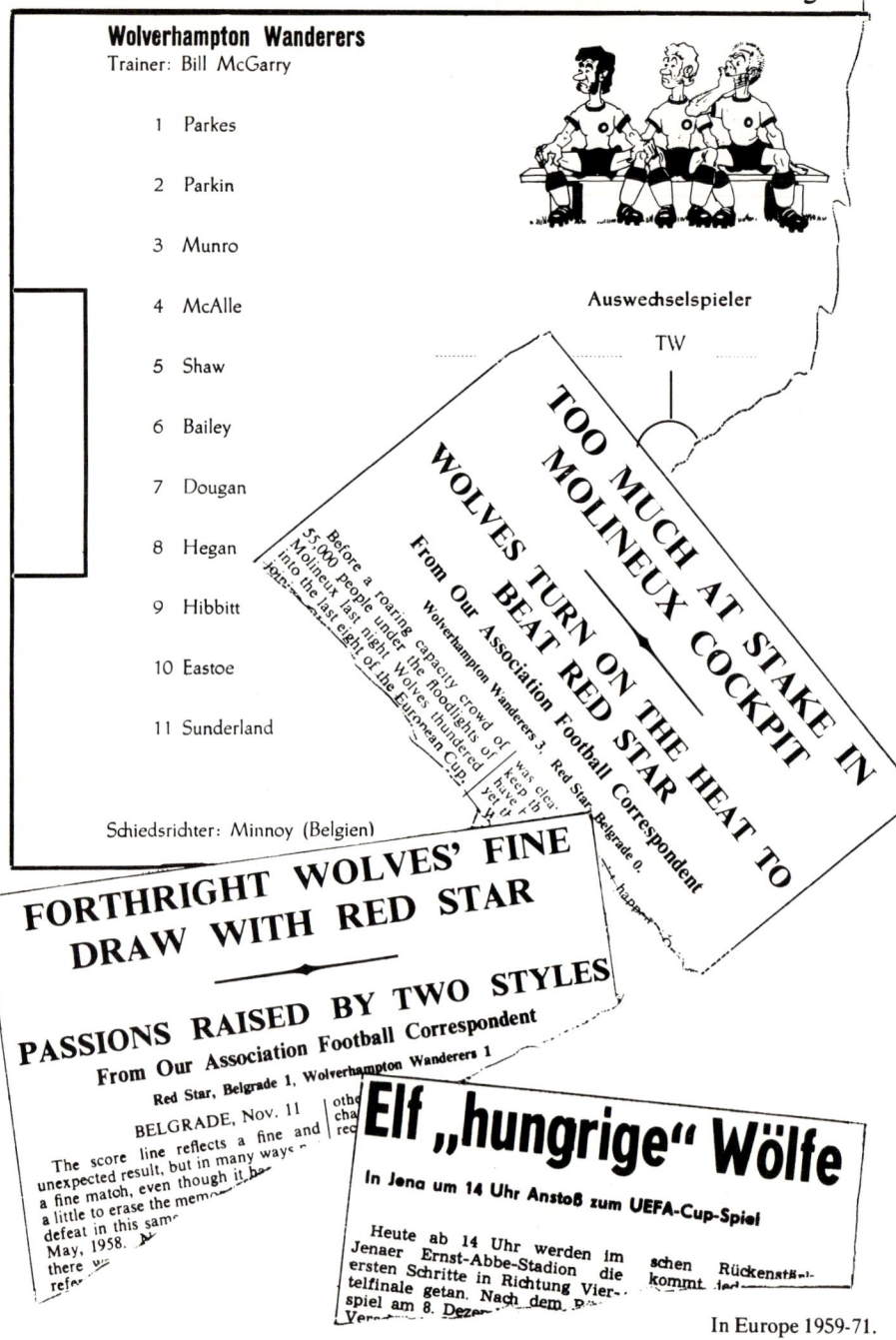

Wolverhampton Wanderers
Trainer: Bill McGarry

1 Parkes

2 Parkin

3 Munro

4 McAlle

5 Shaw

6 Bailey

7 Dougan

8 Hegan

9 Hibbitt

10 Eastoe

11 Sunderland

Auswechselspieler

TW

Schiedsrichter: Minnoy (Belgien)

TOO MUCH AT STAKE IN MOLINEUX COCKPIT
WOLVES TURN ON THE HEAT TO BEAT RED STAR
From Our Association Football Correspondent

Before a roaring capacity crowd of 55,000 people under the floodlights of Molineux last night the Wolves thundered into the last eight of the European Cup.

FORTHRIGHT WOLVES' FINE DRAW WITH RED STAR
PASSIONS RAISED BY TWO STYLES
From Our Association Football Correspondent
Red Star, Belgrade 1, Wolverhampton Wanderers 1

BELGRADE, Nov. 11

The score line reflects a fine and unexpected result, but in many ways a fine match, even though it ha a little to erase the mem defeat in this sam May, 1958.

Elf „hungrige" Wölfe
In Jena um 14 Uhr Anstoß zum UEFA-Cup-Spiel

Heute ab 14 Uhr werden im Jenaer Ernst-Abbe-Stadion die ersten Schritte in Richtung Viertelfinale getan. Nach dem spiel am 8. Deze

In Europe 1959-71.

new style football." On September 30 the visit of a team from South Africa enabled the players to test the lights albeit at rather less than full strength. Wolves won 3-1. Their first thorough experience under lights was on October 7, at Bury, when the match was prefaced by a male voice choir and a brass band. A week later there was a match on at Molineux, against Glasgow Celtic, in which two artistic goals by Wilshaw ensured a comfortable 2-0 win. The *Express and Star* commented "... the football club realise that they are now in the pure entertainment business in a big way." Four years later new lights were installed at a cost of £25,000, the old ones being acquired by Blackpool. Set on four pylons, rising 146 feet above the pitch, their propriety was debated at the time and a minority of aesthetically minded councillors wondered what their effect on the skyline would be. However that may be, those lights illuminated some of the more historic occasions of modern football; and whatever the future may bring it was the pioneering of Wolves that helped to put English club football on a broad international canvas. In many of the early floodlit matches against foreign teams gates of 50,000 were the rule rather than the exception.

In 1893 the reputation of Wolves was recognised in France. A little more than sixty years later the fame of the club was world-wide. In 1950 there was an American baseball team in Harrisburg, Pennsylvania, called the Wolverhampton Baseball Club; an admiring gesture by some transatlantic supporter of obviously bipartisan tendencies. In Hobart, Tasmania, the most eminent football club, founded by an emigrant Wulfrunian, bore the title of the Wanderers F.C. Visitors to Molineux may see a flag presented by the South African F.A. at the end of the tour of that country in 1951, when Wolves won all twelve matches played and scored 60 goals against 5. On August 1, 1953, a party of U.S. sailors, in port at Leith, insisted on devoting their shore leave to attendance at the Wolves match at Easter Road, Edinburgh, against a combined Hearts and Hibernians side. That same year photographs of Wolves were published for the better instruction of the American people in the magazine *Life*. In 1954 a request to the club for a picture of the victorious League side came from another unexpected quarter; from an inmate of H.M. Prison at Parkhurst in the Isle of Wight.

On October 13 1954 First Vienna played a goal-less draw at Molineux, to balance a summer fixture in Vienna in honour of the sixtieth anniversary of the Austrian club, after which the Austrian goalkeeper had remarked that 'Wolves are the best English team seen in Vienna since the war'. After First Vienna on October 28 came the Israel champions Maccabi, who tumbled to catastrophe in a 10-0 defeat. On November 15—against which fixture Wolves trained on a Sunday (November 14) for the first time for seventy-seven years—the Muscovite team Spartak. In a brilliant finish—for there were no first-half goals—Wolves submerged the Russians by 4-0, Hancocks scoring two goals, and Wilshaw and Swinbourne one each. On December 13 Honved came from Hungary. Among the Honved forwards were Kocsis, Puskas, and Czibor, three of the finest players in the world. At half-time the Hungarians were leading by 2-0. A penalty for a foul on Hancocks was taken by Hancocks himself (a 'penalty king' if ever there was one) to reduce the deficit. With Puskas and Kocsis now reduced to relative impotence by the fleetness of Slater and Flowers, with all the half-backs playing as auxiliary forwards and each, therefore, doing the work of two men, Wolves attacked remorselessly. Swinbourne scored two goals. The *Daily Mail* hailed Wolves as 'Champions of the World' and *Punch* noted the occasion in a parody of an unusually ecstatic report by *The Times*. In the summer of 1955 Wolves visited Russia. The consequence of this was the invitation to Molineux of Dynamo—who had won a narrow victory in Moscow. On November 9 they came—and went the same way as all previous invaders, having lost—by 2-1. Thereafter the Rumanian Army team from Bucharest, beaten 5-0 on October 29, 1956 Red Banner from Budapest, on December 12 of that year (1-1) the German team Borussia Dortmund, on March 27, 1957 (Wolves winning by 4-3) Valencia on April 10 (3-0 to Wolves) ... and Real Madrid, the best foreign team, it was said, so far to have visited Molineux. Without Wright—with the England team—and with Stuart as captain the Wolves again turned a half-time deficit into victory, by indefatigable tackling, by the characteristic long-flung pass, and by a directness of approach that showed the Spaniards the virtues of 'traditional English football'. The winning goal, after previous goals from Broadbent and Murray, was scored by Wilshaw, perhaps at his best against Continental opposition, from a pass by Mullen. That was on October 17, 1957—a red-letter day in the Molineux calendar.

At the beginning of July, 1955, James Evans resigned his directorship after 21 years' service. His place was taken by John Ireland, and old Grammar School boy. A well-known amateur footballer and a qualified referee, with considerable business experience and at one time a town councillor, Ireland appeared well qualified to undertake duties which were to absorb his interest more and more over the next two decades. In that year A. H. Oakley added to his other honours in the game a Vice-Presidency of the Football Association, and Miss D. St. C. Mander, a doughty member of the famous family of that name and the keenest of Wolves' supporters travelled to Moscow to see the team play. When she had last been there the Czars still reigned.

On September 27, 1956, the Castlecroft ground, with its own stand and lights, was opened by Sir Stanley Rous, Secretary of the F.A., who was also present at a presentation dinner that night in honour of A. H. Oakley.

In those days it seemed that the good times could never end. For four years running Wolves scored more than 100 goals a season, and for some time the half-back line could count on four English International players being available. In the World Cup team of 1958 Clamp, Wright, and Slater were the middle strength for the match against the Soviet Union, while Ron Flowers, already capped in 1956, was waiting to take the mantle from Wright.

It is always best for his place in posterity that an actor should leave the stage at the zenith of his powers—and also to leave it decisively. Wolves won the Championship in 1959 under the captaincy of Wright. The team for the last match of the season against Everton, at Goodison Park, was:

Finlayson; Stuart, Harris; Slater, Showell, Flowers; Lill, Booth, Murray, Broadbent, Deeley.

On this occasion Clamp and Wright were absent from their customary places in the half-back line. In honour of the team's achievement there was a Civic Banquet, attended by Sir Stanley Rous as Secretary of the F.A. at the time, and other notabilities. One poignant memory is of Joe Mercer, then manager of Aston Villa, learning during the course of the evening's celebration of his own team's relegation through defeat by West Bromwich Albion.

One of the most dedicated of professionals, uncannily skilled in the finer techniques of football strategy, and predominantly the embodiment of "fair play", Wright won 105 international caps.[1] Then, characteristically, he passed into legend when none was looking. On August 8, 1959, he played in a practice match, which among practice matches has the unique distinction of having received coverage on a BBC news bulletin on the previous evening.

After the departure of Wright the curtain went up on the last Act of a drama within a drama. The Cullis era was quite *sui generis*. Nothing that had happened before—even in the age of Buckley—was quite comparable, because Cullis as a football manager was cast in a classical heroic mould. The rise and fall of this man was positively Aristotelean. The beginning of the end came in 1959-60. Runners-up in the League and winners of the F.A. Cup (against a depleted Blackburn side memorable for the presence in it of a young player named Dougan), were denied the "double" by the narrowest of

---

[1] A record only surpassed by Bobby Charlton (106 caps) in 1970, but Charlton's career covered an era when more international matches were played.

margins. On April 30, after winning 5-1 against Chelsea, at Stamford Bridge, the top of the table read:

	P	W	D	L	F	A	Points
Wolves	42	24	6	12	106	67	54
Tottenham	42	21	11	10	86	50	53
Burnley	41	23	7	11	82	60	53

Before the Final, however, Burnley had won the match which made them champions. The Wolves team for Wembley was:

> Finlayson; Showell, Harris; Clamp, Slater (Capt.); Flowers; Deeley, Stobart, Murray, Broadbent, Horne.

It was not long after that Wolves ran into disaster in Spain. After defeating Berlin Vorwaerts and Red Star, Belgrade, in earlier rounds of the European Cup, Wolves went to Barcelona to lose 0-4. The return match was hardly less humbling, the final score being 2-5. By this time the geography of the game had altered. An English club (as Wolves had presciently indicated in their earlier, free enterprise, encounters with the continental powers) in modern times is nothing if it is only an English club.

Within two years Wolves were struggling, with a team now strangely deficient in household names. Flowers was a tower of strength and was to remain such across the lean years to come, and until a fairer climate was reached. But Murray, deft and opportunist, and prolific when injury-free, suffered a gradual *decrescendo* as a goal-scorer, and Broadbent, a distinguished ball player, gave infinite pleasure by his displays but was too seldom given adequate support. Other players having passed their peak went elsewhere, and those who replaced them frequently did not fill the bill. A team, after all, is a team, and not a collection of players uncertain of their relationship with each other and with the management.

At the end of the 1961-2 season relegation was avoided by four points, and there was a flutter of hope the next year. In the first match of the season—Flowers's first as captain—almost every shot at goal became a goal. The score against Manchester City—whose team included the great German goalkeeper, Trautmann, and David Wagstaffe—won 8-1. Four of the goals came from Ted Farmer, at centre-forward. But is was Alan Hinton (whose career reached its climax some seasons later at Derby) whose meteoric rise caught the eye. He scored 19 goals that year, and at Wolves—after the opening extravaganza—twice scored seven goals and finished respectably in the league, it seemed that an awkward corner had been negotiated. On the other hand there was a residual quantum of depression in the inability of the club to win more than one cup-tie in four seasons. On July 29, 1964, John Ireland took over as Chairman of the club.

September brought about a dramatic situation in which separate anxieties caused the kind of conflict in an organisation that arises when those who reluctantly come to be seen as contesting parties are guilty only of caring too much. Statistically, Wolves gained one point from the first seven matches. But within this detail lay the fact that Stanley Cullis was ill. For 30 years he had driven himself, his players, and his friends by an intense, consuming passion for the ideals (not all within football) in which he believed. At this point he went.

History is strewn with the names of such men—and some women—as a warning to some and an inspiration to others. The epitaph on Cullis as the centrifugal force at Molineux for a considerable part of the club's first hundred years is contained in a phrase of John Arlott: "Stanley Cullis is that strange contradiction, a passionate puritan".[1] That phrase incorporates the notion that times had changed—of which the developing career—and status-consciousness of the footballer is the main evidence. Cullis, 30 years at Molineux, had gone through a whole generation.

[1] "This Passionate Puritan", *The Observer*, May 1, 1960.

13

Interregnum

THE calamities of the autumn of 1964 were quickly passed by. First, the departure of Cullis in September left a legacy of mistrust, as well as a vacant chair which proved difficult to fill. The insecurities of the profession of football management are notorious, and Molineux at that time did not appear as a safe haven. A compromise between having a manager and not having one was arrived at when Andrew Beattie arrived with the unofficial status of "caretaker manager". Beattie, dubbed "the flying doctor", had distinguished himself previously in peripatetic consultancy at Nottingham Forest and Plymouth Argyle. When revealed, the "Beattie plan" boiled down to an anticlimax: it was no more than "an earnest wish that the players should enjoy their football". The period inaugurated in this way was lugubrious in that in attempting to bury the past it seemed that the future also was being interred. This is one of the penalties of a long tradition, that the past and the future go inexorably together. It was at this point that Phil Shaw, who had played amateur football, as assistant to Jack Howley began a long association with the club.

On the field the progress towards disaster begun in the autumn intensified. In eight League matches four or more goals were surrendered and in seven there were three on the debit side. In all 29 players made League appearances during the season, and of these some were palpably birds of passage. Flowers, Gerry Harris, Bobby Thomson and Terry Wharton were most regular, but two other players who were to become prominent were often in the headlines. One was David Wagstaffe, who came from Manchester City on Beattie's recommendation, the other Peter Knowles. The former was to play a distinguished and artistic part in the affairs of the club for a decade, the other to compel attention, first by the skills from which he had too little time to remove the blemishes of impetuosity, second by his renunciation of his profession in favour of a proselytising vocation.

Every relegated club hopes to recover its lost fortunes at once. After losing four of the first six matches of the new season, Wolves seemed to take the task of restoration seriously. Hugh McIlmoyle looked promising; Peter Knowles scored two hat-tricks, but then came disaster at Southampton on September 18, when there was an avalanche of twelve goals—of which the home team claimed nine. Beattie was relieved of his post and Ronnie Allen, former Albion and England player, coach at Molineux for a few months already, became manager. Ernie Hunt was signed, and as there was freedom from defeat until December 4—when the game at Bolton was lost narrowly—it seemed that return to the First Division might yet be achieved. In fact the condition in which the club had found itself at the end of October was more or less consistently held, so that at the season's end the final placing was sixth. But there was a remarkable flow of goals, which left Wolves as the most prolific scorers in the Division. It was during this season, on November 19, that Tom Phillipson, famous player of long ago, and sometime Mayor, died.

The resolution and leadership of Bailey, who joined the club in March 1966, the brilliant flowering of Wagstaffe's artistry, and the integrity of the last performances of Flowers gave a good deal of hope, and as the 1966-67 season marched on it became apparent that Wolves—by Christmas sharing the top of the table with Coventry—were likely to prove better than mere pace-makers. In the spring of 1967 Allen made what turned out to be a master-stroke. He signed Derek Dougan—in common understanding regarded as the man of many clubs, with the explosive temperament that often accompanies genius—from Leicester City. Allen hoped that this accomplished player, albeit seemingly in the evening of his career, could provide the additional thrust needed for the last stretch. Characteristically, Dougan threw himself tumultuously into the front-line operations. In his first match in Wolves colours at Molineux, against Hull City, he scored a hat-trick. None was ever more aware of the necessity for matching gesture to opportunity. The team against Hull was:

Parkes; Taylor, Thomson; Bailey, Woodfield, Holsgrove; Wharton, Hunt, Dougan, Knowles, Wagstaffe.

Of these Taylor and Woodfield, of overlapping periods, deserve mention as among the constants of club football; players whose resolution to do their part remains undiminished by behind-the-scenes efforts in the Central League. Phil Parkes, by now established as a regular first choice goalkeeper, was also to prove himself by loyalty and endeavour in the chapter that was to open with re-entry into the First Division.

Wolves went back as runners-up to Coventry in the Second Division. For

Coventry that represented complete satisfaction. The Championship of the Division was won from old and neighbourly rivals, over whom the double had been achieved. The last match of the season for Wolves was at Crystal Palace and all the old inconsistencies once more revealed themselves, as the team tumbled to defeat by 4-1.

In the summer Wolves, masquerading as "Los Angeles Wolves", played in a North American league thought up by a Canadian millionaire and won that competition. The consequences were remarkable in that the millionaire entrepreneur made a million dollar bid to buy the Wolves with a view to maintaining the club as a winter show in England and a summer entertainment in the United States. After these frivolities the realities again obtruded themselves.

The first season of return ended on a melancholy note, the final placing of 17th more or less recovering the anxious forebodings of four seasons earlier. There was, however, one difference. In the two years prior to relegation the last of the old dispensation was disappearing. In 1967 the process of reconstruction was under way. From that of five years earlier only three names were to be found on the team-sheet: Knowles, Wharton, and Woodfield. Among the newcomers who were to retain secure places in the affections of supporters were Frank Munro, a centre-half from Aberdeen who was to represent his country, and Derek Parkin, a defender from Huddersfield. Both these players were adventurous, inclined at times to prefer imagination to industry and thus to raise unexpected hopes at one end of the field and equally unexpected fears at the other.

This vignette, perhaps, is a not inaccurate summary of the whole record of Wolves when this is reviewed in its enterprising entirety. In what are now recalled as the "great days" there was always excitement, with the disappointments born of excitement also. In the last ten years there has been a continuity of the tradition, with safety not always the first consideration.

In the 1967-68 season Dougan and Knowles could be, and often were, devastating. And Alan Evans appeared as a young player with a golden future—which never materialised. It was, however, an uneasy season. Ernie Hunt's brief career at Molineux ended and he went to Everton—who had beaten Wolves at Goodison Park a short while before—for £80,000, and Ron Flowers, after fifteen years of loyal and distinguished service, went to Northampton Town. Too many goals thrown away generated frustration, which was only partially relieved at the end of the season when Frank Wignall, signed from Nottingham Forest, scoring two goals in a 6-1 defeat of his old club, and when an easy victory over Chelsea ensured survival in the First Division. Survival is not enough, and when the 1968-9 season opened it was not long before sounds of insurrection were in the air.

Matters came to a head on September 28 when Wolves, at home, lost to Liverpool by 6-0. Two goals came from Evans, lately transferred from Wolves for £100,000. In a matter of weeks Ronnie Allen found that he was no longer manager.

Having pulled the club out of the darkness into which it had fallen and, at least, pointed the way towards the light, Allen went with quiet dignity. Behind him he left players who were to become dominant figures in the next phase. Among them were John Richards, Ken Hibbitt, and John McAlle.

On November 25, Bill McGarry, long wanted by the Wolves directorate, came to Molineux, from Ipswich bringing with him his trainer-coach, Sammy Chung.

14

Varied Fortunes

A notable feature of the age in which we live is an unwillingness to recognise that facts are as they are. It is thought to be a scientific, a technological age: but it would be delusory to conclude that, in general, the logic which is the beginning and end of science is evident either in the technological outcome of science, or in the structure of contemporary opinion. Even in an era of disbelief—in the theological sense—there is still a sad confidence in the possibility of miraculous solutions to apparently intractable problems. In the case of a struggling football team—and most teams discover that they are struggling for long periods—the coming of a new manager (in the Molineux setting there is always the hope of a "second coming") is thought to hold Messianic possibilities. In the event it was another, quite unexpected, contemplation of the Messianic which placed worldly—more exactly, earthly—values at risk at Molineux.

For none of the young Wolves was a fairer future predicted than for Peter Knowles—at his best gracefully gifted and incisive, at his worst exhibiting personality problems through erratic spasms of tiresome showmanship. It was hoped that all would be there—in the football sense—when maturity was achieved. But Knowles, for reasons which must command respectful sympathy, walked out of football to become an active worker for the "Jehovah's Witnesses". That loss to Wolves might certainly be taken to have been an "Act of God".

The unexpected absense of Dougan for eight weeks was not to be seen in quite the same way. Dougan, whose "image" as a tear-away Irishman was sedulously touched up by romantically inclined sports writers in search of a Cuchullin where none was, became a victim of the cult of "disciplinary action", at a time when the footballer was a convenient scapegoat for a society trying to exculpate itself. As a consequence of incidents at Hillsborough on 16 August and at Molineux on October 4 he was suspended for a total period of eight weeks. No sooner was Dougan returned from exile than Munro was removed from the scene, suspended for a month.

Misfortunes, as is beginning to be made clear, never come singly. Mike O'Grady, transferred from Leeds, was injured almost immediately after arrival at Molineux. That was followed by a severe injury to Dougan who had only just been restored to the team, and lesser injuries to Wagstaffe and Bailey.

Rebuilding a team—McGarry's initial task—was proving both expensive and frustrating. Jim McCalliog and Hugh Curran, with O'Grady, made up a costly trio, their coming setting the club back by something like £220,000. A proper balance in a team is the most important consideration, and when the most skilful players are unable to strike up a convincing combination their efforts are largely wasted. So it was in the first full McGarry season. The top of the League table was far out of sight, even if the colder climate at the bottom was not too uncomfortably close.

The next season was a different matter, albeit it began with a run of 16 matches of which none were won. But a more positive approach came with the developing understanding of a forward line more aggressive and more opportunist than had been seen for a long time. Bobby Gould (who was to return to Wolves in 1976 after spells elsewhere), was signed from Arsenal, was top-scorer in the League, closely followed by Curran—a similarly thrustful and bustling centre-forward of traditional character—and Dougan. The prompting of these players by McCalliog's wit and Ken Hibbitt's blossoming tactical skills, with support from an improved defence to which Munro came as a No. 5 convert from a No. 8 posting, and with Bailey's urgent leadership, made for a considerable improvement in morale both on the field and on the terraces. That was the year of the "Texaco International League Competition", brightly described at the time by a local sports-writer as "a firmly established part of the British football scene", in which teams from the senior British Leagues who were not current trophy-holders were offered the chance of fairly easy pickings. The "Texaco Cup" fixtures of the 1970-71 season were amiably interspersed among more serious events. To the well travelled it was pleasant to see Dundee, Morton, Derry City, and Hearts in matches against Wolves, whose winning of the competition fanned the embers of optimism into a hopeful glow. A Dougan goal against Burnley on May 1 was more significant, however, as the means whereby entry to the UEFA (formerly Fairs) Cup competition was assured.

Four factors marked the 1971-2 season. These were: the culmination of the creative and Thespian genius of Dougan; the impressive, craftsmanlike development of John Richards; the manner in which, after a Grand Tour in classical style, the sought-after UEFA Cup was dashed from the lips at the last stage; and an inconsistency bred from a marriage between *joie de vivre* and fearful carelessness. In that season there were reflections of past history, both in regard to the treatment of foreign teams, and the sheer excitement generated by certain outstanding matches in the domestic programme.

Two matches especially stand out from the League competition—that against Arsenal at Molineux on November 20, 1971, and that against Leeds, also at Molineux, on May 8, 1972.

The Arsenal match was one of those which would naturally go into an anthology of English football; for hardly anywhere else in the world would the game have been played in the prevailing conditions. To some extent it was a three-sided contest, with two courageous teams pitting their skills not only against each other, but also against the elements. There was swirling snow throughout. It was bitterly cold. Through the one and against the other the players set up a kaleidoscope of brilliant endeavour, with goals being taken from improbable positions and at unlikely moments. After half an hour Kennedy scored for Arsenal from long range—a curling, dipping ball. After 50 minutes Wagstaffe produced a facsimile, and the scores were level. Then Wolves rampaged as in olden days, producing four more goals from the night air.

The contrasting match, against Leeds, was almost a midsummer night's dream. Leeds were within grasp of the Cup and League double. In 90 minutes the one prize was lost—as shortly afterwards the other was also to be lost. Before a crowd of 53,379, Wolves were tenacious, and goals by Munro and Dougan left Leeds, even when thus provoked, with too much to do to pick up a face-saving point. When Bremner scored in the second half it did look, however, as though their reserves of skill and stamina might prevail. It was a tense affair, from which the real winners were Derby, who thereby became champions.

The pattern of the season saw the League programme (the F.A. and League Cup competitions quickly went out of sight) interwoven with the saga of the UEFA Cup competition. This was dramatic all the way, and especially memorable because of Dougan's nine goals—which included a hat-trick against the Portuguese side Academica Coimbra, Parkes's two penalty saves against the Budapest team Ferencvaros, and the growing authority of Richards, which took him into the England Under 23 side. David Wagstaffe, already seven years with Wolves, whose nimble accuracy and old style passes from the wing seemed to come from a familiar store of Molineux skills, was at his best that year and went into the Football League side against the Scottish League. Many would think that to have been a meagre reward for exceptional talents in a generally fallow period.

The UEFA progress had an auspicious start at Molineux against Coimbra, and a three goal lead (McAlle, Richards, Dougan), was more than a sufficient basis for ultimate victory. In Portugal the home side collapsed, and McAlle added another goal to Dougan's three—which he had anticipated in a recent hat-trick against Nottingham Forest. Against the Dutch team Den Haag Wolves scored three goals away from home in the first leg (Dougan, McCalliog, Hibbitt) and four at Molineux (one from Dougan; the others all self-inflicted). The next round called for versatility. On an ice-bound pitch, on a leaden afternoon, underneath the high snow-covered east German Thuringian hills, John Richards slipped through an otherwise tightly bound Karl Zeiss Jena defence to score an all-important goal. In the second leg two goals from Dougan, and one from Hibbitt were less than the mastery of Wolves merited.

The further the competition went the more severe it inevitably became. Juventus, one of the most celebrated of Italian teams, held (or were held by) Wolves to a draw at home, Wolves' goal coming from McCalliog. At Molineux the luck of the Irish (it might be thought) held, and Danny Hegan and Dougan scored the necessary goals. Hegan, known to McGarry at Ipswich, came to Molineux at the beginning of the 1970-71 season, and was just on the point of making a major contribution to Northern Irish history by membership of the team victorious over England on May 23, 1972.

The semi-final was won in large part through Parkes's magnificent reflexes, but Richards and Munro, by scoring ensured a draw in Hungary, and goals by Daley and Munro gave Wolves the game, by the best of three, at Molineux.

The Final was against Spurs and was the first time a major European competition involved two English clubs. On account of a greater consistency in recent times the Spurs were taken to be favourites everywhere except in the Midlands. In the event, those who backed the favourites acted wisely. After the event, those who were Wolves supporters were sadder, and possibly wiser. On May 4, 1972, two men defeated Wolves; Chivers, who scored two goals in the 2-1 win, and Jennings. It seemed unnecessary, somehow, to have brought three officials all the way from the USSR to supervise this game, which—as is said—was contested in the best spirit. The second leg on May 17 was determined by Jennings, without whom there could not have been, as there was, a drawn game, a goal by Wagstaffe cancelling one from Mullery.

Meanwhile there were rumours abroad that Coventry were interested in enticing McGarry to Highfield Road. Three days after the second part of the UEFA final it was announced that he had signed a five year contract with Wolves.

The reverse in the UEFA Cup Final, after a colourful progress to that stage, may in retrospect be seen as a turning point in the more recent history of the Club. The Wolves' style is by tradition free-flowing, improvisatory, carefree (even, alas! sometimes careless), and eminently spectator-worthy. In parenthesis it may also be said that it develops a commendable on-the-field spirit of camaraderie. But all of this is the antithesis of burglar-proof defences and calculated opportunism. "Reducing football to an academic problem of defence v attack may be fascinating for the committed and the expert but, when it reduces the game to an arid stalemate, the public become bored."[1] the Wolves have never been exponents of the negative type of football produced by contemporary techniques (or, lack of techniques); but therein lies a problem, not to be solved by one club alone.

In the 1972-3 season Wolves coasted along with a minimum of discomfort, finished fifth in the League and reached the semi-finals of both League and F.A. Cups. In the former there was a carry-over from the previous season's UEFA Cup, Wolves coming apart against Spurs once more. After a 1-1 draw at Molineux, Spurs won by the odd goal in three at home. In the FA Cup the tight play of Leeds was just too inexorable. Wolves lost a gripping match at Maine Road by the only goal of the afternoon. But never did they look quite near enough to infallibility to shake Leeds. The manner in which Leeds were destroyed by Sunderland in the Final, however, shows that football is still unpredictable. Nevertheless in the long term there is a kind of calculable statistical analysis available derived from and pointing to persistent weaknesses and lack of consistent understanding and their opposites. This is the higher mathematics of the game.

At that time it seemed that Richards was on the edge of a great future. The leading goal-scorer in Division 1, with 33, League and Cup goals, and a member of the England team that beat Northern Ireland at Goodison Park, he was in official favour. The subsequent lack of full realisation of this player's dynamic potentialities is—at the time of writing—one of the mysteries and sadnesses of the game.

At the beginning of the 1973-4 season Wolves could look back on two seasons in which they had played 27 cup-ties—in League, FA, and UEFA—of which 17 were won, 5 drawn, and 5 lost. By any normal standards that is a good record; but success tends to go with satisfactory records according to abnormal standards—the standards prescribed by the dourness of point gathering over a too fully occupied league programme. In the 1973-4 season one saw, perhaps, the breaking of a new dawn, in the manner in which young players tutored at Molineux were making places for themselves. Among them

[1] *F.A. Year Book 1973-4.* p.68.

were Palmer, Powell (since gone to Coventry), Sunderland, (whose rise to proficiency was impeded by a serious injury) and Steve Daley.

Wolves went through the major competitions with zest, but inconsistently. In the UEFA Cup grotesque errors in Leipzig in the second round resulted in the necessity of overtaking a 3-0 deficit in the second leg. With great spirit this was done, but winning by 4-1 left the visitors statistically on top by reason of a goal scored away from home. When this happened at the beginning of November, having won only three league games, Wolves were perilously within the relegation area. Fortunately the double thrust of Dougan and Richards was still a decisive factor. Not only was the league position stabilised, the team finished in fifth place; far more satisfactory than had at one time seemed predictable.

Meanwhile in the League Cup a series of pipe-openers against sides from lower divisions prefaced fine victories over Liverpool and Norwich in the fifth and sixth rounds. The milestones thus far were six goals from Richards. These, of course, were not solo exercises, but the completion of operations by what could be a finely tuned attack mechanism. On March 2, 1974, in the week of a General Election, Wolves were at Wembley for the first time since 1960. The only survivor of that occasion was Dougan, who had then been wearing Blackburn colours. The other finalists in 1974 were Manchester City, and—as might be deduced from the team as given below—they were favourites.

Manchester City: McRae; Pardoe, Donachie; Doyle, Booth, Towers; Summerbee, Bell, Lee, Law, Marsh (sub: Carrodus).

Wolves: Pierce; Palmer, Parkin; Bailey, Munro, McAlle; Hibbitt, Sunderland, Richards, Dougan, Wagstaffe (sub: Powell).

Wembley held the statutory 100,000 crowd, which paid £161,500 to see a scintillating game between two sides which in the end proved to be so evenly matched that for either to lose was something of an injustice. But a drawn game would also have been an injustice to the quality of this probing, penetrative football. Wolves went in at half-time with the inestimable advantage of the goal scored by Hibbitt two minutes previously. Not long after the interval Bell put Manchester right back in the game. Indeed, more than this, as the movement developed the probability seemed to be that they would take the lead. But this was the game that Gary Pierce—on his 23rd birthday, choses to make his prize offering to the club. The way in which he dealt with a lethal centre from Lee and an equally peril-laden header from Marsh was other-worldly. And five minutes before the end Richards, alert throughout, decided the issue with a fine goal.

Although it did not seem so at the time—one writer proposing that the League Cup win "could herald a new era at Molineux"—March 2 1974 was the day when the shadows began to lengthen. Richards did not play for the rest of the season, and when he returned in the autumn it was without the magic that had been his previous distinction. Peter Withe, a Lancastrian who came to Molineux by way of South Africa where he had commended himself to Derek Dougan, made his entry as a striker a week after the League Cup Final. This was in a game against Ipswich which, being the first home win against that club for four years, went against recent tradition. Withe had strength and purpose, but being without outstanding ideas his appearances were spasmodic and before long he was transferred to Birmingham City.

At the end of March Wolves were uncomfortably short of points, and a sequence of unbroken defeat could have led to disaster. A striking 4-0 victory over Derby, however, with two goals from Steve Kindon, did lift the hearts of supporters, even if the extent of this victory by way of contrast did serve to underwrite the baneful influence of inconsistency. Kindon had come from Burnley two seasons previously and, as heir-presumptive to Dougan, had been kept waiting his main chance. This now appeared to have come. But the best laid plans do not always produce the desired effect.

As the curtain came down on the season Peter Eastoe went to Swindon, and Dave Woodfield—of an older generation—enjoyed a testimonial. The defensive quadrilateral of Munro and the matured McAlle, with Palmer (an Under-23 player) and Parkin was thought by many to be reaching an assurance on which future hopes could be soundly rested. The League Cup was the symbol of McGarry's first palpable achievement at Molineux. But the new era that was hoped for would require more evidence than that provided by a handsome piece of silver snatched from the blue with a certain entertaining show of impudence.

R. Flowers in action.

Peak year 1958.

G. Showell, E. Clamp, G. Harris, J. Gardiner, M. Finlayson, J. Murray, W. J. Slater, R. Flowers, E. A. Stuart, R. Mason, N. Deeley, W. A. Wright, S. Cullis, P. Broadbent, C. Booth, J. Mullen, J. Henderson. Birmingham League. Worcestershire. Football League. F.A. Youth. Central League. Worcs. Combination Trophies.

F.A. Cup winners 1960.

Molineux Ground 1972.

15

Full Circle

OUT of the last dozen matches of the 1973-4 season David Wagstaffe—for whom the affection of supporters was only matched by the exasperation felt at the frequency with which he was overturned by crudity of opposition—played only in four. For him, as for Dougan, the writing was on the wall, and John Farley had been acquired from Watford, for £50,000 to replace him.

After six minutes of the start of the new season, on August 17, John Richards scored a fine goal to set Wolves off to a good start with a win at Burnley. A goal-less draw at Molineux with Liverpool in mid-week was not unsatisfactory, and four days later Newcastle were destroyed in a remarkable game. After a few minutes Wolves were a goal in arrears—signs of irresolution in defence were symptomatic but hardly yet ominous—and for a quarter of an hour it looked as though they would find difficulties even in getting on equal terms. In the 21st minute, however, Richards slid an irreproachable pass to Hibbitt, who scored. A few moments later, Richards having been pulled down, Hibbitt converted a penalty. Soon after half-time the same player responded to a ricochet from the post—from a shot by Sunderland—and put Wolves further ahead. After Tudor had scored for Newcastle Hibbitt produced another goal three minutes from the end of the match. Such prolificacy had not been seen for a long time.

Those who thought this auspicious, however, thought wrong. From that point six league matches went by without one victory. Additionally, carelessness had caused visions of success in UEFA and League Cup competitions to expire. A moderate Portuguese team, FC Porto, had been responsible for the first disappointment, and Second Division Fulham for the second. On September 28 the drought was relieved by a match-winning Richards goal against Chelsea at Stamford Bridge.

In the dull days of autumn and early winter a goal by Dougan at Middlesbrough was a collector's piece, but a reminder of fading time. Dougan's appearances were scarce during that season, his gifts being tutorially employed for much of the time in the reserves.

It had been hoped at the end of October that Willie Carr might join the club and negotiations had been concluded with Coventry which would then have required an outlay of more than £200,000. In the event the deal fell through after cartilaginous doubts had been raised. In November it looked as though goals might come to compensate for defects in defence which were beginning to appear as chronic, but an accident to Sunderland in training put his leg into plaster and him out of action for the rest of the season. All of this brought a poetic reflection from McGarry that, "there was a cold wind blowing down the corridors of Molineux".

Kindon sparkled by fits and starts and began to look as the suitable partner, as well as foil, to Richards, who scored a goal in the third round of the FA Cup on January 4 1975. Unfortunately Ipswich produced two goals—one from a parabolic free-kick—and Wolves were removed from a third cup competition that season at the first attempt. By February the team was riding uneasily four or five places from the bottom of the League table.

On March 15 the fans had something to shout about, rather than at. Carr, who had scored an impertinent goal against Wolves at Coventry in January, had after all joined the club (at a considerably reduced cost) and he soon made his presence felt. The visitors were Chelsea, and Richards scored after 20 minutes. Two minutes later Carr, engaged primarily for his creativity, scored his initiation goal. After pulling one goal back, Chelsea—well along the route to relegation—collapsed, the final score being 7-1.

Although the season showed the worst away results of any since returning to the First Division in 1968, it ended in a blaze of glory. On March 29 Dougan played his last match for the club. That is to say, he played for all but the last ten minutes when he came off for his protégé Peter Withe (since gone to Birmingham) to take his place. On April 26 Wolves played Leeds, European Cup finalists—at Molineux. Named as substitute, Dougan was in fact the hero of the hour. Tumultuously acclaimed before the match when being presented with a silver salver from the *Express and Star,* he replaced Kindon and presided over the last twenty minutes of a fascinating and eventful game punctuated by the brilliance that itself promotes.

The 1970's will go down in the memory of many as the Dougan era. More than most British players of modern times he has combined technical skills of a high order with an imaginative perception of the communicative purpose of the game. One in which he was participant was never dull. Even when not actually playing he could be relied upon to exasperate tired convention. For instance—appropriately on St. Patrick's Day, 1973—having been stunned into insensibility by a blow on the temple from a ball fortuitously kicked in his direction by Kindon before the start of the match, he recovered well enough to head Coventry City into ignominious defeat through his service of passes to Richards. But Dougan was eloquent off the field; in the interests of his fellow-players (to whom, as Chairman of PFA, he was as a Lord Protector), of his fellow-countrymen, and of the handicapped to whose welfare he unremittingly dedicated himself. The greatest tribute to Dougan, perhaps, was that from an anonymous Cockney *graffiti* composer who decorated the side of Charing Cross Railway Bridge with the simple eloquence of DOOG.

On October 30 1975 Dougan's ritual leave-taking took the form of a Testimonial Match—Wolves v a "Don Revie Select XI". The referee, in his own right no less remarkable than the beneficiary of the occasion—was Jack Taylor, Britain's most celebrated referee and one of the best in the world.

Contemporary football is vastly different from that enjoyed (or endured) by our grandparents. Whereas once it was a folk-ritual, attended by solemnities, it is now an adjunct to the entertainment industry. On account of its simplicity—the virtue that made it the dominant world game—it is superficially easy to understand, and being colourful it is eminently televiewable. As a consequence of this the demand for "personalities" has arisen—a demand which began in part to be met when contractual obligations on players became more liberal. For this, Dougan—a natural choice for the designation "personality"—as a negotiator was partly responsible.

In the 1975-6 season, relatively at least, Wolves appeared personality-less both collectively and individually. There was, on the other hand, what in older times was termed "character", which usually was taken as indication of a willingness to attempt repairs to damaged situations. Unfortunately the season was an almost unbroken sequence of such situations, and as it passed the writing on the wall became larger and clearer, so that the threat of relegation became relegation itself. That this was so was due less to the season's results than to the backlog of insecurity accumulated over the previous few seasons. In this context insecurity requires new corrective methods. A generation ago Buckley was looking for the philosopher's stone. Although not always looking in the right direction he would seem to have had the right idea. Since his time psychological processes in general are better understood, but they are not always applied. The British game has suffered from insularity, and as one looks at the world scene one notices an intellectuality of approach that is a challenge to complacency.

The British game is one which provides drama and the 1975-6 season at Molineux was one of intense excitement and dramatic dénouement. A final match—postponed beyond the normal terminus—on which depend both championship and relegation and in which two clubs other than those directly involved have direct interest, and yet another with some influence on the total result, is surely unique. When on May 4 1976 Wolves met Liverpool at Molineux the position was that: Wolves must win and Birmingham (playing Sheffield United at Sheffield) lose for Birmingham rather than Wolves to be relegated; Wolves must win for Queen's Park Rangers rather than Liverpool to become champions; Wolves must draw (except by 3-3 or more) or lose for Liverpool to win the championship.

The match was played before 50,000—with many persons unable to get into the ground dispersed all over the town and neighbourhood—and in the fourteenth minute it seemed as if many prayers had been sympathetically heard when Kindon scored. While Wolves were ahead at Molineux, Sheffield United were leading Birmingham by 1-0 at Bramall Lane.

But miracles do not happen in the modern world. Efficiency wins in the end—and the operative word is the last. So Liverpool—the most efficient team in England—bided their time, knowing that McAlle and Munro were missing from the heart of the Wolves defence. With an accumulation of offence during the second half defensive positions were rendered untenable and thirteen minutes from full time Keegan made the scores equal. That of course was the moment of truth, but in the last five minutes Liverpool made clear that their cup of delight was not to be supplied from half-measures. Toshack and Kennedy scored and Liverpool fans of the ruder kind went about Wolverhampton like Hunnish despoilers of ancient times. This was Bailey's 500th match for Wolves, in none of which could he said to have given less than the best of what he was capable.

A season of bits and pieces—in which McNab was surprisingly signed from Arsenal, and Gould more surprisingly re-signed from West Ham—saw many disappointments and three remarkable close matches with Manchester United. At Old Trafford in December Manchester's victory was so long delayed that the BBC gave 0-0 as a final score before discovering a goal by Hill from a corner by Coppell in the dying embers of injury time. The odd goal—as it is loosely called—in the final issue was the death of Wolves, for in match after match a single lapse sufficed to lead to disaster. In March, having bravely reached the sixth round of the FA Cup, Wolves first drew with the United at Old Trafford and then proceeded to confound prophecy further. Through sublime opportunism by Kindon and Richards Wolves went two goals ahead in the replay, but adverse fates brought the United to equality by the end of full time and a decisive goal in extra time. A simple epitaph on that match would have been, "we were robbed", but one should never be put into the position of having to adopt that posture.

Apart from occasional moments of exhilaration the main interest in the season centred on the promise of youth; on the displays of the reserves and of the youth team which went as far as the final of the Youth Cup, to lose to West Bromwich Albion. The story of Wolverhampton Wanderers began with youth. It is fitting that the second century of the club's history should commence similarly, with the names of Bell, O'Hara, Daly, Hazell, Berry, standing where once were Baynton, Cliff, Mason, Brodie, Cliff... After the curtain had been rung down on the 1975-6 season changes in the administration of the club took place. John Ireland was named as President for life, his position as Chairman being taken by Harry Marshall, who had succeeded his father as a director some twelve years previously. Predictably, Bill McGarry relinquished his appointment, and his place was taken by Sammy Chung. Some managers of the Wolves in the past achieved fame through their efforts at Molineux. Wisely ignoring the "big name" principle the directors acted in the belief that given the opportunity team and manager may yet again travel together towards success.

Maybe the best is yet to be. An historian dare not be other than an optimist.

INTERNATIONAL PLAYERS

A—Argentine; Au—Austria; B—Belgium; Br—Brazil; Bul—Bulgaria; C—Czechoslovakia; Ch—Chile; Cy—Cyprus; D—Denmark; E—Eire; En—England; F—France; Fi—Finland; FIFA—International Federation of Football Association: G—Germany (also Federal Republic); GDR—German Democratic Republic; Ho—Holland; Hu—Hungary; I—Ireland (also Northern Ireland); Is—Israel; It—Italy; L—Luxembourg; M—Mexico; N—Norway; Pe—Peru; Po—Poland; P—Portugal; R—Rumania; Ru—Russia; S—Scotland; Sp—Spain; Sw—Sweden; Swit—Switzerland; Tu—Turkey; U—Uruguay; USA—United States of America; W—Wales; Y—Yugoslavia.

The following references relate only to appearances during membership of Wolves.

For England

H. Allen, 1888,9,90 (S), 1888 (W,I); T. Baddeley, 1903,4 (S,I), 1904 (W); R. Baugh, 1890 (I); W. M. Beats, 1901 (W), 1902 (S); P. Broadbent, 1958 (Ru), 1959, (S,W,I,It,Br), 1960 (S); J. B. Brodie, 1889 (S), 18891-91 (I); E. Clamp, 1958 (Ru 2,Br,Au); C. Crowe, 1963 (F); S. Cullis, 1938 (S,W,I,F,C), 1939 (S,I, Rest of Europe, N,R,It,Y); N. Deeley, 1959 (Br,Pe 2); A. Fletcher, 1889-90 (W); R. Flowers, 1955 (F); 1959 (S,W,It,Br,Pe,USA,M-sub); 1960 W,I,S,Sw,Y,Sp,Hu), 1961 (I,W,S,L,P,Sw,M,It,Au), 1962 (W,I,S,Au,Pe,L,P, Hu,A,Bul,Br), 1963 (I,W,S,F 2,Switz), 1964 (E,USA,P), 1965 (W,Ho,G,N,); T. Galley, 1937 (N,Sw); J. Hancocks, 1949 (Switz), 1950 (W), 1951 (Y); A. Hinton, 1963 (F); G. Kinsey, 1892 (W), 1893 (S); A. Lowder, 1889 (W); C. Mason, 1887 (I), 1888 (W), 1890 (I); W. Morris, 1939 (S,I,R); J. Mullen, 1946 (B-Victory International), 1947 (S), 1949 (N,F), 1950 (B-sub, Ch, USA), 1954 (W,I,S,FIFA,Sw,Y); J. Pye, 1946 (B-Victory International), 1949 (E); J. Richards, 1973 (I); W. C. Rose, 1884 (S,W,I); 1886 (I), 1891 (I); W. J. Slater 1955 (W,G), 1958 (S,P,Y,Ru 2,Br,Au,Ru), 1959 (Ru), 1960 (S); T. Smalley, 1937 (W); R. Thomson, 1964 (I,USA,P,A), 1965 (B,Ho,I,W); B. F. Williams, 1946 (W,F-Victory Internationals), 1949 (F), 1950 (S,W,Ecuador, It,P,B,Ch,USA), 1951 (I,W,S,Y,A,P), 1952 (W,F), 1954 (Sw,FIFA), 1955 (S,G,Fi,Sp,P), 1956 (W); D. Wilshaw, 1954 (W), 1955 (S,F,Sp,P), 1956 (W,I,Fi,G), 1957 (I); H. Wood, 1890 (I,S), 1896 (I); W. Wooldridge, 1901 (G); W. A. Wright, 1946 (S,B,Switz,F-Victory Internationals), 1947 (S,W,I,E, Hu,F,Switz,P), 1948 (S,W,I,B,Switz,It), 1949 (S,W,I,D,Switz,Sw,N,F), 1950 (S,W,I,E,It,P,B,Ch,USA,Sp), 1951 (S,W,I,A), 1952 (S,W,I,Au 2, It,Switz), 1953 (S,W,I,B,A,Ch,U,USA), 1954 (S,W,I,FIFA,Hu 2, Y,B,Switz,U), 1955 (S,W,I,G,F,Sp,P), 1956 (S,W,I,D,Sp,Br,Fi,G), 1957 (S,W,I,Y,D 2, E 2), 1958 (S,W,I,F,P,Y,Ru,Br,Au,Ru), 1959 (W,I,S,Ru,E,Br 2, Pe,M,USA).

Under-23
C. Booth, 1957 (F-sub); P. Broadbent, 1954 (It); E. Farmer, 1962 (Is,N); R. Flowers, 1955 (It,S); G. Harris, 1958 (Bul,R,S,W); K. Hibbitt, 1971 (W-sub); A. Hinton, 1963 (Y,R), 1964 (W); J. Kirkham, 1961 (W,S); P. Knowles, 1968 (W,It), 1969 (W,N); G. Mannion, 1960 (P,Is); J. Murray, 1958 (S), 1959 (F); G. Palmer, 1974 (W), 1975 (P); D. Parkin, 1970 (W,Ru,Bul,S), 1971 (S); B. Powell, 1974 (S), 1975 (C,P,-sub, S); J. Richards, 1972 (GDR,Po,Ru), 1973 (S), 1974 (Po-sub, W); A. Sunderland, 1974 (S-sub); R. Thomson, 1963 (Y), 1964 (W,G,F), 1965 (R,C 2, G,A), 1966 (F,Y,Tu), 1967 (W,A).

For Scotland
F. Munro, 1971 (I-sub,En-sub,D,Ru), 1975 (Sw,W-sub,I,En,R).

Under-23
F. Munro, 1970 (F,En,W-sub), 1971 (W).

For Wales
J. C. Bowdler, 1894 (En); J. Davies, 1892 (En), 1893 (En); B. Jones, 1935 (I), 1936 (En,S,I), 1937 (En,S,I), 1938 (En,S,I,); E. J. Peers, 1914 (I,S,En), 1920 (En,S), 1921 (S,I,En); C. Phillips, 1931 (I), 1932 (En), 1933 (S), 1934 (En,S,I), 1935 (E,S,I), 1936 (S); D. Richards, 1931 (I), 1933 (En,S,I), 1934 (En,S,I), 1935 (En,S,I), 1936 (En,S,I); R. W. Richards, 1920 (E,S), 1921 (I), 1922 (E,S); C. Sidlow, 1946 (En, S, Victory Internationals).

For Northern Ireland
J. Brown, 1935 (En,W), 1936 (En); A. D. Dougan 1967 (W), 1968 (S,W,Is,Tu-2), 1969 (En,S,W), 1970 (S,En,Ru 2), 1971 (Cy 2,Sp,En,S,W), 1972 (Ru 2,En,S,W), 1973 (Bu,Cy); W. Halligan, 1912 (for Ireland v En); D. Hegan, 1972 (Ru,En,S,W), 1973 (Bu,Cy); A. Lutton, 1970 (S,E); D. Martin, 1935 (En), 1936 (W); P. McParland, 1962 (Hol); S. Smyth, 1948 (En,S,W), 1949 (S,W), 1950 (E,S,W).

Results of every competition game played by Wolverhampton Wanderers F.C., together with League appearances, and goalscorers. (Prepared by Tony Pullein).

1883/84

F.A. CUP
1 — Long Eaton Rangers (h) 4-1
2 — Wednesbury Old Athletic (a) 2-4

1884/85

1 — Derby St. Luke's (h) 0-0
    (a) 2-4

1885/86

F.A. CUP
1 — Derby St. Luke's (h) 7-0
2 — Stafford Road (h) 4-2
3 — Walsall Swifts (h) 2-1
4 — W.B.A. (a) 1-3

1886/87

F.A. CUP
1 — Matlock (h) 6-0
2 — Crosswell's Brewery (h) 14-0
 — Aston Villa (a) 2-2
    (h) 1-1
    (h) 3-3
    (a) 0-2

1887/88

F.A. CUP
1 — Walsall Swifts (a) 2-1
2 — Aston Shakespeare (h) 3-0
3 — W.B.A. (a) 0-2

1888/89

FOOTBALL LEAGUE
Division 1

	Home	Away
Accrington	4-0	4-4
Aston Villa	1-1	1-2
Blackburn	2-2	2-2
Bolton	3-2	1-2
Burnley	4-1	4-0
Derby	4-1	0-3
Everton	4-0	2-1
Notts. Co.	2-1	0-3
Preston	0-4	2-5
Stoke	4-1	1-0
W.B.A.	2-1	3-1

F.A. CUP
1 — Old Carthusians (h) 4-3
2 — Walsall Town Swifts (h) 6-1
3 — Sheff. Wednesday (h) 5-0
S.F. — Blackburn
    (at Crewe) 1-1
    (at Crewe) 3-1
F. Preston
    (at The Oval) 0-3

League appearances:
Allen, H. 22; Anderson, 2; Baugh, R. 22; Baynton, J. M. 18; Benton, J. 1; Brodie, J. B. 14; Cannon, A. 6; Cooper, J. 21; Dudley 1; Fletcher, A. 16; Hunter, T. 20; Knight, T. 17; Lowder, A. 18; Mason, C. 20; Rose, W. C. 4; White, 4; Wood, H. 17; Wykes, D. 18; Yates, J. 1.

League scorers:
Wood 16, Brodie 11, Cooper 7, Knight 7, Hunter 4, White 4, Wykes 1.

Final Table

	P	W	D	L	F	A	P
1. Preston N. E.	22	18	4	0	74	15	40
2. Aston Villa	22	12	5	5	61	43	29
3. Wol'hampton W.	22	12	4	6	50	37	28
4. Blackburn R.	22	10	6	6	66	45	26
5. Bolton W.	22	10	2	10	63	59	22
6. W. B. Albion	22	10	2	10	40	46	22
7. Accrington	22	6	8	8	48	48	20
8. Everton	22	9	2	11	35	46	20
9. Burnley	22	7	3	12	42	62	17
10. Derby County	22	7	2	13	41	60	16
11. Notts. County	22	5	2	15	39	73	12
12. Stoke	22	4	4	14	26	51	12

1889/90

FOOTBALL LEAGUE
Division 1

	Home	Away
Accrington	2-1	3-6
Aston Villa	1-1	1-2
Blackburn	2-4	3-4
Bolton	5-1	1-4
Burnley	9-1	2-1
Derby	2-1	3-3
Everton	2-1	1-1
Notts. County	2-0	2-0
Preston	0-1	2-0
Stoke	2-2	1-2
W.B.A.	1-1	4-1

APPENDIX

F.A. CUP
1 — Old Carthusians		(h)	2-0
2 — Birmingham		(h)	2-1
3 — Stoke		(h)	4-0
replay after protest		(h)	8-0
S.F. — Blackburn			
(at Derby)			0-1

League appearances:
Aldershaw, 1; Allen, H. 21; Baugh, R. 20; Booth, C. 22; Brodie, J. B. 14; Cooper, J. 1; Fletcher, A. 21; Knight, T. 5; Lowder, A. 20; Mason, C. 21; Mason, J. 3; Perry, W. 8; Rose, W. C. 22; Wood, H. 21; Worrall, A. 20; Wykes, D. 22.

League scorers:
Wykes 15, Wood 13, Worrall 9, Brodie 8, Perry 3, Booth 2, Allen 1.

Final Table

	P	W	D	L	F	A	P
1. Preston N. E.	22	15	3	4	71	30	33
2. Everton	22	14	3	5	65	40	31
3. Blackburn Rov.	22	12	3	7	78	41	27
4. Wol'hampton W.	22	10	5	7	51	38	25
5. W. B. Albion	22	11	3	8	47	50	25
6. Accrington	22	9	6	7	53	56	24
7. Derby County	22	9	3	10	43	55	21
8. Aston Villa	22	7	5	10	43	51	19
9. Bolton W.	22	9	1	12	54	65	19
10. Notts. County	22	6	5	11	43	51	17
11. Burnley	22	4	5	13	36	65	13
12. Stoke	22	3	4	15	27	69	10

1890/91

FOOTBALL LEAGUE
Division 1

	Home	Away
Accrington	3-0	2-1
Aston Villa	2-1	2-6
Blackburn	2-0	3-2
Bolton	1-0	0-6
Burnley	3-1	2-4
Derby	5-1	0-9
Everton	0-1	0-5
Notts. County	1-1	1-1
Preston	2-0	1-5
Sunderland	0-3	4-3
W.B.A.	4-0	1-0

F.A. CUP
1 — Long Eaton Rangers	(a)	2-1
2 — Accrington	(a)	3-2
3 — Blackburn	(a)	0-2

League appearances:
Allen, H. 22; Baugh, R. 20; Booth, C. 21; Bowdler, J. C. H. 15; Brodie, J. B. 15; Brown 1; Cooper, J. 1; Fletcher, A. 21; Griffiths, H. 2; Lowder, A. 9; Mason, C. 19; Rose, W. C. 21; Rutter, 1; Thompson, S. 20; Topham, R. 1; Wood, H. 19; Worrall, A. 13; Wykes, D. 21.

League scorers:
Thompson 10, Wood 10, Wykes 6, Booth 4, Brodie 3, Bowdler 2, Topham 2, Allen 1, Worrall 1.

Final Table

	P	W	D	L	F	A	P
1. Everton	22	14	1	7	63	29	29
2. Preston N. E.	22	12	3	7	44	23	27
3. Notts. County	22	11	4	7	52	35	26
4. Wol'hampton W.	22	12	2	8	39	50	26
5. Bolton W.	22	12	1	9	47	34	25
6. Blackburn R.	22	11	2	9	52	43	24
7. Sunderland	22	10	5	7	51	31	23*
8. Burnley	22	9	3	10	52	63	21
9. Aston Villa	22	7	4	11	45	58	18
10. Accrington S.	22	6	4	12	28	50	16
11. Derby County	22	7	1	14	47	81	15
12. W. B. Albion	22	5	2	15	34	57	12

*Two points deducted for playing ineligible player.

1891/1892

FOOTBALL LEAGUE
Division 1

	Home	Away
Accrington	5-0	2-3
Aston Villa	2-0	6-3
Blackburn	6-1	0-2
Bolton	1-2	0-3
Burnley	0-0	1-1
Darwen	2-2	4-1
Derby	1-3	1-2
Everton	5-1	1-2
Notts. County	2-1	2-2
Preston	3-0	0-2
Stoke	4-1	3-1
Sunderland	1-3	2-5
W.B.A.	2-1	3-4

F.A. CUP
1 — Crewe	(h)	2-2
	(a)	4-1
2 — Sheff. United	(h)	3-1
3 — A. Villa	(h)	1-3

League appearances:
Allen, H. 22; Bailey, H. 1; Baker, C. 24; Baugh, R. 24; Booth, C. 19; Bowdler, J. C. H. 8; Bradley, C. 6; Burleigh, J. 2; Davies, J. 14; Devey, W. 25; Dunn, T. 6; Heath, W. 8; Johnston, J. 4; Kinsey, G. 25; Lowder, A. 1; Malpass, A. W. 10; Mason, C. 19; Rose, W. C. 26; Swift, G. 3; Topham, R. 10; Wood, H. 8; Wykes, D. 21.

League scorers:
Devey 18, Wykes 9, Baker 6, Booth 6, Wood 6, Topham 4, Allen 3, Johnson 3, Heath 2, Bowdler 1, Porteous (Sunderland) 1.

Final Table

	P	W	D	L	F	A	P
1. Sunderland	26	21	0	5	93	36	42
2. Preston N. E.	26	18	1	7	61	31	37
3. Bolton W.	26	17	2	7	51	37	36
4. Aston Villa	26	15	0	11	89	56	30
5. Everton	26	12	4	10	49	49	28
6. Wol'hampton W.	26	11	4	11	59	46	26
7. Burnley	26	11	4	11	49	45	26
8. Notts. County	26	11	4	11	55	51	26
9. Blackburn R.	26	10	6	10	58	65	26
10. Derby County	26	10	4	12	46	52	24
11. Accrington	26	8	4	14	40	78	20
12. W. B. Albion	26	6	6	14	51	58	18
13. Stoke	26	5	4	17	38	61	14
14. Darwen	26	4	3	19	38	112	11

1892/93
FOOTBALL LEAGUE
Division 1

	Home	Away
Accrington	5-3	0-4
Aston Villa	2-1	0-5
Blackburn	4-2	3-3
Bolton	1-2	1-3
Burnley	1-0	0-2
Derby	2-1	2-2
Everton	2-4	2-3
Newton Heath	2-0	1-10
Nottm. Forest	2-2	1-3
Notts. County	3-0	0-3
Preston	2-1	0-4
Sheffield Wed.	2-0	1-0
Stoke	1-0	1-2
Sunderland	2-0	2-5
W.B.A.	1-1	1-2

F.A. CUP
1 — Bolton (a) 1-1
  (h) 2-1
2 — Middlesbrough (h) 2-1
3 — Darwen (h) 5-0
S.F. — Blackburn
  (at Nottingham) 3-1
F. — Everton
  (at Fallowfield) 1-0

League appearances:
Allen, H. 29; Baker, C. 13; Baugh, R. 30; Butcher, J. H. 21; Davies, J. 18; Devey, W. 15; Fletcher, A. 2; Griffiths, H. 2; Griffin, A. 8; Hassall, J. 9; Johnston, J. 18; Kinsey, G. 19; Lawrence 2; Malpass, A. W. 23; Rose, W. C. 21; Swift, G. 30; Topham, R. 6; Wilson, 1; Wood, H. 27; Woodhall, G. H. 15; Wykes, D. 21.

League scorers:
Butcher 15, Wood 13, Wykes 8, Devey 5, Johnson 2, Allen 1, Kinsey 1, Swift 1, Topham 1.

Final Table

	P	W	D	L	F	A	P
1. Sunderland	30	22	4	4	100	36	48
2. Preston N. E.	30	17	3	10	57	39	37
3. Everton	30	16	4	10	74	51	36
4. Aston Villa	30	16	3	11	73	62	35
5. Bolton W.	30	13	6	11	56	55	32
6. Barnsley	30	13	4	13	51	44	30
7. Stoke City	30	12	5	13	58	48	29
8. W. B. Albion	30	12	5	13	58	69	29
9. Blackburn R.	30	8	13	9	47	56	29
10. Nottingham F.	30	10	8	12	48	52	28
11. W'hampton W.	30	12	4	14	47	68	28
12. Sheffield W.	30	12	3	15	55	65	27
13. Derby County	30	9	9	12	52	64	27
14. Notts County	30	10	4	16	53	61	24
15. Accrington S.	30	6	11	13	57	81	23
16. Newton Heath	30	6	6	18	50	85	18

1893/94
FOOTBALL LEAGUE
Division 1

	Home	Away
A. Villa	3-0	1-1
Blackburn	5-1	0-3
Bolton	2-1	0-2
Burnley	1-0	2-4
Darwen	2-1	1-3
Derby	2-4	1-4
Everton	2-0	0-3
Newton Heath	2-0	0-1
Nottingham F.	3-1	1-7
Preston	0-0	3-1
Sheffield Un.	3-4	2-3
Sheffield Wed.	3-1	4-1
Stoke	4-2	3-0
Sunderland	2-1	0-6
W.B.A.	0-8	0-0

F.A. CUP
1 — A. Villa (a) 2-4

League appearances:
Allen, H. 7; Baugh, R. 19; Black, D. 18; Butcher, J. H. 25; Dunn, T. 15; Edge, H. 18; Griffin, A. 27; Griffiths, H. 27; Hassall, J. 7; Haynes, H. 2; Kinsey, G. 25; Malpass, A. W. 12; Owen, W. 18; Robson, D. 1; Rose, W. C. 23; Swift, G. 25; Wood, H. 30; Woodhall, G. H. 3; Wykes, D. 28.

APPENDIX

League scorers:
Butcher 16, Wood 11, Edge 8, Wykes 7, Black 3, Griffin 2, Haynes 1, Kinsey 1, Malpass 1, Owen 1, Woodhall 1.

Final Table
Division 1 — Season 1893/94

		P	W	D	L	F	A	P
1.	Aston Villa	30	19	6	5	84	42	44
2.	Sunderland	30	17	4	9	72	44	38
3.	Derby County	30	16	4	10	73	62	36
4.	Blackburn R.	30	16	2	12	69	53	34
5.	Burnley	30	15	4	11	61	51	34
6.	Everton	30	15	3	12	90	57	33
7.	Nottingham F.	30	14	4	12	57	48	32
8.	W. B. Albion	30	14	4	12	66	59	32
9.	Wol'hampton W.	30	14	3	13	52	63	31
10.	Sheffield United	30	13	5	12	47	61	31
11.	Stoke City	30	13	3	14	65	79	29
12.	Sheffield Wed.	30	9	8	13	48	57	26
13.	Bolton Wand.	30	10	4	16	38	52	24
14.	Preston N. E.	30	10	3	17	44	56	23
15.	Darwen	30	7	5	18	37	83	19
16.	Newton Heath	30	6	2	22	36	72	14

1894/95

FOOTBALL LEAGUE
Division 1

	Home	Away
A. Villa	0-4	2-2
Blackburn	3-3	1-5
Bolton	4-2	1-6
Burnley	1-0	1-2
Derby	2-2	3-1
Everton	1-0	1-2
Liverpool	3-1	3-3
Nottingham F.	1-1	2-0
Preston	1-3	0-2
Sheffield Un.	0-3	0-1
Sheffield Wed.	2-0	1-3
Small Heath	2-1	3-4
Stoke	0-0	0-0
Sunderland	1-4	0-2
W.B.A.	3-1	1-5

F.A. CUP

1 — Darwen	(a) 0-0
	(h) 2-0
2 — Stoke	(h) 2-0
3 — W.B.A.	(a) 0-1

League appearances:
Baugh, R. 25; Bell, J. 6; Black, D. 29; Brockstropp, A. 3; Butcher, J. H. 19; Dunn, T. 27; Edge, R. 4; Fleming, G. 17; Griffin, A. 23; Griffiths, H. 26; Hamilton, J. 4; Hassall, J. 30; Haynes, H. 22; Lester, F. 1; Malpass, A.

W. 26; Nurse, D. G. 4; Reynolds, J. 14; Roberts, J. 1; Robson, D. 4; Wood, H. 28; Wykes, D. 17.

League scorers:
Griffin 11, Wood 10, Fleming 5, Reynolds 5, Wykes 4, Butcher 2, Haynes 2, Black 1, Edge 1, McQueen 1, McLean (Liverpool) 1.

Final Table
Division 1 — Season 1894/95

		P	W	D	L	F	A	P
1.	Sunderland	30	21	5	4	80	37	47
2.	Everton	30	18	6	6	82	50	42
3.	Aston Villa	30	17	5	8	82	43	39
4.	Preston N. E.	30	15	5	10	62	46	35
5.	Blackburn R.	30	11	10	9	59	49	32
6.	Sheffield United	30	14	4	12	57	55	32
7.	Nottingham F.	30	13	5	12	50	56	31
8.	Sheffield W.	30	12	4	14	50	55	28
9.	Burnley	30	11	4	15	44	56	26
10.	Bolton W.	30	9	7	14	61	62	25
11.	Wol'hampton W.	30	9	7	14	43	63	25
12.	Birmingham C.	30	9	7	14	50	74	25
13.	W. B. Albion	30	10	4	16	51	66	24
14.	Stoke City	30	9	6	15	50	67	24
15.	Derby County	30	7	9	14	45	68	23
16.	Liverpool	30	7	8	15	51	70	22

1895/96

FOOTBALL LEAGUE
Division 1

	Home	Away
Aston Villa	1-2	1-4
Blackburn	1-2	1-3
Bolton	5-0	0-4
Burnley	5-1	1-3
Bury	1-0	0-3
Derby	2-0	2-5
Everton	2-3	0-2
Nottingham F.	6-1	2-3
Preston	2-1	3-4
Sheffield Un.	4-1	1-2
Sheffield Wed.	4-0	1-3
Small Heath	7-2	2-3
Stoke	1-0	1-4
Sunderland	1-3	2-2
W.B.A.	1-2	1-2

F.A. CUP

1 — Notts Co.	(a) 2-2
	(h) 4-3
2 — Liverpool	(h) 2-0
3 — Stoke	(h) 3-0
S.F. — Derby	
(at Villa Park)	2-1
F. — Sheffield Wed.	
(at Crystal Palace)	1-2

League appearances:
Baugh, R. 30; Beats, W. M. 27; Black, D. 23; Bunch, W. 2; Dunn, T. 28; Fleming, G. 7; Griffin, A. 14; Griffiths, H. 9; Henderson, C. 30; Malpass, A. W. 28; Miller, J. 2; Nurse, D. G. 18; Owen, W. 30; Rose, W. C. 19; Swallow, J. E. 2; Tennant, W. 9; Tonks, J. 18; Topham, R. 2; Wood, H. 27; Wykes, D. 5.

League scorers:
Beats 16, Wood 12, Henderson 9, Black 7, Tonks 5, Wykes 4, Malpass 3, Griffin 2, Owen 1, Topham 1, Allsop (Nottingham Forest) 1.

League appearances:
Beats, W. M. 26; Black, D. 3; Bunch, W. 5; Dunn, T. 10; Eccles, G. S. 19; Edge, R. 2; Fleming, G. 16; Griffiths, H. 29; Lyden, J. 8; Malpass, A. W. 24; McMain, J. 18; Miller, J. 20; Nicholls, 3; Nurse, D. G. 1; Owen, W. 30; Pheasant, E. 8; Smith, W. 20; Tennant, W. 30; Tonks, J. 28; Wood, H. 30.

League scorers:
Beats 9, McMain 5, Miller 5, Smith 5, Tonks 5, Wood 4, Lyden 3, Nicholls 2, Owen 2, Black 1, Eccles 1, Edge 1, Gow (Sunderland) 1.

Final Table
Division 1 — Season 1895/96

	P	W	D	L	F	A	P
1. Aston Villa	30	20	5	5	78	45	45
2. Derby County	30	17	7	6	68	35	41
3. Everton	30	16	7	7	66	43	39
4. Bolton W.	30	16	5	9	49	37	37
5. Sunderland	30	15	7	8	52	41	37
6. Stoke City	30	15	0	15	56	47	30
7. Sheffield W.	30	12	5	13	44	53	29
8. Blackburn R.	30	12	5	13	40	50	29
9. Preston N. E.	30	11	6	13	44	48	28
10. Burnley	30	10	7	13	48	44	27
11. Bury	30	12	3	15	50	54	27
12. Sheffield Utd.	30	10	6	14	40	50	26
13. Nottingham F.	30	11	3	16	42	57	25
14. Wol'hampton W.	30	10	1	19	61	65	21
15. Small Heath	30	8	4	18	39	79	20
16. W. B. Albion	30	6	7	17	30	59	19

Final Table
Division 1 — Season 1896/97

	P	W	D	L	F	A	P
1. Aston Villa	30	21	5	4	73	38	47
2. Sheffield United	30	13	10	7	42	29	36
3. Derby County	30	16	4	10	70	50	36
4. Preston N. E.	30	11	12	7	55	40	34
5. Liverpool	30	12	9	9	46	38	33
6. Sheffield Wed.	30	10	11	9	42	37	31
7. Everton	30	14	3	13	62	57	31
8. Bolton W.	30	12	6	12	40	43	30
9. Bury	30	10	10	10	39	44	30
10. Wol'hampton W.	30	11	6	13	45	41	28
11. Nottingham F.	30	9	8	13	44	49	26
12. W. B. Albion	30	10	6	14	33	56	26
13. Stoke City	30	11	3	16	48	59	25
14. Blackburn R.	30	11	3	16	35	62	25
15. Sunderland	30	7	9	14	34	47	23
16. Burnley	30	6	7	17	43	61	19

1896/97

FOOTBALL LEAGUE
Division 1

	Home	Away
A. Villa	1-2	0-5
Blackburn	1-1	0-2
Bolton	4-0	2-1
Burnley	2-0	3-0
Bury	1-1	2-3
Derby	1-0	3-4
Everton	0-1	0-0
Liverpool	1-2	0-3
Nottingham F.	4-1	2-1
Preston	1-1	0-4
Sheffield Un.	1-1	3-1
Sheffield Wed.	2-0	0-0
Stoke	1-2	1-2
Sunderland	0-1	3-0
W.B.A.	6-1	0-1

F.A. CUP
| 1 — Millwall | | (a) 2-1 |
| 2 — Blackburn | | (a) 1-2 |

1897/98

FOOTBALL LEAGUE
Division 1

	Home	Away
A. Villa	1-1	2-1
Blackburn	3-2	3-2
Bolton	2-0	1-2
Bury	3-0	1-2
Derby	2-0	2-3
Everton	2-3	0-3
Liverpool	2-1	0-1
Nottingham F.	0-0	1-1
Notts Co.	3-1	2-2
Preston	3-0	2-1
Sheffield Un.	1-1	1-2
Sheffield Wed.	5-0	0-2
Stoke	4-2	2-0
Sunderland	4-2	2-3
W.B.A.	1-1	2-2

F.A. CUP
| 1 — Notts Co. | | (a) 1-0 |
| 2 — Derby | | (h) 0-1 |

APPENDIX

League appearances:
Baddeley, T. 29; Beats, W. M. 28; Blackett, J. 30; Chadburn, J. 6; Davies, H. 4; Eccles, G. S. 18; Fleming, G. 30; Greatwich, F. E. 1; Griffiths, H. 25; Harper, G. 2; Harris, G. 1; Malpass, A. W. 9; Matthias, J. S. 4; McMain, J. 9; Miller, J. 29; Nurse, D. G. 1; Owen, W. 28; Smith, J. 2; Smith, W. 23; Tonks, J. 23; Tuft, W. 1; Wood, H. 27.

League scorers;
Beats 12, Wood (Harry) 11, Smith 8, Tonks 7, Miller 6, McMain 4, Harper 2, Blackett 1, Chadburn 1, Fleming 1, Griffiths 1, Owen 1, Turner 1, Fryer (Derby County) 1.

Final Table
Division 1 — Season 1897/98

	P	W	D	L	F	A	P
1. Sheffield United	30	17	8	5	56	31	42
2. Sunderland	30	16	5	9	43	30	37
3. Wol'hampton W.	30	14	7	9	57	41	35
4. Everton	30	13	9	8	48	39	35
5. Sheffield W.	30	15	3	12	51	42	33
6. Aston Villa	30	14	5	11	61	51	33
7. W. B. Albion	30	11	10	9	44	45	32
8. Nottingham F.	30	11	9	10	47	49	31
9. Liverpool	30	11	6	13	48	45	28
10. Derby County	30	11	6	13	57	61	28
11. Bolton W.	30	11	4	15	28	41	26
12. Preston N. E.	30	8	8	14	35	43	24
13. Notts County	30	8	8	14	36	46	24
14. Bury	30	8	8	14	39	51	24
15. Blackburn R.	30	7	10	13	39	54	24
16. Stoke City	30	8	8	14	35	55	24

1898/99

FOOTBALL LEAGUE
Division 1

	Home	Away
A Villa	4-0	1-1
Blackburn	2-1	2-2
Bolton	1-0	1-2
Burnley	4-0	2-4
Bury	1-2	2-0
Derby	2-2	2-6
Everton	1-2	1-2
Liverpool	0-0	0-1
Newcastle	0-0	4-2
Nottingham F.	0-2	0-3
Notts County	1-0	2-0
Preston	0-0	1-2
Sheffield Un.	4-1	0-1
Sheffield Wed.	0-0	0-3
Stoke	3-2	4-2
Sunderland	2-0	0-3
W.B.A.	5-1	2-1

F.A. CUP
1 — Bolton	(h)	0-0
	(a)	1-0
2 — Derby	(a)	1-2

League appearances:
Annis, W. 3; Baddeley, T. 30; Beats, W. M. 26; Blackett, J. 33; Chadburn, J. 5; Davies, H. 22; Davies, R. 11; Fleming, G. 34; Griffiths, H. 32; Harper, G. 4; Harris, G. 4; Malpass, A. W. 5; Matthias, J. S. 23; McMain, J. 19; Miller, J. 33; Nurse, D. G. 2; Pheasant, E. 24; Platt 1; Smith, W. 14; Tonks, J. 29; Tuft, W. 4; Worton, A. J. 16.

League scorers:
Miller 11, Beats 10, Blackett 9, McMain 7, Worton 5, Tonks 4, Smith 3, Davis 2, Fleming 1, Harper 1, Nurse 1.

Final Table
Division 1 — Season 1898/99

	P	W	D	L	F	A	P
1. Aston Villa	34	19	7	8	76	40	45
2. Liverpool	34	19	5	10	49	33	43
3. Burnley	34	15	9	10	45	47	39
4. Everton	34	15	8	11	48	41	38
5. Notts County	34	12	13	9	47	51	37
6. Blackburn R.	34	14	8	12	60	52	36
7. Sunderland	34	15	6	13	41	41	36
8. Wol'hampton W.	34	14	7	13	54	48	35
9. Derby County	34	12	11	11	62	57	35
10. Bury	34	14	7	13	48	49	35
11. Nottingham F.	34	11	11	12	42	42	33
12. Stoke	34	13	7	14	47	52	33
13. Newcastle Un.	34	11	8	15	49	48	30
14. W.B.A.	34	12	6	16	42	57	30
15. Preston N. E.	34	10	9	15	44	47	29
16. Sheffield Un.	34	9	11	14	45	51	29
17. Bolton W.	34	9	7	18	37	51	25
18. Sheffield Wed.	34	8	8	18	32	61	24

1899/1900

FOOTBALL LEAGUE
Division 1

	Home	Away
A. Villa	0-1	0-0
Blackburn	4-0	1-2
Burnley	3-0	1-0
Bury	1-0	0-3
Derby	3-0	2-0
Everton	2-1	1-0
Glossop	4-0	3-2
Liverpool	0-1	1-1
Manchester C.	1-1	1-1
Newcastle	1-1	1-0

Nottingham F.	2-2	0-0	Derby	0-0	5-4
Notts County	2-2	0-0	Everton	1-1	1-5
Preston	1-3	0-2	Liverpool	2-1	0-1
Sheffield Un.	1-2	2-5	Manchester City	1-0	2-3
Stoke	0-2	3-1	Newcastle	1-0	1-3
Sunderland	1-0	2-1	Nottingham F.	1-0	1-2
W.B.A.	2-0	2-3	Notts County	3-2	1-4
			Preston	2-2	1-1
			Sheffield Un.	3-0	1-1
			Sheffield Wed.	1-1	0-2
			Stoke	0-2	0-3
			Sunderland	2-2	2-7
			W.B.A.	0-0	2-1

F.A. CUP
1 — Q.P.R.   (a) 1-1
             (h) 0-1

League appearances:
Baddeley, T. 33; Beats, W. M. 22; Blackett, J. 33; Bowen, G. 18; Bryan 9; Colley 7; Davies, H. 24; Fleming, G. 34; Griffiths, H. 28; Harper, G. 26; Harris, G. 1; Matthias, J. S. 8; Miller, J. 30; Nurse, D. G. 6; Owen, T. 11; Pheasant, E. 34; Platt, 5; Tonks, J. 9; Tuft, W. 3; Worton, A. J. 33.

League scorers:
Harper 11, Beats 9, Bowen 6, Worton 5, Miller 4, Owen (Trevor) 4, Pheasant 3, Bryan 2, Tonks 2, Johnson (Sheffield United) 1, Needham (Sheffield United) 1.

F.A. CUP
1 — New Brighton Tower   (h) 5-1
2 — Notts County   (a) 3-2
3 — Sheffield United   (h) 0-4

League appearances:
Annis, W. 28; Baddeley, T. 34; Barker, 13; Beats, W. M. 33; Bowen, G. 30; Colley 1; Davies, H. 17; Fleming, G. 33; Griffiths, H. 1; Harper, G. 29; Howell, R. 1; Jones, J. W. 6; Matthias, J. S. 8; Miller, J. 28; Nurse, D. G. 6; Pheasant, E. 34; Pope 1; Poppitt, J. 20; Walker, G. 26; Wooldridge, W. T. 17; Worton, A. J. 8.

League scorers:
Wooldridge 8, Bowen 6, Harper 6, Beats 4, Miller 4, Pheasant 4, Poppitt 3, Annis 1, Colley 1, Fleming 1, Worton 1.

Final Table

Division 1 — Season 1899/1900

	P	W	D	L	F	A	P
1. Aston Villa	34	22	6	6	77	35	50
2. Sheffield Un.	34	18	12	4	63	33	48
3. Sunderland	34	19	3	12	50	35	41
4. Wol'hampton W.	34	15	9	10	48	37	39
5. Newcastle United	34	13	10	11	53	43	36
6. Derby County	34	14	8	12	45	43	36
7. Manchester City	34	13	8	13	50	44	34
8. Nottingham F.	34	13	8	13	56	55	34
9. Stoke	34	13	8	13	37	45	34
10. Liverpool	34	14	5	15	49	45	33
11. Everton	34	13	7	14	47	49	33
12. Bury	34	13	6	15	40	44	32
13. W.B.A.	34	11	8	15	43	51	30
14. Blackburn R.	34	13	4	17	49	61	30
15. Notts County	34	9	11	14	46	60	29
16. Preston N. E.	34	12	4	18	38	48	28
17. Burnley	34	11	5	18	34	54	27
18. Glossop	34	4	10	20	31	74	18

1900/01

FOOTBALL LEAGUE
Division 1

	Home	Away
A. Villa	0-0	0-0
Blackburn	2-2	0-2
Bolton	1-1	0-1
Bury	1-1	1-0

Final Table

Division 1 — Season 1900/01

	P	W	D	L	F	A	P
1. Liverpool	34	19	7	8	59	35	45
2. Sunderland	34	15	13	6	57	26	43
3. Notts County	34	18	4	12	54	46	40
4. Nottingham F.	34	16	7	11	53	36	39
5. Bury	34	16	7	11	53	37	39
6. Newcastle United	34	14	10	10	42	37	38
7. Everton	34	16	5	13	55	42	37
8. Sheffield W.	34	13	10	11	52	42	36
9. Blackburn R.	34	12	9	13	39	47	33
10. Bolton W.	34	13	7	14	39	55	33
11. Manchester City	34	13	6	15	48	58	32
12. Derby County	34	12	7	15	55	42	31
13. Wol'hampton W.	34	9	13	12	39	55	31
14. Sheffield Un.	34	12	7	15	35	52	31
15. Aston Villa	34	10	10	14	45	51	30
16. Stoke	34	11	5	18	46	57	27
17. Preston N. E.	34	9	7	18	49	75	25
18. W.B.A.	34	7	8	19	35	62	22

1901/02

FOOTBALL LEAGUE
Division 1

	Home	Away
A. Villa	0-2	1-2
Blackburn	3-1	0-2
Bolton	1-2	2-2
Bury	1-0	1-2
Derby	0-0	1-3
Everton	2-1	1-6
Grimsby	2-0	0-3
Liverpool	3-1	1-4
Manchester C.	0-0	0-3
Newcastle	3-0	1-3
Nottingham F.	2-0	0-2
Notts County	3-1	3-5
Sheffield Un.	1-1	0-0
Sheffield Wed.	1-0	1-1
Small Heath	2-1	2-1
Stoke	4-1	0-3
Sunderland	4-2	0-2

F.A. CUP
1 — Bolton (h) 0-2

League appearances:
Annis, W. 32; Baddeley, T. 33; Beats, W. M. 21; Betterley, R. H. 1; Dean, J. 3; Fellows, A. 26; Gueilliam, 2; Haywood, A. 30; Jones, J. 34; Jones, J. W. 9; Miller, J. 30; Pheasant, E. 33; Pope 2; Poppitt, J. 1; Preston, H. 9; Robotham, H. 6; Stringer, J. 4; Swift, G. 1; Walker, G. 30; Whitehouse, J. 33; Wooldridge, W. T. 34.

League Scorers:
Wooldridge 14, Beats 8, Pheasant 6, Haywood 5, Miller 4, Fellows 3, Gueilliam 1, Jones, J. 1. Pope 1, Preston 1, Robotham 1, Swift 1.

Final Table
Division 1 — Season 1901/02

	P	W	D	L	F	A	P
1. Sunderland	34	19	6	9	50	35	44
2. Everton	34	17	7	10	53	35	41
3. Newcastle United	34	14	9	11	48	34	37
4. Blackburn R.	34	15	6	13	52	48	36
5. Nottingham F.	34	13	9	12	43	43	35
6. Derby County	34	13	9	12	39	41	35
7. Bury	34	13	8	13	44	38	34
8. Aston Villa	34	13	8	13	42	40	34
9. Sheffield W.	34	13	8	13	48	52	34
10. Sheffield United	34	13	7	14	53	48	33
11. Liverpool	34	10	12	12	42	38	32
12. Bolton W.	34	12	8	14	51	56	32
13. Notts County	34	14	4	16	51	57	32
14. Wol'hampton W.	34	13	6	15	46	57	32
15. Grimsby Town	34	13	6	15	44	60	32
16. Stoke	34	11	9	14	45	55	31
17. Small Heath	34	11	8	15	47	45	30
18. Manchester City	34	11	6	17	42	58	28

1902/03

FOOTBALL LEAGUE
Division 1

	Home	Away
A. Villa	2-1	1-3
Blackburn	2-0	0-1
Bolton	3-1	1-4
Bury	3-2	0-4
Derby	3-0	1-3
Everton	1-1	1-2
Grimsby	3-0	2-1
Liverpool	0-2	1-4
Middlesbrough	2-0	0-2
Newcastle	3-0	4-2
Nottingham F.	2-1	0-2
Notts County	2-0	0-0
Sheffield Un.	1-3	0-3
Sheffield Wed.	2-1	1-1
Stoke	1-0	0-3
Sunderland	3-3	0-3
W.B.A.	1-2	2-2

F.A. CUP
1 — Bury (a) 0-1

League appearances:
Adams, W. 1; Annis, W. 32; Baddeley, T. 26; Beats, W. M. 19; Betterley, R. H. 34; Bowen, G. 3; Dean, J. 1; Fellows, A. 27; Haywood, A. 25; Holyhead, J. 6; Jones, J. 34; Miller, J. 34; Pheasant, E. 11; Preston, H. 1; Robotham, H. 1; Smith, J. 21; Smith, W. H. 4; Stringer, J. 8; Walker, G. 21; Whitehouse, J. 31; Wooldridge, W. T. 34.

League scorers:
Haywood 11, Smith, J. 9, Wooldridge 8, Fellows 6, Miller 5, Beats 4, Walker 2, Bowen 1, Jones 1, Pheasant 1.

Final Table
Division 1 — Season 1902/03

	P	W	D	L	F	A	P
1. Sheffield Wed.	34	19	4	11	54	36	42
2. Aston Villa	34	19	3	12	61	40	41
3. Sunderland	34	16	9	9	51	36	41
4. Sheffield Un.	34	17	5	12	58	44	39
5. Liverpool	34	17	4	13	68	49	38
6. Stoke City	34	15	7	12	46	38	37
7. W. B. Albion	34	16	4	14	54	53	36
8. Bury	34	16	3	15	54	43	35
9. Derby County	34	16	3	15	50	47	35
10. Nottingham F.	34	14	7	13	49	47	35
11. Wol'hampton W.	34	14	5	15	48	57	33
12. Everton	34	13	6	15	45	47	32
13. Middlesbrough	34	14	4	16	41	50	32
14. Newcastle United	34	14	4	16	41	51	32
15. Notts County	34	12	7	15	41	49	31
16. Blackburn R.	34	12	5	17	44	63	29
17. Grimsby Town	34	8	9	17	43	62	25
18. Bolton W.	34	8	3	23	37	73	19

1903/04
FOOTBALL LEAGUE
Division 1

	Home	Away
A. Villa	3-2	0-2
Blackburn	1-0	1-1
Bury	0-0	0-0
Derby	2-2	1-2
Everton	2-2	0-2
Liverpool	4-2	2-1
Manchester City	1-6	1-4
Middlesbrough	2-2	2-1
Newcastle	3-2	0-3
Nottingham F.	3-2	0-5
Notts County	1-1	2-0
Sheffield Un.	1-0	2-7
Sheffield Wed.	2-1	0-4
Small Heath	1-0	0-3
Stoke	0-0	1-5
Sunderland	2-1	1-2
W.B.A.	1-0	2-1

F.A. CUP
1 — Stockton (a) 4-1
2 — Derby (a) 2-2
　　　　　　　(h) 2-2
　　(at Villa Park) 0-1

League appearances:
Annis, W. 31; Baddeley, T. 31; Baynham, A. 34; Betterley, R. H. 33; Bevan, F. W. 9; Haywood, A. 34; Jones, J. 34; Miller, J. 30; Pheasant, E. 14; Pilsbury, C. 1; Preston, H. 11; Smith, C. 20; Smith, J. E. 1; Smith, J. 1; Stringer, J. 3; Walker, G. 1; Walker, J. 22; Whitehouse, J. 34; Wooldridge, W. T. 30.

League scorers:
Wooldridge 16, Haywood 6, Miller 6, Smith, C. 5, Baynham 2, Bevan 2, Pheasant 2, Jones 1. Pilsbury 1. Preston 1, Whitehouse 1, Montgomery (Notts County) 1.

Final Table
Division 1 — Season 1903/04

	P	W	D	L	F	A	P
1. Sheffield Wed.	34	20	7	7	48	28	47
2. Manchester City	34	19	6	9	71	45	44
3. Everton	34	19	5	10	59	32	43
4. Newcastle United	34	18	6	10	58	45	42
5. Aston Villa	34	17	7	10	70	48	41
6. Sunderland	34	17	5	12	63	49	39
7. Sheffield United	34	15	8	11	62	57	38
8. Wol'hampton W.	34	14	8	12	44	66	36
9. Nottingham F.	34	11	9	14	57	57	31
10. Middlesbrough	34	9	12	13	46	47	30
11. Birmingham City	34	11	8	15	39	52	30
12. Bury	34	7	15	12	40	53	29
13. Notts County	34	12	5	17	37	61	29
14. Derby County	34	9	10	15	58	60	28
15. Blackburn R.	34	11	6	17	48	60	28
16. Stoke City	34	10	7	17	54	57	27
17. Liverpool	34	9	8	17	49	62	26
18. W. B. Albion	34	7	10	17	36	60	24

1904/05
FOOTBALL LEAGUE
Division 1

	Home	Away
A. Villa	1-1	0-3
Blackburn	2-0	0-3
Bury	2-0	1-3
Derby	2-0	1-2
Everton	0-3	1-2
Manchester City	0-3	1-5
Middlesbrough	5-3	1-3
Newcastle	1-3	0-3
Nottingham F.	3-2	2-2
Notts County	3-1	4-3
Preston	0-0	2-2
Sheffield Un.	4-2	2-4
Sheffield Wed.	1-0	0-4
Small Heath	0-1	1-4
Stoke	1-3	1-2
Sunderland	1-0	0-3
Woolwich Arsenal	4-1	0-2

F.A. CUP
1 — Sunderland (a) 1-1
　　　　　　　　(h) 1-0
2 — Southampton (h) 2-3

League appearances:
Annis, W. 9; Baddeley, T. 22; Baynham, A. 14; Betterley, R. H. 32; Bevan, F. W. 19; Grosvenor 2; Haywood, A. 18; Hopkins, J. 18; Jones, J. 31; Juggins, E. 9; Layton 14; Lunn, T. H. 12; Miller, J. 16; Preston, H. 4; Smith, J. 32; Smith, J. E. 12; Vesey, R. H. 2; Walker, D. 2; Walker, G. 24; Whitehouse, J. 27; Williams, W. 24; Wooldridge, W. T. 31.

League scorers:
Smith J. 14, Wooldridge 13, Bevan 6, Haywood 4, Hopkins 3, Baynham 2, Vesey 2, Betterley 1, Jones 1, Miller 1.

Final Table
Division 1 — Season 1904/05

	P	W	D	L	F	A	P
1. Newcastle United	34	23	2	9	72	33	48
2. Everton	34	21	5	8	63	36	47
3. Manchester City	34	20	6	8	66	37	46
4. Aston Villa	34	19	4	11	63	43	42
5. Sunderland	34	16	8	10	60	44	40
6. Sheffield United	34	19	2	13	64	56	40
7. Small Heath	34	17	5	12	54	38	39
8. Preston N. E.	34	13	10	11	42	37	36
9. Sheffield W.	34	14	5	15	61	57	33
10. Woolwich Arsenal	34	12	9	13	36	40	33
11. Derby County	34	12	8	14	37	48	32
12. Stoke	34	13	4	17	40	58	30
13. Blackburn R.	34	11	5	18	40	51	27
14. Wol'hampton W.	34	11	4	19	47	73	26
15. Middlesbrough	34	9	8	17	36	56	26
16. Nottingham F.	34	9	7	18	40	61	25
17. Bury	34	10	4	20	47	67	24
18. Notts County	34	5	8	21	36	69	18

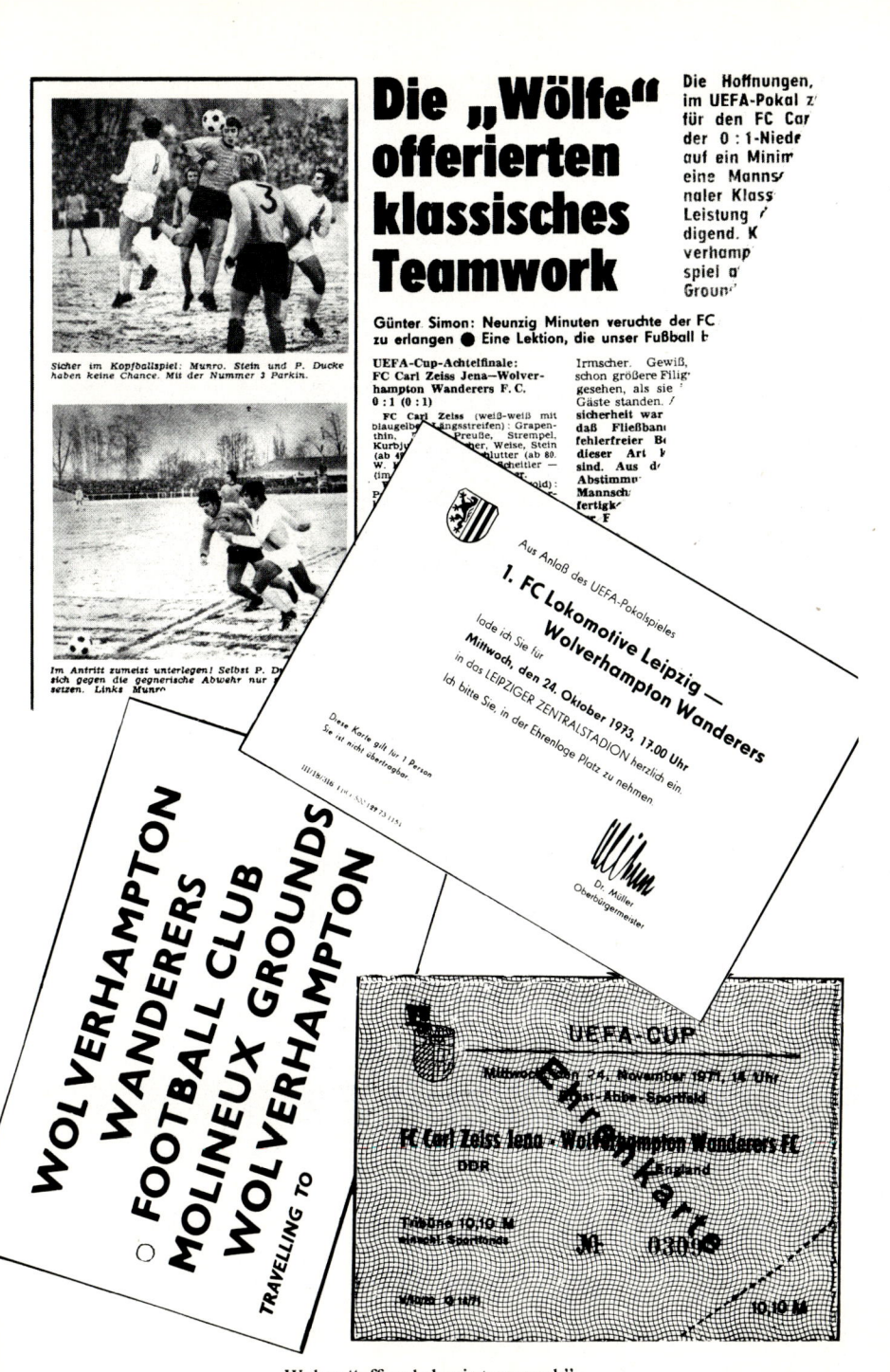

Wolves "offered classic teamwork",
UEFA journeys to Jena and Leipzig, 1971-3.

J. McAlle scores, v Coimbra.

Ado Scores penalty for Den Haag, (1971, UEFA Cup).

A. D. Dougan in prayerful mood 1973.

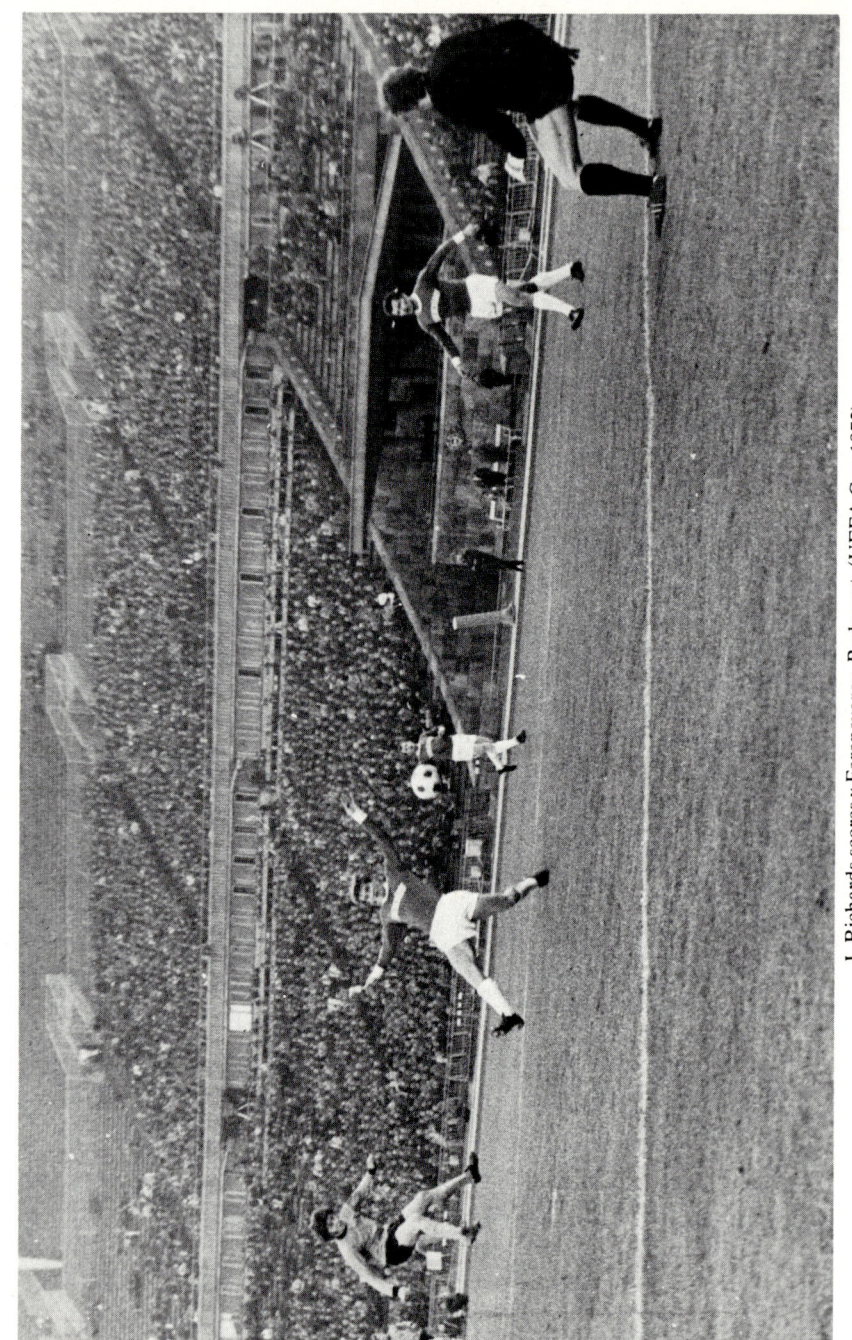

J. Richards scores v Ferencvaros, Budapest. (UEFA Cup 1972).

1905/06

FOOTBALL LEAGUE
Division 1

	Home	Away
A. Villa	4-1	0-6
Birmingham	0-0	3-3
Blackburn	2-1	1-3
Bolton	2-0	2-3
Bury	2-2	1-0
Derby	7-0	0-2
Everton	2-5	2-2
Liverpool	0-2	0-4
Manchester City	2-3	0-4
Middlesbrough	0-0	1-3
Newcastle	0-2	0-8
Nottingham F.	2-1	1-3
Notts County	6-1	2-5
Preston	2-1	2-3
Sheffield Un.	1-1	1-4
Sheffield Wed.	0-0	1-5
Stoke	1-2	0-4
Sunderland	5-2	2-7
Woolwich Arsenal	0-2	1-2

F.A. CUP
1 — Bishop Auckland (a) 3-0
2 — Bradford City (a) 0-5

League scorers:
Wooldridge 12, Pedley 10, Smith 10, Hopkins 5, Jones 4, Corfield 3, Layton 3, Pope 3, Breakwell 2, Gorman 2, Baynham 1, Boon 1, Lloyd 1, Williams, W. 1.

Final Table
Division 1 — Season 1905/06

	P	W	D	L	F	A	P
1. Liverpool	38	23	5	10	79	46	51
2. Preston N. E.	38	17	13	8	54	39	47
3. Sheffield W.	38	18	8	12	63	52	44
4. Newcastle United	38	18	7	13	74	48	43
5. Manchester City	38	19	5	14	73	54	43
6. Bolton W.	38	17	7	14	81	67	41
7. Birmingham City	38	17	7	14	65	59	41
8. Aston Villa	38	17	6	15	72	56	40
9. Blackburn R.	38	16	8	14	54	52	40
10. Stoke City	38	16	7	15	54	55	39
11. Everton	38	15	7	16	70	66	37
12. Arsenal	38	15	7	16	62	64	37
13. Sheffield United	38	15	6	17	57	62	36
14. Sunderland	38	15	5	18	61	70	35
15. Derby County	38	14	7	17	39	58	35
16. Notts County	38	11	12	15	55	71	34
17. Bury	38	11	10	17	57	74	32
18. Middlesbrough	38	10	11	17	56	71	31
19. Nottingham F.	38	13	5	20	58	79	31
20. Wol'hampton W.	38	8	7	23	58	99	23

League appearances:
Baddeley, T. 35; Baynham, A. 23; Betterley, R. H. 13; Bevan, F. W. 7; Boon 3; Breakwell, A. J. 19; Corfield, S. 27; Goodall, J. 7; Gorman, J. 1; Henshall, H. Y. 2; Hopkins, J. 10; Hughes 9; James 17; Jones, J. 38; Juggins, E. 6; Layton 15; Lloyd, A. 17; Lunn, T. H. 3; Pedley, J. 21; Pope 8; Radford 2; Raybould, T. 6; Smith, J. 26; Stanley, J. 19; Whitehouse, J. 23; Wilkes 1; Williams, G. 4; Williams, W. 23; Wooldridge, W. T. 33.

1906/07

FOOTBALL LEAGUE
Division 2

	Home	Away
Barnsley	5-1	1-0
Blackpool	1-1	2-1
Bradford City	1-1	3-2
Burnley	3-0	0-3
Burslem P. V.	6-2	0-0
Burton U.	3-0	1-4
Chelsea	1-2	0-4
Chesterfield	2-1	2-3
Clapton Orient	6-1	0-4
Gainsborough	1-0	0-1
Glossop	4-0	1-2
Grimsby	5-0	1-2
Hull	1-1	1-5
Leeds	3-2	0-2
Leicester	1-0	0-2
Lincoln	3-0	4-0
Nottingham F.	2-0	0-1
Stockport	1-1	0-0
W.B.A.	0-3	1-1

F.A. CUP
1 — Sheffield Wed. (a) 2-3

League appearances:
Baddeley, T. 27; Bishop, A. J. 38; Breakwell, A. J. 5; Corbett, P. B. 2; Corfield, S. 17; Gorman, J. 8; Hawkins, A. 20; Hedley, G. A. 37; Hopkins, J. 15; Hunt, K. R. G. 3; Jones, J. 38; Juggins, E. 7; Lloyd, A. 35; Lunn, T. H. 11; Pedley, J. 38; Price, A. 1; Raybould, T. 9; Roberts, J. 24; Ward, S. 29; Williams, W. 22; Wooldridge, W. T. 32.

League scorers:
Roberts 15, Hedley 11, Hawkins 9, Pedley 5, Wooldridge 5, Hopkins 4, Jones 4, Bishop 3, Williams 3, Gorman 2, Breakwell 1, Corbett 1, Raybould 1, Ward 1, Dixon (Burnley) 1.

Final Table

Division II — Season 1906/07

	P	W	D	L	F	A	P
1. Nottingham F.	38	28	4	6	74	36	60
2. Chelsea	38	26	5	7	80	34	57
3. Leicester Fosse	38	20	8	10	62	39	48
4. W. B. Albion	38	21	5	12	83	45	47
5. Bradford City	38	21	5	12	70	53	47
6. Wol'hampton W.	38	17	7	14	66	53	41
7. Burnley	38	17	6	15	62	47	40
8. Barnsley	38	15	8	15	73	55	38
9. Hull City	38	15	7	16	65	57	37
10. Leeds City	38	13	10	15	55	63	36
11. Grimsby Town	38	16	3	19	57	62	35
12. Stockport County	38	12	11	15	42	52	35
13. Blackpool	38	11	11	16	33	51	33
14. Gainsborough T.	38	14	5	19	45	72	33
15. Glossop N. E.	38	13	6	19	53	79	32
16. Burslem P. Vale	38	12	7	19	60	83	31
17. Clapton Orient	38	11	8	19	45	67	30
18. Chesterfield T.	38	11	7	20	50	66	29
19. Lincoln City	38	12	4	22	46	73	28
20. Burton Utd.	38	8	7	23	34	68	23

League appearances:
Bishop, A. J. 33; Bould, G. 6; Callanan, W. D. 3; Cartwright, A. 2; Collins, E. 33; Corbett, P. B. 4; Ferris, W. F. 2; Fownes, W. 1; Harrison, W. E. 31; Hedley, G. A. 30; Holt, S. 8; Hunt, K. R. G. 21; Jeavons, W. H. 1; Jones, J. 31; Lloyd, A. 26; Lunn, T. H. 34; Mason, J. 4; Metcalf, T. C. 7; Payne, C. E. 2; Pedley, J. 34; Radford, W. R. 25; Shelton, J. 24; Tatem, F. E. 2; Wake, B. 4; Ward, S. 13; Williams, W. 8; Wood, S. 1; Wooldridge, W. T. 28.

League scorers:
Hedley 12, Radford 9, Shelton 9, Harrison 4, Pedley 4, Wooldridge 4, Corbett 2, Lloyd 2, Bould 1, Jones 1, Mason 1, Wake 1.

Final Table

Division II — Season 1907/08

	P	W	D	L	F	A	P
1. Bradford City	38	24	6	8	90	42	54
2. Leicester Fosse	38	21	10	7	72	47	52
3. Oldham Athletic	38	22	6	10	76	42	50
4. Fulham	38	22	5	11	82	49	49
5. W.B.A.	38	19	9	10	61	39	47
6. Derby County	38	21	4	13	77	45	46
7. Burnley	38	20	6	12	67	50	46
8. Hull City	38	21	4	13	73	62	46
9. Wol'hampton W.	38	15	7	16	50	45	37
10. Stoke	38	16	5	17	57	52	37
11. Gainsborough T.	38	14	7	17	47	71	35
12. Leeds City	38	12	8	18	53	65	32
13. Stockport County	38	12	8	18	48	67	32
14. Clapton Orient	38	11	10	17	40	65	32
15. Blackpool	38	11	9	18	51	58	31
16. Barnsley	38	12	6	20	54	68	30
17. Glossop	38	11	8	19	54	74	30
18. Grimsby Town	38	11	8	19	43	71	30
19. Chesterfield T.	38	6	11	21	46	92	23
20. Lincoln City	38	9	3	26	46	83	21

1907/08

FOOTBALL LEAGUE
Division 2

	Home	Away
Barnsley	0-1	0-5
Blackpool	1-0	2-0
Bradford City	0-0	2-6
Burnley	5-1	0-1
Chesterfield	0-0	0-2
Clapton Orient	2-0	1-1
Derby	2-2	2-3
Fulham	2-0	1-2
Gainsborough	1-0	1-0
Glossop	5-0	1-1
Grimsby	5-1	1-0
Hull	1-2	0-2
Leeds	2-0	1-3
Leicester	0-0	0-1
Lincoln	3-0	1-3
Oldham	2-1	0-2
Stockport	0-1	3-1
Stoke	2-0	0-0
W.B.A.	1-2	0-1

F.A. CUP

1 — Bradford C.	(a)	1-1
	(h)	1-0
2 — Bury	(h)	2-0
3 — Swindon	(h)	2-0
4 — Stoke	(a)	1-0
S.F. — Southampton		
(at Stamford Bridge)		2-0
F. — Newcastle		
(at Crystal Palace)		3-1

1908/09

FOOTBALL LEAGUE
Division 2

	Home	Away
Barnsley	2-0	1-1
Birmingham	2-0	1-1
Blackpool	2-2	1-3
Bolton	1-2	1-1
Bradford	1-1	1-4
Burnley	2-1	5-3
Chesterfield	3-0	1-1
Clapton Orient	5-1	3-1
Derby	1-1	1-2
Fulham	0-1	1-1
Gainsborough	4-0	0-1
Glossop	0-0	2-3

APPENDIX

Grimsby	0-0	0-3
Hull	3-0	1-0
Leeds	2-1	2-5
Oldham	1-1	1-2
Stockport	2-0	0-1
Tottenham	1-0	0-3
W.B.A.	0-1	2-0

F.A. CUP
1 — C. Palace   (h) 2-2
                       (a) 2-4

League appearances:
Arrowsmith, A. 1; Bishop, A. J. 36; Blunt, W. 15; Collins, E. 37; Conway, A. J. 2; Gregory, J. T. 1; Hardware, J. 8; Harris, W. T. 5; Harrison, W. E. 35; Hedley, G. A. 19; Hoskins, A. H. 9; Hunt, K. R. G. 10; Jeavons, W. H. 7; Jones, J. 37; Lunn, T. H. 36; Mason, J. 4; May, G. J. 15; Metcalf, T. C. 2; Payne, C. E. 4; Pedley, J. 34; Pemble, A. 2; Radford, W. R. 37; Shelton, J. 33; Ward, S. 2; Wooldridge, W. T. 27.

League scorers:
Radford 21, Hedley 11, Blunt 9, Harrison 4, Pedley 3, Shelton 3, Jones 2, Harris 1, Hoskins 1, Hunt 1.

Final Table
Division II — Season 1908/09

	P	W	D	L	F	A	P
1. Bolton Wand.	38	24	4	10	59	28	52
2. Tottenham H.	38	20	11	7	67	32	51
3. W.B.A.	38	19	13	6	56	27	51
4. Hull City	38	19	6	13	63	39	44
5. Derby Co.	38	16	11	11	55	41	43
6. Oldham Ath.	38	17	6	15	55	43	40
7. Wol'hampton W.	38	14	11	13	56	48	39
8. Glossop	38	15	8	15	57	53	38
9. Gainsborough Tr.	38	15	8	15	49	70	38
10. Fulham	38	13	11	14	58	48	37
11. Birmingham	38	14	9	15	58	61	37
12. Leeds City	38	14	7	17	43	53	35
13. Grimsby Town	38	14	7	17	41	54	35
14. Burnley	38	13	7	18	51	58	33
15. Clapton Orient	38	12	9	17	37	49	33
16. Bradford P. A.	38	13	6	19	51	59	32
17. Barnsley	38	11	10	17	48	57	32
18. Stockport Co.	38	14	3	21	39	71	31
19. Chesterfield T.	38	11	8	19	37	67	30
20. Blackpool	38	9	11	18	46	68	29

1909/10

FOOTBALL LEAGUE
Division 2

	Home	Away
Barnsley	1-0	1-7
Birmingham	4-2	0-1
Blackpool	2-1	0-2
Bradford	0-2	3-2
Burnley	3-1	2-4
Clapton Orient	3-1	0-1
Derby	2-3	0-5
Fulham	1-1	0-0
Gainsborough	0-0	2-0
Glossop	3-1	0-2
Grimsby	8-1	0-1
Hull	2-2	2-2
Leeds	5-0	0-1
Leicester	4-1	1-2
Lincoln	4-2	0-1
Man. City	3-2	0-6
Oldham	1-0	0-3
Stockport	2-1	1-1
W.B.A.	3-1	1-0

F.A. CUP
1 — Reading   (a) 5-0
2 — West Ham   (h) 1-5

League appearances:
Bishop, A. J. 38; Blunt, W. 34; Boxley, F. 4; Collins, E. 29; Conway, A. J. 28; Garratly, G. 13; Groves, A. 1; Hardware, J. 1; Harrison, W. E. 35; Hedley, G. A. 34; Hill, J. T. 1; Hoskins, A. H. 4; Hunt, K. R. G. 7; Jones, J. 34; Lunn, T. H. 33; Needham, J. 1; Payne, C. E. 6; Pedley, J. 29; Perrett, W. 1; Radford, W. R. 21; Shelton, J. 26; Shinton, B. 1; Walker, A. J. 1; Wooldridge, W. T. 36.

League scorers:
Blunt 23, Radford 11, Hedley 10, Harrison 6, Pedley 3, Shelton 3, Jones 2, Bishop 1, Needham 1, Payne 1, Shinton 1, Wooldridge 1, Jackson (Lincoln) 1.

Final Table
Division II — Season 1909/10

	P	W	D	L	F	A	P
1. Man. City	38	23	8	7	81	40	54
2. Oldham Ath.	38	23	7	8	79	39	53
3. Hull City	38	23	7	8	80	46	53
4. Derby Co.	38	22	9	7	72	47	53
5. Leicester Fosse	38	20	4	14	79	58	44
6. Glossop	38	18	7	13	64	57	43
7. Fulham	38	14	13	11	51	43	41
8. Wol'hampton W.	38	17	6	15	64	63	40
9. Barnsley	38	16	7	15	62	59	39
10. Bradford P. A.	38	17	4	17	64	59	38
11. W.B.A.	38	16	5	17	58	56	37
12. Blackpool	38	14	8	16	50	52	36
13. Stockport Co.	38	13	8	17	50	47	34
14. Burnley	38	14	6	18	62	61	34
15. Lincoln C.	38	10	11	17	42	69	31
16. Clapton Orient	38	12	6	20	37	60	30
17. Leeds City	38	10	7	21	46	80	27
18. Gainsborough Tr.	38	10	6	22	33	75	26
19. Grimsby Town	38	9	6	23	50	77	24
20. Birmingham	38	8	7	23	42	78	23

1910/11

FOOTBALL LEAGUE
Division 2

	Home	Away
Barnsley	1-0	2-2
Birmingham	3-1	3-1
Blackpool	0-3	0-2
Bolton	3-0	1-4
Bradford	0-0	0-1
Burnley	1-0	1-1
Chelsea	0-0	0-2
Clapton Orient	1-0	1-3
Derby	1-2	0-2
Fulham	5-1	1-0
Gainsborough	1-1	3-1
Glossop	2-0	1-5
Huddersfield	0-3	1-3
Hull	0-0	2-2
Leeds	3-1	0-1
Leicester	1-0	3-2
Lincoln	2-1	5-1
Stockport	0-0	0-1
W.B.A.	2-3	1-2

F.A. CUP
1 — Accrington (h) 2-0
2 — Man. City (h) 1-0
3 — Chelsea (h) 0-2

League scorers:
Needham J. 14, Hedley 11, A. Harrison 9, Blunt 6, Needham 6, Walker, A. S. 2, Bishop 1, Deakin 1, Wooldridge 1.

Final Table
Division II — Season 1910/11

	P	W	D	L	F	A	P
1. W. B. Albion	38	22	9	7	67	41	53
2. Bolton Wand.	38	21	9	8	69	40	51
3. Chelsea	38	20	9	9	71	35	49
4. Clapton Orient	38	19	7	12	44	35	45
5. Hull City	38	14	16	8	55	39	44
6. Derby Co.	38	17	8	13	73	52	42
7. Blackpool	38	16	10	12	49	38	42
8. Burnley	38	13	15	10	45	45	41
9. Wol'hampton W.	38	15	8	15	51	52	38
10. Fulham	38	15	7	16	52	48	37
11. Leeds City	38	15	7	16	58	56	37
12. Bradford P. A.	38	14	9	15	53	55	37
13. Huddersfield	38	13	8	17	57	58	34
14. Glossop	38	13	8	17	48	62	34
15. Leicester Fosse	38	14	5	19	52	62	33
16. Birmingham	38	12	8	18	42	64	32
17. Stockport Co.	38	11	8	19	47	79	30
18. Gainsborough Tr.	38	9	11	18	37	55	29
19. Barnsley	38	7	14	17	52	62	28
20. Lincoln City	38	7	10	21	28	72	24

League appearances:
Bishop, A. J. 38; Blunt, W. 8; Boxley, F. 36; Brookes, A. W. 6; Collins, E. 37; Deakin, E. 5; Fownes, W. 7; Garratly, G. 38; Groves, A. 38; Harrison, W. E. 33; Hedley, G. A. 31; Hill, J. T. 2; Hunt, K. R. G. 4; Jones, J. 5; Micklewright, W. 5; Needham, A. 33; Needham, J. 35; Walker, A. 4; Walker, A. S. 26; Wooldridge, W. T. 27.

1911/12

FOOTBALL LEAGUE
Division 2

	Home	Away
Barnsley	5-0	1-2
Birmingham	1-0	1-3
Blackpool	3-0	0-1
Bradford	1-1	2-0
Bristol City	3-1	3-0
Burnley	2-0	1-2
Chelsea	3-1	0-4
Clapton Orient	0-1	0-1
Derby	0-1	1-1
Fulham	0-0	1-1
Gainsborough	1-0	1-0
Glossop	1-1	1-0
Grimsby	1-2	0-0
Huddersfield	1-2	1-1
Hull	8-0	0-3
Leeds	5-0	1-1
Leicester	1-0	1-1
Nottingham F.	1-0	0-0
Stockport	4-0	2-1

F.A. CUP
1 — Watford (a) 0-0
              (h) 10-0
2 — Lincoln (h) 2-1
3 — Blackburn (a) 2-3

League appearances:
Bishop, A. J. 35; Blunt, W. 1; Boxley, F. 27; Brookes, A. W. 3; Brooks, S. 13; Collins, E. 37; Fownes, W. 4; Garratly, G. 38; Groves, A. 37; Halligan, W. 35; Harrison, W. E. 38; Hedley, G. A. 32; Hunt, K. R. G. 2; Jones, J. 2; Needham, J. 36; Parsonage, H. 9; Peers, E. J. 11; Perrett, W. 3; Sheargold, A. L. 4; Young, R. 25; Yule, T. 26.

League scorers:
Halligan 20, Hedley 7, Needham 7, Harrison 6, Yule 6, Young 5, Parsonage 4, Brooks 1, Garratly 1.

Final Table
Division II — Season 1911/12

	P	W	D	L	F	A	P
1. Derby Co.	38	23	8	7	74	28	54
2. Chelsea	38	24	6	8	64	34	54
3. Burnley	38	22	8	8	77	41	52
4. Clapton Orient	38	21	3	14	61	44	45
5. Wol'hampton W.	38	16	10	12	57	33	42
6. Barnsley	39	15	12	11	45	42	42
7. Hull City	38	17	8	13	54	51	42
8. Fulham	38	16	7	15	66	58	39
9. Grimsby Town	38	15	9	14	48	55	39
10. Leicester Fosse	38	15	7	16	49	66	37
11. Bradford P. A.	38	13	9	16	44	45	35
12. Birmingham	38	14	6	18	55	59	34
13. Bristol City	38	14	6	18	41	60	34
14. Blackpool	38	13	8	17	32	52	34
15. Nottingham F.	38	13	7	18	46	48	33
16. Stockport Co.	38	11	11	16	47	54	33
17. Huddersfield T.	38	13	6	19	50	64	32
18. Glossop	38	8	12	18	42	56	28
19. Leeds City	38	10	8	20	50	78	28
20. Gainsborough Tr.	38	5	13	20	30	64	23

1912/13

FOOTBALL LEAGUE
Division 2

	Home	Away
Barnsley	3-0	2-3
Birmingham	2-2	0-0
Blackpool	4-0	2-1
Bradford	0-0	1-5
Bristol City	1-1	1-3
Burnley	0-2	2-4
Bury	3-1	0-1
Clapton Orient	1-1	0-0
Fulham	2-1	2-4
Glossop	3-1	3-1
Grimsby	3-0	1-2
Huddersfield	2-0	1-2
Hull	0-1	1-0
Leeds	2-2	2-2
Leicester	1-1	1-0
Lincoln	2-0	1-2
Nottingham F.	2-3	0-2
Preston	2-0	1-1
Stockport	1-0	1-5

F.A. CUP
1 — London Call.   (h) 3-1
2 — Bradford   (a) 0-3

League appearances:
Bishop, A. J. 36; Brookes, A. W. 6; Brooks, S. 34; Collins, E. 38; Crabtree, J. 1; Dunn, R. 1; Garratly, G. 32; Groves, A. 37; Halligan, W. 32; Harrison, W. E. 34; Hedley, G. A. 11; Hunt, K. R. G. 2; Jones, J. 1; Jordan, W. C. 3; Mulholland, T. 6; Needham, J. 35; Parsonage, H. 11; Peers, E. J. 38; Price, A. 15; Smart, B. 3; Young, R. 34; Yule, T. 8.

League scorers:
Halligan 15, Needham 9, Brooks 7, Groves 6, Parsonage 4, Harrison 3, Hedley 3, Young 3, Garratly 1, Jones 1, Jordan 1, Mulholland 1, Yule 1, Tufnell (Barnsley) 1.

Final Table
Division II — Season 1912/13

	P	W	D	L	F	A	P
1. Preston N. E.	38	19	15	4	56	33	53
2. Burnley	38	21	8	9	88	53	50
3. Birmingham City	38	18	10	10	59	44	46
4. Barnsley	38	19	7	12	57	47	45
5. Huddersfield T.	38	17	9	12	66	40	43
6. Leeds City	38	15	10	13	70	64	40
7. Grimsby Town	38	15	10	13	51	50	40
8. Lincoln City	38	15	10	13	50	52	40
9. Fulham	38	17	5	16	65	55	39
10. Wol'hampton W.	38	14	10	14	56	54	38
11. Bury	38	15	8	15	53	57	38
12. Hull City	38	15	6	17	60	56	36
13. Bradford	38	14	8	16	60	60	36
14. Clapton Orient	38	10	14	14	34	47	34
15. Leicester Fosse	38	13	7	18	50	65	33
16. Bristol City	38	9	15	14	46	72	33
17. Nottingham F.	38	12	8	18	58	59	32
18. Glossop N. E.	38	12	8	18	49	68	32
19. Stockport County	38	8	10	20	56	78	26
20. Blackpool	38	9	8	21	39	69	26

1913/14

FOOTBALL LEAGUE
Division 2

	Home	Away
Barnsley	0-1	1-2
Birmingham	1-0	1-4
Blackpool	1-0	0-2
Bradford	1-0	0-1
Bristol City	0-2	0-0
Bury	3-0	4-1
Clapton Orient	2-1	2-2
Fulham	1-0	0-1
Glossop	1-0	2-1
Grimsby	4-1	0-1
Huddersfield	2-2	0-0
Hull	1-0	1-7
Leeds	1-3	0-5
Leicester	2-1	3-2
Lincoln	1-0	0-1
Nottingham F.	4-1	3-1
Notts County	4-1	0-2
Stockport	3-1	0-0
Woolwich Arsenal	1-2	1-3

F.A. CUP

1 — Southampton	(h)	3-0
2 — Sheffield Wed.	(h)	1-1
	(a)	0-1

League appearances:
Bishop, A. J. 34; Brookes, A. W. 3; Brooks, A. 11; Brooks, S. 32; Collins, E. 37; Crabtree, J. 9; Francis, E. 10; Garratly, G. 27; Griffiths, C. R. 4; Groves, A. 31; Harrison, W. E. 35; Hayes, W. 2; Howell, H. 15; Hughes, W. H. 21; Lea, T. 2; Lloyd, H. 8; Lockett, W. C. 6; Marr, A. 3; Needham, J. 33; Peers, E. J. 36; Price, F. 38; Richards, R. W. 10; Riley, A. 1; Streets, J. W. 2; Young, R. 8.

League scorers:
Brooks, S. 11, Hughes 10, Needham 7, Harrison 6, Francis 3, Groves 3, Richards 3, Griffiths 2, Lockett 2, Young 2, Garratly 1, Lloyd 1.

Final Table
Division II — Season 1913/14

	P	W	D	L	F	A	P
1. Notts County	38	23	7	8	77	36	53
2. Bradford	38	23	3	12	71	47	49
3. Woolwich A.	38	20	9	9	54	38	49
4. Leeds City	38	20	7	11	76	46	47
5. Barnsley	38	19	7	12	51	45	45
6. Clapton Orient	38	16	11	11	47	35	43
7. Hull City	38	16	9	13	53	37	41
8. Bristol City	38	16	9	13	52	50	41
9. Wol'hampton W.	38	18	5	15	51	52	41
10. Bury	38	15	10	13	39	40	40
11. Fulham	38	16	6	16	46	43	38
12. Stockport County	38	13	10	15	55	57	36
13. Huddersfield T.	38	13	8	17	47	53	34
14. Birmingham City	38	12	10	16	48	60	34
15. Grimsby Town	38	13	8	17	42	58	34
16. Blackpool	38	9	14	15	33	44	32
17. Glossop N. E.	38	11	6	21	51	67	28
18. Leicester Fosse	38	11	4	23	45	61	26
19. Lincoln City	38	10	6	22	36	66	26
20. Nottingham F.	38	7	9	22	37	76	23

1914/15

FOOTBALL LEAGUE
Division 2

	Home	Away
Barnsley	4-1	1-2
Birmingham	0-0	2-1
Blackpool	2-0	0-1
Bristol City	2-2	1-0
Bury	1-1	1-4
Clapton Orient	0-0	1-1
Derby	0-1	1-3
Fulham	2-0	1-0
Glossop	4-0	2-0
Grimsby	0-1	4-1
Huddersfield	4-1	0-2
Hull	1-2	1-5
Leeds	5-1	3-2
Leicester	7-0	3-0
Lincoln	3-1	2-2
Nottingham F.	5-1	1-3
Preston	2-0	3-5
Stockport	4-1	2-2
Woolwich Arsenal	1-0	1-5

F.A. CUP

1 — Reading	(a)	1-0
2 — Sheffield Wed.	(a)	0-2

League appearances:
Bishop, A. J. 38; Brookes, A. W 1; Brooks, A. 4; Brooks, S. 37; Collins, E. 37; Curtis, F. 37; Dunn, R. 14; Garratly, G. 34; Griffiths, C. R. 9; Groves, A. 31; Harrison, W. E. 35; Howell, H. 12; Langford, T. S. 7; Lea, T. 3; Needham, J. 32; Parfitt, G. 1; Peers, E. J. 38; Price, F. 35; Richards, R. W. 3; Riley, A. 10.

League scorers:
Curtis 25, Brooks, S. 18, Needham 15, Howell 4, Dunn 3, Garratly 3, Langford 3, Richards 3, Bishop 1, Grove, 1, Harrison 1.

Final Table
Division II — Season 1914/15

	P	W	D	L	F	A	P
1. Derby Co.	38	23	7	8	71	33	53
2. Preston N. E.	38	20	10	8	61	42	50
3. Barnsley	38	22	3	13	51	51	47
4. Wol'hampton W.	38	19	7	12	77	52	45
5. Birmingham	38	17	9	12	62	39	43
6. Arsenal	38	19	5	14	69	41	43
7. Hull City	38	19	5	14	65	54	43
8. Huddersfield	38	17	8	13	61	42	42
9. Clapton Orient	38	16	9	13	50	48	41
10. Blackpool	38	17	5	16	58	57	39
11. Bury	38	15	8	15	61	56	38
12. Fulham	38	15	7	16	53	47	37
13. Bristol City	38	15	7	16	62	56	37
14. Stockport Co.	38	15	7	16	54	60	37
15. Leeds City	38	14	4	20	65	64	32
16. Lincoln City	38	11	9	18	46	65	31
17. Grimsby Town	38	11	9	18	48	76	31
18. Nottingham F.	38	10	9	19	43	77	29
19. Leicester Fosse	38	10	4	24	47	88	24
20. Glossop	38	6	6	26	31	87	18

1919/20

FOOTBALL LEAGUE
Division 2

	Home	Away
Barnsley	2-4	1-4
Birmingham	0-2	0-2
Blackpool	0-3	1-1
Bristol City	3-1	1-1
Bury	0-1	0-2
Clapton Orient	1-2	0-0
Coventry	2-0	0-1
Fulham	2-1	1-1
Grimsby	6-1	1-0
Huddersfield	2-3	0-2
Hull	4-2	3-10
*{ Leeds City / Port Vale	2-4	1-1
Leicester	1-1	2-1
Lincoln	4-0	0-4
Nottingham F.	4-0	0-1
Rotherham	0-1	0-2
South Shields	0-0	0-0
Stockport	2-2	1-4
Stoke	4-0	0-3
Tottenham	1-3	2-4
West Ham	1-1	0-4

F.A. CUP
1 — Blackburn (a) 2-2
               (h) 1-0
2 — Cardiff (h) 1-2

*Wolves played both games against Leeds City who were later expelled. Their results were transferred to Port Vale who took over their fixtures.

League appearances:
Bate, W. 11; Bansond 1; Baugh, R. 26; Bird, H. 3; Bishop, A. J. 31; Brooks, S. 34; Curtis, F. 3; Cutler, E. 13; Garratly, G. 35; Green, J. A. 6; Groves, A. 25; Harrison, W. E. 31; Higgs, H. 3; Hodnett, J. E. 12; Howell, H. 11; Hunt, K. R. G. Rev. 1; Jones, J. 18; Lea, T. 11; Needham, J. 14; Nightingale, J. G. 3; Parfitt, G. 3; Peers, E. J. 30; Price, J. 28; Richards, R. W. 27; Riley, A. 26; Roper, F. L. 1; Rostance, J. C. 9; Sambrook, J. H. 15; Smart, B. 4; Woodward, M. 9; Wright, H. F. 18.

League scorers:
Richards 10, Brooks 6, Bate, Needham, Sambrook each 5, Cutler, Groves, Wright each 4, Harrison 3, Howell, Lea each 2, Green, Hodnett, Smart, Woodward, Williams (Barnsley) each 1.

Final Table
Division II — Season 1919/20

		P	W	D	L	F	A	P
1.	Tottenham H.	42	32	6	4	102	32	70
2.	Huddersfield T.	42	28	8	6	97	38	64
3.	Birmingham C.	42	24	8	10	85	34	56
4.	Blackpool	42	21	10	11	65	47	52
5.	Bury	42	20	8	14	60	44	48
6.	Fulham	42	19	9	14	61	50	47
7.	West Ham Un.	42	19	9	14	47	40	47
8.	Bristol City	42	13	17	12	46	43	43
9.	Gateshead	42	15	12	15	58	48	42
10.	Stoke City	42	18	6	18	60	54	42
11.	Hull City	42	18	6	18	78	72	42
12.	Barnsley	42	15	10	17	61	55	40
13.	Leeds City & Port Vale*	42	16	8	18	59	62	40
14.	Leicester City	42	15	10	17	41	61	40
15.	Leyton Orient	42	16	6	20	51	59	38
16.	Stockport County	42	14	9	19	52	61	37
17.	Rotherham Un.	42	13	8	21	51	83	34
18.	Nottingham F.	42	11	9	22	43	73	31
19.	Wol'hampton W.	42	10	10	22	55	80	30
20.	Coventry City	42	9	11	22	35	73	29
21.	Lincoln City	42	9	9	24	44	101	27
22.	Grimsby Town	42	10	5	27	34	75	25

*Port Vale took over fixtures in October after Leeds City had been disbanded by the F.A.

1920/21

FOOTBALL LEAGUE
Division 2

	Home	Away
Barnsley	1-1	2-3
Birmingham	0-3	1-4
Blackpool	3-1	0-3
Bristol City	0-0	0-2
Bury	2-1	1-3
Cardiff	1-3	0-2
Clapton Orient	0-2	1-0
Coventry	1-0	0-4
Fulham	1-0	0-2
Hull	1-3	1-0
Leeds	3-0	0-3
Leicester	3-0	0-0
Nottingham F.	2-1	1-1
Notts County	1-0	1-2
Port Vale	2-2	3-2
Rotherham	3-0	0-1
Sheffield Wed.	1-2	0-6
South Shields	3-0	2-1
Stockport	2-0	2-1
Stoke	3-3	0-1
West Ham	1-2	0-1

F.A. CUP

1 — Stoke	(h)	3-2
2 — Derby	(a)	1-1
	(h)	1-0
3 — Fulham	(a)	1-0
4 — Everton	(a)	1-0
S.F. — Cardiff (Anfield)		0-0
(Old Trafford)		3-1
F. — Tottenham		
(at Stamford Bridge)		0-1

League appearances:
R. Baugh 20; S. Brooks 33; F. Burrill 33; C. N Caddick 4; E. R. Cutler 5; G. Edmonds 37; N. George 8; V. Gregory 32; F. F. Hales 2; W. E. Harrison 10; Hartland 1; J. Hodnett 26; J. Jones 18; T. Lea 16; G. H. Marshall 38; P. Newell 3; E. J. Peers 33; A. Potts 28; J. Price 11; W. R. Richards 21; A. Riley 40; J. H. S. Sambrook 6; D. Stokes 7; A. Thomas 9; M. Woodward 21.

League scorers:
Edmonds 11, Potts, Burrell each 9, Brooks 6, Hodnett 3, Gregory, Richards, Sambrook each 2, Hales, Harrison, Jones, Price, Riley each 1.

Final Table
Division II — Season 1920/21

	P	W	D	L	F	A	P
1. Birmingham C.	42	24	10	8	79	38	58
2. Cardiff City	42	24	10	8	59	32	58
3. Bristol City	42	19	13	10	49	29	51
4. Blackpool	42	20	10	12	54	42	50
5. West Ham Un.	42	19	10	13	51	30	48
6. Notts County	42	18	11	13	55	40	47
7. Leyton Orient	42	16	13	13	43	42	45
8. Gateshead	42	17	10	15	61	46	44
9. Fulham	42	16	10	16	43	47	42
10. Sheffield W.	42	15	11	16	48	48	41
11. Bury	42	15	10	17	45	49	40
12. Leicester City	42	12	16	14	39	46	40
13. Hull City	42	10	20	12	43	53	40
14. Leeds United	42	14	10	18	40	45	38
15. Wol'hampton W.	42	16	6	20	49	66	38
16. Barnsley	42	10	16	16	48	50	36
17. Port Vale	42	11	14	17	43	49	36
18. Nottingham F.	42	12	12	18	48	55	36
19. Rotherham Un.	42	12	12	18	37	53	36
20. Stoke City	42	12	11	19	46	56	35
21. Coventry City	42	12	11	19	39	70	35
22. Stockport Co.	42	9	12	21	42	75	30

1921/22

FOOTBALL LEAGUE
Division 2

	Home	Away
Barnsley	2-0	1-2
Blackpool	4-0	3-1
Bradford	5-0	0-0
Bristol City	2-2	0-2
Bury	1-1	1-2
Clapton Orient	0-2	0-1
Coventry	1-0	1-3
C. Palace	0-1	1-1
Derby	0-3	3-2
Fulham	0-0	0-1
Hull	0-2	0-2
Leeds	0-0	0-0
Leicester	1-1	1-0
Nottingham F.	2-0	0-0
Notts County	1-2	0-4
Port Vale	2-0	2-0
Rotherham	3-1	0-1
Sheffield Wed.	0-0	1-3
South Shields	3-2	2-0
Stoke	1-1	0-3
West Ham	0-1	0-2

F.A. CUP

1 — Preston	(a)	0-3

League scorers:
Edmonds 13, Bisset 9, Hargreaves 5, Burrill, Richards each 4, Baugh 3, Brooks 2, Caddick, Lea, Marshall, Smart each 1.

Final Table
Division II — Season 1921/22

	P	W	D	L	F	A	P
1. Nottingham F.	42	22	12	8	51	30	56
2. Stoke	42	18	16	8	60	44	52
3. Barnsley	42	22	8	12	67	52	52
4. West Ham Utd.	42	20	8	14	52	39	48
5. Hull City	42	19	10	13	51	41	48
6. South Shields	42	17	12	13	43	38	46
7. Fulham	42	18	9	15	57	38	45
8. Leicester City	42	14	17	11	39	34	45
9. Leeds Utd.	42	16	13	13	48	38	45
10. Sheffield W.	42	15	14	13	47	50	44
11. Bury	42	15	10	17	54	55	40
12. Derby Co.	42	15	9	18	60	64	39
13. Notts Co.	42	12	15	15	47	51	39
14. C. Palace	42	13	13	16	45	51	39
15. Clapton O.	42	15	9	18	43	50	39
16. Rotherham Co.	42	14	11	17	32	43	39
17. Wol'hampton W.	42	13	11	18	44	49	37
18. Port Vale	42	14	8	20	43	57	36
19. Blackpool	42	15	5	22	44	57	35
20. Coventry City	42	12	18	20	51	60	34
21. Bristol City	42	12	9	21	37	58	33
22. Bradford P. A.	42	12	9	21	46	62	33

League appearances:
Baugh, R. 40; Bissett, G. 25; Brooks, S. 34; Burrill, F. 17; Caddick, C. N. 28; Carter, E. T. 10; Edmonds, G. W. 39; George, N. 42; Gregory, V. 39; Gill, J. 7; Hargreaves, H. 28; Hodnett, J. 14; Lea, T. 15; Marshall, G. H. 34; Mayson, T. 2; Newell, P. 1; Potts, A. 7; Price, J. 2; Richards, R. W. 27; Riley, A. 32; Rouse 5; Smart, F. L. 3; Thomas, A. 2; Watson, E. 6; Woodward, M. 3.

1922/23

FOOTBALL LEAGUE
Division 2

	Home	Away
Barnsley	3-3	0-1
Blackpool	3-4	1-3
Bradford City	4-1	1-1
Bury	1-1	0-3
Clapton Orient	1-3	1-4
Coventry	1-2	1-7
C. Palace	1-0	0-5
Derby	0-1	1-1
Fulham	0-0	0-2
Hull	3-0	0-0
Leeds	0-1	0-1
Leicester	1-2	0-7
Man. United	0-1	0-1
Notts County	1-0	1-4
Port Vale	3-0	0-1
Rotherham	3-2	2-3
Sheffield Wed.	2-0	0-1
Southampton	0-0	0-3
South Shields	1-0	1-1
Stockport	3-1	1-1
West Ham	1-4	0-1

F.A. CUP
1 — Merthyr (a) 1-0
2 — Liverpool (h) 0-2

League appearances:
Baugh, R. 21; Best, R. 22; Bissett, G. 16; Brewster, G. 11; Burrill, F. 11; Caddick, W. 26; Carter, E. T. 6; Edmonds, G. W. 38; Fazackerley, S. 23; George, N. 24; Getgood, G. 17; Gregory, V. 25; Hampton, J. W. 18; Hargreaves, H. 26; Hodnett, J. 23; Kay, A. E. 25; Lees, H. H. 3; McCall, W. 15; McMillan, S. T. 22; Marshall, G. H. 30; Newell, P. 6; Picken, A. H. 7; Rhodes, L. 19; Riley, A. 3; Watson, E. 11; Whatmore, E. 2; White, E. 11; White, J. 1.

League scorers:
Edmonds 14, Fazackerley 12, Burrill, Hargreaves, White (E) each 3, Baugh, Bissett, Caddick, Hodnett, McCall, McMillan, Rhodes each 1.

Final Table
Division II — Season 1922/23

	P	W	D	L	F	A	P
1. Notts County	42	23	7	12	46	34	53
2. West Ham Un.	42	20	11	11	63	38	51
3. Leicester City	42	21	9	12	65	44	51
4. Manchester Un.	42	17	14	11	51	36	48
5. Blackpool	42	18	11	13	60	43	47
6. Bury	42	18	11	13	55	46	47
7. Leeds United	42	18	11	13	43	36	47
8. Sheffield Wed.	42	17	12	13	54	47	46
9. Barnsley	42	17	11	14	62	51	45
10. Fulham	42	16	12	14	43	32	44
11. Southampton	42	14	14	14	40	40	42
12. Hull City	42	14	14	14	43	45	42
13. South Shields	42	15	10	17	35	44	40
14. Derby County	42	14	11	17	46	50	39
15. Bradford City	42	12	13	17	41	45	37
16. Crystal Palace	42	13	11	18	54	62	37
17. Port Vale	42	14	9	19	39	51	37
18. Coventry City	42	15	7	20	46	63	37
19. Clapton Orient	42	12	12	18	40	50	36
20. Stockport County	42	14	8	20	43	58	36
21. Rotherham Co.	42	13	9	20	44	63	35
22. Wol'hampton W.	42	9	9	24	42	77	27

1923/24

FOOTBALL LEAGUE
Division 3 (North)

	Home	Away
Accrington	5-1	0-1
Ashington	1-0	7-1
Barrow	3-0	2-2
Bradford	2-0	1-0
Chesterfield	2-1	0-0
Crewe	1-0	0-0
Darlington	2-0	1-1
Doncaster	1-0	2-0
Durham	2-1	3-2
Grimsby	4-1	0-2
Halifax	4-0	2-2
Hartlepool	2-1	1-0
Lincoln	3-0	0-0
New Brighton	5-1	1-0
Rochdale	0-0	0-0
Rotherham	3-0	1-1
Southport	2-1	0-0
Tranmere	3-0	0-0
Walsall	0-0	1-2
Wigan	3-3	1-1
Wrexham	3-0	2-2

F.A. CUP
1 — Darlington (h) 3-1
2 — Charlton (a) 0-0
  (h) 1-0
3 — W.B.A. (a) 1-1
  (h) 0-2

APPENDIX

League appearances:
Baugh, R. 1; Bowen, T. 4; Bradford, J. 2; Caddick, W. 36; Carter, E. T. 1; Crew, W. 7; Davison, T. R. 6; Edmonds, G. W. 1; Edwards, E. 38; Fazackerley, S. 34; George, N. 42; Getgood, G. 36; Harrington, J. 27; Kay, A. E. 38; Lees, H. 40; Legge, E. 11; McMillan, S. T. 14; Marston, F. 3; Martin, J. C. 11; Phillipson, T. W. 23; Picken, A. H. 4; Shaw, H. 37; Timmins, T. 5; Watson, E. 41.

League scorers:
Lees 21, Fazackerley 13, Phillipson 12, Edwards 7, Martin 6, McMillan 4, Harrington and Legge each 3, Marston 2, Bowen, Davison, Getgood, Kay and Huddart (Barrow) each 1.

Final Table
Division III (North) — Season 1923/24

	P	W	D	L	F	A	P
1. Wol'hampton W.	42	24	15	3	76	27	63
2. Rochdale	42	25	12	5	60	26	62
3. Chesterfield	42	22	10	10	70	39	54
4. Rotherham Un.	42	23	6	13	70	43	52
5. Bradford	42	21	10	11	69	43	52
6. Darlington	42	20	8	14	70	53	48
7. Southport	42	16	14	12	44	42	46
8. Ashington	42	18	8	16	39	61	44
9. Doncaster Rovers	42	15	12	15	59	53	42
10. Wigan Athletic	42	14	14	14	55	53	42
11. Grimsby Town	42	14	13	15	49	47	41
12. Tranmere Rovers	42	13	15	14	51	60	41
13. Accrington St.	42	16	8	18	48	61	40
14. Halifax Town	42	15	10	17	42	59	40
15. Durham City	42	15	9	18	59	60	39
16. Wrexham	42	10	18	14	37	44	38
17. Walsall	42	14	8	20	44	59	36
18. New Brighton	42	11	13	18	40	53	35
19. Lincoln City	42	10	12	20	48	59	32
20. Crewe Alex.	42	7	13	22	32	58	27
21. Hartlepools Un.	42	7	11	24	33	70	25
22. Barrow	42	8	9	25	35	80	25

1924/25

FOOTBALL LEAGUE
Division 2

	Home	Away
Barnsley	0-1	0-0
Blackpool	2-0	4-2
Bradford City	2-0	1-3
Chelsea	0-1	0-1
Clapton Orient	1-2	1-2
Coventry	3-1	4-2
C. Palace	3-1	1-2
Derby	0-4	1-0
Fulham	2-1	0-1
Hull	2-1	1-0
Leicester	0-1	0-2
Man. United	0-0	0-3
Middlesbrough	1-0	0-2
Oldham	2-0	0-2
Portsmouth	0-5	2-2
Port Vale	1-0	3-1
Sheffield Wed.	1-0	0-2
Southampton	3-0	1-1
South Shields	2-1	3-3
Stockport	3-0	1-1
Stoke	1-0	3-0

F.A. CUP
1 — Hull		
	(a)	1-1
	(h)	0-1

League appearances:
Bowen, T. 27; Bradford, J. 38; Bradley, J. 1; Caddick, W. 39; Davidson, T. 3; Edwards, E. 25; Fazackerley, S. 12; Fox, W. V. 8; George, N. 42; Getgood, G. 2; Gummery, W. 10; Harrington, J. 22; Harris, J. 6; Kay, A. E. 9; Lees, H. 39; Legge, A. E. 13; Marson, F. 5; Mitton, J. 36; O'Connor, J. 11; Phillipson, T. W. 36; Picken, A. 1; Shaw, H. 31; Timmins, R. 5; Tyler, S. 4; Watson, E. 37.

League scorers:
Phillipson 15, Lees 14, Bowen 8, Edwards 5, Fazackerley 3, Harris, Marson, Mitton and O'Connor each 2, Gummery and Harrington each 1.

Final Table
Division II — Season 1924/25

	P	W	D	L	F	A	P
1. Leicester City	42	24	11	7	90	32	59
2. Man. United	42	23	11	8	57	23	57
3. Derby County	42	22	11	9	71	36	55
4. Portsmouth	42	15	18	9	58	50	48
5. Chelsea	42	16	15	11	51	37	47
6. Wol'hampton W.	42	20	6	16	55	51	46
7. Southampton	42	13	18	11	40	36	44
8. Port Vale	42	17	8	17	48	56	42
9. South Shields	42	12	17	13	42	38	41
10. Hull City	42	15	11	16	50	49	41
11. Clapton Orient	42	14	12	16	42	42	40
12. Fulham	42	15	10	17	41	56	40
13. Middlesbrough	42	10	19	13	36	44	39
14. Sheffield Wed.	42	15	8	19	50	56	38
15. Barnsley	42	13	12	17	46	59	38
16. Bradford City	42	13	12	17	37	50	38
17. Blackpool	42	14	9	19	65	61	37
18. Oldham Athletic	42	13	11	18	35	51	37
19. Stockport County	42	13	11	18	37	57	37
20. Stoke	42	12	11	19	34	46	35
21. C. Palace	42	12	10	20	38	54	34
22. Coventry City	42	11	9	22	45	84	31

1925/26

FOOTBALL LEAGUE
Division 2

	Home	Away
Barnsley	7-1	1-1
Blackpool	0-0	0-4
Bradford City	1-1	2-1
Chelsea	0-0	3-3
Clapton Orient	3-0	1-2
Darlington	1-0	4-3
Derby	2-0	0-2
Fulham	0-0	2-1
Hull	3-1	1-3
Middlesbrough	3-1	1-4
Nottingham F.	4-0	4-1
Oldham	2-1	2-1
Portsmouth	4-1	0-3
Port Vale	3-1	0-3
Preston	3-0	0-1
Sheffield Wed.	1-2	1-2
Southampton	4-1	2-4
South Shields	2-0	1-3
Stockport	5-1	0-1
Stoke	5-1	0-0
Swansea	2-3	4-2

F.A. CUP
3 — Arsenal (h) 1-1
(a) 0-1

League scorers:
Phillipson 36, Price 8, Bowen 7, Keetley, Kerr, Lees and Scott each 5, Harrington, Mitton, Caddick and Hann each 2, Meek, Homer, Briscoe, Barrett (Nottingham Forest) and Barnett (Barnsley) each 1.

Final Table
Division II — Season 1925/26

	P	W	D	L	F	A	P
1. Sheffield Wed.	42	27	6	9	88	48	60
2. Derby County	42	25	7	10	77	42	57
3. Chelsea	42	19	14	9	76	49	52
4. Wol'hampton W.	42	21	7	14	84	60	49
5. Swansea Town	42	19	11	12	77	57	49
6. Blackpool	42	17	11	14	76	69	45
7. Oldham Athletic	42	18	8	16	74	62	44
8. Middlesbrough	42	21	2	19	77	68	44
9. South Shields	42	18	8	16	74	65	44
10. Port Vale	42	19	6	17	79	69	44
11. Portsmouth	42	17	10	15	79	74	44
12. Preston N. E.	42	18	7	17	71	84	43
13. Hull City	42	16	9	17	63	61	41
14. Southampton	42	15	8	19	63	63	38
15. Darlington	42	14	10	18	72	77	38
16. Barnsley	42	12	12	18	58	84	36
17. Nottingham F.	42	14	8	20	51	73	36
18. Bradford City	42	13	10	19	47	66	36
19. Fulham	42	11	12	19	46	77	34
20. Clapton Orient	42	12	9	21	50	65	33
21. Stoke City	42	12	8	22	54	77	32
22. Stockport County	42	8	9	25	51	97	25

League appearances:
Bowen, T. 16; Bradford, J. 14; Bradley, P. 2; Burns, W. 1; Caddick, W. 12; Canavon, A. 2; Charnley, T. 29; Fox, W. V. 12; George, N. 23; Hampton, J. 17; Hann, C. W. 5; Homer, S. 18; Keetley, J. S. 10; Kerr, P. 13; Kay, A. E. 29; Lees, H. 21; Harrington, J. 19; Legge, A. 6; McDougall, A. 3; Meek, H. L. 6; Mitton, J. 39; Phillipson, T. 31; Price, E. 35; Scott, H. 28; Shaw, H. 37; Timmins, B. 1; Tyler, S. 6; Watson, E. 27.

1926/27

FOOTBALL LEAGUE
Division 2

	Home	Away
Barnsley	9-1	1-4
Blackpool	4-1	3-2
Bradford City	7-2	2-1
Chelsea	0-3	0-1
Clapton Orient	5-0	0-2
Darlington	2-1	1-3
Fulham	2-1	1-4
Grimsby	3-4	0-6
Hull	5-2	0-1
Man. City	4-1	1-2
Middlesbrough	1-2	0-2
Nottingham F.	2-0	1-1
Notts County	0-1	2-2
Oldham	1-1	0-2
Portsmouth	0-1	1-2
Port Vale	1-2	1-1
Preston	1-2	0-2
Reading	1-1	2-1
Southampton	2-2	0-1
South Shields	2-0	2-1
Swansea	2-2	1-4

F.A. CUP
3 — Carlisle (a) 2-0
4 — Nottingham F. (h) 2-0
5 — Hull (h) 1-0
6 — Arsenal (a) 1-2

League appearances:
Baker, E. 3; Boswell, W. 8; Bowen, T. 23; Bradford, J. 22; Caddick, W. 3; Chadwick, W. 30; Charnley, S. 19; Fox, V. 2; George, N. 28; Hampton, J. 14; Hann, C. W. 9; Harrington 23; Higham, F. 17; Homer, S. 11; Kay, A. E. 31; Kerr, R. 5; Lees, H. 12; Legge, A. 20; Mitton, J. 25; McDougall, A. 5; Phillipson, T. 32; Price, F. 4; Bradley, P. 2; Scott, H. 7; Shaw, H. 40; Tyler, S. 8; Watson, E. 34; Weaver, W. 25.

League scorers:
Phillipson 31; Chadwick 12, Weaver 8, Bowen 3, Boswell 5, Lees, Watson, Legge, Harrington and Kerr each 2, Mitton, Scott, McDougall and Highman each 1.

Final Table
Division II — Season 1926/27

	P	W	D	L	F	A	P
1. Middlesbrough	42	27	8	7	122	60	62
2. Portsmouth	42	23	8	11	87	49	54
3. Manchester City	42	22	10	10	108	61	54
4. Chelsea	42	20	12	10	62	52	52
5. Nottingham F.	42	18	14	10	80	55	50
6. Preston N. E.	42	20	9	13	74	72	49
7. Hull City	42	20	7	15	63	52	47
8. Port Vale	42	16	13	13	88	78	45
9. Blackpool	42	18	8	16	95	80	44
10. Oldham Athletic	42	19	6	17	74	84	44
11. Barnsley	42	17	9	16	88	87	43
12. Swansea Town	42	16	11	15	68	72	43
13. Southampton	42	15	12	15	60	62	42
14. Reading	42	16	8	18	64	72	40
15. Wol'hampton W.	42	14	7	21	73	75	35
16. Notts County	42	15	5	22	70	96	35
17. Grimsby Town	42	11	12	19	74	91	34
18. Fulham	42	13	8	21	58	92	34
19. South Shields	42	11	11	20	71	96	33
20. Clapton Orient	42	12	7	23	60	96	31
21. Darlington	42	12	6	24	79	98	30
22. Bradford City	42	7	9	26	50	88	23

1927/28
FOOTBALL LEAGUE
Division 2

	Home	Away
Barnsley	2-1	2-2
Blackpool	2-4	0-3
Bristol City	5-2	1-4
Chelsea	1-2	0-2
Clapton Orient	5-3	0-0
Fulham	3-1	0-7
Grimsby	0-1	1-0
Hull	1-1	0-2
Leeds	0-0	0-3
Man. City	2-2	0-3
Nottingham F.	1-0	2-3
Notts County	2-2	2-1
Oldham	3-1	0-3
Port Vale	2-1	2-2
Preston	2-3	4-5
Reading	2-1	1-2
Southampton	2-1	1-4
South Shields	2-1	2-2
Stoke	1-2	2-2
Swansea	1-1	0-6
W.B.A.	4-1	0-4

F.A. CUP
3 — Chelsea	(h)	2-1
4 — Sheffield Un.	(a)	1-3

League appearances:
Baker, E. 10; Baxter, T. W. 24; Boswell, W. 1; Botto, L. 16; Bowen, T. 16; Bradford, J. 1; Bryce, F. 2; Canavon, A. 11; Chadwick, W. 33; Charnley, S. 5; Cock, D. 3; Fox, V. 22; George, N. 13; Green, F. 7; Harrington, J. W. 16; Higham, F. 20; Kay, A. E. 36; Lees, H. 5; Legge, A. 3; McDougall, A. 12; Marshall, G. H. 11; Phillipson, T. 22; Pritchard, T. 35; Richards, D. 3; Richards, W. 25; Rotton, W. H. 4; Shaw, H. 21; Watson, E. 28; Weaver, R. 22; Weaver, W. 21; Williams, L. 14; Williams, W. J. 3.

League scorers:
Chadwick 19, Weaver (R) 11, Phillipson 10, Bowen 5, Baxter, Marshall and Weaver (W) each 3, Watson 2, Charnley, Cock, Green, Harrington, Higham, Richards (W) and Rotton each 1.

Final Table
Division II — Season 1927/28

	P	W	D	L	F	A	P
1. Man. City	42	25	9	8	100	59	59
2. Leeds United	42	25	7	10	98	49	57
3. Chelsea	43	23	8	11	75	45	54
4. Preston N. E.	42	22	9	11	100	66	53
5. Stoke City	42	22	8	12	78	59	52
6. Swansea Town	42	18	12	12	75	63	48
7. Oldham Ath.	42	19	8	15	75	51	46
8. W. B. Albion	42	17	12	13	90	70	46
9. Port Vale	42	18	8	16	68	57	44
10. Nottingham F.	42	15	10	17	83	84	40
11. Grimsby Town	42	14	12	16	69	83	40
12. Bristol City	42	15	9	18	76	79	39
13. Barnsley	42	14	11	17	65	85	39
14. Hull City	42	12	15	15	41	54	39
15. Notts County	42	13	12	17	68	74	38
16. Wol'hampton	42	13	10	19	63	91	36
17. Southampton	42	14	7	21	68	77	35
18. Reading	42	11	13	18	53	75	35
19. Blackpool	42	13	8	21	83	101	34
20. Clapton Orient	42	11	12	19	55	85	34
21. Fulham	42	13	7	22	68	89	33
22. Gateshead	42	7	9	26	56	111	23

1928/29
FOOTBALL LEAGUE
Division 2

	Home	Away
Barnsley	3-1	2-2
Blackpool	1-5	0-3

APPENDIX 177

Bradford	3-1	1-4
Bristol City	2-1	2-3
Chelsea	1-1	2-0
Clapton Orient	3-2	0-2
Grimsby	2-2	0-2
Hull	2-4	3-1
Middlesbrough	3-3	3-8
Millwall	0-1	5-0
Nottingham F.	2-3	1-2
Notts County	3-1	0-3
Oldham	0-0	4-0
Port Vale	4-0	4-1
Preston	1-2	1-5
Reading	2-0	0-3
Southampton	1-1	1-2
Stoke	4-0	3-4
Swansea	0-0	0-2
Tottenham	4-2	2-3
W.B.A.	0-1	2-0

F.A. CUP
3 — Mansfield (h) 0-1

League scorers:
Weaver 18, Green 16, Chadwick 13, Baxter 10, Ferguson 4, Featherby, Marshall and Pritchard each 3, Hartill and Johnson each 2, Coundon, Richards and Priestley (Grimsby) each 1.

Final Table
Division II — Season 1928/29

	P	W	D	L	F	A	P
1. Middlesbrough	42	22	11	9	92	57	55
2. Grimsby Town	42	24	5	13	82	61	53
3. Bradford P. A.	42	22	4	16	88	70	48
4. Southampton	42	17	14	11	74	60	48
5. Notts County	42	19	9	14	78	65	47
6. Stoke City	42	17	12	13	74	51	46
7. W. B. Albion	42	19	8	15	80	79	46
8. Blackpool	42	19	7	16	92	76	45
9. Chelsea	42	17	10	15	64	65	44
10. Tottenham H.	42	17	9	16	75	81	43
11. Nottingham F.	42	15	12	15	71	70	42
12. Hull City	42	13	14	15	58	63	40
13. Preston N. E.	42	15	9	18	78	79	39
14. Millwall	42	16	7	19	71	86	39
15. Reading	42	15	9	18	63	86	39
16. Barnsley	42	16	6	20	69	66	38
17. Wol'hampton W.	42	15	7	20	77	81	37
18. Oldham Athletic	42	16	5	21	54	75	37
19. Swansea Town	42	13	10	19	62	75	36
20. Bristol City	42	13	10	19	58	72	36
21. Port Vale	42	15	4	23	71	86	34
22. Clapton Orient	42	12	8	22	45	72	32

League appearances:
Baker, J. E. 3; Barraclough, W. 3; Baxter, T. W. 26; Brown, W. 34; Burns, W. 3; Chadwick, W. 34; Coundon, C. 13; Cross, C. A. 3; Featherby, L. W. 12; Ferguson, J. J. 20; Gardiner, J. 3; Green, F. 29; Hartill, W. J. 7; Hetherington, J. A. 13; Hollingworth, R. 10; Johnson, M. 8; Kay, A. E. 32; Lewis, A. N. 29; Marshall, G. H. 17; Pritchard, T. 21; Rhodes, R. A. 2; Richards, D. 12; Richards, W. E. 5; Shaw, H. V. 39; Thorpe, A. E. 1; Toothill, A. 6; Turner, J. A. 7; Watson, E. 9; Weaver, R. 28; Weaver, W. 28; Williams, L. H. 33.

1929/30

FOOTBALL LEAGUE
Division 2

	Home	Away
Barnsley	3-0	1-3
Blackpool	1-2	2-3
Bradford	4-4	0-0
Bradford City	6-0	2-2
Bristol City	1-0	2-1
Bury	2-0	1-3
Cardiff	4-0	0-0
Charlton	0-4	0-2
Chelsea	0-1	1-1
Hull	4-2	0-2
Millwall	1-1	0-4
Nottingham F.	2-1	2-5
Notts County	5-1	3-0
Oldham	1-1	0-6
Preston	4-0	1-1
Reading	2-1	1-3
Southampton	2-0	1-3
Stoke	2-1	0-3
Swansea	4-1	2-2
Tottenham	3-0	2-4
W. B. Albion	2-4	3-7

F.A. CUP
3 — Oldham (a) 0-1

League appearances:
Barraclough, W. 20; Bartley, J. 2; Bellis, G. 24; Crook, M. S. 31; Davies, R. 9; Deacon, J. 36; Featherby, L. 8; Forshaw, R. 6; Griffiths, J. 1; Green, F. 1; Hartill, W. 36; Hetherington, J. 22; Hollingworth, R. 12; Kay, A. E. 25; Lax, G. 40; Lowton, W. 40; Marshall, G. 25; Phillips, C. 5; Rhodes, R. A. 11; Richards, D. 28; Richardson, J. T. 3; Shaw, H. 29; Shaw, S. 1; Tootill, A. 41; Walker, W. 1; White, R. 3; Williams, L. 2.

League scorers:
Hartill 34, Deacon 9, Hetherington and Marshall each 7, Rhodes 5, Featherby and Forshaw each 3; Lowton and White each 2, Barraclough, Crooks, Richards, Bisby (Notts County) and Cable (Tottenham Hotspur) each 1.

Final Table
Division II — Season 1929/30

	P	W	D	L	F	A	P
1. Blackpool	42	27	4	11	98	67	58
2. Chelsea	42	22	11	9	74	46	55
3. Oldham Athletic	42	21	11	10	90	51	53
4. Bradford	42	19	12	11	91	70	50
5. Bury	42	22	5	15	78	67	49
6. W. B. Albion	42	21	5	16	105	73	47
7. Southampton	42	17	11	14	77	76	45
8. Cardiff City	42	18	8	16	61	59	44
9. Wol'hampton W.	42	16	9	17	77	79	41
10. Nottingham F.	42	13	15	14	55	69	41
11. Stoke City	42	16	8	18	74	72	40
12. Tottenham H.	42	15	9	18	59	61	39
13. Charlton Athletic	42	14	11	17	59	63	39
14. Millwall	42	12	15	15	57	73	39
15. Swansea Town	42	14	9	19	57	61	37
16. Preston N. E.	42	13	11	18	65	80	37
17. Barnsley	42	14	8	20	56	71	36
18. Bradford City	42	12	12	18	60	77	36
19. Reading	42	12	11	19	54	67	35
20. Bristol City	42	13	9	20	61	83	35
21. Hull City	42	14	7	21	51	78	35
22. Notts County	42	9	15	18	54	70	33

1930/31

FOOTBALL LEAGUE
Division 2

	Home	Away
Barnsley	2-0	0-3
Bradford	1-1	1-1
Bradford City	0-1	1-4
Bristol City	0-1	3-0
Burnley	2-4	2-4
Bury	7-0	0-1
Cardiff	4-1	3-0
Charlton	1-1	2-1
Everton	3-1	0-4
Millwall	2-0	1-1
Nottingham F.	4-2	4-3
Oldham	3-0	0-2
Plymouth	4-3	2-3
Port Vale	3-0	1-0
Preston	2-0	4-5
Reading	3-1	0-3
Southampton	3-2	0-2
Stoke	5-1	2-1
Swansea	3-1	1-1
Tottenham	3-1	0-1
W. B. Albion	1-4	1-2

F.A. CUP

3 — Wrexham	(h) 9-1
4 — Bradford City	(a) 0-0
	(h) 4-2
5 — Barnsley	(a) 3-1
6 — W. B. Albion	(a) 1-1
	(h) 1-2

League appearances:
Anderson, E. 3; Barraclough, W. 27; Bellis, G. 1; Bottrill, W. 35; Crook, M. 5; Deacon, J. 36; Deacon, R. 3; Griffiths, J. R. 1; Hartill, W. 33; Hatfield, E. 3; Hemmingway, C. 4; Hetherington, J. 15; Hollingworth, R. 41; Kay, A. E. 23; Lax, G. 19; Lowton, W. 38; Lumberg, A. 11; Martin, T. 12; Phillips, C. 37; Reed, J. 1; Rhodes, R. 28; Richards, D. 31; Shaw, C. 9; Smith, A. 4; Tootill, A. 36; Whittaker, P. 6.

League scorers:
Harthill 25, Bottrill 14, Deacon (J) 12, Martin and Phillips each 8, Lowton 7, Hetherington 4, Hollingworth 2, Barraclough, Deacon (R), Lax and Thompson (Nottingham Forest) each 1.

Final Table
Division II — Season 1930/31

	P	W	D	L	F	A	P
1. Everton	42	28	5	9	121	66	61
2. W. B. Albion	42	22	10	10	83	49	54
3. Tottenham H.	42	22	7	13	88	55	51
4. Wol'hampton W.	42	21	5	16	84	67	47
5. Port Vale	42	21	5	16	67	61	47
6. Bradford	42	18	10	14	97	66	46
7. Preston N. E.	42	17	11	14	83	64	45
8. Burnley	42	17	11	14	81	77	45
9. Southampton	42	19	6	17	74	62	44
10. Bradford City	42	17	10	15	61	63	44
11. Stoke City	42	17	10	15	64	71	44
12. Oldham Athletic	42	16	10	16	61	72	42
13. Bury	42	19	3	20	75	82	41
14. Millwall	42	16	7	19	71	80	39
15. Charlton Ath.	42	15	9	18	59	86	39
16. Bristol City	42	15	8	19	54	82	38
17. Nottingham F.	42	14	9	19	80	85	37
18. Plymouth Argyle	42	14	8	20	76	84	36
19. Barnsley	42	13	9	20	59	79	35
20. Swansea Town	42	12	10	20	51	74	34
21. Reading	42	12	6	24	72	96	30
22. Cardiff City	42	8	9	25	47	87	25

APPENDIX

1931/32
FOOTBALL LEAGUE
Division 2

	Home	Away
Barnsley	2-0	2-2
Bradford	6-0	1-2
Bradford City	3-1	2-2
Bristol City	4-2	4-0
Burnley	3-1	3-1
Bury	6-0	0-1
Charlton	3-1	2-3
Chesterfield	6-0	2-1
Leeds	1-1	1-2
Man. United	7-0	2-3
Millwall	5-0	2-1
Nottingham F.	0-0	0-2
Notts County	0-0	1-3
Oldham	7-1	2-0
Plymouth	2-0	3-3
Port Vale	2-0	7-1
Preston	3-2	2-4
Southampton	5-1	3-1
Stoke	0-1	1-2
Swansea	2-0	1-1
Tottenham	4-0	3-3

F.A. CUP
3 — Luton (a) 2-1
4 — Preston (a) 0-2

League scorers:
Hartill 30, Bottrill 21, Phillips 18, Deacon 13, Lowton 9, Barraclough 7, Buttery 6, Hollingworth 4, Crook 2, Martin, Redfern, Richards, Smalley and Ward (Bradford) each 1.

Final Table
Division II — Season 1931/32

	P	W	D	L	F	A	P
1. Wol'hampton W.	42	24	8	10	115	49	56
2. Leeds United	42	22	10	10	78	54	54
3. Stoke City	42	19	14	9	69	48	52
4. Plymouth Argyle	42	20	9	13	100	66	49
5. Bury	42	21	7	14	70	58	49
6. Bradford P. A.	42	21	7	14	72	63	49
7. Bradford City	42	16	13	13	80	61	45
8. Tottenham H.	42	16	11	15	87	78	43
9. Millwall	42	17	9	16	61	61	43
10. Charlton Ath.	42	17	9	16	61	66	43
11. Nottingham F.	42	16	10	16	77	72	42
12. Man. United	42	17	8	17	71	72	42
13. Preston N. E.	42	16	10	16	75	77	42
14. Southampton	42	17	7	18	66	77	41
15. Swansea Town	42	16	7	19	73	75	39
16. Notts County	42	13	12	17	75	75	38
17. Chesterfield	42	13	11	18	64	86	37
18. Oldham Ath.	42	13	10	19	62	84	36
19. Burnley	42	13	9	20	59	87	35
20. Port Vale	42	13	7	22	58	89	33
21. Barnsley	42	12	9	21	55	91	33
22. Bristol City	42	6	11	25	39	78	23

League appearances:
Barraclough, W. 40; Bellis, G. 10; Bottrill, W. 38; Buttery, A. 10; Crook, M. 5; Deacon, J. 30; Griffiths, R. 4; Hartill, W. 37; Hetherington, J. 1; Hollingworth, R. 32; Kay, A. E. 31; Lax, G. 2; Lowton, W. 41; Martin, T. 3; Phillips, C. 38; Redfern, L. 5; Rhodes, R. 40; Richards, D. 33; Shaw, C. 8; Smalley, T. 2; Smith, J. 9; Tootill, A. 42.

1932/33
FOOTBALL LEAGUE
Division 1

	Home	Away
Arsenal	1-7	2-1
A. Villa	2-4	3-1
Birmingham	1-0	0-0
Blackburn	5-3	0-1
Blackpool	2-3	2-2
Bolton	4-1	0-2
Chelsea	1-2	1-3
Derby	3-1	4-4
Everton	4-2	1-5
Huddersfield	6-4	2-3
Leeds	3-3	0-2
Leicester	1-1	2-2
Liverpool	3-1	1-5
Man. City	1-2	1-4
Middlesbrough	2-0	1-2
Newcastle	1-1	2-3
Portsmouth	5-2	0-2
Sheffield Un.	5-1	0-0
Sheffield Wed.	3-5	0-2
Sunderland	0-2	1-0
W. B. Albion	3-3	1-4

F.A. CUP
3 — Derby (h) 3-6

League appearances:
Barraclough, W. 36; Bellis, G. 9; Bottrill, W. 30; Bryant 4; Crook, M. 24; Deacon, J. 38; Ellis, J. 21; Farrow, G. 10; Hartill, W. 42; Hetherington, J. 14; Heelbeck, L. 6; Hollingworth, R. 12; Ivill, E. 4; Lowton, W. 37; Lumberg, A. 9; Nelson, J. 22; Phillips, C. 18; Pincott, F. 2; Redfern, L. 1; Rhodes, R. 24; Richards, D. 36; Shaw, C. 20; Smalley, T. 3; Smith, J. 14; Smith, W. 4; Tootill, A. 13; Wildman 9.

League scorers:
Hartill 33, Deacon 15, Crook 8, Bottrill 7, Hetherington 6, Barraclough 4, Phillips 2, Lowton, Young (Huddersfield) Richards, Nelson and Rhodes each 1.

Final Table
Division I — Season 1932/33

		P	W	D	L	F	A	P
1.	Arsenal	42	25	8	9	118	61	58
2.	Aston Villa	42	23	8	11	92	67	54
3.	Sheffield Wed.	42	21	9	12	80	68	51
4.	W. B. Albion	42	20	9	13	83	70	49
5.	Newcastle U.	42	22	5	15	71	63	49
6.	Huddersfield	42	18	11	13	66	53	47
7.	Derby County	42	15	14	13	76	69	44
8.	Leeds United	42	15	14	13	59	62	44
9.	Portsmouth	42	18	7	17	74	76	43
10.	Sheffield U.	42	17	9	16	74	80	43
11.	Everton	42	16	9	17	81	74	41
12.	Sunderland	42	15	10	17	63	80	40
13.	Birmingham	42	14	11	17	57	57	39
14.	Liverpool	42	14	11	17	79	84	39
15.	Blackburn R.	42	14	10	18	76	102	38
16.	Man. City	42	16	5	21	68	71	37
17.	Middlesbrough	42	14	9	19	63	73	37
18.	Chelsea	42	14	7	21	63	73	35
19.	Leicester City	42	11	13	18	75	89	35
20.	W'ampton W.	42	13	9	20	80	96	35
21.	Bolton W.	42	12	9	21	78	92	33
22.	Blackpool	42	14	5	23	69	85	33

League appearances:
Barraclough, W. 38; Beattie, J. M. 26; Bryant, W. 1; Clayton, G. 1; Crook, M. 7; Deacon, J. 8; Ellis, J. 5; Goddard, G. 16; Hartill, W. 26; Harwood, I. 6; Hetherington, A. 14; Heelbeck, L. 2; Hollingworth, R. 16; Jones, B. 27; Lowton, W. 38; Morris, W. 2; Nelson, J. 31; Phillips, C. 38; Preece, J. 2; Rhodes, R. 15; Richards, L. 36; Shaw, C. 42; Smalley, T. 29; Smith, J. 2; Spiers, C. 4; Weare 1; Wildman, F. 32.

League scorers:
Phillips and Hartill each 13, Godard 12, Jones 10, Beattie 7, Lowton 6, Barraclough 5, Hetherington 4, Nelson 2, Richards and Davidson (Newcastle) each 1.

Final Table
Division I — Season 1933/34

		P	W	D	L	F	A	P
1.	Arsenal	42	25	9	8	75	47	59
2.	Huddersfield	42	23	10	9	90	61	56
3.	Tottenham	42	21	7	14	79	56	49
4.	Derby County	42	17	11	14	68	54	45
5.	Man. City	42	17	11	14	65	72	45
6.	Sunderland	42	16	12	14	81	56	44
7.	W. B. Albion	42	17	10	15	78	70	44
8.	Blackburn	42	18	7	17	74	81	43
9.	Leeds	42	17	8	17	75	66	42
10.	Portsmouth	42	15	12	15	52	55	42
11.	Sheffield Wed.	42	16	9	17	62	67	41
12.	Stoke	42	15	11	16	58	71	41
13.	Aston Villa	42	14	12	16	78	75	40
14.	Everton	42	12	16	14	62	63	40
15.	Wolves	42	14	12	16	74	86	40
16.	Middlesbrough	42	16	7	19	68	80	39
17.	Leicester	42	14	11	17	59	74	39
18.	Liverpool	42	14	10	18	79	87	38
19.	Chelsea	42	14	8	20	67	69	36
20.	Birmingham	42	12	12	18	54	56	36
21.	Newcastle	42	10	14	18	68	77	34
22.	Sheffield United	42	12	7	23	58	101	31

1933/34

FOOTBALL LEAGUE
Division 1

	Home	Away
Arsenal	0-1	2-3
A. Villa	4-3	2-6
Birmingham	2-0	0-0
Blackburn	5-3	1-7
Chelsea	1-1	2-5
Derby	3-0	1-3
Everton	2-0	2-1
Huddersfield	5-2	1-3
Leeds	2-0	3-3
Leicester	1-1	1-1
Liverpool	3-2	1-1
Man. City	8-0	0-4
Middlesbrough	0-1	0-0
Newcastle	2-1	1-5
Portsmouth	1-1	1-1
Sheffield Un.	3-2	1-3
Sheffield Wed.	6-2	1-2
Stoke	0-2	1-1
Sunderland	1-6	3-3
Tottenham	1-0	0-4
W. B. Albion	0-0	0-2

F.A. CUP
3 — Newcastle (h) 1-0
4 — Derby (a) 0-3

1934/35

FOOTBALL LEAGUE
Division 1

	Home	Away
Arsenal	1-1	0-7
A. Villa	5-2	1-2
Birmingham	3-1	1-1
Blackburn	2-1	2-4
Chelsea	6-1	2-4
Derby	5-1	0-2
Everton	4-2	2-5
Grimsby	0-3	1-2
Huddersfield	2-3	1-4
Leeds	1-2	1-1
Leicester	3-1	1-1

Snow scene in Jena 1971.

Defeat of Juventus 1972.

Winning the League Cup 1974.

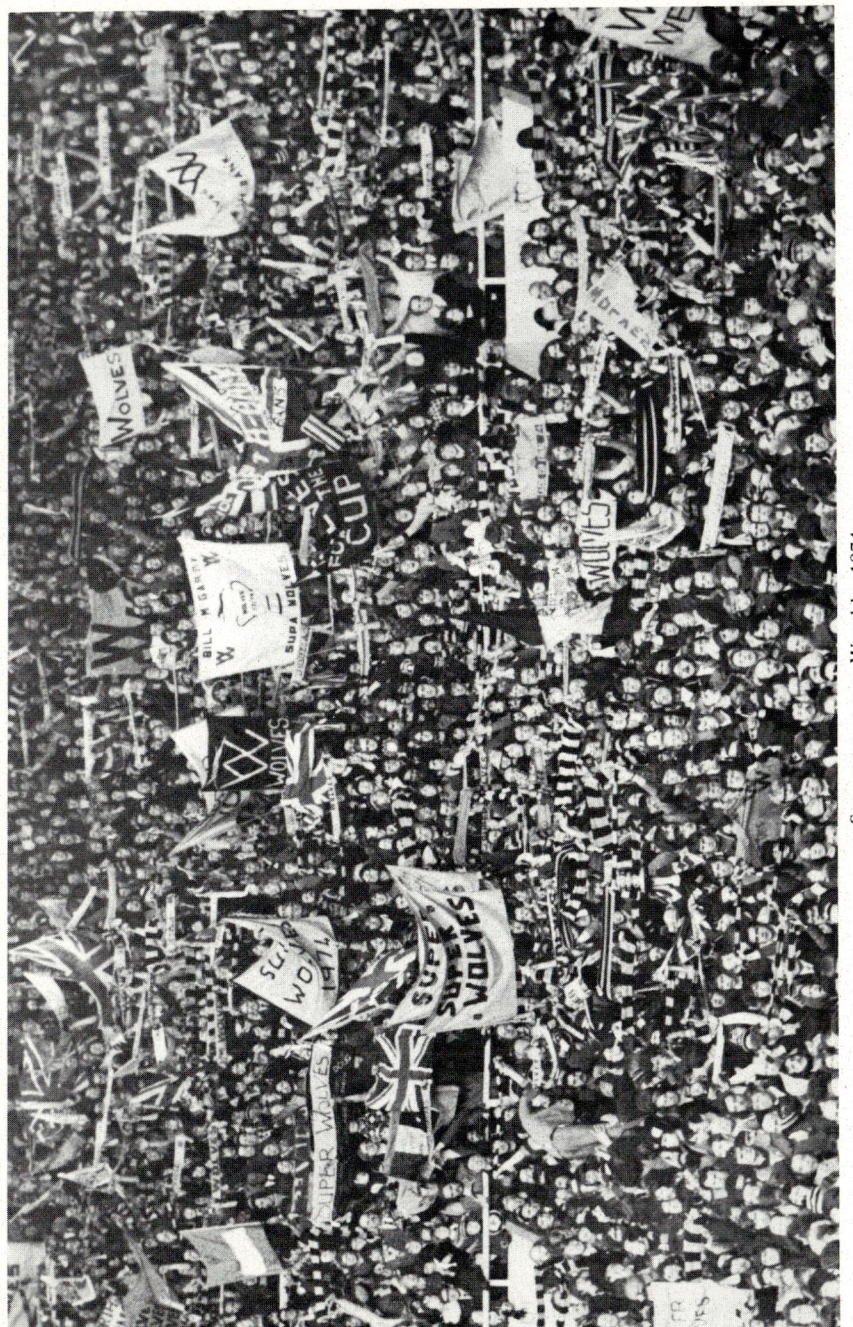

Supporter power, Wembley 1974.

Contrasts: 1884 and 1974.

APPENDIX

Liverpool	5-3	1-2
Manchester City	5-0	0-5
Middlesbrough	5-3	2-2
Portsmouth	2-3	1-0
Preston	2-2	1-2
Sheffield Wed.	2-2	1-3
Stoke	2-1	2-1
Sunderland	1-2	0-0
Tottenham	6-2	1-3
W. B. Albion	3-2	2-5

F.A. CUP
3 — Notts Co. (h) 4-0
4 — Sheffield Wed. (h) 1-2

League appearances:
Astill, 2; Barraclough, W. 8; Beattie, J. M. 18; Bowen, J. 6; Brown, J. 7; Clayton, G. 4; Crook, M. 5; Cullis, 3; Deacon, J. 1; Down 1; Galley 6; Gardiner 1; Goddard, G. 1; Greene 2; Hartill, W. 40; Hetherington, A. 16; Hollingworth, R. 35; Iverson, R. T. J. 9; Jones, B. 33; Lowton, W. 4; Lutterlock 2; Martin, D. 9; Morris, W. 8; Nelson, J. 21; Phillips, C. 32; Richards, D. 31; Rhodes, R. 22; Shaw, C. 42; Smalley, T. 35; Spiers, C. 4; Utterson, J. 11; Weare 13; Wildman, F. 14; Wrigglesworth, W. 16.

League scorers:
Hartill 27, Phillips 11, Jones, Martin and Wrigglesworth each 7, Beattie 6, Iverson 4, Clayton, Crook and Hetherington each 3, Shaw 2, Galley, Richards, Rhodes, Deacon, Nelson, Hollingworth, Spencer (Stoke City) and Stuart (Middlesbrough) each 1.

Final Table
Division I — Season 1934/35

	P	W	D	L	F	A	P
1. Arsenal	42	23	12	7	115	46	58
2. Sunderland	42	19	16	7	90	51	54
3. Sheffield Wed.	42	18	13	11	70	64	49
4. Man. City	42	20	8	14	82	67	48
5. Grimsby	42	17	11	14	78	60	45
6. Derby County	42	18	9	15	81	66	45
7. Liverpool	42	19	7	16	85	88	45
8. Everton	42	16	12	14	89	88	44
9. W. B. Albion	42	17	10	15	83	83	44
10. Stoke City	42	18	6	18	71	70	42
11. Preston	42	15	12	15	62	67	42
12. Chelsea	42	16	9	17	73	82	41
13. Aston Villa	42	14	13	15	74	88	41
14. Portsmouth	42	15	10	17	71	72	40
15. Blackburn R.	42	14	11	17	66	78	39
16. Huddersfield	42	14	10	18	76	71	38
17. Wolves	42	15	8	19	88	94	38
18. Leeds	42	13	12	17	75	92	38
19. Birmingham	42	13	10	19	63	81	36
20. Middlesbrough	42	10	14	18	70	90	34
21. Leicester	42	12	9	21	61	86	33
22. Tottenham	42	10	10	22	54	93	30

1935/36

FOOTBALL LEAGUE
Division 1

	Home	Away
Arsenal	2-2	0-4
A. Villa	2-2	2-4
Birmingham	3-1	0-0
Blackburn	8-1	0-1
Bolton	3-3	3-0
Brentford	3-2	0-5
Chelsea	3-3	2-2
Derby	0-0	1-3
Everton	4-0	1-4
Grimsby	1-0	1-2
Huddersfield	2-2	0-3
Leeds	3-0	0-2
Liverpool	3-1	2-0
Man. City	4-3	1-2
Middlesbrough	4-0	2-4
Portsmouth	2-0	0-1
Preston	4-2	0-2
Sheffield Wed.	2-1	0-0
Stoke	1-1	1-4
Sunderland	3-4	1-3
W. B. Albion	2-0	1-2

F.A. CUP
3 — Leeds (h) 1-1
(a) 1-3

Final Table
Division I — Season 1935/36

	P	W	D	L	F	A	P
1. Sunderland	42	25	6	11	109	74	56
2. Derby Co.	42	18	12	12	61	52	48
3. Huddersfield	42	18	12	12	59	56	48
4. Stoke City	42	20	7	15	57	57	47
5. Brentford	42	17	12	13	81	60	46
6. Arsenal	42	15	15	12	78	48	45
7. Preston	42	18	8	16	67	64	44
8. Chelsea	42	15	13	14	65	72	43
9. Man. City	42	17	8	17	68	60	42
10. Portsmouth	42	17	8	17	54	67	42
11. Leeds	42	15	11	16	66	64	41
12. Birmingham	42	15	11	16	61	63	41
13. Bolton	42	14	13	15	67	76	41
14. Middlesbrough	42	15	10	17	84	70	40
15. Wolves	42	15	10	17	77	76	40
16. Everton	42	13	13	16	89	89	39
17. Grimsby	42	17	5	20	65	73	39
18. W. B. Albion	42	16	6	20	89	88	38
19. Liverpool	42	13	12	17	60	64	38
20. Sheffield W.	42	13	12	17	63	77	38
21. Aston Villa	42	13	9	20	81	110	35
22. Blackburn R.	42	12	9	21	55	96	33

League appearances:
Ashall, G. H. 12; Brown, J. 13; Clayton, G. 4; Cullis, S. 12; Curnow, J. 6; Dowen, J. 1; Galley, T. 23; Gardiner, J. 19; Greene, C. 5; Henson, G. 6; Hollingworth, R. 12; Iverson, R. 19; Jones, B. 40; Laking, G. 18; Marsden, F. 1; Martin, D. 16; Morris, W. 39; Phillips, C. 23; Rhodes, R. 6; Richards, D. 8; Shaw, C. 42; Scott, R. A. 11; Smalley, T. 42; Taylor, J. 10; Thompson, H. 22; Utterson, J. 1; Weare, A. J. 24; Whittam, E. A. 1; Wrigglesworth, W. 26.

League scorers:
Wrigglesworth 12, Martin 10, Jones and Smalley each 9, Phillips 7, Thompson and Shaw each 6, Brown and Ashall each 3, Clayton, Green, Iverson and Gardiner each 2, Henson, Morris, Turner (Stoke) and Crook (Blackburn Rovers) each 1.

1936/37

FOOTBALL LEAGUE
Division 1

	Home	Away
Arsenal	2-0	0-3
Birmingham	2-1	0-1
Bolton	2-3	2-1
Brentford	4-0	2-3
Charlton	6-1	0-4
Chelsea	1-2	1-0
Derby	3-1	1-5
Everton	7-2	0-1
Grimsby	5-2	1-1
Huddersfield	3-1	0-4
Leeds	3-0	1-0
Liverpool	2-0	0-1
Man. City	2-1	1-4
Man. United	3-1	1-1
Middlesbrough	0-1	0-1
Portsmouth	1-1	1-1
Preston	5-0	3-1
Sheffield Wed.	4-3	3-1
Stoke	2-1	1-2
Sunderland	1-1	2-6
W. B. Albion	5-2	1-2

F.A. CUP
3 — Middlesbrough	(h)	6-1
4 — Sheffield United	(h)	2-2
	(a)	2-1
5 — Grimsby	(a)	1-1
	(h)	6-2
6 — Sunderland	(h)	1-1
	(a)	2-2
(at Hillsborough)		0-4

League appearances:
Ashall, G. H. 40; Brown, J. 7; Clayton, G. 31; Coley, W. E. 2; Cullis, S. 24; Dowen, J. 1; Galley, T. 36; Gardiner, J. 25; Gold, W. 10; Iverson, R. 7; Jones, B. 27; Jones, E. 3; Jordan, D. 3; Keeley, A. 2; Laking, G. 9; Maguire, J. E. 14; Morris, W. 36; Ordish, C. S. 1; Scott, R. A. 28; Shaw, C. 12; Smalley, T. 39; Taylor, F. 6; Taylor, J. 29; Thompson, H. 19; Waring, T. 10; Weare, A. J. 4; Westcott, D. 8; Wharton, G. 21; Wrigglesworth, W. 8.

League scorers:
Clayton 24, Galley 13, Jones (B) 11, Ashall 10, Thompson 7, Westcott 5, Brown and Waring each 3, Wharton and Wrigglesworth each 2, Morris, Iversin, Goodall (Huddersfield) and Shaw (C) (West Bromwich Albion) each 1.

Final Table
Division I — Season 1936/37

	P	W	D	L	F	A	P
1. Man. City	42	22	13	7	107	61	57
2. Charlton	42	21	12	9	58	49	54
3. Arsenal	42	18	16	8	80	49	52
4. Derby Co.	42	21	7	14	96	90	49
5. Wolves	42	21	5	16	84	67	47
6. Brentford	42	18	10	14	82	78	46
7. Middlesbrough	42	19	8	15	74	71	46
8. Sunderland	42	19	6	17	89	87	44
9. Portsmouth	42	17	10	15	62	66	44
10. Stoke City	42	15	12	15	72	57	42
11. Birmingham	42	13	15	14	64	60	41
12. Grimsby	42	17	7	18	86	81	41
13. Chelsea	42	14	13	15	52	55	41
14. Preston N. E.	42	14	13	15	56	67	41
15. Huddersfield	42	12	15	15	62	64	39
16. W. B. Albion	42	16	6	20	77	98	38
17. Everton	42	14	9	19	81	78	37
18. Liverpool	42	12	11	19	62	84	35
19. Leeds	42	15	4	23	60	80	34
20. Bolton	42	10	14	18	43	66	34
21. Man. United	42	10	12	20	55	78	32
22. Sheffield W.	42	9	12	21	53	69	30

1937/38

FOOTBALL LEAGUE
Division 1

	Home	Away
Arsenal	3-1	0-5
Birmingham	3-2	0-2
Blackpool	1-0	2-0
Bolton	1-1	2-1
Brentford	2-1	1-2
Charlton	1-1	1-4
Chelsea	1-1	2-0
Derby	2-2	2-1

APPENDIX

Everton	2-0	1-0
Grimsby	1-1	0-1
Huddersfield	1-4	0-1
Leeds	1-1	2-1
Leicester	10-1	1-1
Liverpool	2-0	1-0
Man. City	3-1	4-2
Middlesbrough	0-1	3-0
Portsmouth	5-0	0-1
Preston	0-0	0-2
Stoke	2-2	1-1
Sunderland	4-0	0-1
W. B. Albion	2-1	2-2

F.A. CUP
3 — Swansea	(a)	4-0
4 — Arsenal	(h)	1-2

League appearances:
Ardish 1; Ashall, G. H. 32; Clayton, G. 7; Cullis, S. 36; Dorsett 10; Dowen, J. 3; Galley, T. 35; Gardiner, J. 38; Jones, B. 36; Kirkham 8; Langley 7; M'Intosh 8; Maguire, J. E. 33; Morris, W. 40; Scott, R. A. 39; Sidlow 3; Smalley, T. 29; Smith 2; Taylor, F. 2; Taylor, J. 39; Thompson, H. 17; Westcott, D. 26; Wharton, G. 8; Wright, W. A. 3.

League scorers:
Westcott 19, Jones (B) 15, Galley 11, Dorsett 6, Clayton and Maguire each 5, Langley and Thompson each 3, Kirkham 2, Smalley, Ashall and Howe (Derby County) each 1.

Final Table
Division I — Season 1937/38

	P	W	D	L	F	A	P
1. Arsenal	42	21	10	11	77	44	52
2. Wol'hampton W.	42	20	11	11	72	49	51
3. Preston N. E.	42	16	17	9	64	44	49
4. Charlton Ath.	42	16	14	12	65	51	46
5. Middlesbrough	42	19	8	15	72	65	46
6. Brentford	42	18	9	15	69	59	45
7. Bolton W.	42	15	15	12	64	60	45
8. Sunderland	42	14	16	12	55	57	44
9. Leeds United	42	14	15	13	64	69	43
10. Chelsea	42	14	13	15	65	65	41
11. Liverpool	42	15	11	16	65	71	41
12. Blackpool	42	16	8	18	61	66	40
13. Derby County	42	15	10	17	66	87	40
14. Everton	42	16	7	19	79	75	39
15. Huddersfield	42	17	5	20	55	68	39
16. Leicester City	42	14	11	17	54	75	39
17. Stoke City	42	13	12	17	58	59	38
18. Birmingham	42	10	18	14	58	62	38
19. Portsmouth	42	13	12	17	62	68	38
20. Grimsby Town	42	13	12	17	51	68	38
21. Man. City	42	14	8	20	80	77	36
22. W. B. Albion	42	14	8	20	74	91	36

1938/39

FOOTBALL LEAGUE
Division 1

	Home	Away
Arsenal	0-1	0-0
A. Villa	2-1	2-2
Birmingham	2-1	2-3
Blackpool	1-1	0-1
Bolton	1-1	0-0
Brentford	5-2	1-0
Charlton	3-1	4-0
Chelsea	2-0	3-1
Derby	0-0	2-2
Everton	7-0	0-1
Grimsby	5-0	4-2
Huddersfield	3-0	2-1
Leeds	4-1	0-1
Leicester	0-0	2-0
Liverpool	2-2	2-0
Man. United	3-0	3-1
Middlesbrough	6-1	0-1
Portsmouth	3-0	0-1
Preston	3-0	2-4
Stoke	3-0	3-5
Sunderland	0-0	1-1

F.A. CUP
3 — Bradford	(h)	3-1
4 — Leicester	(h)	5-1
5 — Liverpool	(h)	4-1
6 — Everton	(h)	2-0
S.F. — Grimsby (at Maine Road)		5-0
F. — Portsmouth (at Wembley)		1-4

Final Table
Division I — Season 1938/39

	P	W	D	L	F	A	P
1. Everton	42	27	5	10	88	52	59
2. Wol'hampton W.	42	22	11	9	88	39	55
3. Charlton Ath.	42	22	6	14	75	59	50
4. Middlesbrough	42	20	9	13	93	74	49
5. Arsenal	42	19	9	14	55	41	47
6. Derby County	42	19	8	15	66	55	46
7. Stoke City	42	17	12	13	71	68	46
8. Bolton Wand.	42	15	15	12	67	58	45
9. Preston N. E.	42	16	12	14	63	59	44
10. Grimsby Town	42	16	11	15	61	69	43
11. Liverpool	42	14	14	14	62	63	42
12. Aston Villa	42	15	11	16	71	60	41
13. Leeds United	42	16	9	17	59	67	41
14. Man. United	42	11	16	15	57	65	38
15. Blackpool	42	12	14	16	56	68	38
16. Sunderland	42	13	12	17	54	67	38
17. Portsmouth	42	12	13	17	47	70	37
18. Brentford	42	14	8	20	53	74	36
19. Huddersfield	42	12	11	19	58	64	35
20. Chelsea	42	12	9	21	64	80	33
21. Birmingham	42	12	8	22	62	84	32
22. Leicester City	42	9	11	22	48	82	29

APPENDIX

League appearances:
Barlow 3; Brown 2; Burton, S. 28; Cullis, S. 40; Dorsett 35; Galley, T. 42; Gardiner, J. 38; Goddard, 4; Kirkham 5; Maguire, J. E. 32; Marshall 1; M'Aloon 2; M'Donald\ 2; M'Intosh 33; M'Mahon 1; Morris, W. 40; Mullen, J. 8; Myers 3; Parker 2; Rooney 2; Scott, R. A. 41; Sidlow, C. 1; Tagg 1; Taylor, J. 42; Steen 1; Thompson, H. 11; Westcott, D. 37; Wright 5.

League scorers:
Westcott 32; Dorset 26; Galley 11; M'Intosh 7, Burton and Kirkham each 3; Maguire 2, Barlow, M'Aloon, Steen and Wright each 1.

1939/40

This campaign had to be abandoned, after only three games had been played, due to the outbreak of war. Results were expurged from official records.

1945/46

Though the Football League programme did not get under way again until the following season, the F.A. Cup was played on a two-legged basis for the first, and only, time in its history.

F.A. CUP
3 — Lovells Ath.		(a)	4-2
		(h)	8-1
4 — Charlton		(a)	2-5
		(h)	1-1

1946/47

FOOTBALL LEAGUE
Division 1

	Home	Away
Arsenal	6-1	1-1
A. Villa	1-2	0-3
Blackburn	3-3	2-1
Blackpool	3-1	0-2
Bolton	5-0	3-0
Brentford	1-2	1-4
Charlton	2-0	4-1
Chelsea	6-4	2-1
Derby	7-2	1-2
Everton	2-3	2-0
Grimsby	2-0	0-0
Huddersfield	6-1	1-0
Leeds	1-0	1-0
Liverpool	1-2	5-1
Man. United	3-2	1-3
Middlesbrough	2-4	1-1
Portsmouth	3-1	1-1
Preston	4-1	2-2
Sheffield United	3-1	0-2
Stoke	3-0	3-0
Sunderland	2-1	1-0

F.A. CUP
3 — Rotherham	(h)	3-0
4 — Sheffield United	(h)	0-0
	(a)	0-2

League appearances:
Alderton, J. H. 11; Chatham, R. H. 2; Crook, W. C. 39; Cullis, S. 37; Dorsett, R. 1; Dunn, J. 3; Elliott, E. 3; Forbes, W. 27; Galley, T. 35; Hancocks, J. 40; King, F. A. 6; McIntosh, A. 3; McLean, A. 41; Miller, D. 2; Morris, W. 10; Mullen, J. 38; Pritchard, R. T. 4; Pye, J. 34; Ramscar, F. T. 16; Ratcliffe, P. C. 2; Westcott, D. 35; Williams, B. F. 39; Wright, W. A. 34.

League scorers:
Westcott, 37, Pye 20, Mullen 12, Hancocks 10, Forbes 8, Galley 4, King 3, Crook, Dunn, Ramscar, Wright each 1.

Final Table
Division I — Season 1946/47

	P	W	D	L	F	A	P
1. Liverpool	42	25	7	10	84	52	57
2. Man. United	42	22	12	8	95	54	56
3. Wol'hampton W.	42	25	6	11	98	56	56
4. Stoke City	42	24	7	11	90	53	55
5. Blackpool	42	22	6	14	71	70	50
6. Sheffield United	42	21	7	14	89	75	49
7. Preston N. E.	42	18	11	13	76	74	47
8. Aston Villa	42	18	9	15	67	53	45
9. Sunderland	42	18	8	16	65	66	44
10. Everton	42	17	9	16	62	67	43
11. Middlesbrough	42	17	8	17	73	68	42
12. Portsmouth	42	16	9	17	66	60	41
13. Arsenal	42	16	9	17	72	70	41
14. Derby County	42	18	5	19	73	79	41
15. Chelsea	42	16	7	19	69	84	39
16. Grimsby Town	42	13	12	17	61	82	38
17. Blackburn R.	42	14	8	20	45	53	36
18. Bolton W.	42	13	8	21	57	69	34
19. Charlton Ath.	42	11	12	19	57	71	34
20. Huddersfield	42	13	7	22	53	79	33
21. Brentford	42	9	7	26	45	88	25
22. Leeds United	42	6	6	30	45	90	18

1947/48

FOOTBALL LEAGUE
Division 1

	Home	Away
Arsenal	1-1	2-5
A. Villa	4-1	2-1
Blackburn	5-1	0-1

Blackpool	1-1	2-2
Bolton	1-0	2-3
Burnley	1-1	1-1
Charlton	2-0	1-5
Chelsea	1-0	1-1
Derby	1-0	2-1
Everton	2-4	1-1
Grimsby	8-1	4-0
Huddersfield	2-1	1-0
Liverpool	1-2	1-2
Manchester City	1-0	3-4
Manchester United	2-6	2-3
Middlesbrough	1-3	4-2
Portsmouth	3-1	0-2
Preston	4-2	3-1
Sheffield United	1-1	2-2
Stoke	1-2	3-2
Sunderland	2-1	1-2

F.A. CUP
3 — Bournemouth (a) 2-1
4 — Everton (h) 1-1
(a) 2-3

League appearances:
Brice, G. H. J. 12; Chatham, R. H. 6; Crook, W. C. 31; Dunn, J. 26; Elliot, E. 4; Forbes, W. 20; Galley, T. 6; Hancocks, J. 37; Kelly, L. 21; McLean, A. 31; Mullen, J. 34; Mynard, L. D. 3; Pritchard, R. T. 20; Pye, J. 32; Shorthouse, W. H. 30; Simpson, A. 1; Smith, I. J. 2; Smyth, S. 30; Springthorpe, T. A. 11; Stevenson, E. 6; Westcott, D. 22; Williams, B. F. 38; Wright, W. A. 39.

Final Table
Division I — Season 1947/48

	P	W	D	L	F	A	P
1. Arsenal	42	23	13	6	81	32	59
2. Man. United	42	19	14	9	81	48	52
3. Burnley	42	20	12	10	56	43	52
4. Derby County	42	19	12	11	77	57	50
5. Wol'hampton	42	19	9	14	83	70	47
6. Aston Villa	42	19	9	14	65	57	47
7. Preston N. E.	42	20	7	15	67	68	47
8. Portsmouth	42	19	7	16	68	50	45
9. Blackpool	42	17	10	15	57	41	44
10. Man. City	42	15	12	15	52	47	42
11. Liverpool	42	16	10	16	65	61	42
12. Sheffield Un.	42	16	10	16	65	70	42
13. Charlton Ath.	42	17	6	19	57	66	40
14. Everton	42	17	6	19	52	66	40
15. Stoke City	42	14	10	18	41	55	38
16. Middlesbrough	42	14	9	19	71	73	37
17. Bolton W.	42	16	5	21	46	58	37
18. Chelsea	42	14	9	19	53	71	37
19. Huddersfield	42	12	12	18	51	60	36
20. Sunderland	42	13	10	19	56	67	36
21. Blackburn R.	42	11	10	21	54	72	32
22. Grimsby Town	42	8	6	28	45	111	22

League scorers:
Pye, Hancocks each 16, Westcott 11, Dunn 9, Smyth, Mullen, Forbes each 8, Wright 5, Galley, McLean each 1.

1948/49

FOOTBALL LEAGUE
Division 1

	Home	Away
Arsenal	1-3	1-3
A. Villa	4-0	1-5
Birmingham	2-2	1-0
Blackpool	2-1	3-1
Bolton	2-0	5-0
Burnley	3-0	0-0
Charlton	2-0	3-2
Chelsea	1-1	1-4
Derby	2-2	2-3
Everton	1-0	0-1
Huddersfield	7-1	0-4
Liverpool	0-0	0-0
Manchester City	1-1	3-3
Manchester United	3-2	0-2
Middlesbrough	0-3	4-4
Newcastle	3-0	1-3
Portsmouth	3-0	0-5
Preston	2-1	1-1
Sheffield United	6-0	1-1
Stoke	3-1	1-2
Sunderland	0-1	3-3

F.A. CUP
3 — Chesterfield (h) 6-0
4 — Sheffield United (a) 3-0
5 — Liverpool (h) 3-1
6 — W. B. Albion (h) 1-0
S.F. — Manchester United
(at Hillsborough) 1-1
Manchester United
(at Goodison Park) 1-0
F. — Leicester (at Wembley) 3-1

League appearances:
Baxter, W. 5; Chatham, R. H. 4; Crook, A. R. 1; Crook, W. C. 36; Dunn, J. 28; Forbes, W. 16; Hancocks, J. 38; Kelly, L. 21; McLean, J. 13; Mullen, J. 38; Parsons, D. R. 1; Pritchard, R. T. 30; Pye, J. 33; Russell, E. T. 4; Shorthouse, W. H. 39; Simpson, A. 1; Sims, N. D. 4; Smith, L. J. 7; Smyth, S. 39; Springthorpe, R. A. 19; Stevenson, E. 2; Williams, B. F. 37; Wilshaw, D. 11; Wright, W. A. 35.

League scorers:
Pye 17, Smyth 16, Hancocks, Mullen each 12, Wilshaw 10, Dunn 6, Forbes, Wright each 2, Ferrier (Portsmouth), McDowell (Manchester City) each 1.

Final Table
Division I — Season 1948/49

		P	W	D	L	F	A	P
1.	Portsmouth	42	25	8	9	84	42	58
2.	Man. United	42	21	11	10	77	44	53
3.	Derby County	42	22	9	11	74	55	53
4.	Newcastle United	42	20	12	10	70	56	52
5.	Arsenal	42	18	13	11	74	44	49
6.	Wol'hampton W.	42	17	12	13	79	66	46
7.	Man. City	42	15	15	12	47	51	45
8.	Sunderland	42	13	17	12	49	58	43
9.	Charlton Athletic	42	15	12	15	63	67	42
10.	Aston Villa	42	16	10	16	60	76	42
11.	Stoke City	42	16	9	17	66	68	41
12.	Liverpool	42	13	14	15	53	43	40
13.	Chelsea	42	12	14	16	69	68	38
14.	Bolton W.	42	14	10	18	59	68	38
15.	Burnley	42	12	14	16	43	50	38
16.	Blackpool	42	11	16	15	54	67	38
17.	Birmingham City	42	11	15	16	36	38	37
18.	Everton	42	13	11	18	41	63	37
19.	Middlesbrough	42	11	12	19	46	57	34
20.	Huddersfield	42	12	10	20	40	69	34
21.	Preston N. E.	42	11	11	20	62	75	33
22.	Sheffield United	42	11	11	20	57	78	33

1949/50

FOOTBALL LEAGUE
Division 1

	Home	Away
Arsenal	3-0	1-1
Aston Villa	2-3	4-1
Birmingham	6-1	1-1
Blackpool	3-0	2-1
Bolton	1-1	4-2
Burnley	0-0	1-0
Charlton	2-1	3-2
Chelsea	2-2	0-0
Derby	4-1	2-1
Everton	1-1	2-1
Fulham	1-1	2-1
Huddersfield	7-1	0-1
Liverpool	1-1	2-0
Manchester City	3-0	1-2
Manchester United	1-1	0-3
Middlesbrough	3-1	0-2
Newcastle	2-1	0-2
Portsmouth	1-0	1-1
Stoke	2-1	1-2
Sunderland	1-3	1-3
W. B. Albion	1-1	1-1

F.A. CUP

3 — Plymouth	(a)	1-1
	(h)	3-0
4 — Sheffield United	(h)	0-0
	(a)	4-3
5 — Blackpool	(h)	0-0
	(a)	0-1

League appearances:
Baxter, W. 3; Chatham, R. H. 9; Crook, W. C. 34; Dunn, J. 7; Forbes, W. 8; Hancocks, J. 38; Kelly, L. 18; McLean, A. 32; Mullen, J. 40; Parsons, D. R. 5; Pye, J. 39; Pritchard, R. T. 26; Rowley, K. 1; Russell, E. T. 13; Shorthouse, W. H. 39; Sims, N. D. 1; Smith, L. J. 4; Smyth, S. 29; Springthorpe, T. A. 5; Swinbourne, R. H. 20; Walker, J. H. 12; Williams, B. F. 36; Wilshaw, D. 8; Wright, W. A, 35.

League scorers:
Pye 18, Mullen, Hancocks each 10, Smyth 9, Walker 8, Swinbourne 7, Forbes 5, Wilshaw, Wright each 3, Dunn, McLean, Dorman (Birmingham) each 1.

Final Table
Division I — Season 1949/50

		P	W	D	L	F	A	P
1.	Portsmouth	42	22	9	11	74	38	53
2.	Wol'hampton W.	42	20	13	9	76	49	53
3.	Sunderland	42	21	10	11	83	62	52
4.	Man. United	42	18	14	10	69	44	50
5.	Newcastle United	42	19	12	11	77	55	50
6.	Arsenal	42	19	11	12	79	55	49
7.	Blackpool	42	17	15	10	46	35	49
8.	Liverpool	42	17	14	11	64	54	48
9.	Middlesbrough	42	20	7	15	59	48	47
10.	Burnley	42	16	13	13	40	40	45
11.	Derby County	42	17	10	15	69	61	44
12.	Aston Villa	42	15	12	15	61	61	42
13.	Chelsea	42	12	16	14	58	65	40
14.	W. B. Albion	42	14	12	16	47	53	40
15.	Huddersfield	42	14	9	19	52	73	37
16.	Bolton W.	42	10	14	18	45	59	34
17.	Fulham	42	10	14	18	41	54	34
18.	Everton	42	10	14	18	42	66	34
19.	Stoke City	42	11	12	19	45	75	34
20.	Charlton Athletic	42	13	6	23	53	65	32
21.	Man. City	42	8	13	21	36	68	29
22.	Birmingham City	42	7	14	21	31	67	28

1950/51

FOOTBALL LEAGUE
Division 1

	Home	Away
Arsenal	0-1	1-2
Aston Villa	2-3	0-1
Blackpool	1-1	1-1
Bolton	7-1	1-2
Burnley	0-1	0-2
Charlton	2-3	2-3
Chelsea	2-1	1-2
Derby	2-3	2-1
Everton	4-0	1-1

Fulham	1-1	1-2
Huddersfield	3-1	2-1
Liverpool	2-0	4-1
Man. United	0-0	1-2
Middlesbrough	3-4	2-1
Newcastle	0-1	1-1
Portsmouth	2-3	4-1
Sheffield Wednesday	4-0	2-2
Stoke	2-3	1-0
Sunderland	2-1	0-0
Tottenham	2-1	1-2
W. B. Albion	3-1	2-3

F.A. CUP
3 — Plymouth	(a) 2-1
4 — Aston Villa	(h) 3-1
5 — Huddersfield	(h) 2-0
6 — Sunderland	(a) 1-1
	(h) 3-1
S.F. — Newcastle (at Hillsborough)	0-0
Newcastle (at Huddersfield)	1-2

League appearances:
Baxter, W. 2; Broadbent, P. F. 9; Chatham, R. H. 21; Crook, W. C. 26; Dunn, J. 32; Hancocks, J. 31; McLean, A. 27; Mullen, J. 31; Parsons, D. R. 6; Pritchard, R. T. 29; Pye, J. 23; Russell, E. T. 13; Short, J. 18; Shorthouse, W. H. 37; Smith, L. J. 5; Smyth, S. 3; Swinbourne, R. H. 41; Walker, J. H. 20; Williams, B. F. 36; Wilshaw, D. 14; Wright, W. A. 38.

Final Table
Division I — Season 1950/51

	P	W	D	L	F	A	P
1. Tottenham	42	25	10	7	82	44	60
2. Man. United	42	24	8	10	74	40	56
3. Blackpool	42	20	10	12	79	53	50
4. Newcastle United	42	18	13	11	62	53	49
5. Arsenal	42	19	9	14	73	56	47
6. Middlesbrough	42	18	11	13	76	65	47
7. Portsmouth	42	16	15	11	71	68	47
8. Bolton W.	42	19	7	16	64	61	45
9. Liverpool	42	16	11	15	53	59	43
10. Burnley	42	14	14	14	48	43	42
11. Derby County	42	16	8	18	81	75	40
12. Sunderland	42	12	16	14	63	73	40
13. Stoke City	42	13	14	15	50	59	40
14. Wol'hampton W.	42	15	8	19	74	61	38
15. Aston Villa	42	12	13	17	66	68	37
16. W. B. Albion	42	13	11	18	53	61	37
17. Charlton Athletic	42	14	9	19	63	80	37
18. Fulham	42	13	11	18	52	68	37
19. Huddersfield	42	15	6	21	64	92	36
20. Chelsea	42	12	8	22	53	65	32
21. Sheffield Wed.	42	12	8	22	64	83	32
22. Everton	42	12	8	22	48	86	32

League scorers:
Swinbourne 20, Hancocks 19, Walker 11, Dunn 7, Mullen, Wilshaw each 5, Pye 4, Crook, Smith, Broadbent each 1.

1951/52

FOOTBALL LEAGUE
Division 1

	Home	Away
Arsenal	2-1	2-2
Aston Villa	1-2	3-3
Blackpool	3-0	2-3
Bolton	5-1	2-2
Burnley	1-2	2-2
Charlton	2-2	0-1
Chelsea	5-3	1-0
Derby	1-2	3-1
Fulham	2-2	2-2
Huddersfield	0-0	7-1
Liverpool	2-1	1-1
Manchester City	2-2	0-0
Manchester United	0-2	0-2
Middlesbrough	4-0	0-4
Newcastle	3-0	1-3
Portsmouth	1-1	3-2
Preston	1-4	0-3
Stoke	3-0	0-1
Sunderland	0-3	1-1
Tottenham	1-2	2-4
W. B. Albion	1-4	1-2

F.A. CUP
3 — Manchester City	(a) 2-2
	(h) 4-1
4 — Liverpool	(a) 1-2

League appearances:
Baxter, W. 20; Birch, P. 3; Broadbent, P. F. 16; Chatham, R. H. 23; Clews, M. D. 1; Crook, W. C. 20; Deeley, N. V. 6; Dunn, J. 26; Gibbons, L. 22; Gutteridge, W. D. 2; Hancocks, J. E. 30; Mullen, J. 40; Parsons, D. R. 11; Pritchard, R. T. 19; Pye, J. 27; Short, J. 25; Shorthouse, W. H. 37; Sims, N. D. 4; Smith, L. J. 15; Smyth, S. 1; Stuart, E. A. 2; Swinbourne, R. H. 19; Walker, J. H. 5; Whitfield, K. 9; Williams, B. F. 26; Wilshaw, D. 14; Wright, W. A. 39.

League scorers:
Pye 15, Hancocks 12, Mullen 11, Dunn 9, Smith 7, Wilshaw 5, Swinbourne 4, Whitfield 3, Walker 2, Baxter, Birch, Broadbent, Smyth, Stuart each 1.

APPENDIX

Final Table
Division I — Season 1951/52

	P	W	D	L	F	A	P
1. Man. United	42	23	11	8	95	52	57
2. Tottenham	42	22	9	11	76	51	53
3. Arsenal	42	21	11	10	80	61	53
4. Portsmouth	42	20	8	14	68	58	48
5. Bolton	42	19	10	13	65	61	48
6. Aston Villa	42	19	9	14	79	70	47
7. Preston	42	17	12	13	74	54	46
8. Newcastle	42	18	9	15	98	73	45
9. Blackpool	42	18	9	15	64	64	45
10. Charlton	42	17	10	15	68	63	44
11. Liverpool	42	12	19	11	57	61	43
12. Sunderland	42	15	12	15	70	61	42
13. W. B. Albion	42	14	13	15	74	77	41
14. Burnley	42	15	10	17	56	63	40
15. Man. City	42	13	13	16	58	61	39
16. Wolves	42	12	14	16	73	73	38
17. Derby Co.	42	15	7	20	63	80	37
18. Middlesbrough	42	15	6	21	64	88	36
19. Chelsea	42	14	8	20	52	72	36
20. Stoke City	42	12	7	23	49	88	31
21. Huddersfield	42	10	8	24	49	82	28
22. Fulham	42	8	11	23	58	77	27

League appearances:
Baxter, W. 8; Broadbent, P. 25; Chatham, R. H. 10; Crook, W. C. 10; Dunn, J. 1; Flowers, R. 20; Gibbons, L. 2; Gutteridge, W. H. 2; Hancocks, J. 27; Mullen, J. 41; Pritchard, R. T. 40; Short, J. 29; Shorthouse, W. H. 39; Sims, N. D. 13; Smith, L. J. 15; Stockin, R. 15; Swinbourne, R. H. 41; Slater, W. J. 17; Taylor, J. E. 10; Whitfield, K. 1; Williams, B. F. 29; Wilshaw, D. 29; Wright, W. A. 38.

League scorers:
Swinbourne 21, Wilshaw 17, Mullen 11, Hancocks 10, Smith, Stockin each 7, Broadbent 5, Slater 3, Taylor, Flowers, Wright, Curtis (Sheffield Wed.), Batty (Newcastle) each 1.

Final Table
Division I — Season 1952/53

	P	W	D	L	F	A	P
1. Arsenal	42	21	12	9	97	64	54
2. Preston N. E.	42	21	12	9	85	60	54
3. Wol'hampton W.	42	19	13	10	86	63	51
4. W. B. Albion	42	21	8	13	66	60	50
5. Charlton Athletic	42	19	11	12	77	63	49
6. Burnley	42	18	12	12	67	52	48
7. Blackpool	42	19	9	14	71	70	47
8. Man. United	42	18	10	14	69	72	46
9. Sunderland	42	15	13	14	68	82	43
10. Tottenham H.	42	15	11	16	78	69	41
11. Aston Villa	42	14	13	15	63	61	41
12. Cardiff City	42	14	12	16	54	46	40
13. Middlesbrough	42	14	11	17	70	77	39
14. Bolton W.	42	15	9	18	61	69	39
15. Portsmouth	42	14	10	18	74	83	38
16. Newcastle United	42	14	9	19	59	70	37
17. Liverpool	42	14	8	20	61	82	36
18. Sheffield W.	42	12	11	19	62	72	35
19. Chelsea	42	12	11	19	56	66	35
20. Man. City	42	14	7	21	72	87	35
21. Stoke City	42	12	10	20	53	66	34
22. Derby County	42	11	10	21	59	74	32

1952/53

FOOTBALL LEAGUE
Division 1

	Home	Away
Arsenal	1-1	3-5
Aston Villa	2-1	1-0
Blackpool	2-5	0-2
Bolton	3-1	1-2
Burnley	5-1	0-0
Cardiff	1-0	0-0
Charlton	1-2	2-2
Chelsea	2-2	2-1
Derby	3-1	3-2
Liverpool	3-0	1-2
Man. City	7-3	1-3
Man. United	6-2	3-0
Middlesbrough	3-3	1-1
Newcastle	2-0	1-1
Portsmouth	4-1	2-2
Preston	0-2	1-1
Sheffield Wed.	3-1	3-2
Stoke	3-0	2-1
Sunderland	1-1	2-5
Tottenham	0-0	2-3
W. B. Albion	2-0	1-1

F.A. CUP
3 — Preston (a) 2-5

1953/54

FOOTBALL LEAGUE
Division 1

	Home	Away
Arsenal	0-2	3-2
A. Villa	1-2	2-1
Blackpool	4-1	0-0
Bolton	1-1	1-1
Burnley	1-2	1-4
Cardiff	3-1	3-1
Charlton	5-0	2-0
Chelsea	8-1	2-4

Huddersfield	4-0	1-2	
Liverpool	2-1	1-1	
Man. City	3-1	4-0	
Man. United	3-1	0-1	
Middlesbrough	2-4	3-3	
Newcastle	3-2	2-1	
Portsmouth	4-3	0-2	
Preston	1-0	1-0	
Sheffield United	6-1	3-3	
Sheffield Wed.	4-1	0-0	
Sunderland	3-1	2-3	
Tottenham	2-0	3-2	
W. B. Albion	1-0	1-0	

F.A. CUP
3 — Birmingham (h) 1-2

League appearances:
Baxter, W. 5; Broadbent, P. 36; Chatham, R. H. 1; Clamp, E. 2; Deeley, N. V. 6; Flowers, R. 15; Gibbons, L. 1; Gutteridge, W. H. 2; Hancocks, J. 42; Mullen, J. 38; Pritchard, R. T. 27; Short, J. 26; Shorthouse, W. H. 40; Sims, N. D. 8; Slater, W. J. 39; Smith, L. J. 4; Stockin, R. 6; Stuart, E. A. 12; Swinbourne, R. H. 40; Williams, B. F. 34; Wilshaw, D. 39; Wright, W. A. 39.

League scorers:
Wilshaw, Hancocks each 25, Swinbourne 24, Broadbent 12, Mullen 7, Slater 2, Smith 1.

1954/55

FOOTBALL LEAGUE
Division 1

	Home	Away
Arsenal	3-1	1-1
Aston Villa	1-0	2-4
Blackpool	1-0	2-0
Bolton	1-2	1-6
Burnley	5-0	0-1
Cardiff	1-1	2-3
Charlton	2-1	3-1
Chelsea	3-4	0-1
Everton	1-3	2-3
Huddersfield	6-4	0-2
Leicester	5-0	2-1
Man. City	2-2	0-3
Man. United	4-2	4-2
Newcastle	2-2	3-2
Portsmouth	2-2	0-0
Preston	1-1	3-3
Sheffield United	4-1	2-1
Sheffield Wed.	4-2	2-2
Sunderland	2-0	0-0
Tottenham	4-2	2-3
W. B. Albion	4-0	0-1

F.A. CUP
3 — Grimsby (a) 5-2
4 — Arsenal (h) 1-0
5 — Charlton (h) 4-1
6 — Sunderland (a) 0-2

Final Table
Division I — Season 1953/54

	P	W	D	L	F	A	P
1. Wolves	42	25	7	10	96	56	57
2. W. B. Albion	42	22	9	11	86	63	53
3. Huddersfield	42	20	11	11	78	61	51
4. Man. United	42	18	12	12	73	58	48
5. Bolton	42	18	12	12	75	60	48
6. Blackpool	42	19	10	13	80	69	48
7. Burnley	42	21	4	17	78	67	46
8. Chelsea	42	16	12	14	74	68	44
9. Charlton	42	19	6	17	75	77	44
10. Cardiff	42	18	8	16	51	71	44
11. Preston	42	19	5	18	87	58	43
12. Arsenal	42	15	13	14	75	73	43
13. Aston Villa	42	16	9	17	70	68	41
14. Portsmouth	42	14	11	17	81	89	39
15. Newcastle Utd.	42	14	10	18	72	77	38
16. Tottenham	42	16	5	21	65	76	37
17. Man. City	42	14	9	19	62	77	37
18. Sunderland	42	14	8	20	81	89	36
19. Sheffield Wed.	42	15	6	21	70	91	36
20. Sheffield Utd.	42	11	11	20	69	90	33
21. Middlesbrough	42	10	10	22	60	91	30
22. Liverpool	42	9	10	23	68	97	28

Final Table
Division I — Season 1954/55

	P	W	D	L	F	A	P
1. Chelsea	42	20	12	10	81	57	52
2. Wolves	42	19	10	13	89	70	48
3. Portsmouth	42	18	12	12	74	62	48
4. Sunderland	42	15	18	9	64	54	48
5. Man. United	42	20	7	15	84	74	47
6. Aston Villa	42	20	7	15	72	73	47
7. Man. City	42	18	10	14	76	69	46
8. Newcastle Utd.	42	17	9	16	89	77	43
9. Arsenal	42	17	9	16	69	63	43
10. Burnley	42	17	9	16	51	48	43
11. Everton	42	16	10	16	62	68	42
12. Huddersfield	42	14	13	15	63	68	41
13. Sheffield Utd.	42	17	7	18	70	86	41
14. Preston N. E.	42	16	8	18	83	64	40
15. Charlton	42	15	10	17	76	75	40
16. Tottenham	42	16	8	18	72	73	40
17. W. B. Albion	42	16	8	18	76	96	40
18. Bolton	42	13	13	16	62	69	39
19. Blackpool	42	14	10	18	60	64	38
20. Cardiff	42	13	11	18	62	76	37
21. Leicester	42	12	11	19	74	86	35
22. Sheffield Wed.	42	8	10	24	63	100	26

APPENDIX

League appearances:
Baillie, J. 1; Booth, C. 3; Broadbent, P. F. 38; Clamp, E. 10; Deeley, N. V. 7; Flowers, R. 37; Hancocks, J. 32; McDonald, T. 1; Mullen, J. 17; Pritchard, R. T. 7; Russell, P. 2; Shorthouse, W. H. 36; Showell, G. W. 8; Sims, N. D. 3; Slater, W. J. 38; Smith, L. J. 34; Stuart, E. A. 33; Swinbourne, R. H. 36; Taylor, D. 3; Williams, B. F. 39; Wilshaw, D. 38; Wright, W. A. 39.

League scorers:
Hancocks 25, Wilshaw 20, Swinbourne 14, Smith 6, Broadbent, Mullen, Flowers each 5, Slater 4, Wetton (Tottenham Hotspur) 2, Deeley, Wright, Cockburn (Manchester United) each 1.

League scorers:
Hancocks 18, Swinbourne 17, Murray 11, Broadbent 10, Booth 7, Mullen 7, Slater 7, Wilshaw 6, McDonald, Shorthouse, Clamp, Flowers and Deeley each 1. Opponents 1.

Final Table

Division I — Seasonal 1955-56

	P	W	D	L	F	A	P
1. Man. United	42	25	10	7	83	51	60
2. Blackpool	42	20	9	13	86	62	49
3. Wolves	42	20	9	13	89	65	49
4. Man. City	42	18	10	14	82	69	46
5. Arsenal	42	18	10	14	60	61	46
6. Birmingham City	42	18	9	15	75	57	45
7. Burnley	42	18	8	16	64	54	44
8. Bolton Wand.	42	18	7	17	71	58	43
9. Sunderland	42	17	9	16	80	95	43
10. Luton Town	42	17	8	17	66	64	42
11. Newcastle United	42	17	7	18	85	70	41
12. Portsmouth	42	16	9	17	78	85	41
13. W. B. Albion	42	18	5	19	58	70	41
14. Charlton Athletic	42	17	6	19	75	81	40
15. Everton	42	15	10	17	55	69	40
16. Chelsea	42	14	11	17	64	77	39
17. Cardiff City	42	15	9	18	55	69	39
18. Tottenham H.	42	15	7	20	61	71	37
19. Preston N. E.	42	14	8	20	73	72	36
20. Aston Villa	42	11	13	18	52	69	35
21. Huddersfield T.	42	14	7	21	54	83	35
22. Sheffield United	42	12	9	21	63	77	33

1955/56

FOOTBALL LEAGUE
Division 1

	Home	Away
Arsenal	3-3	2-2
Aston Villa	0-0	0-0
Birmingham	1-0	0-0
Blackpool	2-3	1-2
Bolton	4-2	1-2
Burnley	3-1	2-1
Cardiff	0-2	9-1
Charlton	2-0	2-0
Chelsea	2-1	3-2
Everton	1-0	1-2
Huddersfield	4-0	3-1
Luton	1-2	1-5
Man. City	7-2	2-2
Man. United	0-2	3-4
Newcastle	2-1	1-3
Portsmouth	3-1	1-2
Preston	2-1	0-2
Sheffield Utd.	3-2	3-3
Sunderland	3-1	1-1
Tottenham	5-1	1-2
W. B. Albion	3-2	1-1

F.A. CUP
3 — W. B. Albion (h) 1-2

League appearances:
Booth, C. 26; Broadbent, P. F. 39; Clamp, E. 27; Deeley, N. V. 8; Flowers, R. 18; Hancocks, J. 28; Howells, R. 7; Jones, G. 1; McDonald, T. 4; Mason, R. H. 1; Middleton, H. 1; Mullen, J. 36; Murray, J. R. 25; Russell, P. 1; Shorthouse, W. H. 38; Showell, G. W. 10; Sims, N. D. 5; Slater, W. J. 34; Smith, L. J. 2; Stuart, E. A. 37; Swinbourne, R. H. 14; Williams, B. F. 38; Wilshaw, D. 25; Wright, W. A. 37.

1956/57

FOOTBALL LEAGUE
Division 1

	Home	Away
Arsenal	5-2	0-0
Aston Villa	3-0	0-4
Birmingham	3-0	2-2
Blackpool	4:1	2-3
Bolton	3-2	3-0
Burnley	1-2	0-3
Cardiff	3-1	2-2
Charlton	7-3	1-2
Chelsea	3-1	3-3
Everton	2-1	1-3
Leeds	1-2	0-0
Luton	5-4	0-1
Man. City	5-1	3-2
Man. United	1-1	0-3
Newcastle	2-0	1-2
Portsmouth	6-0	0-1
Preston	4-3	0-1
Sheffield Wed.	2-1	1-2
Sunderland	2-2	3-2
Tottenham	3-0	1-4
W. B. Albion	5-2	1-1

APPENDIX

F.A. CUP
3 — Swansea (h) 5-3
4 — Bournemouth (h) 0-1

League appearances:
Bonson, J. 10; Booth, C. 20; Broadbent, P. F. 35; Clamp, E. 13; Deeley, N. 10; Finlayson, M. J. 13; Flowers, R. 39; Harris, G. 31; Hooper, H. 39; Jones, G. 2; Mason, R. H. 8; Mullen, J. 30; Murray, J. 33; Neil, P. 4; Shorthouse, W. H. 9; Showell, G. W. 13; Slater, W. J. 32; Stuart, E. A. 30; Tether, C. 1; Thomson, R. 1; Williams, B. F. 29; Wilshaw, D. 20; Wright, W. A. 40.

League scorers:
Hooper 19, Broadbent, Murray 17, Wilshaw 10, Booth 9, Bonson, Slater 4, Mullen, Flowers, Mason 3, Neil, P. Clamp, Thompson, Deeley 1, Opponents 1.

Final Table
Division I — Season 1956/57

		P	W	D	L	F	A	P
1.	Man. United	42	28	8	6	103	54	64
2.	Tottenham H.	42	22	12	8	104	56	56
3.	Preston N. E.	42	23	10	9	84	56	56
4.	Blackpool	42	22	9	11	93	65	53
5.	Arsenal	42	21	8	13	85	69	50
6.	Wolves	42	20	8	14	94	70	48
7.	Burnley	42	18	10	14	56	50	46
8.	Leeds United	42	15	14	13	72	63	44
9.	Bolton Wand.	42	16	12	14	65	65	44
10.	Aston Villa	42	14	15	13	65	55	43
11.	W. B. Albion	42	14	14	14	59	61	42
12.	Birmingham C.	42	15	9	18	69	69	39
13.	Chelsea	42	13	13	16	73	73	39
14.	Sheffield Wed.	42	16	6	20	82	88	38
15.	Everton	42	14	10	18	61	79	38
16.	Luton Town	42	14	9	19	58	76	37
17.	Newcastle Utd.	42	14	8	20	67	87	36
18.	Manchester City	42	13	9	20	78	88	35
19.	Portsmouth	42	10	13	19	62	92	33
20.	Sunderland	42	12	8	22	67	88	32
21.	Cardiff City	42	10	9	23	53	88	29
22.	Charlton Ath.	42	9	4	29	62	120	22

1957/58

FOOTBALL LEAGUE
Division 1

	Home	Away
Arsenal	1-2	2-0
Aston Villa	2-1	3-2
Birmingham	5-1	5-1
Blackpool	3-1	2-3
Bolton	6-1	1-1
Burnley	2-1	1-1
Chelsea	2-1	2-1
Everton	2-0	0-1
Leeds	3-2	1-1
Leicester	5-1	3-2
Luton	1-1	1-3
Man. City	3-3	4-3
Man. United	3-1	4-0
Newcastle	3-1	1-1
Nottingham F.	2-0	4-1
Portsmouth	1-0	1-1
Preston	2-0	2-1
Sheffield Wed.	4-3	1-2
Sunderland	5-0	2-0
Tottenham	4-0	0-1
W. B. Albion	1-1	3-0

F.A. CUP
3 — Lincoln (a) 1-0
4 — Portsmouth (h) 5-1
5 — Darlington (h) 6-1
6 — Bolton (a) 1-2

League appearances:
Booth, C. 13; Broadbent, P. 40; Clamp, E. 41; Deeley, N. 41; Dwyer, N. 5; Finlayson, M. 37; Flowers, R. 28; Harris, G. 39; Henderson, J. 1; Howells, R. 2; Jackson, A. 2; Jones, G. 2; Lill, M. 1; Mason, R. 20; Mullen, J. 38; Murray, J. 41; Showell, G. 7; Slater, W. 14; Stuart, E. 40; Wilshaw, D. 12; Wright, W. 38.

League scorers;
Murray 29, Deeley 23, Broadbent 17, Clamp 10, Mason 7, Mullen 4, Wilshaw 4, Flowers 3, Booth 2, Showell 1, Lill 1, Opponents 2.

Final Table
Division I — Season 1957/58

		P	W	D	L	F	A	P
1.	Wolves	42	28	8	6	103	47	64
2.	Preston N. E.	42	26	7	9	100	51	59
3.	Tottenham H.	42	21	9	12	93	77	51
4.	W. B. Albion	42	18	14	10	92	70	50
5.	Man. City	42	22	5	15	104	100	49
6.	Burnley	42	21	5	16	80	74	47
7.	Blackpool	42	19	6	17	80	67	44
8.	Luton Town	42	19	6	17	69	63	44
9.	Man. United	42	16	11	15	85	75	43
10.	Nottingham F.	42	16	10	16	69	63	42
11.	Chelsea	42	15	12	15	83	79	42
12.	Arsenal	42	16	7	19	73	85	39
13.	Birmingham C.	42	14	11	17	76	89	39
14.	Aston Villa	42	16	7	19	73	86	39
15.	Bolton Wand.	42	14	10	18	65	87	38
16.	Everton	42	13	11	18	65	75	37
17.	Leeds United	42	14	9	19	51	63	37
18.	Leicester City	42	14	5	23	91	112	33
19.	Newcastle Utd.	42	12	8	22	73	81	32
20.	Portsmouth	42	12	8	22	73	88	32
21.	Sunderland	42	10	12	20	54	97	32
22.	Sheffield Wed.	42	12	7	23	69	92	31

1958/59

FOOTBALL LEAGUE
Division 1

	Home	Away
Arsenal	6-1	1-1
Aston Villa	4-0	3-1
Birmingham	3-1	3-0
Blackburn	5-0	2-1
Blackpool	2-0	1-0
Bolton	1-2	2-2
Burnley	3-3	2-0
Chelsea	1-2	2-6
Everton	1-0	1-0
Leeds	6-2	3-1
Leicester	3-0	0-1
Luton	5-0	1-0
Man. City	2-0	4-1
Man. United	4-0	1-2
Newcastle	1-3	4-3
Nottingham F.	5-1	3-1
Portsmouth	7-0	5-3
Preston	2-0	2-1
Tottenham	1-1	1-2
W. B. Albion	5-2	1-2
West Ham	1-1	0-2

F.A. CUP
3 — Barrow (a) 4-2
4 — Bolton (h) 1-2

EUROPEAN CHAMPIONS CUP
1 — Schalke '04 (h) 2-2
(a) 1-2

Final Table
Division I — Season 1958/59

		P	W	D	L	F	A	P
1.	Wolves	42	28	5	9	110	49	61
2.	Man. United	42	24	7	11	103	66	55
3.	Arsenal	42	21	8	13	88	68	50
4.	Bolton W.	42	20	10	12	79	66	50
5.	W. B. Albion	42	18	13	11	88	68	49
6.	West Ham Utd.	42	21	6	15	85	70	48
7.	Burnley	42	19	10	13	81	70	48
8.	Blackpool	42	18	11	13	66	49	47
9.	Birmingham C.	42	20	6	16	84	68	46
10.	Blackburn Rov.	42	17	10	15	76	70	44
11.	Newcastle U.	42	17	7	18	80	80	41
12.	Preston N. E.	42	17	7	18	70	77	41
13.	Nottingham F.	42	17	6	19	71	74	40
14.	Chelsea	42	18	4	20	77	98	40
15.	Leeds Utd.	42	15	9	18	57	74	39
16.	Everton	42	17	4	21	71	87	38
17.	Luton Town	42	12	13	17	68	71	37
18.	Tottenham H.	42	13	10	19	85	95	36
19.	Leicester City	42	11	10	21	67	98	32
20.	Man. City	42	11	9	22	64	95	31
21.	Aston Villa	42	11	8	23	58	87	30
22.	Portsmouth	42	6	9	27	64	112	21

League appearances:
Booth, C. 13; Broadbent, P. 40; Clamp, E. 26; Deeley, N. 38; Durandt, C. 1; Finlayson, M. 39; Flowers, R. 31; Harris, G. 40; Henderson, J. 8; Horne, R. 8; Jackson, A. 2; Jones, G. 4; Kelly, P. 1; Lill, M. 18; Mason, R. 34; Mullen, J. 16; Murray, J. 28; Showell, G. 8; Sidebottom, G. 3; Slater, W. 27; Stuart, E. 38; Wright, W. 39.

League scorers:
Murray 21, Broadbent 20, Deeley 17, Mason 13, Lill 12, Booth 7, Mullen 4, Henderson 3, Horne 3, Clamp 3, Showell 2, Harris 1, Jackson 1, Opponents 2.

1959/60

FOOTBALL LEAGUE
Division 1

	Home	Away
Arsenal	3-3	4-4
Birmingham	2-0	1-0
Blackburn	3-1	1-0
Blackpool	1-1	1-3
Bolton	0-1	1-2
Burnley	6-1	1-4
Chelsea	3-1	5-1
Everton	2-0	2-0
Fulham	9-0	1-3
Leeds	4-2	3-0
Leicester	0-3	1-2
Luton	3-2	5-1
Man City	4-2	6-4
Man. United	3-2	2-0
Newcastle	2-0	0-1
Nottingham F.	3-1	0-0
Preston	3-3	3-4
Sheffield Wed.	3-1	2-2
Tottenham	1-3	1-5
W. B. Albion	3-1	1-0
West Ham	5-0	2-3

F.A. CUP
3 — Newcastle (h) 2-2
(a) 4-2
4 — Charlton (h) 2-1
5 — Luton (a) 4-1
6 — Leicester (a) 2-1
S.F. — A. Villa
(at West Bromwich) 1-0
F. — Blackburn
(at Wembley) 3-0

EUROPEAN CHAMPIONS CUP
Prel. — Voerwaerts (a) 1-2
(h) 2-0
1 — Red Star, Belgrade (a) 1-1
(h) 3-0
2 — Barcelona (a) 0-4
(h) 2-5

APPENDIX

League appearances:
Booth, C. 3; Broadbent, P. 33; Clamp, E. 38; Deeley, N. 37; Durandt, C. 7; Finlayson, M. 35; Flowers, R. 35; Harris, G. 36; Horne, D. 26; Jones, G. 6; Kelly, P. 4; Kirkham, J. 3; Lill, M. 11; Mannion, G. 10; Mason, R. 37; Murray, J. 40; Showell, G. 32; Sidebottom, G. 7; Slater, W. 30; Stobart, B. 4; Stuart, E. 28.

League scorers:
Murray 29, Broadbent 14, Deeley 14, Mason 13, Horne 9, Clamp 8; Mannion 6, Flowers 4, Slater 2, Stobart 2, Lill 2, Booth 1, Opponents 2.

Final Table
Division I — Season 1959/60

	P	W	D	L	F	A	P
1. Burnley	42	24	7	11	85	61	55
2. Wolves	42	24	6	12	106	67	54
3. Tottenham H.	42	21	11	10	86	50	53
4. W. B. Albion	42	19	11	12	83	57	49
5. Sheffield Wed.	42	19	11	12	80	59	49
6. Bolton W.	42	20	8	14	59	51	48
7. Man. United	42	19	7	16	102	80	45
8. Newcastle Utd.	42	18	8	16	82	78	44
9. Preston N. E.	42	16	12	14	79	76	44
10. Fulham	42	17	10	15	73	80	44
11. Blackpool	42	15	10	17	59	71	40
12. Leicester City	42	13	13	16	66	75	39
13. Arsenal	42	15	9	18	68	80	39
14. West Ham Utd.	42	16	6	20	75	91	38
15. Man. City	42	17	3	22	78	84	37
16. Everton	42	13	11	18	73	78	37
17. Blackburn R.	42	16	5	21	60	70	37
18. Chelsea	42	14	9	19	76	91	37
19. Birmingham	42	13	10	19	63	80	36
20. Nottingham F.	42	13	9	20	50	74	35
21. Leeds United	42	12	10	20	65	92	34
22. Luton Town	42	9	12	21	50	73	30

1960/61

FOOTBALL LEAGUE
Division 1

	Home	Away
Arsenal	5-3	5-1
A. Villa	3-2	2-0
Birmingham	5-1	2-1
Blackburn	0-0	1-2
Blackpool	1-0	2-5
Bolton	3-1	2-0
Burnley	2-1	3-5
Cardiff	2-2	2-3
Chelsea	6-1	3-3
Everton	4-1	1-3
Fulham	2-4	3-1
Leicester	3-2	0-2

Man. City	1-0	4-2
Man. United	2-1	3-1
Newcastle	2-1	4-4
Nottingham F.	5-3	1-1
Preston	3-0	2-1
Sheffield Wed.	4-1	0-0
Tottenham	0-4	1-1
W. B. Albion	4-2	1-2
West Ham	4-2	0-5

F.A. CUP
| 3 — Huddersfield | (h) 1-1 |
| | (a) 1-2 |

EUROPEAN CUP-WINNERS' CUP
Q.F. — F. K. Austria	(a) 0-2
	(h) 5-0
S.F. — Rangers	(a) 0-2
	(h) 1-1

LEAGUE CUP
Did not enter

League appearances:
Broadbent, P. 36; Brodie, C. 1; Clamp, E. 40; Cocker, L. 1; Deeley, N. 40; Durandt, C. 22; Farmer, E. 27; Finlayson, M. 23; Flowers, R. 36; Harris, G. 26; Horne, D. 6; Kelly, P. 4; Kirkham, J. 3; Mannion, G. 10; Mason, R. 28; Murray, J. 31; Showell, G. 34; Sidebottom, G. 18; Slater, W. 34; Stobart, B. 10; Stuart, E. 30.

League scorers:
Farmer 28, Murray 23, Broadbent 11, Deeley 8, Durandt 8, Mason 6, Flowers 5, Stobart 5, Horne 4, Kirkham 2, Mannion 1, Opponents 2.

Final Table
Division I — Season 1960/61

	P	W	D	L	F	A	P
1. Tottenham H.	42	31	4	7	115	55	66
2. Sheffield Wed.	42	23	12	7	78	47	58
3. Wolves	42	25	7	10	103	75	57
4. Burnley	42	22	7	13	102	77	51
5. Everton	42	22	6	14	87	69	50
6. Leicester City	42	18	9	15	87	70	45
7. Man. United	42	18	9	15	88	76	45
8. Blackburn R.	42	15	13	14	77	76	43
9. Aston Villa	42	17	9	16	78	77	43
10. W. B. Albion	42	18	5	19	67	71	41
11. Arsenal	42	15	11	16	77	85	41
12. Chelsea	42	15	7	20	98	100	37
13. Man. City	42	13	11	18	79	90	37
14. Nottingham F.	42	14	9	19	62	78	37
15. Cardiff City	42	13	11	18	60	85	37
16. West Ham Utd.	42	13	10	19	77	88	36
17. Fulham	42	14	8	20	72	95	36
18. Bolton Wand.	42	12	11	19	58	73	35
19. Birmingham	42	14	6	22	62	84	34
20. Blackpool	42	12	9	21	68	73	33
21. Newcastle Utd.	42	11	10	21	86	109	32
22. Preston N. E.	42	10	10	22	43	71	30

1961/62

FOOTBALL LEAGUE
Division 1

	Home	Away
Arsenal	2-3	1-3
Aston Villa	2-2	0-1
Birmingham	2-1	6-3
Blackburn	0-2	1-2
Blackpool	2-2	2-7
Bolton	5-1	0-1
Burnley	1-1	3-3
Cardiff	1-1	3-2
Chelsea	1-1	5-4
Everton	0-3	0-4
Fulham	1-3	1-0
Ipswich	2-0	2-3
Leicester	1-1	0-3
Man. City	4-1	2-2
Man. United	2-2	2-0
Nottingham F.	2-1	1-3
Sheffield Un.	0-1	1-2
Sheffield Wed.	3-0	2-3
Tottenham	3-1	0-1
W. B. Albion	1-5	1-1
West Ham	3-2	2-4

F.A. CUP
3 — Carlisle (h) 3-1
4 — W. B. Albion (h) 1-2

LEAGUE CUP
Did not enter

Final Table
Division I — Season 1961/62

	P	W	D	L	F	A	P
1. Ipswich	42	24	8	10	93	67	56
2. Burnley	42	21	11	10	101	67	53
3. Tottenham H.	42	21	10	11	88	69	52
4. Everton	42	20	11	11	88	54	51
5. Sheffield Un.	42	19	9	14	61	69	47
6. Sheffield Wed.	42	20	6	16	72	58	46
7. Aston Villa	42	18	8	16	65	56	44
8. West Ham Un.	42	17	10	15	76	82	44
9. W. B. Albion	42	15	13	14	83	67	43
10. Arsenal	42	16	11	15	71	72	43
11. Bolton W.	42	16	10	16	62	66	42
12. Man. City	42	17	7	18	78	81	41
13. Blackpool	42	15	11	16	70	75	41
14. Leicester City	42	17	6	19	72	71	40
15. Man. United	42	15	9	18	72	75	39
16. Blackburn R.	42	14	11	17	50	58	39
17. Birmingham	42	14	10	18	65	81	38
18. Wolves	42	13	10	19	73	86	36
19. Nottingham F.	42	13	10	19	63	79	36
20. Fulham	42	13	7	22	66	74	33
21. Cardiff City	42	9	14	19	50	81	32
22. Chelsea	42	9	10	23	63	94	28

League appearances:
Broadbent, P. 33; Clamp, E. 17; Crowe, C. 14; Davies, F. 12; Deeley, N. 13; Durandt, C. 13; Farmer, E. 11; Finlayson, M. 30; Flowers, R. 35; Goodwin, F. 1; Harris, J. 2; Harris, G. 12; Hinton, A. 16; Jones, G. 7; Kelly, P. 7; Kirkham, J. 29; Lazarus, M. 9; Mason, R. 18; McParland, P. 15; Murray, J. 38; Showell, G. 10; Slater, W. 38; Stobart, B. 5; Stuart, E. 36; Thomson, R. 14; Woodfield, D. 2; Wharton, T. 25.

League scorers:
Murray 16, Wharton 11, McParland 7; Crowe 7, Hinton 5, Broadbent 5, Farmer 5, Kirkham 4, Flowers 4, Lazarus 3, Mason 2, Deeley 2, Slater 1, Durandt 1.

1962/63

FOOTBALL LEAGUE
Division 1

	Home	Away
Arsenal	1-0	4-5
Aston Villa	3-1	2-0
Birmingham	0-2	4-3
Blackburn	4-2	1-5
Blackpool	2-0	2-0
Bolton	4-0	0-3
Burnley	7-2	0-2
Everton	0-2	0-0
Fulham	2-1	5-0
Ipswich	0-0	3-2
Leicester	1-3	1-1
Leyton Orient	2-1	4-0
Liverpool	3-2	1-4
Man. City	8-1	3-3
Man. United	2-3	1-2
Nottingham F.	1-1	0-2
Sheffield United	0-0	2-1
Sheffield Wed.	2-2	1-3
Tottenham	2-2	2-1
W. B. Albion	7-0	2-2
West Ham	0-0	4-1

F.A. CUP
3 — Nottingham F. (a) 3-4

LEAGUE CUP
Did not enter

League appearances:
Broadbent, P. 27; Crowe, C. 37; Davies, F. 41; Farmer, E. 13; Finlayson, M. 1; Flowers, R. 40; Galley, J. 3; Goodwin, F. 15; Harris, G. 7; Harris, J. 1; Hinton, A. 38; Kirkham, J. 29; McParland. P. 6; Murray, J. 29; Showell, G. 35; Slater, W. 7; Stobart, B. 23; Thomson R. 42; Wharton, T. 34; Woodfield, D. 34.

APPENDIX

League scorers:
Hinton 19, Wharton 16, Stobart 12, Crowe 11, Farmer 9, Murray 8, Broadbent 5, Kirkham 4, McParland 3, Galley 2, Flowers 2, Opponents 2.

Final Table
Division I — Season 1962/63

	P	W	D	L	F	A	P
1. Everton	42	25	11	6	84	42	61
2. Tottenham H.	42	23	9	10	111	62	55
3. Burnley	42	22	10	10	78	57	54
4. Leicester City	42	20	13	10	79	53	52
5. Wolves	42	20	10	12	93	65	50
6. Sheffield Wed.	42	19	10	13	77	63	48
7. Arsenal	42	18	10	14	86	77	46
8. Liverpool	42	17	10	15	71	59	44
9. Nottingham F.	42	17	10	15	67	69	44
10. Sheffield Un.	42	16	12	14	58	60	44
11. Blackburn R.	42	15	12	15	79	71	42
12. West Ham Un.	42	14	12	16	73	69	40
13. Blackpool	42	13	14	15	58	64	40
14. W. B. Albion	42	16	7	19	71	79	39
15. Aston Villa	42	15	8	19	62	68	38
16. Fulham	42	14	10	18	50	71	38
17. Ipswich Town	42	12	11	19	59	78	35
18. Bolton Wand.	42	15	5	22	55	75	35
19. Man. United	42	12	10	20	67	81	34
20. Birmingham	42	10	13	19	63	90	33
21. Man. City	42	10	11	21	58	102	31
22. Leyton Orient	42	6	9	27	37	81	21

1963/64

FOOTBALL LEAGUE
Division 1

	Home	Away
Arsenal	2-2	3-1
Aston Villa	3-3	2-2
Birmingham	5-1	2-2
Blackburn	1-5	1-1
Blackpool	1-1	2-1
Bolton	2-2	4-0
Burnley	1-1	0-1
Chelsea	4-1	3-2
Everton	0-0	3-3
Fulham	4-0	1-4
Ipswich	2-1	0-1
Leicester	1-2	1-0
Liverpool	1-3	0-6
Man. United	2-0	2-2
Nottingham F.	2-3	0-3
Sheffield Un.	1-1	3-4
Sheffield Wed.	1-1	0-5
Stoke	2-1	2-0
Tottenham	1-4	3-4
W. B. Albion	0-0	1-3
West Ham	0-2	1-1

F.A. CUP
3 — Arsenal (a) 1-2

LEAGUE CUP
Did not enter

League appearances:
Barron, J. 7; Broadbent, P. 32; Crawford, R. 34; Crowe, C. 32; Davies, F. 34; Farmer, E. 6; Finlayson, M. 1; Flowers, R. 40; Goodwin, F. 21; Harris, G. 7; Hinton, A. 21; Kirkham, J. 15; Knowles, P. 14; Le Flem, R. 13; Melia, J. 9; Murray, J. 8; Showell, G. 36; Stobart, B. 7; Thomson, R. 42; Wharton, T. 38; Woodfield, D. 35; Woodruff, D. 10.

League scorers:
Crawford 26, Wharton 9, Crowe 6, Hinton 5, Broadbent 4, Le Flem 4, Knowles 4, Melia 4, Flowers 3, Farmer 2, Murray 1, Kirkham 1, Stobart 1.

Final Table
Division I — Season 1963/64

	P	W	D	L	F	A	P
1. Liverpool	42	26	5	11	92	45	57
2. Man. United	42	23	7	12	90	62	53
3. Everton	42	21	10	11	84	64	52
4. Tottenham H.	42	22	7	13	97	81	51
5. Chelsea	42	20	10	12	72	56	50
6. Sheffield Wed.	42	19	11	12	84	67	49
7. Blackburn R.	42	18	10	14	89	65	46
8. Arsenal	42	17	11	14	90	82	45
9. Burnley	42	17	10	15	71	64	44
10. W. B. Albion	42	16	11	15	70	61	43
11. Leicester City	42	16	11	15	61	58	43
12. Sheffield Un.	42	16	11	15	61	64	43
13. Nottingham F.	42	16	9	17	64	68	41
14. West Ham Utd.	42	14	12	16	69	74	40
15. Fulham	42	13	13	16	58	65	39
16. Wolves	42	12	15	15	70	80	39
17. Stoke City	42	14	10	18	77	78	38
18. Blackpool	42	13	9	20	52	73	35
19. Aston Villa	42	11	12	19	62	71	34
20. Birmingham	42	11	7	24	54	92	29
21. Bolton Wand.	42	10	8	24	48	80	28
22. Ipswich Town	42	9	7	26	56	121	25

1964/65

FOOTBALL LEAGUE
Division 1

	Home	Away
Arsenal	0-1	1-4
Aston Villa	0-1	2-3
Birmingham	0-2	1-0
Blackburn	4-2	1-4
Blackpool	1-2	1-1

APPENDIX

Burnley	1-2	1-1
Chelsea	0-3	1-2
Everton	2-4	0-5
Fulham	0-0	0-2
Leeds	0-1	2-3
Leicester	1-1	2-3
Liverpool	1-3	1-2
Man. United	2-4	0-3
Nottingham F.	1-2	2-0
Sheffield Un.	1-0	2-0
Sheffield Wed.	3-1	0-2
Stoke	3-1	2-0
Sunderland	3-0	2-1
Tottenham	3-1	4-7
W. B. Albion	3-2	1-5
West Ham	4-3	0-5

F.A. CUP

3 — Portsmouth	(h)	0-0
	(a)	3-2
4 — Rotherham	(h)	2-2
	(a)	3-0
5 — Aston Villa	(h)	1-1
	(a)	0-0
		3-1
6 — Man. United	(h)	3-5

LEAGUE CUP
Did not enter

League scorers:
Crawford 13, Woodruff 11, Wharton 8, McIlmoyle 7, Knowles 6, Miller 3, Buckley 3, Woodfield 2, Thompson 1, Harris 1, Le Flem 1, Wagstaffe 1, Kirkham 1, Flowers 1.

Final Table
Division I — Season 1964/65

	P	W	D	L	F	A	P
1. Man. United	42	26	9	7	89	39	61
2. Leeds United	42	26	9	7	83	52	61
3. Chelsea	42	24	8	10	89	54	56
4. Everton	42	17	15	10	69	60	49
5. Nottingham F.	42	17	13	12	71	67	47
6. Tottenham H.	42	19	7	16	87	71	45
7. Liverpool	42	17	10	15	67	73	44
8. Sheffield Wed.	42	16	11	15	57	55	43
9. West Ham Utd.	42	19	4	19	82	71	42
10. Blackburn R.	42	16	10	16	83	79	42
11. Stoke City	42	16	10	16	67	66	42
12. Burnley	42	16	10	16	70	70	42
13. Arsenal	42	17	7	18	69	75	41
14. W. B. Albion	42	13	13	16	70	65	39
15. Sunderland	42	14	9	19	64	74	37
16. Aston Villa	42	16	5	21	57	82	37
17. Blackpool	42	12	11	19	67	78	35
18. Leicester City	42	11	13	18	69	85	35
19. Sheffield United	42	12	11	19	50	64	35
20. Fulham	42	11	12	19	60	78	34
21. Wolves	42	13	4	25	59	89	30
22. Birmingham	42	8	11	23	64	96	27

League appearances:
Barron, J. 1; Broadbent, P. 13; Buckley, P. 14; Crawford, R. 23; Davies, F. 32; Flowers, R. 39; Farrington, J. 2; Ford, C. 2; Galley, J. 2; Goodwin, F. 7; Harris, G. 34; Hawkins, G. 1; Kemp, F. 3; Kirkham, J. 16; Knighton, K. 4; Knowles, P. 23; Le Flem, R. 6; MacLaren, D. 9; McIlmoyle, H. 25; Melia, J. 15; Miller, G. 28; Showell, G. 8; Thompson, D. 8; Thomson, R. 40; Wagstaffe, D. 11; Wharton, T. 40; Wilson, J. 6; Woodfield, D. 21; Woodruff, R. 29.

1965/66

FOOTBALL LEAGUE
Division 2

	Home	Away
Birmingham	2-0	2-2
Bolton	3-1	1-2
Bristol City	1-1	1-0
Bury	3-0	0-1
Cardiff	2-1	4-1
Carlisle	3-0	1-2
Charlton	2-2	1-1
Coventry	0-1	1-2
C. Palace	1-0	1-0
Derby	4-0	2-2
Huddersfield	2-1	1-1
Ipswich	4-1	2-5
Leyton Orient	2-1	3-0
Man. City	2-4	1-2
Middlesbrough	3-0	1-3
Norwich	2-1	3-0
Plymouth	0-0	2-2
Portsmouth	8-2	0-2
Preston	3-0	2-2
Rotherham	4-1	3-4
Southampton	1-1	3-9

F.A. CUP

3 — Altrincham	(h)	5-0
4 — Sheffield United	(h)	3-0
5 — Man. United	(h)	2-4

LEAGUE CUP
Did not enter

League appearances:
Bailey, M. 11; Buckley, P. 6; Davies, F. 8; Flowers, R. 38; Goodwin, F. (1); Harris, G. 2; Hawkins, G. 10; Holsgrove, J. 22; Hunt, E. 31; Knighton, K. 4, (3); Knowles, P. 31; MacLaren, D. 34; McIlmoyle, H. 41; Miller, G. 9; Thomson, R. 41; Wagstaffe, D. 38; Wilson, L. 1; Wilson, J. 37; Wharton, T. 39; Woodfield, D. 39, (2); Woodruff, R. 20.

Wolves v Porto 1974, two scenes.

Wolves Youth team, Switzerland 1976.

WOLVERHAMPTON WANDERERS F.C.

Proudly Present

The Final Act of

"The Great First Division Drama"

Starring: Your very own

Wolverhampton Wanderers

Needing two points tonight to maintain a Division One billing—provided rivals Birmingham City are beaten at Sheffield.

Also

The pride of the Kop

LIVERPOOL

They seek a win here tonight (maybe one point will do) and the Football League Championship is theirs for a record nine times.

Curtain rises at 7.30 p.m.
Tuesday, 4th May, 1976 at Molineux Grounds, Wolverhampton.

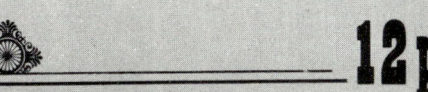

12p

Official programme

"Test Match" 1976.

Vale et ave: W. McGarry, S. Chung.

APPENDIX 197

League scorers:
Knowles 19, McIlmoyle 15, Wharton 10, Hunt 10, Wagstaffe 9, Woodfield 7, Woodruff 7, Holsgrove 2, Buckley 2, Flowers 1, Opponents 5.

F.A. CUP
3 — Oldham	(a)	2-2
	(h)	4-1
4 — Everton	(h)	1-1
	(a)	1-3

Final Table
Division II — Season 1965/66

	P	W	D	L	F	A	P
1. Man. City	42	22	15	5	76	44	59
2. Southampton	42	22	10	10	85	56	54
3. Coventry City	42	20	13	9	73	53	53
4. Huddersfield T.	42	19	13	10	62	36	51
5. Bristol City	42	17	17	8	63	48	51
6. Wolves	42	20	10	12	87	61	50
7. Rotherham	42	16	14	12	75	74	46
8. Derby Co.	42	16	11	15	71	68	43
9. Bolton Wand.	42	16	9	17	62	59	41
10. Birmingham	42	16	9	17	70	75	41
11. C. Palace	42	14	13	15	47	52	41
12. Portsmouth	42	16	8	18	74	78	40
13. Norwich City	42	12	15	15	52	52	39
14. Carlisle Utd.	42	17	5	20	60	63	39
15. Ipswich Town	42	15	9	18	58	66	39
16. Charlton Ath.	42	12	14	16	61	70	38
17. Preston N. E.	42	11	15	16	62	70	37
18. Plymouth	42	12	13	17	54	63	37
19. Bury	42	14	7	21	62	76	35
20. Cardiff City	42	12	10	20	71	91	34
21. Middlesbrough	42	10	13	19	58	86	33
22. Leyton Orient	42	5	13	24	38	80	23

LEAGUE CUP
2 — Mansfield	(h)	2-1
3 — Fulham	(a)	0-5

League appearances:
Bailey, M. A. 41; Buckley, P. M. 2; Burnside, D. G. 25 (2); Davies, F. 27; Dougan, A. D. 11; Farrington, J. R. 4; Flowers, R. 14; Hatton, R. 10; Hawkins, G. N. 12(4); Holsgrove, J. W. 25(2); Hunt, R. P. 37; Knighton K. 5; Knowles, P. R. 21(2); MacLaren, D. 1; McIlmoyle, H. 24; Parkes, P. 14; Taylor, G. W. 17; Thomson, R. A. 39; Wagstaffe, D. 42; Wallace —(1); Wharton, T. J. 35(1); Wilson, J. 16; Wilson, L. 2(2); Woodfield, D. 38.

League scorers:
Hunt 20, McIlmoyle 13, Wharton 13, Dougan 9, Knowles 8, Hatton 7, Wagstaffe 6, Burnside 4, Bailey 3, Woodfield 2, Buckley 1, Holsgrove 1, Thomson 1.

1966/67

FOOTBALL LEAGUE
Division 2

	Home	Away
Birmingham	1-2	2-3
Blackburn	4-0	0-0
Bolton	5-2	0-0
Bristol City	1-1	0-1
Bury	4-1	1-2
Cardiff	7-1	3-0
Carlisle	1-1	3-1
Charlton	1-0	3-1
Coventry	1-3	1-3
C. Palace	1-1	1-4
Derby	5-3	3-0
Huddersfield	1-0	1-0
Hull	4-0	1-3
Ipswich	0-0	1-3
Millwall	2-0	1-1
Northampton	1-0	4-0
Norwich	4-1	2-1
Plymouth	2-1	1-0
Portsmouth	3-1	3-2
Preston	3-2	2-1
Rotherham	2-0	2-2

Final Table
Division II — Season 1966/67

	P	W	D	L	F	A	P
1. Coventry City	42	23	13	6	74	43	59
2. Wolves	42	25	8	9	88	48	58
3. Carlisle United	42	23	6	13	71	54	52
4. Blackburn R.	42	19	13	10	56	46	51
5. Ipswich T.	42	17	16	9	70	54	50
6. Huddersfield T.	42	20	9	13	58	46	49
7. C. Palace	42	19	10	13	61	55	48
8. Millwall	42	18	9	15	49	58	45
9. Bolton Wand.	42	14	14	14	64	58	42
10. Birmingham	42	16	8	18	70	66	40
11. Norwich City	42	13	14	15	49	55	40
12. Hull City	42	16	7	19	77	72	39
13. Preston N. E.	42	16	7	19	65	67	39
14. Portsmouth	42	13	13	16	59	70	39
15. Bristol City	42	12	14	16	56	62	38
16. Plymouth Argyle	42	14	9	19	59	58	37
17. Derby Co.	42	12	12	18	68	72	36
18. Rotherham Un.	42	13	10	19	61	70	36
19. Charlton Ath.	42	13	9	20	49	53	35
20. Cardiff City	42	12	9	21	61	87	33
21. Northampton	42	12	6	24	47	84	30
22. Bury	42	11	6	25	49	83	28

1967/68

FOOTBALL LEAGUE
Division 1

	Home	Away
Arsenal	3-2	2-0
Burnley	3-2	1-1
Chelsea	3-0	0-1
Coventry	2-0	0-1
Everton	1-3	2-4
Fulham	3-2	2-1
Leeds	2-0	1-2
Leicester	1-3	1-3
Liverpool	1-1	1-2
Man. City	0-0	0-2
Man. United	2-3	0-4
Newcastle	2-2	0-2
Nottingham F.	6-1	1-3
Sheffield United	1-3	1-1
Sheffield Wed.	2-3	2-2
Southampton	2-0	1-1
Stoke	3-4	2-0
Sunderland	2-1	0-2
Tottenham	2-1	1-2
W. B. Albion	3-3	1-4
West Ham	1-2	2-1

F.A. CUP
3 — Rotherham (a) 0-1

LEAGUE CUP
2 — Huddersfield (a) 0-1

Final Table
Division I — Season 1967/68

	P	W	D	L	F	A	P
1. Manchester City	42	26	6	10	86	43	58
2. Man. United	42	24	8	10	89	55	56
3. Liverpool	42	22	11	9	71	40	55
4. Leeds United	42	22	9	11	71	41	53
5. Everton	42	23	6	13	67	40	52
6. Chelsea	42	18	12	12	62	68	48
7. Tottenham H.	42	19	9	14	70	59	47
8. W. B. Albion	42	17	12	13	75	62	46
9. Arsenal	42	17	10	15	60	56	44
10. Newcastle United	42	13	15	14	54	67	41
11. Nottingham F.	42	14	11	17	52	64	39
12. West Ham	42	14	10	18	73	69	38
13. Leicester City	42	13	12	17	64	69	38
14. Burnley	42	14	10	18	64	71	38
15. Sunderland	42	13	11	18	51	61	37
16. Southampton	42	13	11	18	66	83	37
17. Wolves	42	14	8	20	66	75	36
18. Stoke City	42	14	7	21	50	73	35
19. Sheffield Wed.	42	11	12	19	51	63	34
20. Coventry City	42	9	15	18	51	71	33
21. Sheffield United	42	11	10	21	49	70	32
22. Fulham	42	10	7	25	56	98	27

League appearances:
Bailey, M. A. 41; Buckley, P. M. 5(1); Burnside, D. G. 13; Davies, F. 2; Hawkins, G. N. 5(2); Dougan, A. D. 38; Holsgrove, J. W. 42; Hunt, R. P. 6; Kenning, M. J. 17(1); Knowles, P. R. 35(1); McAlle 1(1); Munro, F. M. 7(1); Parkes, P. 27; Parkin, D. 15; Ross, S. 1(1); Taylor, G. W. 21(1); Thomson, R. A. 36; Wagstaffe, D. 33; Wharton, T. J. 13; Williams, S. E. 13; Wilson, L. J. 14(3); Woodfield, D. 38; Wignall, F. 12.

League scorers:
Dougan 17, Knowles 12, Wignall 8, Evans 5, Bailey 4, Holsgrove 3, Kenning 3, Buckley 2, Hunt 2, Parkin 2, Wharton 2, Burnside 1, Farrington 1, Thomson 1, Wilson 1, Woodfield 1, Opponents 1.

1968/69

FOOTBALL LEAGUE
Division 1

	Home	Away
Arsenal	0-0	1-3
Burnley	1-1	1-1
Chelsea	1-1	1-1
Coventry	1-1	1-0
Everton	1-2	0-4
Ipswich	1-1	0-1
Leeds	0-0	1-2
Leicester	1-0	0-2
Liverpool	0-6	0-1
Man. City	3-1	2-3
Man. United	2-2	0-2
Newcastle	5-0	1-4
Nottingham F.	1-0	0-0
Q.P.R.	3-1	1-0
Sheffield Wed.	0-3	2-0
Southampton	0-0	1-2
Stoke	1-1	1-4
Sunderland	1-1	0-2
Tottenham	2-0	1-1
W. B. Albion	0-1	0-0
West Ham	2-0	1-3

F.A. CUP
3 — Hull (a) 3-1
4 — Tottenham (a) 1-2

LEAGUE CUP
2 — Southend (h) 1-0
3 — Millwall (h) 5-1
4 — Blackpool (a) 1-2

APPENDIX

League appearances:
Bailey, M. A. 34; Boswell, A. H. 10; Clarke, D. 1(3); Curran, H. 10; Dougan, D. 39; Evans, A. 1(1); Farrington, J. R. 18(1); Galvain, D. 5; Hibbitt, K. —(1); Holsgrove, J. W. 41; Kenning, M. J. 18(5); Knowles, P. R. 39; Lutton, R. J. 3; McAlle, J. E. 9(5); McVeigh, J. 2; Munro, F. M. 12(4); Parkes, P. 32; Parkin, D. 42; Ross S. —(1); Seal, J. 1; Taylor, G. W. 11; Thompson, 2; Thomson, R. A. 21(1); Wagstaffe, D. 26; Walker, P. G. 2(1); Wignall, F. 20; Wilson, L. J. 37; Woodfield, D. 26.

League scorers:
Dougan 11, Knowles 9, Wignall 6, Curran 4, Gailey 3, Kenning 2, Munro 2, Wilson 2, Farrington 1, Wagstaffe 1.

Final Table
Division I — Season 1968/69

	P	W	D	L	F	A	P
1. Leeds United	42	27	13	2	66	26	67
2. Liverpool	42	25	11	6	63	24	61
3. Everton	42	21	15	6	77	36	57
4. Arsenal	42	22	12	8	56	27	56
5. Chelsea	42	20	10	12	73	53	50
6. Tottenham H.	42	14	17	11	61	51	45
7. Southampton	42	16	13	13	57	48	45
8. West Ham	42	13	18	11	66	50	44
9. Newcastle United	42	15	14	13	61	55	44
10. W. B. Albion	42	16	11	15	64	67	43
11. Man. United	42	15	12	15	57	53	42
12. Ipswich Town	42	15	11	16	59	60	41
13. Man. City	42	15	10	17	64	55	40
14. Burnley	42	15	9	18	55	82	39
15. Sheffield Wed.	42	10	16	16	41	54	36
16. Wolves	42	10	15	17	41	58	35
17. Sunderland	42	11	12	19	43	67	34
18. Nottingham F.	42	10	13	19	45	57	33
19. Stoke City	42	9	15	18	40	63	33
20. Coventry City	42	10	11	21	46	64	31
21. Leicester City	42	9	12	21	39	68	30
22. Q.P.R.	42	4	10	28	39	95	18

1969/70

FOOTBALL LEAGUE
Division 1

	Home	Away
Arsenal	2-0	2-2
Burnley	1-1	3-1
Chelsea	3-0	2-2
Coventry	0-1	0-1
C. Palace	1-1	1-2
Derby	1-1	0-2
Everton	2-3	0-1
Ipswich	2-0	1-1
Leeds	1-2	1-3
Liverpool	0-1	0-0
Man. City	1-3	0-1
Man. United	0-0	0-0
Newcastle	1-1	1-1
Nottingham F.	3-3	2-4
Sheffield Wed.	2-2	3-2
Southampton	2-1	3-2
Stoke	3-1	1-1
Sunderland	1-0	1-2
Tottenham	2-2	1-0
W. B. Albion	1-0	3-3
West Ham	1-0	0-3

F.A. CUP
3 — Burnley (a) 0-3

LEAGUE CUP
2 — Tottenham (h) 1-0
3 — Brighton (a) 3-2
4 — Q.P.R. (a) 1-3

League appearances:
Bailey, M. A. 38; Clarke, D. 1; Curran, H. 38; Dougan, D. 26; Farrington, J. R. 1; Holsgrove, J. W. 39; Kent, M. —(1); Knowles, P. 8; Lutton, R. J. 12(4); McCalliog, J. 42; McAlle, J. E. 5(7); Munro, F. M. 32(1); O'Grady, M. 20; Oldfield, J. S. 14; Parkes, P. 28; Parkin, 42; Richards, J. P. 4; Shaw, B. 10(2); Taylor, G. W. 19; Wagstaffe, D. 31; Walker, P. G. 9(7); Wilson, L. J. 26(5); Woodfield, D. 17(1).

Final Table
Division I — Season 1969/70

	P	W	D	L	F	A	P
1. Everton	42	29	8	5	72	34	66
2. Leeds United	42	21	15	6	84	49	57
3. Chelsea	42	21	13	8	70	50	55
4. Derby County	42	22	9	11	64	37	53
5. Liverpool	42	20	11	11	65	42	51
6. Coventry	42	19	11	12	58	48	49
7. Newcastle United	42	17	13	12	57	35	47
8. Man. United	42	14	17	11	66	61	45
9. Stoke City	42	15	15	12	56	52	45
10. Man. City	42	16	11	15	55	48	43
11. Tottenham H.	42	17	9	16	54	55	43
12. Arsenal	42	12	18	12	51	49	42
13. Wolves	42	12	16	14	55	57	40
14. Burnley	42	12	15	15	56	61	39
15. Nottingham F.	42	10	18	14	50	71	38
16. W. B. Albion	42	14	9	19	58	66	37
17. West Ham	42	12	12	18	51	60	36
18. Ipswich Town	42	10	11	21	40	63	31
19. Southampton	42	6	17	19	46	67	29
20. Crystal Palace	42	6	15	21	34	68	27
21. Sunderland	42	6	14	22	30	68	26
22. Sheffield Wed.	42	8	9	25	40	71	25

League scorers:
Curran 20, Dougan 8, McCalliog 7, O'Grady 4, Wilson 4, Bailey 3, Knowles 3, Lutton 1, Munro 1, Parkin 1, Wagstaffe 1, Woodfield 1, Opponents 1.

1970/71
FOOTBALL LEAGUE
Division 1

	Home	Away
Arsenal	0-3	1-2
Blackpool	1-0	2-0
Burnley	1-0	3-2
Chelsea	1-0	2-2
Coventry	0-0	1-0
C. Palace	2-1	1-1
Derby	2-4	2-1
Everton	2-0	2-1
Huddersfield	3-1	2-1
Ipswich	0-0	3-2
Leeds	2-3	0-3
Liverpool	1-0	0-2
Man. City	3-0	0-0
Man. United	3-2	0-1
Newcastle	3-2	2-3
Nottingham F.	4-0	1-4
Southampton	0-1	2-1
Stoke	1-1	0-1
Tottenham	0-3	0-0
W. B. Albion	2-1	4-2
West Ham	2-0	3-3

F.A. CUP
3 — Norwich (h) 5-1
4 — Derby (a) 1-2

LEAGUE CUP
2 — Oxford (a) 0-1

League appearances:
Bailey, M. A. 34; Curran, H. 27(3); Dougan, D. 23(2); Gould, R. A. 34; Hegan, D. 6(3); Hibbitt, K. 30(2); Holsgrove, J. W. 9; Lutton, R. J. 1(1); McCalliog, J. 40; McAlle, J. E. 37; Munro, F. M. 36; O'Grady, M. 5(3); Oldfield, J. S. 5; Parkes, P. 37; Parkin, D. 39; Richards, J. P. 4(10); Shaw, B. 36(1); Taylor, G. W. 8; Wagstaffe, D. 39; Walker, P. G. 2(2); Wilson, 10. (L.J.).

League scorers:
Gould 17, Curran 16, Dougan 12, McCalliog 7, Bailey 3, Hibbitt 2, Wagstaffe 2, O'Grady 1, Richards 1, Shaw 1, Opponents 2.

Final Table
Division I — Season 1970/71

	P	W	D	L	F	A	P
1. Arsenal	42	29	7	6	71	29	65
2. Leeds United	42	27	10	5	72	30	64
3. Tottenham H.	42	19	14	9	54	33	52
4. Wolves	42	22	8	12	64	54	52
5. Liverpool	42	17	17	8	42	24	51
6. Chelsea	42	18	15	9	52	42	51
7. Southampton	42	17	12	13	56	44	46
8. Man. United	42	16	11	15	65	66	43
9. Derby Co.	42	16	10	16	56	54	42
10. Coventry City	42	16	10	16	37	38	42
11. Man. City	42	12	17	13	47	42	41
12. Newcastle United	42	14	13	15	44	46	41
13. Stoke City	42	12	13	17	44	48	37
14. Everton	42	12	13	17	54	60	37
15. Huddersfield T.	42	11	14	17	40	49	36
16. Nottingham F.	42	14	8	20	42	61	36
17. W. B. Albion	42	10	15	17	58	75	35
18. C. Palace	42	12	11	19	39	57	35
19. Ipswich Town	42	12	10	20	42	48	34
20. West Ham	42	10	14	18	47	60	34
21. Burnley	42	7	13	22	29	63	27
22. Blackpool	42	4	15	23	34	66	23

1971/72
FOOTBALL LEAGUE
Division 1

	Home	Away
Arsenal	5-1	1-2
Chelsea	0-2	1-3
Coventry	1-1	0-0
C. Palace	1-0	2-0
Derby	2-1	1-2
Everton	1-1	2-2
Huddersfield	2-2	1-0
Ipswich	2-2	1-2
Leeds	2-1	0-0
Leicester	0-1	2-1
Liverpool	0-0	2-3
Man. City	2-1	2-5
Man. United	1-1	3-1
Newcastle	2-0	0-2
Nottingham F.	4-2	3-1
Sheffield United	1-2	2-2
Southampton	4-2	2-1
Stoke	2-0	1-0
Tottenham H.	2-2	1-4
W. B. Albion	0-1	3-2
West Ham	1-0	0-1

F.A. CUP
3 — Leicester (h) 1-1
(a) 0-2

LEAGUE CUP
2 — Man. City (a) 3-4

APPENDIX

UEFA CUP

1 — Academica Coimbra	(h) 3-0
	(a) 4-1
2 — Den Haag	(a) 3-1
	(h) 4-0
3 — Carl Zeiss Jena	(a) 1-0
	(h) 3-0
Q.F. — Juventus	(a) 1-1
	(h) 2-1
S.F. — Ferencvaros	(a) 2-2
	(h) 2-1
F. — Tottenham H.	(h) 1-2
	(a) 1-1

League appearances:
Bailey, M. A. 20; Curran, H. 2(2); Daley, S. 5(5); Dougan, D. 38; Eastoe, P. R. 2(1); Gould, E. M. 5(1); Hegan, D. 21(2); Hibbitt, K. 33(1); Kent, M. J. —(1); McAlle, J. E. 42; McCalliog, J. 38; Munro, F. M. 37; O'Grady, M. 3(1); Parkes, P. 42; Parkin, D. 32; Richards, J. P. 33(2); Shaw, B. 41; Sunderland, A. 5(3); Taylor, G. W. 19(2); Wagstaffe, D. 39; Walker, P. G. 4; Wilson, L. J. 1(1).

League scorers:
Dougan 15, Richards 13, McCalliog 11, Hibbitt 7, Hegan 3, Munro 3, Bailey 2, Daley 2, Parkin 2, Wagstaffe 2, Gould 1, Shaw 1, Taylor 1, Opponents 2.

Final Table
Division I — Season 1971/72

		P	W	D	L	F	A	P
1.	Derby Co.	42	24	10	8	69	33	58
2.	Leeds United	42	24	9	9	73	31	57
3.	Liverpool	42	24	9	9	64	30	57
4.	Man. City	42	23	11	8	77	45	57
5.	Arsenal	42	22	8	12	58	40	52
6.	Tottenham H.	42	19	13	10	63	42	51
7.	Chelsea	42	18	12	12	58	49	48
8.	Man. United	42	19	10	13	69	61	48
9.	Wolves	42	18	11	13	65	57	47
10.	Sheffield United	42	17	12	13	61	60	46
11.	Newcastle United	42	15	11	16	49	52	41
12.	Leicester City	42	13	13	16	41	46	39
13.	Ipswich Town	42	11	16	15	39	53	38
14.	West Ham	42	12	12	18	47	51	36
15.	Everton	42	9	18	15	37	48	36
16.	W. B. Albion	42	12	11	19	42	54	35
17.	Stoke City	42	10	15	17	39	56	35
18.	Coventry City	42	9	15	18	44	67	33
19.	Southampton	42	12	7	23	52	80	31
20.	C. Palace	42	8	13	21	39	65	29
21.	Nottingham F.	42	8	9	25	47	81	25
22.	Huddersfield T.	42	6	13	23	27	59	25

1972/73

FOOTBALL LEAGUE
Division 1

	Home	Away
Arsenal	1-3	2-5
Birmingham	3-2	1-0
Chelsea	1-0	2-0
Coventry	3-0	1-0
Crystal Palace	1-1	1-1
Derby County	1-2	0-3
Everton	4-2	1-0
Ipswich Town	0-1	1-2
Leeds United	0-2	0-0
Leicester City	2-0	1-1
Liverpool	2-1	2-4
Manchester City	5-1	1-1
Manchester United	2-0	1-2
Newcastle United	1-1	1-2
Norwich City	3-0	1-1
Sheffield United	1-1	2-1
Southampton	0-1	1-1
Stoke City	5-3	0-2
Tottenham	3-2	2-2
W.B.A.	2-0	0-1
West Ham	3-0	2-2

F.A. CUP

3 — Man. United	(h)	1-0
4 — Bristol City	(h)	1-0
5 — Millwall	(h)	1-0
6 — Coventry	(h)	2-0
S.F. — Leeds (at Maine Road)		0-1
3/4 — Place Arsenal	(a)	3-1

LEAGUE CUP

2 — Orient	(h)	2-1
3 — Sheffield Wed.	(h)	3-1
4 — Bristol Rovers	(h)	4-0
5 — Blackpool	(h)	1-1
	(a)	1-0
S.F. — Tottenham	(h)	1-2
	(a)	2-2

TEXACO CUP

1 — Kilmarnock	(h)	5-1
	(a)	0-0
2 — Ipswich	(a)	1-2
	(h)	0-1

League appearances:
Bailey, M. 29; Daley, S. 9(3); Dougan, D. 36(1); Eastoe, P. 2; Hegan, D. 17; Hibbitt, K. 31; Jefferson, D. 17; Kindon, S. 16(11); McAlle, J. 41; McCalliog, J. 24(2); Munro, F. 32; O'Grady, M. —(1); Owen, B. 4; Parkes, P. 42; Parkin, D. 18; Powell, B. 10(1); Richards, J. 42; Shaw, B. 26; Sunderland, A. 10(6); Taylor, G. 35; Wagstaffe, D. 21.

League scorers:
Richards 27, Dougan 12, Hibbitt 6, Sunderland 5, Kindon 4, McCalliog 4, Hegan 3, Munro 2, Powell 1, Opponents 2.

Final Table

Division 1 — Season 1972/73

	P	W	D	L	F	A	P
1. Liverpool	42	25	10	7	72	42	60
2. Arsenal	42	23	11	8	57	43	57
3. Leeds United	42	21	11	10	71	45	53
4. Ipswich	42	17	14	11	55	45	48
5. Wolves	42	18	11	13	66	54	47
6. West Ham	42	17	12	13	67	53	46
7. Derby County	42	19	8	15	56	54	46
8. Tottenham	42	16	13	13	58	48	45
9. Newcastle	42	16	13	13	60	51	45
10. Birmingham	42	15	12	15	53	54	42
11. Manchester City	42	15	11	16	57	60	41
12. Chelsea	42	13	14	15	49	51	40
13. Southampton	42	11	18	13	47	52	40
14. Sheffield Un.	42	15	10	17	51	59	40
15. Stoke City	42	14	10	18	61	56	38
16. Leicester City	42	10	17	15	40	46	37
17. Everton	42	13	11	18	41	49	37
18. Man. United	42	12	13	17	44	60	37
19. Coventry City	42	13	9	20	40	55	35
20. Norwich City	42	11	10	21	36	63	32
21. Crystal Palace	42	9	12	21	41	58	30
22. W. B. Albion	42	9	10	23	38	62	28

1973/74

FOOTBALL LEAGUE
Division 1

	Home	Away
Arsenal	3-1	2-2
Birmingham	1-0	1-2
Burnley	0-2	1-1
Chelsea	2-0	2-2
Coventry	1-1	0-1
Derby County	4-0	0-2
Everton	1-1	1-2
Ipswich Town	3-1	0-2
Leeds United	0-2	1-4
Leicester City	1-0	2-2
Liverpool	0-1	0-1
Man. City	0-0	1-1
Man. United	2-1	0-0
Newcastle United	1-0	0-2
Norwich City	3-1	1-1
Q.P.R.	2-4	0-0
Sheffield Un.	2-0	0-1
Southampton	2-1	1-2
Stoke City	1-1	3-2
Tottenham	1-1	3-1
West Ham	0-0	0-0

UEFA CUP
1 — Belenenses	(a) 2-0
	(h) 2-1
2 — Lok. Leipzik	(a) 0-3
	(h) 4-1

F.A. CUP
| 3 — Leeds | (h) 1-1 |
| | (a) 0-1 |

LEAGUE CUP
2 — Halifax	(a) 3-0
3 — Tranmere	(a) 1-1
	(h) 2-1
4 — Exeter	(h) 5-1
5 — Liverpool	(h) 1-0
S.F. — Norwich	(a) 1-1
	(h) 1-0
F — Man. City (at Wembley)	2-1

League appearances:
Bailey, M. 32; Daley, S. 15; Dougan, D. 30(8); Eastoe, P. —(1); Hegan, D. 5(1); Hibbitt, K. 29(4); Jefferson, D. 9(1); Kelly, J. 1; Kindon, S. 13(6); McAlle, J. 39; McCalliog, J. 14(3); Munro, F. 36; Palmer, G. 29; Parkes, P. 28; Parkin, D. 39; Powell, B. 25(2); Pierce, G. 14; Richards, J. 26; Sunderland, A. 31(3); Taylor, G. 17; Wagstaffe, D. 27; Withe, P. 3.

League scorers:
Dougan 10, Richards 9, Sunderland 7, McCalliog 5, Kindon 4, Powell 3, Hibbitt 2, Munro 2, Daley 1, Palmer 1, Wagstaffe 1, Withe 1, own goals 3.

Final Table

Division I — Season 1973/74

	P	W	D	L	F	A	P
1. Leeds	42	24	14	4	66	31	62
2. Liverpool	42	22	13	7	52	31	57
3. Derby Co.	42	17	14	11	52	42	48
4. Ipswich Town	42	18	11	13	67	58	47
5. Stoke City	42	15	16	11	54	42	46
6. Burnley	42	16	14	12	56	53	46
7. Everton	42	16	12	14	50	48	44
8. Q.P.R.	42	13	17	12	56	52	43
9. Leicester	42	13	16	13	51	41	42
10. Arsenal	42	14	14	14	49	51	42
11. Tottenham	42	14	14	14	45	50	42
12. Wolverhampton	42	13	15	14	49	49	41
13. Sheffield United	42	14	12	16	44	49	40
14. Man. City	42	14	16	39	46	40
15. Newcastle United	42	13	12	17	49	48	38
16. Coventry City	42	14	10	18	43	54	38
17. Chelsea	42	12	13	17	56	60	37
18. West Ham	42	11	15	16	55	60	37
19. Birmingham City	42	12	13	17	52	64	37
20. Southampton	42	11	14	17	47	68	36
21. Man. United	42	10	12	20	38	48	32
22. Norwich	42	7	15	20	37	62	29

1974/75

FOOTBALL LEAGUE
Division 1

	Home	Away
Arsenal	1-0	0-0
Birmingham City	0-1	1-1
Burnley	4-2	2-1
Carlisle United	2-0	0-1
Chelsea	7-1	1-0
Coventry City	2-0	1-2
Derby County	0-1	0-1
Everton	2-0	0-0
Ipswich Town	2-1	0-2
Leeds United	1-1	0-2
Leicester City	1-1	2-3
Liverpool	0-0	0-2
Luton Town	5-2	2-3
Man. City	1-0	0-0
Middlesbrough	2-0	1-2
Newcastle United	4-2	0-0
Q.P.R.	1-2	0-2
Sheffield United	1-1	0-1
Stoke City	2-2	2-2
Tottenham H.	2-3	0-3
West Ham	3-1	2-5

UEFA CUP
1 — Porto (a) 1-4
 (h) 3-1

F.A. CUP
3 — Ipswich (h) 1-2

LEAGUE CUP
2 — Fulham (h) 1-3

Final Table
Division I — Season 1974/75

	P	W	D	L	F	A	P
1. Derby County	42	21	11	10	67	49	53
2. Liverpool	42	20	11	11	60	39	51
3. Ipswich Town	42	23	5	14	66	44	51
4. Everton	42	16	18	8	56	42	50
5. Stoke City	42	17	15	10	64	48	49
6. Sheffield United	42	18	13	11	58	51	49
7. Middlesbrough	42	18	12	12	54	40	48
8. Man. City	42	18	10	14	54	54	46
9. Leeds United	42	16	13	13	57	49	45
10. Burnley	42	17	11	14	68	67	45
11. Q.P.R.	42	16	10	16	54	54	42
12. Wolves	42	14	11	17	57	54	39
13. West Ham	42	13	13	16	58	59	39
14. Coventry City	42	12	15	15	51	62	39
15. Newcastle United	42	15	9	18	59	72	39
16. Arsenal	42	13	11	18	47	49	37
17. Birmingham City	42	14	9	19	53	61	37
18. Leicester City	42	12	12	18	46	60	36
19. Tottenham	42	13	8	21	52	63	34
20. Luton Town	42	11	11	20	47	65	33
21. Chelsea	42	9	15	18	42	72	33
22. Carlisle United	42	12	5	25	43	59	29

League appearances:
Bailey, M. 38; Carr, W. 10; Daley, S. 15(8); Dougan, D. 3(3); Farley, J. 18; Gardner, C. 1(2); Hibbitt, K. 41; Jefferson, D. 13; Kindon, S. 29; McAlle, J. 38; Munro, F. 35; Palmer, G. 31; Parkes, P. 22; Parkin, D. 41; Pierce, G. 20; Powell, B. 23(3); Richards, J. 34; Sunderland, A. 15(2); Taylor, G. 3; Wagstaffe, D. 13; Williams, N. 10; Withe, P. 9(5).

League scorers:
Hibbit 17, Richards 13, Kindon 10, Munro 3, Carr 2, Parkin 2, Powell 2, Withe 2, Bailey 1, Daley 1, Dougan 1, Palmer 1, Wagstaffe 1, own goal.

1975/76

FOOTBALL LEAGUE
Division 1

	Home	Away
Arsenal	0-0	1-2
Aston Villa	0-0	1-1
Birmingham	2-0	1-0
Burnley	3-2	5-1
Coventry	0-1	1-3
Derby	0-0	2-3
Everton	1-2	0-3
Ipswich	1-0	0-3
Leeds	1-1	0-3
Leicester	2-2	0-2
Liverpool	1-3	0-2
Man. City	0-4	2-3
Man. United	0-2	0-1
Middlesbrough	1-2	0-1
Newcastle	5-0	1-5
Norwich	1-0	1-1
Q.P.R.	2-2	2-4
Sheffield Un.	5-1	4-1
Stoke	2-1	2-2
Tottenham	0-1	1-2
West Ham	0-1	0-0

F.A. CUP
3 — Arsenal (h) 3-0
4 — Ipswich (a) 0-0
 (h) 1-0
5 — Charlton (h) 3-0
6 — Man. United (a) 1-1
 (h) 2-3

LEAGUE CUP
2 — Swindon (a) 2-3
 (h) 3-2
3 — Birmingham (a) 2-0
4 — Mansfield (a) 0-1

Final Table
Division I — Season 1975/76

		P	W	D	L	F	A	P
1.	Liverpool	42	23	14	5	66	31	60
2.	Q.P.R.	42	24	11	7	67	33	59
3.	Man. United	42	23	10	9	68	42	56
4.	Derby	42	21	11	10	75	58	53
5.	Leeds	42	21	9	12	65	46	51
6.	Ipswich	42	16	14	12	54	48	46
7.	Leicester	42	13	19	10	48	51	45
8.	Man. City	42	16	11	15	64	46	43
9.	Tottenham	42	14	15	13	63	63	43
10.	Norwich	42	16	10	16	58	58	42
11.	Everton	42	15	12	15	60	66	42
12.	Stoke	42	15	11	16	48	50	41
13.	Middlesbrough	42	15	10	17	46	45	40
14.	Coventry	42	13	14	15	47	57	40
15.	Newcastle	42	15	9	18	71	62	39
16.	A. Villa	42	11	17	14	51	59	39
17.	Arsenal	42	13	10	19	47	53	36
18.	West Ham	42	13	10	19	48	71	36
19.	Birmingham	42	13	7	22	57	75	33
20.	Wolves	42	10	10	22	51	68	30
21.	Burnley	42	9	10	24	43	66	28
22.	Sheff. United	42	6	10	26	33	82	22

League appearances:
Bailey, M. 32; Bell, N. 11; Carr, W. 35(3); Daly, M. 3(1); Daley, S. 27(4); Farley, J. 13(1); Gould, W. 13(4); Hibbitt, K. 39(2); Jefferson, D. 2; Kelly, J. 9; Kindon, S. 22(6); McAlle, J. 41; McNab, R. 13; Munro, F. 30; O'Hara, G. 5; Palmer, G. 26; Parkes, P. 23; Parkin, D. 30; Patching, M. 2(1); Pierce, G. 19; Richards, J. 38(1); Sunderland, A. 24(5); Taylor, G. 1; Wagstaffe, D. 3; Williams, N. 1.

League scorers:
Richards 17, Hibbitt 8, Carr 7, Daley 6, Kindon 5, Bell 4, Gould 3, Palmer 1.

Index of proper names

Numerous passing references are not noted below because of the exigencies of space. The lists in the Appendix (p.154f), however, contain the names of all those officially recorded as having played in the Wolves first team.

Adams, T. B., 34
Addenbrooke, various members of family, 12, 14, 16, 66
Addenbrooke, J. H., 7, 10, 12, 14, 18, 20, 22, 47, 48, 67, 76
Addenbrooke, Mrs. J. H., 47
Allen, H., 25, 26, 27, 28, 29, 33, 35, 37, 40, 41, 45, 48, 112, 154, 156, 157, 158
Allen, R., 139, 141
Allt, W., 26, 34, 57
Amery, L. S., 64
Archer, R. H., 117, 120
Ashall, G. H., 108, 112, 182, 183

Baddeley, T., 53, 54, 55, 61-2, 154, 161, 162, 163, 164, 165
Bailey, M. A., 139, 197, 198, 199, 200, 201
Baker, C., 18, 157, 158
Baker, J. S., 117, 119, 120, 125
Bakewell, G., 23
Barcroft, W. H., 1, 2, 6, 7
Barker, E., 66, 71, 83
Barlow, J., 11
Barraclough, W., 94, 96, 101, 107, 177, 178, 179, 180, 181
Bate, W., 70, 171
Baugh, R. I., 7, 25, 26, 28, 33, 41, 45, 48, 51, 154, 156, 157, 158, 159, 160
Baugh, R., II, 28, 74, 88, 95, 171, 172, 173, 174
Baxter, W., 132, 186, 187, 188, 189
Baynton, J., 1, 2, 6, 7, 11, 12, 15, 17, 20, 23, 24, 27, 28, 29, 36, 153, 156
Beats, W. M., 48, 51, 54, 55, 154, 160, 161, 162, 163
Beattie, A., 138, 139
Beattie, J. M., 106, 180, 181
Bell, J., 44, 49
Bell, N., 153
Bellis, G., 94, 95, 101, 105, 177, 178, 179
Bentley, J. J., 26, 54
Berry, G., 153
Bishop, A. J., 64, 70, 72, 165, 166, 167, 168, 169, 170, 171

Bisset, G., 78, 173
Black, D., 44, 48, 51, 52, 158, 159, 160
Blackham, T. A., 7, 11, 12, 17, 18, 19, 24
Blakemore, W., 34
Bonson, J., 132, 191
Booth, Charles, 47
Booth, Colin, 129 135, 155, 157, 190, 191, 192, 193
Botto, L., 93, 176
Bottrill, W., 94, 101
Bowdler. J. H., 155, 157
Bowen, G., 57, 162, 163
Bowen, T., 88, 174, 175, 176
Boxley, F., 67, 168
Bradford, J., 83, 84, 174, 175-6
Bradford, R., 108
Bray, M., 34
Brewster, G., 78, 173
Brice, G. H., 123, 124, 185
Broadbent, P., 129, 130, 134, 135, 136, 154, 155, 187, 188, 189, 190, 191, 192, 193, 194, 195, 196
Brodie, J. B., 1, 2, 7, 11, 15, 16, 17, 20, 24, 25, 26, 27, 28, 29, 33, 36, 48, 49-50, 70, 71, 83, 153, 154, 156, 157
Brooks, S., 68, 70, 73, 74, 76, 168, 169, 170, 171, 172, 173
Broome, F., 118
Brown, J., 107, 108, 155, 182
Bryce, F., 93, 176
Buckley, F. C., 80, 90, 91, 92-116, 117, 118, 119, 121, 129, 151
Burrill, F., 74, 172, 173
Burton, S., 113, 184
Butcher, J. H., 36, 37, 41, 48, 49, 158, 159
Buttery, A., 103

Caddick, C. N., 81, 172, 173
Caddick, W., 11, 12, 15
Cadman, G., 11, 12, 14
Canavon, A., 93, 175, 176
Carr, W., 150
Cattell, W. J., 71
Chadwick, W., 86, 88, 175, 176, 177

INDEX

Chapman, H., 84, 92
Chatham, R. H., 124, 128, 132, 184, 185, 186, 187, 188, 189
Chung, S., 141, 153
Churchill, W., 65, 66
Clamp, E., 129, 135, 136, 154, 189, 190, 191, 192, 193, 194
Clayton, G., 108, 180, 181
Clegg, J. C., 27
Cliff, T., 7, 11, 12, 14, 15, 17, 20, 24, 153
Collins, E., 64, 166, 167, 170
Corbett, P. B., 62, 165, 166
Craddock, S., 34, 57
Crichton, R., 11, 12, 14, 20-21
Crook, M. S., 94, 96, 128, 178, 179, 180, 181
Crook, W. C., 119, 126, 127, 132, 184, 185, 186, 187, 188
Crowe, C., 154, 194, 195
Crump, C., 5, 9-10, 18, 20, 29, 32, 34, 57
Crump, S. G., 5
Cullis, S., 45, 108, 110, 111, 112, 113, 114, 117, 122, 124, 125-137, 138, 154, 181, 182, 183, 184
Curran, H., 143, 199, 200, 201

Daley, S., 145, 147, 200, 201
Dallard, H., 34
Dallard, W., 17
Daly, M., 153
Danks, R., 25-6
Davidson, A., 15, 17, 20
Davies, E., 5
Davies, J., 127, 155
Davies, R., 95
Deacon, J., 94, 96, 101, 107, 178, 179, 180, 181
Dean, H., 12
Dean, S., 12
Deans, H., 20
Deeley, N., 129, 132, 135, 136, 154, 187, 189, 190, 191, 192, 193, 194
Dorsett, R., 112, 113, 182, 183, 184
Dougan, A. D., 135, 139, 140, 142, 144, 145, 148, 149, 150, 155, 197, 198, 199, 200, 201
Dunn, J., 119, 123, 124, 126, 127, 128, 129, 132, 184, 185, 186, 187, 188
Dunn, T., 44, 50, 157, 158, 159, 160

Eastoe, P., 145, 201
Edmonds, G. W., 72, 74, 172, 173, 174
Elgar, E., 36, 84
Edwards, E., 81, 83, 174
Evans, A., 140, 141
Evans, J., 117, 134

Farley, J., 149
Farmer, E., 136, 155, 193, 194, 195
Fazackerley, S., 78, 81, 82, 83, 174

Fidler, R., 16
Finlayson, M. J., 135, 136, 191, 192, 193, 194, 195
Fleming, G., 44, 48, 56, 57, 159, 160, 161, 162
Fleming, W., 66
Fletcher, A., 26, 28, 33, 34, 47, 72, 154, 156, 157, 158
Flowers, R., 130, 134, 135, 136, 138, 139, 140, 154, 155, 188, 189, 190, 191, 192, 193, 194, 195, 196, 197
Forbes, W., 124, 184, 185, 186, 187
Forder, C., 34
Forshaw, R., 95, 177
Fowler, Sir H., 66
Fox, W. V., 84, 86, 174, 175, 176

Gale, H., 17
Galley, T., 108, 112, 113, 120, 154, 182, 183, 184, 185
Gardiner, J., 108, 112, 113, 127, 181, 182, 183, 184
Garratly, G., 70, 167, 168, 169, 170, 171
George, V, King, 74
George, N., 73, 74, 76, 81, 83, 86, 88, 93, 95, 172, 173, 174, 175, 176
Getgood, G., 81, 173, 174
Gill, B., 11
Gladstone, W. E., 23 56
Goddard, G., I, 106, 107, 180, 181
Goddard, G., II, 114, 184
Goodall, A., 59
Gould, R. A., 143, 152, 200, 201
Gowland, various members of family, 5
Grant, W., 5
Green, W., 16
Gregory, V., 73, 74, 172, 173
Griffin, A., 36, 41, 48, 50, 158, 159, 160
Griffiths, B., 25
Griffiths, H., 48, 51, 53, 56, 158, 159, 160, 161, 162
Griffiths, Jabez, 18, 25, 51
Griffiths, John, 17, 20, 23, 25, 51
Griffiths, T., 15
Gritton, J., 16
Grossmith, G., 23

Hadley, E., 15, 17, 24
Halligan, W., 68, 155, 169
Hamilton, J., 44
Hancocks, J., 119, 120, 121, 124, 126, 127, 130, 131, 134, 154, 184, 185, 186, 187, 188, 189, 190
Handley, T., 11
Harding, Alice Mary, 1
Harper, J., 8
Harrington, J., 81, 83, 86, 88, 89, 174, 175, 176
Harris, G., 136, 138, 155, 191, 192, 193, 194, 195

INDEX

Harrison, W. E., 64, 65, 67, 165, 166, 167, 168, 169, 170, 171
Hartill, W., 94, 96, 100, 101, 105, 107, 108, 177, 178, 179, 180, 181
Hassall, J., 48, 158, 159
Haynes, H., 49, 158, 159
Hazell, R., 153
Hedley, G. A., 63, 64, 65, 67, 165, 166, 167, 168, 169
Hegan, D., 145, 155, 200
Henderson, C., 48, 51, 160, 161
Hetherington, J. A. 97, 105, 177, 178, 179, 180, 181
Hibbitt, K., 141, 143, 145, 147, 149, 155, 200, 201
Hickman, A., 7, 12, 28, 29, 34, 40, 45, 49, 52, 57, 64; Lady A., 58
Higham, F., 88, 175, 176
Hill, F., 16
Hill, F. C., 71
Hill, J. G., 7, 11, 12, 15, 20, 24
Hinton, A., 136, 154, 155, 194, 195
Hodnett, J. E., 74, 171, 172, 173
Hodson, W., 16
Holley, G., 76
Hollingsworth, A., 29, 31, 38, 45, 48, 52
Hollingsworth, R., 94, 103, 107, 177, 178, 179, 180, 181, 182
Hollins, F. T., 71
Holloway, A. J., 71
Holsgrove, J. W., 139, 197, 198, 199, 200
Hooper, H., 131-2, 191
Horne, D., 136, 193
Hoskins, A. H., 76
Howell, H., 70, 171, 172
Howley, J., 125
Hughes, C. J., 40
Hughes, T., 2
Hunt, R. D., 139, 140, 197, 198
Hunt, K. R. G., 62, 63, 64, 65, 67, 72, 165, 166, 167, 168, 169
Hunt, R. G., 62, 64, 66
Hunter, C. H., 120
Hunter, T., 25, 28, 156

Ireland, J., 134, 137, 153
Irving, H., 23

Jarrad, J., 10
Jeffs, A. G., 66, 71
Jobey, G., 76, 103
Johnson, L., 11, 14-15, 38, 48, 57, 64, 103
Johnson, T., 16
Johnson, W., 16
Jones, B., 106, 108, 109, 110, 112, 155, 181, 182, 183
Jones, E., 5, 18
Jones, E., 108, 182

Jones, H., 67
Jones, J., 62, 64, 67, 165, 166, 167, 168, 169, 170, 171
Jones, "Jackery", 77, 78
Jones, L., 119
Jordon, W. C., 68, 169

Kay, A. E., 81, 88, 94, 100, 173, 174, 175, 176, 177
Kelly, J.,
Kelly, L., 126, 132, 184, 185
Kendrick, W., 6
Kindon, S., 148, 150, 151, 152
Kinnaird, Lord, 27, 40, 65
Kinsey, G., 36, 39, 41, 45, 50, 154, 157, 158
Knight, T., 25, 28, 156, 157
Knowles, P. R., 138, 139, 140, 142, 155, 194, 195, 196, 197
Kynoch, G., 24
Kirkham, J., 155, 193, 194, 195

Laking, G., 108, 110, 182
Langley, F. T., 57
Lawrence, J., 57
Lax, G., 94, 95, 177
Lea, T., 74, 170, 171, 172, 173
Lees, H. H., 81, 82, 83, 173, 174, 175, 176
Legge, A. E., 81, 82, 114, 175, 176
Leicester, C., 16
Lewis, A. N., 93, 177
Lewis, J., 35, 47, 48
Lightfoot, J., 5, 6
Lockett, H., 26
Lowder, A., 7, 12, 15, 19, 20, 23, 25, 28, 33, 154, 156, 157
Lowder, W., 12, 17
Lowton, W. G., 94, 95, 101, 107, 177, 178, 179, 180, 181
Ludlam, J. S., 5, 12
Lumberg, A., 94, 103, 178, 179
Lunn, T. H., 61, 64, 67, 165, 166, 167
Lutton, A., 155, 199, 200

McAlle, J., 141, 145, 147, 148, 150, 198, 199, 200, 201
McBean, F., 12
McCalliog, J., 143, 145, 199, 200, 201
McCann, G., 5
McGarry, W., 125, 141-153
McGregor, O. E., 3, 94
McGregor, W., 24, 26, 32
McKenna, J., 84
McIlmoyle, H., 139, 196, 197
McIntosh, A., 113, 119, 184
McLean, A., 119, 120, 124, 128, 132, 185, 186, 187
McNab, R., 152

INDEX

McParland, P., 155, 194
Maguire, J. E., 113, 182, 183, 184
Malpass, A. W., 36, 40, 41, 48, 50, 51, 56, 157, 158, 159, 160, 161
Mander, C., Sir, 107, 111
Mander, C. T., 30, 41, 57
Mander, Miss D. St. C., 134
Mannion, G., 155, 193
Marindin, F., 27
Marshall, F., 5
Marshall, G. H., 74, 93, 94, 96, 172, 173, 174, 175, 176, 177
Marshall, H. J., 153
Martin, D., 107, 110, 155, 181, 182
Martin, T., 94, 178, 179
Mason, C., 7, 11, 12, 14-15, 17, 20, 23, 26, 28, 33, 36, 153, 154, 156, 157
Mason, J., 1, 7
Matthews, B., 71, 117, 119
Meecham, E., 16
Meek, H. L., 84, 175
Minshull, W., 16
Mitton, J., 84, 88, 175
Morris, W., 110, 120, 154, 180, 181, 182, 183, 184
Morse, E., 72
Mullen, J., 114, 118, 120, 121, 124, 126, 128, 130, 154, 184, 185, 186, 187, 188, 189, 190, 191, 192
Munro, F. M., 140, 142, 143, 144, 145, 147, 148, 151, 155, 198, 199, 200, 201
Murray, J., 131, 134, 135, 136, 155, 184, 185, 191, 192, 193, 194, 195

Needham, J., 70, 167, 168, 170, 171
Nelson, J., 127, 180, 181
Newman, E., 6
Nicholls, A., 5, 18
Nock, B. B., 34

O'Grady, M., 143, 200, 201
O'Hara, G., 153

Oakley, A. H., 83, 107, 109, 117, 134, 135
Owen, T., 57, 162
Owen, W., 48, 51, 56, 158, 160, 161

Palmer, G., 147, 148, 155
Parkes, P., 139, 144, 145, 197, 198, 199, 200, 201
Parkin, D., 140, 147, 148, 155, 198, 199, 200, 201
Parry, J., 1
Parsons, D. R., 132, 185, 186, 187
Pearson, A., 19, 20, 23, 25
Pedley, J., 64, 103, 165, 166, 167

Peers, E. J., 68, 70, 71, 73, 76, 168, 169, 170, 171, 172
Phillips, C., 94, 100, 101, 103, 106, 155, 177, 178, 179, 180, 181, 182
Phillipson, T., 83, 84, 86, 88, 89, 93, 94, 119, 122, 139, 174, 175, 176
Pierce, G., 147
Plowden, W., 34
Potts, A., 70, 165
Powell, B., 147, 148, 155
Price, E., 84, 175
Price, J., 70, 171, 172, 173
Price, W. J., 2
Pritchard, R. T., 119, 124, 126, 127, 130, 132, 184, 185, 186, 187, 188, 189, 190
Pritchard, T., 94, 176, 177

Radford, W. R., 62, 64, 166, 167
Ramscar, F. T., 120, 184
Ray, E., 9, 18
Reynolds, F., 12
Rhodes, R. A., 94, 101, 107, 177, 178, 179, 180, 181
Richards, D., 94, 101, 103, 106, 155, 176, 177,
Richards, R. W., 71, 74, 155, 170, 171, 172, 173
Richards, J. P., 141, 143, 144, 145, 146, 147, 148, 149, 150, 151, 152, 154, 155, 199, 200, 201
Riley, A., 74, 170, 171, 172, 173
Robotham, H., 57, 163
Robson, D., 44, 158, 159
Rose, W. C., 33, 36, 39, 41, 45, 48, 50, 56, 156, 157, 158, 160
Rous, S., 135

Scotchbrook, F., 86, 89
Scott, H., 84, 174, 175
Scott, R. A., 112, 113, 118, 182, 183, 184
Sellman, G. H., 5, 9, 11
Shaw, B., 25
Shaw, C., 101, 103, 108, 112, 178, 179, 180, 181
Shaw, H., 81, 82, 83, 88, 93, 174, 175, 176, 177
Shaw, P., 138
Shelton, J., 64, 67, 166, 167
Shepherd, W., 66
Shipton, W., 19
Short, J., 130, 187, 188, 189
Shorthouse, W. H., 123, 124, 126, 127, 128, 130, 131, 132, 185, 186, 187, 188, 189, 190, 191
Showell, G., 135, 136, 190, 191, 192, 193, 194, 195, 196
Sidlow, C., 118, 123, 155, 183, 184
Sidney, T. H., 48, 57, 66, 67
Sims, N. D., 129, 130, 185, 186, 187

INDEX

Slater, W. J., 129-30, 131, 134, 135, 154, 188, 189, 190, 191, 192, 193, 194
Smalley, T., 103, 112, 119, 154, 170, 180, 181, 182, 183
Smith, L. J., 132, 188, 189, 190
Smith, W., 48, 57, 66, 67
Smyth, S., 123, 126, 127, 128, 155, 185, 186, 187
Spiers, C., 106, 180, 181
Springthorpe, T. A., 126, 127, 185
Stanford, T., 11
Steen, J., 114, 184
Steer, E., 14
Stobart, B., 136, 193, 194, 195
Stockin, R., 130, 188, 189
Straubenzee, A. J. Van, 2
Stuart, E. A., 130, 132, 135, 187, 189, 190, 191, 192, 193, 194
Sudell, W., 26
Sunderland, A., 147, 150, 155
Swift, G., 36, 41, 45, 49, 157, 158
Swinbourne, R. H., 129, 130, 131, 132, 134, 186, 187

Tate, J. J., 34
Taylor, A. F., 11
Taylor, F., 113, 182, 183
Taylor, F. D., 57
Taylor, G. W., 139, 197, 198, 199, 200, 201
Tennant, W., 50, 51, 56, 160
Thomson, R., 138, 139, 154, 155, 194, 195, 196, 197
Tildesley, J. C., 117, 120
Tipper, Hester, 1
Tonks, J. 51, 160, 161, 162
Tootill, A., 94, 101, 177, 178, 179
Topham, R., 36, 37, 39, 40, 41, 50, 157, 158, 160
Turton, H., 18, 23

Utterson, J. 107, 181, 182

Vealey, R. M., 15
Victoria, Queen, 25
Vizard, E., 119-20, 124, 127

Wagstaffe, D., 136, 138, 139, 144, 145, 147, 149, 196, 197, 198, 199, 200, 201
Waldron, J., 15, 17, 19
Walker, A. J., 67, 167
Walter, G. W., 34, 57
Ward, J., 6
Wardle, T., 5
Waring, T., 108, 182
Watson, E., 81, 84, 88, 173, 174, 175, 176, 177
Weaver, R., 93, 94, 108, 176, 177
Weaver, W., 86, 88, 94, 175, 176, 177
Westcott, D., 112, 113, 118, 119, 120, 121, 122, 182, 183, 184, 185
Wharton, T., 138, 139, 140, 194, 195
Whitehead, J., 5, 9, 18
Whitehead, T., 5
Whitehouse, J., 60, 163, 164, 165
Whittaker, P., 94, 178
Whittingham, R., 71
Whitworth, H., 57
Wignall, F., 140, 198, 199
Wilcock, R., 14
Wildman, F., 106, 180, 181
Williams, B. F., 119, 120 124, 126, 127, 128, 130, 131, 132, 154, 184, 185, 186, 187, 188, 189, 190, 191
Williams, D., 2
Wilshaw, D., 119, 129, 130, 131, 132, 133, 134, 154, 185, 186, 187, 188, 189, 190, 191
Withe, P., 148, 150
Wood, H., 20, 23, 28, 41, 46, 48, 51, 56, 154, 156, 157, 158, 159, 160, 161
Wood, G., 23
Woodfield, D., 139, 140, 148, 194, 195, 196, 197, 198, 199
Woodhouse, G., 2
Woodward, M., 72, 74, 76, 171, 172, 173
Wooldridge, W. T., 60, 64, 154, 162, 163, 164, 165, 166, 167, 168
Worrall, A., 17
Worrall, T., 6, 7
Wrigglesworth, W., 108, 181, 182
Wright, W. A., 114, 118, 120, 121, 124, 126, 128, 129, 130, 131, 132, 135, 154, 183, 184, 185, 186, 187, 188, 189, 191, 192
Wykes, D., 34, 57

Yates, C., 15